THE
PRACTICE
OF
PSYCHOTHERAPY

506 Questions and Answers

Lewis R. Wolberg, M.D.

THE PRACTICE OF PSYCHOTHERAPY

506 Questions and Answers

BRUNNER/MAZEL, *Publishers* • New York

Library of Congress Cataloging in Publication Data

Wolberg, Lewis Robert, 1905-
    The practice of psychotherapy.

    Bibliography: p.
    Includes index.
    1. Psychotherapy—Examinations, questions,
etc. I. Title.
RC343.5.W64   616.89'14   81-21724
ISBN 0-87630-290-8   AACR2

Published by
BRUNNER/MAZEL, INC.
19 Union Square
New York, New York 10003

Contents

Preface

Freud once humorously remarked that "Anyone who wants to make a living from the treatment of nervous patients must clearly be able to do something to help them" (S.E. 22:16). It is amazing how frequently this simple precept is ignored and, when a patient does not get well, how often the failure is attributed to lack of proper motivation, diminutive ego strength, latent schizophrenia, and a multitude of assorted resistances. Difficulties that arise during therapy are not due to a deliberate conspiracy of neglect on the part of the therapist. They usually come about because of obstructive situations that develop in work with patients with which the therapist is unprepared to cope. During the past years of my psychiatric career, a good part of which has been spent in teaching and supervising, I have come into contact with many students and graduate therapists who have brought up concerns about psychotherapy that relate to such obstructive situations. Over a period of time, I have collected and collated questions they have asked, with the eventual object of organizing them and their answers into a book. The present volume is the result of this effort.

My original idea was a supplementary volume to my *The Technique of Psychotherapy*, which was being used as a standard reference in a number of training centers. But as the book evolved, it became apparent that it could stand on its own as an independent text. The format, as will be seen, is a main section of several hundred questions dealing with various topics related to psychotherapy and their answers, followed by a concluding chapter which treats implications of the questions for the effective practice of psychotherapy. I have selected for the most part those questions that rank highest in frequency. Where questions were unclear in the original form, I have taken the liberty of rephrasing them without altering the basic ideas behind the questions. I have also in some cases expanded the questions to cover broader areas of more widespread interest. The answers to the questions were generally taken from cassette recordings in the event recordings were made. Otherwise I have tried to recall the questions after lectures and supervisory conferences, and to reconstruct my replies. Where I have felt my answers might have been expanded, I have amplified them, again retaining the original ideas as closely as I could. I have also included references from the literature wherever possible. Obviously, my replies reflect my own biases and some of the answers may not accord with what other professionals would consider appropriate. Where I have been aware of variant answers to a question, I have tried to include these and even to analyze them, again reflecting my biases.

A multitude of the questions deal with the management of the hard-to-treat patient such as affective disorders, borderline personality, schizophrenia, and chronic mental illness, topics of contemporary interest and importance. The use of pharmacotherapy and other adjunctive measures and the handling of transference and countertransference are other issues that are responsible for a good number of questions. Many other subjects are broached; indeed, there is scarcely an area that has not been covered in the queries under discussion.

The points of view that I have advanced are gleaned from 50 years of experience in the psychiatric field. I started my career in psychiatry in 1932 as the Assistant Executive Officer at the Boston Psychopathic Hospital (now the Massachusetts Mental Health Center) under C. Macfie Campbell as overall Director and Karl Bauman as Medical Director. One of my functions was admitting new cases, after which I had an opportunity to follow them as they were being treated by the residents until their discharge or transfer. Consequent to this I worked for the next 13 years with inpatients at the Kings Park State Hospital on Long Island; as Supervising Psychiatrist there I gave lectures to psychiatric nurses and attendants. I was fortunate in being able to participate in organizing one of the first insulin therapy and ECT units in the country. I was also deeply involved in research in hypnosis, out of which issued my books, *Hypnoanalysis* and *Medical Hypnosis*. During this period, I received my psychoanalytic training, personal analysis, and "control" analysis in New York City, first at the New York Psychoanalytic Institute with its brilliant array of teachers like Gregory Zilboorg and Lawrence Kubie, who espoused the classical Freudian viewpoint; and later with the Society for the Advancement of Psychoanalysis with neofreudians like Karen Horney, Clara Thompson and Erich Fromm. I became acquainted with other points of view by contact with innovators like Paul Federn, Sandor Rado and Abram Kardiner. At this time I was on the staff of Flower-Fifth Avenue Hospital and taught a psychiatric course at the New York Medical College. My wife Arlene, Chief Psychiatric Social Worker at the Flower-Fifth Avenue Hospital, and I were responsible for bringing a large group of analysts to the New York Medical College, where the first postgraduate psychoanalytic training program connected with a medical school was founded. I served as a training analyst in this program for a number of years, engaging in lecturing and "control" analyses (supervision) of psychoanalytic candidates. Many of the questions today about psychoanalysis and psychotherapy interestingly are the same as those puzzling my trainees then, and these questions are included in this volume.

Coordinate with the above experience, my wife and I founded the Postgraduate Center for Mental Health in New York City in 1945, an interdisciplinary postgraduate psychoanalytic training and treatment facility with research and community mental health departments. This organization rapidly became the largest mental health center of its kind in the country. As Medical Director and Dean I had an opportunity to make in-depth contact with the training problems of students from various disciplines through lectures, supervision, and follow-up studies. Teaching residents at Bellevue Hospital brought me in touch with the problems of another group of trainees. Moreover, my interests took me to different parts of the United States and Europe, where I lectured on various subjects in the psychiatric field. My work in these different areas inspired several books, including *The Technique of Psychotherapy* and *The Handbook of Short-term Psychotherapy*.

I have taken the liberty of summarizing my background to explain whence springs my dynamic orientation with eclectic overtones. The questions in this present volume are the outcome of this broad spectrum of experience. I have learned a great deal from my students by their questions and in answering these I hope to contribute somewhat to a field that continues to intrigue us with its vast problems and possibilities.

Acknowledgment is made to the many students with whom I have worked whose questions inspired this book, to my colleagues from whose contributions in the field I have drawn liberally, and to the Postgraduate Center for Mental Health who sponsored and supported the research and writing of the volume.

Lewis R. Wolberg, M.D.

THE
PRACTICE
OF
PSYCHOTHERAPY

506 Questions and Answers

I. General Aspects of Psychotherapy

A puzzling phenomenon that vexes many students is the continuing parade of new psychotherapies that burst into the therapeutic arena like lions, only to slink out in defeat like lambs. Is the constant influx of desultory techniques testimony to the sterility of present-day conventional approaches? The facts that approximately two-thirds of all patients improve with psychotherapy, irrespective of type, and that statistical studies reveal little superiority of any one treatment method have raised the knotty point as to whether techniques are mere epiphenomena that are secondary to more important factors operating in the therapeutic situation. Many uncertainties confound the clinician who seeks clarification about amorphous issues that invest psychotherapy. Some of these issues are raised in questions contained in this section. These concern themselves with topics of general interest related to a number of themes including: the basic ingredients of psychotherapy; factors that make for therapeutic change; therapist and patient characteristics that result in good or bad therapy; the utility of eclecticism in method; modes of enhancing a therapeutic alliance; the matching of patients and therapists; the impact of cultural factors; the role of insight; acting-out phenomena; resistance to termination; the effect of changing therapists; present-day training needs and problems; working with cotherapists; the use of paraprofessionals and mental health aides; and the difficulties of informed consent.

Q1: What is the best kind of therapy?

A1: One cannot generalize about what is the best therapy for all people. Different individuals learn most advantageously by interventions that uniquely interlock with their needs. The therapist's clinical judgment should be based on the criterion of what interventions are best employed at a specific time, rather than "shot-gun" methods for all persons. This should not preclude the employment of standard approaches as a way of getting started, but these should be implemented less with the expectation that they will work with all patients than as a way of studying the patient's responses for clues regarding resistances, conflicts, and defenses.

What is good for the patient, however, must accord with what is good for the therapist. Definitive research is yet to be done in the area of selection of the "best" therapy in terms of the therapist, but considering the many factors that enter into the psychotherapeutic situation, that therapy is probably best which works best for each individual therapist, provided, of course, the patient can use it. A behavior therapist will do better with methods organized around the social-learning paradigm than with methods issuing from psychoanalytic theory. A psychoanalyst who has little faith in behavioral, family, group, hypnotic, and other methods will not give these techniques the enthusiastic dedication required to make them optimally effective. Above all, flexibility is the key to determining what is "best" in therapy.

Q2: How would you account for the great proliferation of therapies that we see today?

A2: Professionals develop individual styles of doing psychotherapy, as artists evolve unique ways of painting. They then become wedded to these styles, perfect them, find them effective to their satisfaction, and then sometimes promote them as the "best" of all treatments. A general theory is fabricated sooner or later to provide a rationale which, more or less, draws from their personal lives and intrapsychic experiences. If they are sufficiently persuasive, they may attract a host of followers who are searching for answers to the dilemmas of treatment. And if they possess an abundance of charisma, they may even initiate a "revolution" in the form of a new school, which lasts for a period until sufficient failures in therapy accumulate to convince therapists that the psychiatric messiah has not yet arrived. When we distill out the important essences of all of the existing therapies, the differences are not as profound as they seem on the surface, although several classes of therapies do exist with distinctive goals and operational modes (see Wolberg, 1977, pp. 13-17, 269-281).

Q3: In your opinion, what are the most important ingredients in psychotherapy?

A3: Briefly put, I would say that first and foremost is establishing a good working relationship (rapport, therapeutic alliance). This holds true irrespective of the kind of therapy done. Next, I believe a psychodynamic orientation is an indispensable basis for understanding what has happened to and what is now going on in the patient, in relation to both the evolution and continuing perpetuation of the problem. It is helpful also in tracking the course of therapy and in spotting resistances that interfere with it.

The therapist does not have to be a psychoanalyst to apply dynamic principles. However, he needs to have integrated into his frame of reference information about personality development and dynamics. I am not talking so much about metapsychology, which concerns itself with such speculations as the vicissitudes of drives, instincts, "splitting," structure of the psychic apparatus, and sundry other theoretical constructs. I refer to an understanding of: how past conditionings fashion needs and defenses that survive in the present and pollute a realistic adaptation; conflicts that are relegated to the unconscious and that engender present-day anxiety; defenses and coping measures, some of which generate symptoms; and transference and other resistances that obstruct constructive learning. In short, the therapist needs to know how these dynamic constituents are influencing the patient's present problems and how they affect what is being done for the patient in treatment.

As to the treatment process itself, flexibility and eclecticism of method are, in my opinion, of great advantage, the techniques used being fashioned by the patient's needs and learning capacities. Irrespective of the techniques, many similarities may be found in the processes through which a patient works out his problems. A number of nonspecific healing agencies facilitate the therapeutic process. These include the placebo influence, the impact of the relationship with an empathic nonjudgmental therapist, emotional catharsis, suggestion, dyadic group dynamics fostering identification with the therapist, operant conditioning with the reinforcing of adaptive patterns, growing awareness and understanding of what has produced and is sustaining one's problems (insight), and the testing of new behavioral patterns with evolvement of an increasing sense of mastery.

Finally, in all cases the therapist must recognize his own biases and prejudicial antitherapeutic reactions (countertransference) to avoid stimulating the patient into repeating his pathogenic developmental difficulties.

Q4: Isn't therapeutic change related to the degree of empathy expressed by the therapist?

A4: Empathy is only one of the therapy-enhancing variables and an important one. But the degree of empathy expressed may not be a good index of predicted therapeutic responsiveness. In schizophrenics or borderline patients, for example, too great empathy at the start may be regarded as a seduction and may frighten some patients. While empathy is important, it must be titrated against the extent of patient receptiveness to such empathy. Moreover, there are times during treatment where withdrawal of empathy may be indicated, as when confrontation is utilized to accent the undesirability of certain attitudes or patterns, or where in psychoanalytic therapy one wishes to stir up negative feelings or tension to expedite transference.

Q5: You have mentioned that concern for, interest in, and caring about a patient and what happens to him or her is quite important in the helping process. What happens if you experience none of these things toward your patient?

A5: You simply can't hatch an egg in a refrigerator. Unless you are empathic with your patient and have some notion as to what he is experiencing, you will not be able to communicate essential concern or compassion. How you develop empathy is, of course, a key problem. You can't turn it on if it isn't there. Often, putting yourself in the patient's position and asking yourself how you would feel if you went through what he has gone through may enable you to understand the feelings, thoughts, and motives of the patient and to act accordingly with sympathy and understanding.

Q6: How can a psychotherapist who is having problems in his own personal adjustment, e.g., marital discord, do good psychotherapy?

A6: Considering the stresses and pressures of contemporary society, it is little wonder that all individuals, including psychotherapists, are burdened with some neurotic defenses. Even thoroughly "analyzed" psychoanalysts possess a share of these burdens, which may display themselves in marital and other maladjustments. The fact that some personal difficulties exist should not prevent a psychotherapist from doing good psychotherapy. The role he plays in a therapeutic situation is different from that assumed in personal relationships. The therapist is usually more in control and hence more secure with patients than he may be with his family or with his colleagues. Difficulties will occur, however, where the therapist's neurotic problems are quantitatively too strong and cannot be controlled during therapy, spilling over into the therapeutic situation in the form of unbridled countertransference. This is why personal psychotherapy can be so helpful to a psychotherapist, equipping him to assume greater objectivity in work with patients.

Q7: Isn't the psychotherapeutic process also therapeutically helpful to the therapist?

A7: It can be; in some cases it is even more beneficial for the therapist than for the patient. We are hopeful, of course, that the therapist is somewhat less neurotic than the patient! Seriously speaking, psychotherapy is a two-way process and each participant (patient and therapist) should benefit from it, at least educationally if not in reconstructive change.

Q8: I get mixed up by so many different therapies claiming superiority in results. Can one ever use pieces from different therapies in one's own system?

A8: This is the essence of methodological eclecticism. No one therapy covers every aspect of the therapeutic process. Each therapy seems to have selected a limited zone of pathology and to have focused on this dimension. In an eclectic approach we may employ techniques from different therapies at different phases of the treatment process; for example, we may use some of the methods of the client-centered school during the early stages when we seek to establish a therapeutic alliance; some of the methods of psychoanalysis (dreams, transference, etc.) when we are probing for conflicts; some of the methods of gestalt therapy when confrontation is in order; some of the methods of behavior therapy when we are trying to convert insight into action; and some of the methods of cognitive therapy when we are trying to alter belief systems. We might also try other modalities for specific reasons like drug therapy, marital therapy, sex therapy, family therapy and group therapy. These methods have to be employed selectively, coordinating them with the patient's needs and the objectives we are trying to achieve. The problem with most psychotherapeutic schools is that they try to approach all phases of the therapeutic process with a limited tool. It would be like building a house with a hammer alone when a variety of tools is needed. Naturally, *how* eclectic methods are used and the personality of the therapist are crucial for success.

Q9: There are many psychotherapeutic techniques available. When should a therapist change from one to the next?

A9: This is a personal matter. There is no earthly reason for jumping around from one method to another if therapy is proceeding satisfactorily. Most therapists learn a few techniques thoroughly and do well with them. It would seem to me that only where a patient is not responding to one's habitual techniques, and the therapist is assured the failure is not rooted in transference and other resistances, should he change the interventions. This presupposes that the therapist has learned and has available to him supplementary techniques. The fact that a therapist is eclectic in his methods does not mean that he cannot be discriminating in using them.

Q10: Since a therapeutic alliance is fundamental to doing good psychotherapy, are there ways of enhancing the therapeutic alliance?

A10: Research data exist which endorse certain procedures as facilitative of a therapeutic alliance (Goldstein, 1980, Goldstein and Wolpe

1971). First, preparatory structuring for the patient by the initial screener of what to expect from the assigned therapist and from therapy itself, couched in enthusiastic constructive terms, has a beneficial influence on the patient. After the patient describes the kind of therapist he would like, assurance that the therapist to whom he will be assigned actually possesses the desired qualities appears to promote expectant trust. The screener, in further describing the assigned therapist, makes the patient additionally receptive by indicating the latter's expertise, warmth and capacities to help. Where the therapist comes from the same background as the patient, a statement to that effect has also been shown to facilitate the forthcoming relationship. Finally, role expectancy structuring can be useful in terms of what the patient and therapist will do and what the patient may expect from therapy. This helps eliminate surprise, confusion and negative feelings.

A recommended article is that by Orne and Wender (1968), which details the words to use in a structuring interview. In my 1977 (pp. 506-519) and 1980 (pp. 41-42) books there are also precise ways of structuring the therapeutic situation. Sometimes a cassette tape is given to the patient which contains clarifying instructions of how the patient and the therapist are to behave with each other. Research studies show that modeling or observational learning can add to the attraction potential the patient has for the therapist. Here an audio- or videotape that is played containing an actual or simulated session which brings out the therapist's sympathetic and caring qualities in relation to a patient seems to have an impressive effect on some patients. According to contemporary studies, the higher the expertise and status of the therapist in the mind of the patient, the greater the therapist's confidence in what he is doing, the stronger the activity level and degree of demonstrable conviction, the more manifest the empathy with the patient's feelings—the more attracted the patient will be to the therapist and hence the more likely a therapeutic alliance will develop.

Q11: How important an accelerating factor is faith in and identification with the therapist?

A11: Faith in the therapist and in his techniques expedites the placebo element and makes the patient more receptive to the ministrations of the therapist, whether the latter deserves it or not. It also does a great deal toward neutralizing the initial resistance. The factor of identification with the therapist, particularly with his value systems and modes of managing problems, eventually plays a part in altering some pathogenic attitudes and behavior. This presupposes that the therapist is a well-balanced individual and reflects values and patterns that will prove to be adaptive for the patient. Therapists reared in cognitive approaches tend to minimize the effect of this modeling phenomenon which, an aspect of dyadic group dynamics, nevertheless plays an important part, consciously or unconsciously, in helping to promote change.

Q12: Does the patient's confidence in the therapist influence his convictions?

A12: Enormously important—even when the therapist's ideas of the etiology or dynamics of the patient's difficulty are wrong. The patient's acceptance of explanations proffered with conviction by a therapist in whom there is confidence can have a determining influence on him. They are incorporated into his belief system and sponsor tension reduction and restoration of habitual defenses. Through what means this alchemy takes place is not clearly known, but suggestion, the placebo effect, and the impact of the protecting relationship offered by the therapist undoubtedly play a part.

Q13: How important are nonspecific factors in psychotherapy?

A13: Very important and always present. Since they cannot be avoided, the therapist should graciously (and thankfully?) accept them with humility, realizing that such factors as the placebo influence, relief experienced by emotional catharsis, suggestion, idealization of the therapist, and dyadic group dynamics may counteract his operative errors.

Q14: How would you explain the placebo effect?

A14: Until recently the ranking opinion was that a placebo depended on confidence in the efficacy of a procedure, which psychologically allayed tension and fear and thus helped the individual achieve his customary sense of mastery. Exactly how the suggested effect operated was not even speculated on. With the discovery of endogenous opiate-like substances that reduced pain and substances that acted like a tranquilizer, both of which were manufactured in the brain, a new hypothesis has evolved, namely that both the placebo effect and the effect of suggestion are due to the release of endorphin and kindred chemicals. Whether this hypothesis will hold up with scientific experiment remains to be seen, but so far it is an interesting explanation. Acupuncture, biofeedback, and hypnosis may also, hypothetically, in part at least, exploit the same biochemical mechanism.

Q15: How does the therapeutic relationship act to effectuate change in the patient?

A15: One way is that while the patient may want to cling to his neurotic patterns, he may be willing to experiment with different behaviors solely to please the therapist. Once the patient receives rewards in the form of approving gestures and words for changes in attitudes and behavior, such changes may become solidified. Of importance here is an alteration of the self-image, which contributes to the permanence of change. Modeling oneself after an idealized therapist is another change mechanism and may gear the patient toward new constructive experiences. A relationship with the therapist helps him to tolerate, explore and accept aspects of himself that have been repudiated and repressed. The incorporation of a new image of authority as embodied in the more tolerant, nonjudgmental therapist helps alter a punitive, intolerant superego. There are undoubtedly other mechanisms operative, further exploration of which may be found elsewhere (Wolberg, 1977, pp. 44, 47, 641, 648).

Q16: How can you pragmatically assign a proper therapist for a certain patient?

A16: To date there are no definite studies that indicate we have answers to this question. The best thing one can do is to see that the problems of any patients are within the training and experiential scope of the assigned therapists. Thus severe depressions, schizophrenias, manic states, paranoid conditions and somatic ailments should be handled by medically trained therapists (psychiatrists) who have the proper experience with psychotropic medications and the management of emergencies. Where psychotherapy, psychoanalysis, group therapy, family therapy, couples therapy, biofeedback, hypnosis, behavior therapy and various adjunctive therapies appear indicated, a therapist, irrespective of discipline, who is trained and skilled in these techniques should be able to execute them. Matching patient and therapist on the basis of personality characteristics is still haphazard, even though the Indiana Matching Project (Bergin, 1977) has indicated that the best pairings are those where patient and therapist characteristics complement each other (passive, submissive, inhibited patients doing better with active and dominant therapists and vice versa). Some syndromes seem to be helped more by therapists skilled in certain techniques, e.g., phobias by flooding and in vivo desensitization, obsessive-compulsive reactions by paradoxical intention and behavioral methods, depression by cognitive therapy and antidepressants, schizophrenia by neuroleptics and milieu therapy, etc. (see also p. 338 in the final chapter).

Q17: Are there specific characteristics that make a patient susceptible to chosen psychotherapeutic methods?

A17: A number of attempts have been made to establish criteria for a patient-method alignment, for example, the *symptomatic diagnosis* (like behavior therapy for phobias, an inspirational group such as AA for alcoholism, neuroleptics for schizophrenia, lithium for mania); the *characterologic diagnosis* (like the personality typologies proposed by Horowitz, 1976, 1977); *responses to hypnotic induction* (Spiegel and Spiegel, 1978); and the *developmental diagnosis* (Burke et al., 1979). The latter authors believe that therapeutic methods may be selected that coordinate with the period in development where the most offensive conflicts were sustained.

Except for the symptomatic diagnosis where certain syndromes lend themselves to special interventions, matching patient and method is haphazard. Matching patients and therapists is even more challenging, because of the interference of miscellaneous patient, therapist, environmental, transferential, countertransferential and resistance variables. The very choice of a diagnosis and the identification of the mental conflict around which the therapeutic plan is organized are subject to the therapist's bias, as is the method to which the therapist is dedicated. This bias will prejudice the patient's response. A therapist who applies himself to a favored technique with enthusiasm and conviction will expedite the patient's progress, whereas the same technique used casually and unenthusiastically may have a minimal effect on the patient. The style of some therapists and their investment in their theories will support or militate against the effective use of any of the methods. In summary, at the present stage of our knowledge we cannot be sure that a selected method exists for every patient we treat. Our options must remain open and we must be willing to change our methods when a selected technique does not work.

Q18: Are there certain therapist characteristics that facilitate treatment in selected patients?

A18: Therapists from the same cultural and socioeconomic background, who are able to communicate in the same language forms, and who have similar values, political ideas, and world views, more readily empathize with and establish contact with their patients, and more easily serve as identification models. They also tend more accurately to interpret their patients' unexpressed feelings and attitudes.

Q19: Is acting-out ever caused by arousal of early memories in therapy?

A19: Acting-out can occur when early repudiated memories threaten to break out and the patient resists their revelation to the therapist. Instead of being talked about, they are defensively discharged outside of the session in action tendencies.

Q20: How is acting-out best handled?

A20: Acting-out is best handled by interpretation; sometimes, especially where the acting-out behavior is hazardous, this may mean going a bit beyond the patient's immediate emotional readiness for such interpretation. Any untoward reponse to the interpretation will then have to be handled, but this is better than allowing the patient to plunge into serious troubles through destructive acting-out.

Q21: Patients often show a stubbornness in moving forward in treatment. How is this best handled? Are there differences in the way psychoanalysts and behavior therapists deal with this problem, and is there a good behavioral model one can follow?

A21: Little has been written on how definitely to solve the paradox of the patient who seeks help yet resists any external control or guidance toward change. What would seem to be indicated is a participant model for therapy in which the patient takes responsibility in treatment, monitoring his own behavior and determining the nature of his environment and his future plans.

In psychoanalysis, early in treatment the patient gathers from the passivity of the analyst that he has to make his own decisions and work through his blocks toward utilizing insight in the direction of change. Interpretation of resistances is the prime modality used and the analyst hopes that the patient will in the resolution of these obstructions generalize his learnings in therapy toward making new constructive adaptations.

In psychoanalytically oriented therapy, the therapist is more active and employs techniques in addition to interpretation to help the patient effectuate change. These techniques often draw from many schools and are more or less eclectic in nature.

In behavior therapy, the therapist is highly active, utilizing when necessary a rich assortment of devices, including systematic desensitization, operant conditioning, modeling of preferred behaviors, role-playing, work assignments, and cognitive therapy. These treatments are sometimes blended with counseling.

At the outset it often becomes apparent that what some patients want from therapy is to overcome suffering without giving up attitudes and behaviors that are responsible for their suffering. What is required before any progress can be made is to work toward motivating the patient to change and to formulate worthwhile objectives in treatment.

In his chapter on self-management methods, Kanfer (1980) describes a behavioral model drawn from Skinnerian methods and research findings in social and cognitive psychology as well as current clinical practices. Through various techniques, the patient acquires skills for use in problem-solving. He is also trained in altering noxious elements of his environment. Development of constructive repertoires is conducted through negotiations with the patient. Past experiences are reviewed only to provide information during behavioral analysis on the circumstances surrounding the original conditions when the maladaptive behavior was developed and to point out the present inappropriateness of this behavior.

In controlled environments like a hospital or in military organizations, reinforcement contingencies may be relatively easily applied. But in one's ordinary living environment these are not so readily arranged and it is for this reason that manipulation of cognitive variables through cognitive behavior therapy can be valuable in order to help evolve constructive self-reinforcing attitudes. A good deal of support will be required from the therapist at the start of treatment, but this will diminish as the patient becomes more skilled in self-management. A contract is usually negotiated, details of which spell out the required behavior, the time goal, the reinforcements for fulfillment of obligations, some aversive consequences of non-fulfillment of the contract, and the way reviews and evaluations will be conducted. Where required behaviors occur outside the range of observation of the therapist, self-monitoring is mandatory and here the patient will benefit from keeping a careful record of his behaviors. Assignment of tasks expedites self-observation and hastens the development of new behavioral repertoires. Techniques are employed to set up environmental conditions unfavorable to the undesired behavior, and to establish contingencies for self-reinforcement. Discussions cover the patient's experiences in self-management with the object of helping him transfer his learnings and skills to situations that may develop in the future. There are other models one may follow if one is pursuing a behavioral program, but the one I have outlined seems to cover the essential points.

Q22: How important is knowledge of cultural factors in treating patients from another background?

A22: Very important. Cultural factors influence how the patient regards his problem, as well as his attitude toward the treatment process and the therapist. The individual may be under the influence of misbeliefs, of primitive notions of disease causation, and superstitious ideas of witchcraft and sorcery that can prejudice responses to treatment. Archaic ideas may persist even in educated individuals and among higher socioeconomic classes. Individuals from a culturally different background may believe they can respond only to action-oriented methods and medications. Interviewing and probings for psychological causation leave them cold. It may require a good deal of preparation, best undertaken in a warm empathic relationship, before patients are ready to move from their established values and ideas to those consonant with our own principles of psychotherapeutic technique. It can be done, however, if the therapist is forbearing and handles his own prejudices and countertransferences.

Q23: Does one always have to have insight before he can experience change?

A23: Not necessarily. Behavioral changes can come about purely as a consequence of conditioning and reinforcement. Interestingly, insight regarding what has been responsible for faulty coping patterns may follow such behavioral change. On the other hand, we always strive for some cognitive improvement or change, and often the therapeutic focus is on bringing the individual to an insightful awareness of what is behind his difficulties. This awareness (insight) then can act as a motivating force to inspire the person to take steps to change his patterns.

Q24: Can false insights result in improvement and change?

A24: Yes, if the individual then acts on these to alter his destructive behavioral patterns. Sometimes spurious insights, by bringing about freedom from fear, tension, and anxiety, may halt the use of associated pathological defenses. The individual is then free to pursue behaviors which are constructive and which through reinforcement may lead to a healthy adaptation. On the other hand, if the false insight is a blatantly deceptive canard, the individual will eventually see through it, and he may experience a relapse.

Q25: Is there a difference between emotional insight and intellectual insight?

A25: The difference is a subtle and often blurred one. We can regard an intellectual insight as merely a twinkling of understanding on which the individual does not act to produce behavioral change. It is quite likely that the individual here is not ready to put his insights to the test. An emotional insight may be defined as a "gut" feeling that a revelation is correct. This can inspire behavior that may lead to change. The individual here apparently has resolved sufficient resistances to change and possesses a willingness to forego the secondary gains of his neurosis sufficiently to permit himself to experiment with new behaviors.

Q26: Can people change encrusted character patterns without insight?

A26: Yes, they can and they sometimes do. We rarely see these cases in practice, but instances of persons achieving widespread alterations in values, attitudes, and modes of relating to people and the world are not infrequent. Usually this occurs as a consequence of involvement in a productive human relationship with an empathic and intelligent person through whom a widespread reconditioning process is implemented, the individual working through his customary expectations of rejection, punishment and exploitation. We must consider the possibility that transference will at some point appear and that it will be behaviorally rather than cognitively resolved. Or perhaps a silent kind of insight, which may or may not eventually be verbally expressed, will be acquired subconsciously.

Q27: Why are people so reluctant to change even when they have insight into their problems?

A27: A ponderous, extremely obese person may realize he is digging his grave with his teeth, and even be able to see the connection of his overeating with early rejection, deprivation, or overindulgence. An inveterate smoker may realize that tobacco intensifies his emphysema and cardiac condition and threatens his well-being, if not his life. An alcoholic exposes himself continuously to abuse, suffering, and censorship, in the medium of awareness of what he is doing to himself and recognition of the sources of his insecurity.

These are examples of how little control some people have over aberrant needs and impulses. There are many subversive gratifications a person gets out of the indulgence of neurotic patterns and these can dwarf the value of insight as a deterrent force. It takes a good deal of working-through in the matrix of a constructive relationship before the individual is willing and able to abandon his deviant patterns and to experiment with new, adaptive ones. The therapeutic alliance gives the person an opportunity for this kind of healthy change.

Q28: Why, if insight is not as effective as once believed, should we try to inculcate it in our patients?

A28: Insight is like a roadmap. It may give one the directions to reach the objective of change, but it will not in itself produce change. One still has to travel a tedious path of extinguishing old destructive patterns and acquiring new adaptive ones. The working-through of insight requires a good deal of fortitude, patience, and time. But insight can provide the individual with a substantive motivation for change and turn the spotlight on essential areas of alteration; without it a person may wander about aimlessly in the dark.

Q29: Why do so many patients struggle against terminating therapy?

A29: Patients resist termination for several reasons, including failure to resolve a positive transference, fear of yielding the comfortable niche they have in treatment where everyday decisions are checked with the therapist, terror at facing separation and grief that follows loss of an important object, and the inability or unwillingness of the therapist to let go of the patient (countertransference).

Q30: Does changing therapists in the course of treatment have an adverse effect?

A30: The problem of continuity of therapists in treatment is one that concerns teaching centers where interns and residents rotate after a certain period of time, requiring transfer of patients to new therapists. Does such transfer impede progress? In an experimental program conducted by Muench and Schumacher (1968), patients were divided into three groups. Patients in the first group, which acted as a control group, were given 12 individual therapy sessions with a therapist. The second group received six sessions with a therapist and six more sessions with three different therapists. The third group had six sessions first with three different therapists and six sessions with a new therapist. Results revealed no difference between the control and the rotational groups. Naturally, the *quality* of service is the key factor, and if therapists are capable of doing effective therapy, and the patient is in advance of treatment prepared for possible rotation of therapists, transfer should not have too serious adverse effects.

Q31: Does present-day training, as done in traditional psychoanalytic schools, equip the trainee for practice?

A31: This depends on the school and on the kinds of patients the student will be seeing in practice. My personal opinion is that thorough grounding in psychoanalysis forms an excellent basic structure for practice. But since more patients seen in practice are *not* suitable candidates for psychoanalysis, unless the student has had further training beyond psychoanalysis he will not be able to utilize himself most effectively.

An excellent example of what I am saying is provided in the article in the January 1979 issue of the *Bulletin,* the Newsletter for Area II District Branches of the American Psychiatric Association, by a young psychiatrist, trained to provide long-term psychoanalytically oriented psychotherapy and/or analysis, who claimed that his training did not equip him for the kinds of service required in the area in which he lived (Schreiber, 1979). He wrote: "I was forced to change my Freudian oriented, N.Y.C. training and practice, to the present eclectic, short-term therapy orientation." Millman (1979), in an Editorial reply to this article, avows that more and more psychiatrists are abandoning their long-term constituted philosophies and styles of operation and resorting to short-term methods that coordinate more with the realities of contemporary requirements. Vital, contends Millman, is the fact that psychotherapeutic "training programs must be more responsive to the real needs of the patient population than to the real or imagined needs of the faculty or the trainees. . . . The field should begin to develop alternative practice modes that might serve patients' needs better."

Another example of how traditional training fails to prepare therapists for their functional assignments is provided by Wilder (1979), Associate Dean for Planning and Operations at Albert Einstein College of Medicine. Referring to a clinic suffering from the common problem of overcrowding, he states: "Now this clinic is in real trouble. They have no money, they can't do anything with the legislature, and what they've got is a lot of chronic cases—and maybe a lot of chronic staff too. Anyhow, the chronic patients keep coming back, taking up everybody's time, nobody improves or gets well, everybody's demoralized. Now our problem is what should we try to find out about? What should we ask about? How can we get this problem clinic back on the track? What should we look for?" Clearly a shift in orientation is required. A simple reorganization of staff time, for example, with the bulk of chronic patients seen in groups, may result in a dramatic change for the better in both clinic morale and therapeutic results. Such a shift, however, requires a courageous flexibility and an opening of therapists' minds to the usefulness of new and different modalities. Clearly, comments Wilder, "good programs evolve through good leadership and staff being creative." It is vital that adequate means of self-evaluation be provided.

With the advent of third-party payments and the imminence of accountability and required demonstrations of cost-effectiveness, the efficiency of our present therapeutic operations will need a more critical appraisal. Are we utilizing what is now available to improve our methods? The examples cited indicate that we still have a long way to go.

If I were advising a young therapist regarding what he needed to learn beyond his background in psychoanalysis, I would say: psychoanalytically oriented psychotherapy, group therapy, marital therapy, behavior therapy, family therapy, cognitive therapy, hypnosis, and pharmacotherapy. Obviously no person can be an expert in all of these areas, but at least a working knowledge of these therapies would be important. What analytic training provides is an understanding of dynamic principles that can be applied to the happenings in all kinds of therapy. Transference and resistance can sidetrack the patient from working effectively in treatment, and countertransference may obstructively operate in the therapist to complicate the relationship. Without some dynamic understanding the therapist will be handicapped in recognizing and dealing with these ubiquitous resistance saboteurs. Can a therapist acquire a dynamic understanding without going through a long and expensive psychoanalytic training experience? In some cases, yes. For others formal training will be the only way such knowledge can be acquired and integrated.

Q32: Why is there such a great decrease of medical students going into psychiatry as a specialty?

A32: The fall-off from 10 percent a few years ago to the 1980 figure of 3.5 percent is, I believe, mainly due to economics. Other specialties pay more and many young graduates nowadays are less idealists than practical businessmen. The fact that the government supports primary care and has shifted its financial subsidies and training grants from psychiatry to the specialty of family practice is also an important factor. Some medical schools do not put a high priority on psychiatric teaching and relegate relevant courses to non-medical faculty members, which gives students the impression that psychiatry does not have the grounding in medicine common to other specialties. Added to these facts is the impoverished public image of psychiatry: It tends to be lampooned in the press and downgraded by other members of the medical profession. Some authorities believe that an important way of reversing the situation is by making the fiscal incentives more attractive. This means higher salaries in the public sector and increased fees in the private sector. Unfortunately, psychiatry can never compete compensation-wise with surgery, ophthalmology, dermatology, and other specialties. Additional rewards must be found if we wish to correct the disparity.

Q33: Shouldn't a personal analysis and completion of psychotherapeutic training suffice to equip a therapist to function in a top-notch way in the practice of psychotherapy?

A33: For the most part, yes, but there is no guarantee that personal analysis and training in themselves will be sufficient to make for a really proficient psychotherapist. There are some elusive personality qualities that elicit confidence in the patient, foster a good therapeutic alliance, and aid in the resolution of resistance that some therapists possess and others do not have or acquire even after analysis and training. Countertransference is also a subtle interference that unwittingly may militate against the patient's working-through of problems, and even well-analyzed therapists may display it with certain patients. The important thing is not whether countertransference exists but whether it can be managed during therapy. This is not to depreciate the virtues of personal analysis and adequate training, but other factors also must be taken into account in the making of a top-notch therapist.

Q34: What would you consider the value of the many weekend continuing education courses on techniques in psychotherapy that are available to professionals?

A34: The current practice of offering seminars and workshops in the various psychotherapeutic techniques is commendable in intent but fraught with many caveats. Cursory exposure to such techniques without a thorough understanding of their scientific background, and without a good deal of supervision in their application, can easily lead to misuse and distorted ideas of their values. It takes much experimentation and experience to acquire expertise for the proper employment of psychoanalytically oriented therapy, hypnosis, behavior therapy, family therapy, group therapy and other interventions. Yet after a weekend conference some of the participants are apt to consider themselves sufficiently schooled to plunge into unsupervised practice, to misrepresent themselves as experts, and to offer judgments about the virtues of methods to which they have been cursorily exposed. Equally confounding is the use of such relatively untrained professionals as therapists in research studies of different techniques. Rarely is the background of the therapists revealed by the investigators to permit an evaluation of their competence in management of specific methods. The fact of publication lends authenticity to a piece of research that may actually be worthless. Weekend seminars do, however, have educational value as a brief introduction, provided an aspiring participant is stimulated to acquire further sophisticated instructions.

Q35: What are the advantages and disadvantages of cotherapy?

A35: Cotherapists are able to contribute their individual inputs toward understanding a patient's problems ("two heads are better than one"). The presence of two therapists invites transference feelings originating in relationships with parents or siblings to be differentially projected. Cotherapists are also better able to detect and to correct distortions caused by each other's countertransference. This presupposes that the cotherapists like each other and are not too competitive. Otherwise the therapeutic situation will become a battlefield of opposing opinions which will interfere with a patient's therapy.

Q36: In treating psychotic patients in individual psychotherapy, is it helpful to have an auxiliary therapist?

A36: Very much so. Not only does this help to dilute the transference, which can become disturbing, but it provides a substitute helper when the primary therapist is not available or away. This is an advantage especially where one treats very sick patients like schizophrenics or depressives. A continuity of care is expedient here, and most problems that come up when the primary therapist gets ill or goes on a vacation may be solved or avoided by having a cotherapist available. Transference is attenuated enough so that a negative therapeutic reaction is not so explosive. The alternative therapist may carry on with suitable interventions while the transference to the primary therapist is being worked out.

Q37: Can nonprofessional helpers aid a person with an emotional problem?

A37: Individuals with emotional difficulties are constantly turning to friends and family members for help. Sometimes a great deal of help is forthcoming, especially where the provider of help is empathic, intelligent, and interested in the supplicant. Therapeutic effects are largely the product of important nonspecific factors like the placebo influence, emotional catharsis, the relationship dimension, suggestion, and dyadic group dynamics (which are also operative with professional helpers). What untrained nonprofessional helpers lack is understanding of dynamics, techniques, and useful interventions, as well as recognition of the operations of transference, resistance, and countertransference. They are also less capable of objectivity, being more intimately involved in the supplicant's life, and hence more likely to act out and utilize the latter for their own neurotic needs. This does not mean that all professional helpers are necessarily successful because they may also not be adequately trained and they may be burdened by personality defects that show up in obstructive countertransference. On the whole, however, their results should be better than those of untrained nonprofessional helpers.

Q38: Can paraprofessionals be taught to do good psychotherapy?

A38: This depends on the paraprofessional and on the trainer. My own personal opinion is that a background in the biological and behavioral sciences is very important for those who are going to do psychotherapy. Nevertheless, persons who are intelligent, mature, motivated to help others, and who have capacities for empathy, warmth and honesty, may, without extensive prior academic education, be trained in many counseling and behavioral techniques geared toward problem-solving, attitude change, and behavioral correction. This group of talented helpers and "behavioral technologists" can add to the much needed manpower pool. They should, of course, work under the direction of more extensively trained professionals. Where psychotherapy is to be done, further graduate and postgraduate training will be necessary.

Q39: What about training psychologists and social workers to prescribe drugs when needed?

A39: In view of the relative lack of psychiatrists in numbers sufficient to supply community needs, there are those who favor the intensive training of psychologists, social workers and paraprofessionals in all aspects of mental health service, including the prescription of psychoactive drugs (Abroms, 1972). It is pointed out that a precedent exists for the prescribing of medications by nonmedical persons, such as dentists and podiatrists. The Colorado Child Health Associate Law permits for the first time prescription of the majority of drugs employed in pediatric practice by persons with an education below the doctorate level. It may, however, be expected that there will be a good deal of opposition toward liberalizing prescribing laws for the mental health professions.

Q40: What is involved in the process of "informed consent" when you want to prescribe a drug in a patient who needs it? Do you have to get his consent in all cases?

A40: In an emergency, the California State Laws, for example, permit the use of antipsychotic medications where a drastic change has occurred in a patient's condition "so that action is immediately necessary for the preservation of the life or the prevention of serious bodily harm to the patient and others." Where such a serious situation does not exist and a drug is deemed essential, "informed consent" means informing the patient about the state of his mental condition that requires medications, the possibilities of what will result if he does or does not take the drug, the right to refuse medication at any time once started, what other treatments are possible, the kinds of medications that can be useful and how they are prescribed, and possible and probable side effects. Refusal to take drugs is not a reason for involuntary hospitalization. Written records of the interview should be kept with a notation of the patient's consent or refusal. Obviously, this procedure is a cumbersome one and poses many problems especially where the patient's cognitive functions are impaired by his illness. But considering the current emphasis on "patient's rights," the therapist may have no alternative but to abide by legal rules.

Q41: What can one do when a patient fails to live up to his obligations and pay his fee after repeated bills are sent? Should the therapist telephone the patient and request payment? Should he refer the matter to a collection agency? Should he take the loss and forget the matter?

A41: It is as much a blow to the narcissism of the therapist as it is to to his pocketbook to have a patient with whom he has spent time show no respect for his financial obligations. There are some patients who are exploitative and demanding, and in their consuming "orality" try to get as much as they can without reciprocating. In long-term therapy these trends can be explored. The therapist, aware of such problems in his patient, can insist on per session or weekly payments so that the patient does not groove himself into acting out these trends.

In short-term therapy this is not so possible. In some cases nonpayment is the product of a patient's feeling that his expectations of what should have been done for him have not been fulfilled. In his mind the therapist has not lived up to his part of the contract. Obviously, the therapist will feel angry and wounded at this accusation, particularly if the patient has been helped. Needless to say, many patients expect results that are beyond even divine powers to achieve. There are no standard formulas for retrieving payments after a patient has left therapy. A personal letter inviting the patient to come in to see the therapist to discuss his feelings about his treatment may bring results. A note may also be sent to the effect that if the charge is too difficult to pay at this time, small weekly payments may be made.

II. Psychoanalysis

Psychoanalysis has provided us with concepts and techniques for the recognition and exposure of motivations that operate beyond the zone of awareness. How this information can best be put to use and its serviceability in the treatment of emotional problems are, however, questions that concern present-day clinicians. Most students are no longer willing to accept psychological theories on the basis of faith or literary elegance. Some are relatively unimpressed with both the pronouncements and achievements of psychoanalysis, moving toward active approaches directed practically at symptom relief and problem-solving. Among their expressed doubts are:

1) that psychoanalysis is the best treatment for most problems of an emotional nature;
2) that unconscious conflict is necessarily at the root of all emotional difficulties;
3) that every communication of the patient to the therapist during a session has an unconscious meaning and that through free association one eventually can reach this repudiated core;
4) that verbal unburdening has a greater impact on the individual than behavioral solutions to a problem;

5) that supportive and educational interventions are temporary and inevitably lead to greater avoidance and repression;

6) that an adequate cure of a neurosis necessitates its duplication in treatment through the relationship with the therapist (transference);

7) that psychoanalytic theories can be validated through either research or careful clinical inquiry; and

8) that psychoanalysis is the only method through which reconstructive change can be achieved.

The upshot of these questions is that students are in progressively larger numbers doubting the clinical usefulness of psychoanalysis and the need for extensive personal training in psychoanalytic techniques, with the sacrifices of time, energy and money that disciplined analytic studies would entail. The questions asked and answered in this section relate to these issues.

Q42: What do we mean by "classical psychoanalysis"?

A42: There is general agreement that the term applies to a technique originated by Sigmund Freud in which an analyst intensively works with his patient (the analysand) on a four to five times a week basis, utilizing a couch, free association and dreams, aiming at the development of a transference neurosis which is dealt with by interpretation.

Q43: How really effective is formal psychoanalysis as a technique?

A43: Opinions vary due to the countless variables involved in patient and therapist characteristics. It is often avowed that current pessimistic impressions of the potential of psychoanalysis as a therapy result from the inclusion of reports of outcome made by inexperienced practitioners (Gedo, 1979). Are there any reliable reports of experienced analysts? Summarizing his own work of two decades as an experienced full-time analyst, Gedo is convinced of the effectiveness of the method. His data are drawn from a total caseload of 36 people treated over 20 years of practice, 28 of whom terminated analysis with a "consensus about the satisfactory outcome of the enterprise." The patients were primarily in the higher socioeconomic class. The technique was classical psychoanalysis four or five times weekly, for 600 to 1000 sessions in three to seven years. There was no systematic follow-up study, but the author estimates that failure to contact him "argues for the probability that those who have not been heard from are not simply withholding unfavorable tidings." The author cryptically concludes with the statement that an analyst should not approach clinical work with a personal need to be a healer since "to require patients to improve is an illegitimate infringement on their autonomy."

In reviewing the presented statistics of 28 out of 36 patients improved over a period of 20 years of practice, one would estimate that, irrespective of whether the results justify the conclusion of a "matchless usefulness of the analytic method as a means for personal growth," the classical technique is definitely not designed for the great majority of patients seeking help for emotional problems. This does not in any way invalidate the incorporation of analytic principles in a lesser than long-term program. But to return to the classical analytic technique, could the difficulties encountered with the method be due to a poor selection of candidates? Many authorities believe this to be so.

My own impression is that, given a carefully screened patient and a well-trained analyst, the results with classical analysis can justify the expense and effort. On the other hand, the great majority of patients can be effectively helped by less intensive and costly methods. Where poor results have been obtained with classical psychoanalysis, the chances are that it has been employed with patients who were unsuited for the technique, or that the therapist was by training or personality not capable of working with the method.

Q44: Can you completely eradicate an infantile neurosis through psychoanalysis?

A44: Freud once remarked that one cannot destroy an enemy in effigy. Since he believed that the core problem in many emotional ailments was the infantile neurosis, the best way to eliminate it was to bring it out in the open, activate it in the relationship with the therapist (transference) and resolve it by working it through in a more favorable setting than that which had existed in the individual's childhood. In practice we find that even though we provoke a transference neurosis through intensive therapy and work it through in analysis, the revived memory traces of the infantile neurosis cannot be entirely eliminated. We often have to be satisfied with finding better reality solutions for it so that it does not contaminate our present adjustment and permits us to live as happily and creatively as possible.

Q45: Why do psychoanalysts use such difficult and nebulous language to describe psychopathology?

A45: Fortunately, not all analysts do this. Once a professional accepts and thinks in terms of certain classical hypotheses, e.g., assumptions about instinctual drives and the tripartite structure of the psychic apparatus, he may translate all clinical phenomena into this dialect. Yet he may deviate from some formulations, introducing his own constructions or those of contemporary theorists, further adding to the complexity of his ideas and making them more nebulous for others. He himself knows what he means, but others may have difficulty decoding his expressions and adapting them to their own linguistic systems. Going to lectures or reading articles written by specialists wedded to certain theories may be thus a frustrating experience. In my opinion, the best way to lessen frustration is to read up on the different theories and then translate the concepts described into language that makes sense for oneself.

Q46: Has there been any change in Freud's concepts of the unconscious since he formulated them?

A46: The existence of unconscious mental activity was known before Freud. Freud's enduring contribution was not to discover the unconscious, but to delineate its continuous dynamic influence on behavior, as well as to explore ways of examining it through dreams, symptoms, free association, and transference manifestations. Freud alluded to the unconscious as a cauldron of pleasure-seeking irrationality that wrought havoc on the individual and that had to be subdued by the socially rational conscious mind which was concerned with the demands of reality.

This view has been challenged over the years by many observers who credit to the unconscious not only reservoirs of potential turmoil and pathology, but also characteristics of constructive, creative and insightful problem-solving. What we are coming to is an affirmation of Piaget's idea of the continuity, rather than opposition, of conscious and unconscious ideation (Piaget and Inhelder, 1958). This does not in any way lessen our task of exposing aspects of the unconscious that have been barricaded from awareness and that influence behavior adversely. Therefore, when we deal with unconscious activities we should include not only archaic and useless residues of faulty development, but also inhibited creative impulses that either are seeking expression or have been repressed because of anxiety.

Q47: In actual technique, how does classical psychoanalysis differ from other forms of therapy?

A47: Briefly put, in classical analysis there is a focus on the systematic interpretation of the transference, with strict technical neutrality on the part of the therapist. Intensive self-observation by the patient is constantly encouraged.

Q48: Which patients are most suitable for classical psychoanalysis?

A48: Reviewing 24 separate studies on this question, Bachrach and Leaff (1978) report agreement that the capacity for "analyzability" is best found in persons whose pretreatment adjustment has been relatively good, and whose ego strength and object relations are on a high level. This means that reality-testing, potentiality for sublimation, coping flexibility, communicative aptitude, intellectual ability, and "capacity to regress in the service of the ego" are favorable. The individual's symptoms must not be too severe, diagnostically the patient falling within the "neurotic" zone. (The upshot of these propitious traits is a capacity to develop a working alliance with the therapist and to form a transference neurosis.) Narcissistic pathology should be low and relationships with others good. Early separation and deprivations should have been mastered without loss of "object constancy." There must be an ability to tolerate anxiety, depression, and frustration without losing control or suffering cognitive distortions. In addition, there must be an adequate motivation for change and satisfactory self-understanding. The personality must be suited for psychological exploration ("psychological mindedness"). The "superego is integrated and tolerant." Moreover, suitable candidates are young, "mainly in their twenties or early thirties."

It is doubtful that any human being has all of these "ideal" characteristics, but a good proportion is conceded to be conducive to the best outcome. The fact that there are so few candidates who fulfill these requirements has sponsored in practice many compromises in technique toward greater activity and a veering away from the basic principles of classical psychoanalysis, particularly a setting up and analysis through interpretation of a transference neurosis. However, a good deal of controversy has developed over whether such compromises should be called "psychoanalysis." The term "psychoanalytically oriented psychotherapy" embraces a host of interventions that draw substance from psychoanalytic theory, but address themselves to the more practical issue of treating the large army of people who do not, in addition to lacking "ideal" qualities cited above, have the time, incentive or money to qualify for classical treatments. Whether the outcome of such "diluted" therapies is better or worse than the results with orthodox treatment is a matter that is still being debated.

Assuming that we have selected a patient who has all or most of the characteristics for analyzability, does this mean that success will be inevitable? Obviously not, since the therapist by his singular personality traits and problems (e.g., countertransference) may not be able to provide the kind of relationship with all patients that is conducive to good analysis. This is why a "trial analysis" is indicated to see if both participants are suited for each other.

Q49: Can one decide on the suitability of a patient for psychoanalysis on the basis of the data we get in the initial interview?

A49: The best way of deciding on the suitability for analysis is by an actual "trial analysis." Here we can see whether the relationship between the patient and therapist will "gel" so to speak, and whether the patient is adequately motivated and possesses the suitable qualities for analysis.

Whether the average therapist can arrive at a decision as to analyzability in the initial interview is somewhat doubtful. Experienced analysts may have intuitive hunches about prospective candidates, but even they can be wrong. Proper selection is nevertheless important. In my own practice, I have seen quite a number of analytic failures, some with skilled analysts, that were the result of improper selection. The patient simply was not suitable for analysis. Most of these referrals responded quite satisfactorily to psychoanalytically oriented psychotherapy with treatment geared toward less ambitious goals, such as symptom alleviation or behavioral readjustment.

Q50: Is there any relationship between the degree of illness of a patient and the need for intensive psychoanalysis?

A50: Yes, an inverse ratio. Michels (1980) has pointed out that "a prospective patient must be healthy enough to participate in an analysis," and, citing the recent peer review manual of the American Psychoanalytic Association, lists 11 essential qualifications including "relative absence of significant early trauma" and characteristics more in keeping with a well adjusted than an emotionally ill individual. There are some analysts who claim severe pathology can be treated with modifications of the classical method, but others argue that when this is done we are not doing psychoanalysis. All of which means that with the sicker patients psychotherapy (perhaps along dynamic lines) is more suited for their needs than psychoanalysis.

Q51: Has psychoanalysis been shown to be cost-effective?

A51: Cost-effectiveness of any therapy is related to the population it serves. For the general population psychoanalysis is definitely not cost-effective. For a carefully selected group of patients who are adequately motivated, possess sufficient ego strength, and have other positive characteristics, psychoanalysis performed by a trained, capable psychoanalyst can be cost-effective where reconstructive personality change is the goal. What applies to psychoanalysis in terms of patient selection, goals, and therapist expertise applies also to other therapies.

Q52: What ideas are basic in classicial psychoanalysis and can we call therapies that deviate from these ideas "psychoanalysis"?

A52: A central idea in classical psychoanalysis is that the motivating forces in emotional problems are needs, impulses, and drives which are kept submerged (repressed) by moral prohibitions or environmental pressures. The conflict produced by the opposing forces of drives clashing with defenses (resistances) acts to produce symptoms and aberrations in behavior. Therapy consists of exposing and *working-through* of resistances in order to enable the patient to gain *insight* into his unconscious needs and conflicts. Such insight enables the individual to reconstitute his behavior and to restructure vital aspects of his personality.

In classical analysis an attempt is made to encourage projection of significant past feelings and attitudes into the therapeutic relationship in the phenomenon of *transference*. The actual reproduction in the relationship of important past experiences with parental and other important figures (*transference neurosis*) opens a window into the unconscious and enables the patient to view early developmental happenings and to recognize how these contribute to present-day distortions. Hopefully the patient's neurosis will be worked through in the transference neurosis. The adoption by the therapist of a passive, neutral, non-supportive role encourages the development of transference, and the use of free association and dream analysis permits the therapist to interpret unconscious derivatives toward promotion of essential insight.

Modifications of the classical techniques have occurred since the beginnings of psychoanalysis and have resulted in many deviations,

including greater activity and stronger emphasis on current personality operations as compared to involvement with the past. An object
is attenuation or avoidance of a transference neurosis. Emphasis on
unconscious conflict and the effect of survival of developmental deficits
and defenses are still considered fundamental in dynamically oriented
therapies, but whether these modifications can still rightfully be called
"psychoanalysis" has become more a matter of professional politics
than of scientific substantiality. Proof that many patients do better
with a modified than with a classical approach does little to resolve
this issue. My personal feeling is that while we may utilize some psychoanalytic concepts like the unconscious, repression, resistance, working-through, transference, etc., we should designate the modifications
from classical technique by appropriate terms like dynamic psychotherapy, psychoanalytically oriented therapy, ego analysis, Kleinian
analysis, neofreudian analysis, etc.

**Q53: Why in formal psychoanalysis does the therapist have to
maintain an anonymous and detached attitude when we
know that this does not help establish rapport so essential
in treatment? In fact, it interferes with rapport.**

A53: The anonymous and detached attitude of the analyst and the
couch position are *deliberately designed to induce frustration* by not
gratifying demands for reassurance and support that ordinarily would
be given in other forms of therapy. Normal defenses are bypassed in
this situation and regressive defenses with primary process ideation
usually come to the fore. This fosters the development of a transference
neurosis, the working-through of which will hopefully resolve the infantile neurosis, the paradigm of the transference neurosis and a continuing unconscious source of conflict.

**Q54: What is the difference between psychoanalytically oriented
psychotherapy, dynamically oriented psychotherapy, and
dynamic therapy? How do these differ from psychoanalysis
proper?**

A54: These terms are often used interchangeably. The difference from
classical analysis is that the transference neurosis is not considered
central to the therapeutic process. Whereas in psychoanalysis one con-

centrates on resolution of resistances to the exposure of the infantile conflict with its reliving in the transference neurosis, in the more active therapies the emphasis is away from creation of a transference neurosis and even on its rapid discouragement and dissolution should it appear. The therapeutic relationship is regarded more as a means toward a corrective emotional experience rather than as a vehicle for the exploration of unconscious trends.

Q55: How does psychoanalytically oriented psychotherapy differ in objectives from psychoanalysis proper?

A55: Psychoanalysis aims at a systematic and complete resolution of unconscious conflicts with structural alteration of defenses and the character organization. Psychoanalytically oriented psychotherapy is less ambitious, aiming for the practical and less arduously achieved goals of resolving some conflicts, modifying others, and even retaining and strengthening certain neurotic defenses that permit the individual to contain his anxiety and to function. This does not necessarily make psychoanalysis a "better" kind of treatment than psychoanalytically oriented therapy or vice versa. Some patients fail miserably at one and do quite well with the other. The key issue, I believe, is the proper selection of cases for the two different techniques. Patients who will be exposed to formal analysis, centered around evolvement of a transference neurosis and its resolution through interpretation, will require so many qualifications in terms of personality characteristics, available time, finances, etc. that they are relatively few in number. Most patients, on the other hand, will qualify for psychoanalytically oriented therapy.

Q56: How do psychoanalysis and psychotherapy differentially approach the problem of the ubiquitous infantile neurosis?

A56: All people may be considered as possessing residues of an infantile neurosis to which they are adjusting for better or worse. Those who are "normal" are capable of controlling and living around this neurotic core; those who are "neurotic" are handicapped by a greater or lesser degree of anxiety and by defenses to reduce anxiety. Where an infantile neurosis is feeding present-day maladjustment, its management may call for some kind of psychological treatment. Psychoanalysis offers

itself as a technique that can, if successful, promote maturity by eliminating the infantile neurosis as a source of emotional pollution. Psychotherapy is more modest in its goals. It can help to strengthen the
individual's defenses so as to prevent the infantile neurosis from interfering too much with a reality adaptation. It can also provide guidelines for more competent coping with everyday stress. In this way the
individual is better able to live with his infantile neurosis and to make
an adjustment that is no better or worse than the "normal" individual
who, though he possesses some neurotic defenses, never sees the inside
of a psychotherapist's office and still gets along satisfactorily with life
and people.

Q57: Can all patients achieve reconstruction of the personality with proper psychoanalytic treatment?

A57: Relatively few patients who come for therapy are either motivated
for character reconstruction or are suitable candidates for the intensity
of treatment that is required. Even where the therapist is a trained,
skilled, and experienced psychoanalyst, he will not be able to get far
with many patients because of their unsuitability for analysis. The
latter individuals would, however, be quite suitable for psychotherapy
of a less intensive nature (i.e., where a transference neurosis is deliberately avoided). This does not mean that we cannot employ dynamic
concepts in such a psychotherapeutic program which may, over a long
period after therapy has ended, in the medium of life experience itself,
foster continuing personality change in some patients and even reconstructive characterologic alterations.

Q58: In the event a patient is suffering from the effects of un- resolved nuclear conflicts, wouldn't he need deep probing psychoanalysis to resolve these before he experiences re- lief?

A58: It must be emphasized that while nuclear conflicts exist in all
people and give rise to many secondary derivative conflicts, the existing
defensive structures may be sufficiently flexible to permit an adequate
adjustment to most responsibilities of life. However, where some severe
crisis shatters security or markedly undermines self-esteem, the defenses may not be able to safeguard the individual from catastrophic

feelings of helplessness. Early conflicts customarily held in check may then surface, and anachronistic, inadequate coping measures may then be brought into play, which promote rather than neutralize anxiety, creating neurotic symptoms and behavioral disturbances.

The fact that historical antecedents exist that account for character distortions and provide provocative stimuli for the present emotional upset does not mean that identification and exploration of these antecedents will in any way help in immediate problem-solving. Indeed, there is a good deal of evidence that defenses may sometimes be restored more adequately through simple counseling and behaviorally oriented interventions, the individual being brought back more or less rapidly to his customary equilibrium. In many cases, perhaps in most cases, this is all that the patient wants done or that can practically be done. In no way does this imply that more could not have been accomplished through a depth-oriented approach. But we have to balance off possible reconstructive personality gains against the rigorous inconveniences, the stringent financial expense, and the grim risks of embarking on a long and sometimes unrewarding journey into the recesses of the unconscious. On the other hand, we may have no alternative to initiating a program designed to deal with developmentally inspired mischief mongers where these operate as unmovable resistances to productive problem-solving. Fortunately, we now have enough understanding of the therapeutic process to avoid making many of the blunders with dynamically directed techniques that in the past have led to interminable therapy or outright failure.

Q59: Can narcissistic personalities be psychoanalyzed?

A59: Some analysts say "no" since narcissistic personalities do not seem to be able to form a transference neurosis, which makes them unanalyzable. Other analysts do not agree that the narcissistic personality cannot form a transference neurosis. Indeed they claim success with the use of traditional classical techniques. Still others, like Modell (1980), believe that psychoanalysis is possible in some cases through "modification in the analytic process itself."

According to Modell, the analytic setting, rather than the transference neurosis, becomes the major focus. The couch position is used; there is no support or reassurance. Active measures like those used in psychotherapy are avoided. The consequence is "a true analytic result ... comparable to that achieved in the transference neurosis." During the initial period of therapy, the therapist must recognize that the patient will seal himself off and will not allow himself to engage too deeply. The middle phase is often associated with a negativistic reaction, perhaps as a consequence of resentment that the therapist is not as omniscient and powerful as the patient would like. Finally, patients who are analyzable will relate transferentially and here real therapeutic work may be accomplished. An empathic stance by the therapist in the opening phase provides symbolic gratification for early unmet needs. Interpretations at the beginning are usually futile and may be resented; their later acceptance is a true mark of progress. In the final phase of therapy free association may be possible in some patients and a transference neurosis may occur. Should this happen we can say that the patient is truly in an analytic situation, merely warming up to it in the prior phases of treatment.

Narcissistic personalities who are unanalyzable, according to Modell, are those in whom self-object differentiation is severely impaired and who harbor a degree of sadism which outwardly directed makes for paranoid anxiety, and inwardly focused produces unconscious guilt. Not all analysts would agree with Modell's formulations (e.g. Stone, 1980; Kernberg, 1980). Be this as it may, there is increasing interest in the narcissistic personality and new concepts, such as those of Kohut (1971), are influencing treatment ideas so that the prognosis for analyzability in these difficult patients is not as hopeless as was once imagined.

Q60: Why is a transference neurosis important and when would you consider the development and use of a transference neurosis necessary?

A60: There are some symptom-sponsoring conflicts and memories, associated with early traumatic experiences and fantasies related to parents and other significant persons, that are so deeply repressed that they require an emotional atom bomb to blast them to the surface. This is what a transference neurosis provides, since the relationship with the therapist here duplicates to some extent what went on in childhood and liberates buried affects and memories related to this period. No other therapeutic experience parallels this phenomenon in dramatic intensity. On the wave of the aroused emotions the patient then is given a second chance to rectify the hurts and distortions experienced when the ego was too weak to deal with overpowering emotions. In the guise of a new parental figure who is tolerant and understanding, the therapist may be able to provide the patient with an opportunity to get insight into the origins of pathogenic conflicts, to recognize his own role and that of his parents in producing these, to see how they are related to his personality difficulties and to the symptoms for which he seeks relief in treatment. He still has to work through his insights to produce changes in behavioral patterns. Because his habits are rigidly set this will require continuing experiment with new ways of behaving over a period of time. Even though established habits change with great reluctance, persistence is hopefully rewarded so that eventually cognitions, emotions, and behavior become more attuned to reality. A good therapeutic relationship offers the best conditions for working-through, although insightful, motivated patients living in favorable settings can carry on the working-through process in life experience itself.

From this we should not assume that treatment oriented around the transference neurosis is the only way people can overcome problems. In many instances the source of psychopathology lies in areas other than unconscious conflicts so that their exposure is unnecessary. In most cases conflicts and memories are not so pathogenic nor so deeply repressed that they cannot be understood and worked through by less intensive methods than the major surgery of a transference neurosis. Even with short-term dynamic psychotherapy, sufficient understanding may ensue to allow for continuing working-through and change after termination of treatment.

Among the caveats embracing our encouraging a transference neurosis is the fact that there are some patients who cannot tolerate and who should not be exposed to the major psychological surgery procedure of a transference neurosis, even though their problems are embedded in unconscious conflict. Their ego structure is too infirm and their defenses too shaky to endure the rigors of the experience. These patients are particularly unsuited for classical psychoanalysis which, as we know, through its techniques is designed most elegantly to stimulate and manage a transference neurosis.

Q61: Aren't the results with setting up and working through of a transference neurosis more extensive and more permanent than any other method and shouldn't this therefore be the objective in good therapy?

A61: With patients who have the ideal characteristics to qualify for classical psychoanalysis, and who have the good fortune to be treated by a trained, experienced and empathic psychoanalyst the results can be most gratifying. But in terms of numbers such endowed individuals are few. To try to encourage a transference neurosis in the less qualified candidates, in the hopes of blasting away resistances to the exposure of nuclear conflicts, is less than productive, and in the case of sicker patients dangerous, opening up a Pandora's Box of trouble for both the patient and therapist. Other forms of treatment are more expedient and more effective. For the average patient consequently, psychotherapy, preferably with a dynamic orientation, is the best approach.

Q62: How important are nontransferential reactions in analytic therapies? Also aren't we moving away from the idea that the patient is in constant transference with the analyst whether he shows it or not?

A62: Many reactions of a nontransferential nature occur during analysis, neglect of which may be antitherapeutic. Thus, a negative response to therapy is not always a manifestation of negative transference. Insistence on the latter may not get at crucial resistances. Where a therapist is wedded to the concept that transference is the exclusive agency around which all therapeutic transactions operate, he may easily overestimate its importance. There is, on the other hand, danger in minimization of transference as a most potent factor in understanding the ongoing psychodynamics and in providing a means of rectifying underlying psychopathology.

Today, we witness a tendency to soften Ferenczi's (1926) contention that "every dream, every gesture, every faulty action, every worsening or improvement in the state of the patient above all is an expression of transference." Yet, there are still many analysts who agree with Ferenczi and insist that every piece of behavior, acting-out, affect or resistance during the analytic hours originates in transference. Some explain this on the basis that the analyst's confrontations and interpretations keep the unconscious determinants associated with himself. Moreover, all of the activities of the patient during the analytic hour are communicated to the analyst verbally or nonverbally and this is what ties the analyst to the patient and encourages transference reactions. To answer your question, in summary, we must in analysis—and in all therapies for that matter—deal with both transferential and nontransferential reactions.

III. Psychoanalytically Oriented (Dynamic) Psychotherapy

Utilized selectively, classical psychoanalysis still has an unmatched utility for a small number of suitable patients seeking reconstructive personality change. For the great majority of patients, however, other techniques are far more practical and effective. But some principles of psychoanalysis can still be universally useful, and attempts have been made to extract from the body of psychoanalytic theory and method worthy aspects that can be adapted to other modalities. The ensuing products are often regarded as "psychodynamic" or "psychoanalytically oriented."

The incorporation of psychoanalytic concepts into technical operations has led to a wide divergence of methods that are active, that sometimes employ supportive and educational tactics, that shy away from deeper unconscious content, that manipulate the relationship by limiting transference reactions and avoiding a transference neurosis, that focus on here-and-now problems rather than on aspects of the past, that deal both behaviorally and interpretively with resistance, and that utilize various adjunctive instrumentalities. This has opened the door to many questions, including how extensive the penetration should be into early childhood experience, whether a prescribed avoidance of intense transference reactions violates analytic principles, the bolstering effect on repression of active maneuvers, the possible by-passing of pathogenic conflicts through the concentration on present surface issues, and whether reconstructive change is possible with the compromises imposed by the manipulative techniques.

Q63: When you talk about dynamic therapy or dynamically oriented therapy, what do you mean by "dynamic"?

A63: The word dynamic was coined to describe the interaction of intrapsychic forces as the core etiological factor in emotional illness. Many of these forces operate outside the zone of awareness and wreak their havoc by creating conflicts. In dynamic therapy we acknowledge the operation of these unconscious intrapsychic elements and we attempt to uncover, mediate, and, if necessary, resolve them.

Q64: Isn't the goal of dynamic or psychoanalytically oriented psychotherapy always a resolution of the oedipus complex?

A64: This is a much too truncated characterization of therapeutic objectives in dynamic psychotherapy. A good deal of the argumentation that has split the analytic school has centered around the designation of the oedipus complex as the polestar of all pathology. While upsetting oedipal problems do require attention in therapy, they are not the only celestial mischief mongers in the galaxy of human adversity. It is no more correct to say that the exclusive goal of dynamic therapy is the resolution of the oedipus complex than to particularize the objective as an overcoming of oral dependency, or of self-destructive masochism, or of intemperate narcissism, or of omnipotent grandiosity. Probably all of these components will require correction if they are pathologically implicated.

Q65: Is psychoanalysis as it is practiced today different from the way it was done in past years?

A65: The classical psychoanalytic technique is still practiced by some analysts, but, by and large, many, perhaps most analysts employ a modified psychoanalytic technique which differs from the orthodox form. Among a sizeable number of questionnaires sent out by the Research Committee on Psychoanalytic Practice of the American Academy of Psychoanalysis (Tabachnick, 1973), only six percent of the patients being treated by the respondees were seen four times a week, and a mere one percent five times a week. The great majority of the patients were treated in the sitting-up rather than in the couch position. Group, family and marital therapy were occasionally utilized, and

94 percent of those polled sometimes prescribed drugs. We might speculate from this that either the bulk of patients were not suited for intensive psychoanalytic work, or that the analysts in the survey believed that psychoanalysis could be done with less than the classical four-to-five-time-per-week sessions, or that most patients could not afford paying for more frequent visits, or that the members of the American Academy of Psychoanalysis were less rigorous than their colleagues in the more orthodox American Psychoanalytic Association. My hunch is that this survey truly reflects what is going on in contemporary psychoanalysis, and that even the most orthodox analysts are not utilizing the classical technique for most of their patients. My further hunch, which is reinforced by conversations with a sizeable number of psychoanalysts of various schools, is that the brand of psychoanalytic practice being done today is more in the nature of a psychoanalytically oriented treatment than the classical type, irrespective of what analysts themselves say they are doing.

Q66: With the growing criticism of psychoanalysis and loss of its popularity, isn't this a sign that psychoanalytic therapy is on the way out?

A66: The glittering allure of psychoanalysis was never destroyed by attacks on its theories or methods. The reason for this lies not in man's reluctance to abandon traditional beliefs, but in the solemn fact that some of the contentions and methods of psychoanalysis continue to be substantially useful. Psychoanalytic therapies, in contrast to symptom-oriented therapies, have an appeal because they direct themselves toward expanding self-awareness, altering the nature of one's mental functioning, as well as the quality of relationships with others. This in no way depreciates what symptom-oriented and problem-solving therapies do. But the objectives of the dynamic therapies add an important dimension.

Q67: Where you use active manipulative techniques in psychoanalytically oriented therapy, doesn't this encourage the repressive forces that you are trying to modulate?

A67: Not necessarily. I believe it is necessary to emphasize that repression is not always a neurotic manifestation. It is as much a parcel of good therapy to build up constructive repression as it is to soften those destructive repressions that prevent the individual from fulfilling himself creatively and productively. What I am trying to emphasize is the need to differentiate these two kinds of repression and to deal differentially with their manifestations and effects. In psychopathic personalities, for example, where the individual has poor impulse control and frequently is at the mercy of anarchic drives that seek fulfillment irrespective of the consequences on society and the self, a reinforcing of repressive controls is a mandatory goal in therapy. In hysterical personalities, on the other hand, repression may be too severe, preventing expression of normal needs and drives. Here their tempering and modification may be important.

Q68: Can you do psychoanalytically oriented psychotherapy without considering the transference?

A68: I doubt it. Nor can you avoid dealing with unconscious needs and defenses. However, in psychoanalytically oriented psychotherapy transference is not deliberately encouraged or intensified to the point of a transference neurosis. One might imagine that watering down transference would dilute results. This, in my opinion, does not happen in well conducted therapy.

Q69: In psychoanalytic psychotherapy how much time should be spent in probing the past?

A69: Too much concentration on the past can be counterproductive. The past must be related to what is going on in the present. This does not mean we should neglect working with the past during some phases of therapy. But since we do not want to inspire too much regression and precipitate a transference neurosis, the focus should be on the here-and-now.

Q70: By dealing with here-and-now problems in psychoanalytically oriented therapy aren't you avoiding the basic source of neurosis in unconscious conflict?

A70: Here-and-now problems are frequently bracketed to personality difficulties, which in turn may be linked to unconscious conflicts. In good psychoanalytically oriented therapy we always alert ourselves to manifestations of these conflicts, conscious and unconscious, as they reveal themselves in transference, acting-out tendencies, dreams, fantasies and free association.

Q71: I always had the impression that psychoanalysts considered modifications of the classical psychoanalytic technique a compromise resulting in a second-best type of therapy. Is this true?

A71: This is definitely not so for the vast bulk of problems that are seen in treatment. As a matter of fact, the reverse is true. Psychoanalysis is suited for only a small selected group of patients and its results in unselected patients leave much to be desired. Some research studies bear this out. For example, in the extensive Psychotherapy Research Project at the Menninger Foundation (Kernberg et al., 1972; Applebaum, 1975) the prediction that patients would respond to psychoanalysis with more extensive and stable changes than to less intensive therapies like psychoanalytically oriented psychotherapy was not substantiated by the research. Even where the transference was not uncovered or interpreted, several patients maintained stable changes. What seemed to be most important was the character of the therapeutic alliance. Modification of the classical technique for most patients would seem to be the preferred method.

Q72: Can psychoanalytically oriented psychotherapy achieve reconstructive personality changes that are as thorough as those in psychoanalysis?

A72: Reconstructive personality change is difficult to achieve for many reasons with any therapy, even with prolonged intensive psychoanalysis, but it is not impossible where the patient is adequately motivated for such change, where the need for a neurotic adjustment (like masochistic self-punishment) is not too great, where secondary gains are not too strong, where a good working relationship exists, where the therapist is well-trained and knows how to manage transference and other resistances, where countertransference can be used productively, and where the environment will support healthier patterns in the patient. Personality change under these circumstances can be obtained by psychoanalytically oriented psychotherapy as well as by psychoanalysis. But failures can also occur in both.

Q73: How can we expedite the treatment process in psychoanalytically oriented therapy?

A73: Experience does confirm the wisdom of providing each individual with as much information about himself and his conflicts as can be tolerated. Since significant conflicts are more or less unconscious, and because resistance is always present to prevent understanding from nurturing constructive change, the implementation of this kind of depth dynamic approach, however desirable it may be, becomes an arduous and often prolonged procedure. While dynamic schema explain why and how emotional difficulties develop, this insight in itself rarely produces change. It can, however, act as a catalyst to expedite change. Toward this objective we may use facilitating techniques in the form of active, eclectic stratagems which are derived from psychoanalytic, behavioral, cognitive, and other methodologies. In other words, interpretation should be supplemented with other methods that expedite learning and toward this end the therapist has a great variety of group and individual procedures to choose from.

IV. Behavior Therapy (Behavior Modification)

Modern clinical and experimental research has contributed to the sophistication of behavioral interventions and has extended their usefulness for dealing with many syndromes, ranging from adjustment and habit disorders, to neurotic symptomatology (e.g., phobias, obsessions, compulsions, and depressions), to problems of retardates and psychotics. Questions continue to be asked about the utilities and dangers of behavior therapy, many based on misconceptions, for example, the ideas that the method is too authoritarian, coercive, controlling and punitive; that behavior therapists avoid history-taking and extensive data-gathering; that symptom removal often results in symptom substitution or in only temporary benefits; and that the therapist-patient relationship is not considered to be too important.

Accusations are still levied at behavior therapists to the effect that they disregard inner nonmeasurable aspects of experience like feelings and fantasies, and even that some therapists are so tied to a simple stimulus-response ideology that they consider the human brain "an irrelevant and unnecessary intervening variable." These ideas are

51

largely erroneous, and contribute to the existing climate of misunderstanding. Although analysts and behavior therapists are becoming more tolerant of each other's ideas, there is still a good deal of distance and distrust between them which, hopefully, time and constructive dialogue will resolve.

Q74: Can a dynamically oriented psychotherapist utilize some of the techniques of behavior therapy?

A74: Yes, especially during the phase of treatment where we desire to translate insight into action. The patient's psychological responses to behavioral techniques may be studied and dreams examined for unconscious conflicts and transference manifestations. A good deal of valuable information may be obtained which will be helpful in the analytic process, the working-through of which will expedite the resolving of resistances to the behavioral techniques.

Q75: What are some of the basic concepts of behavior therapy?

A75: In a dynamic approach maladaptive behavior is regarded as a symbolic expression of inner conflict as well as a defense against it. Psychoanalysis works toward the exploration, exposure, and defusing of unconscious conflict, resolution of which is presumed to dissipate pathogenic defenses and symptoms. Adaptive, socially appropriate behavior then has the best opportunity to follow. Behavior theory rejects this thesis, contending that symptoms are not a by-product of intrapsychic problems, but rather constitute the problems themselves. All behavior is learned and sustained by reinforcements. In treating symptoms, the focus is on achieving different respones to stimuli provided by new environmental contingencies. Maladaptive behavior is replaced by adaptive activities when reinforcements favor the latter rather than the former.

The actual conduct of behavior therapy differs from that of dynamic psychotherapy. The therapist is highly directive. Little attention is paid to the patient's complaints (negative reinforcement), while acceptable pursuits are greeted with rewards and approval. The patient is distracted from talking about his historical past; he focuses on immediate tasks that will bring reinforcements. On the contrary, the dynamic therapist is nondirective, accepting and warm, guiding the patient into talking about his past and his present, about fantasies and dreams. The patient, rather than the therapist, more or less determines the content of the interviews.

A basic premise of behavioral approaches is that problems for which people seek help are maintained by ongoing current behaviors and relationships. Accordingly, therapy is directed at what maintains problem behaviors and relationships. What is deemed essential is as precise an identification of the problem as possible, recognition and delineation of the consequences of the problem for the patient and others, identification of the contingencies that maintain the problem or prevent it from being resolved, and designation of ways in which the maintaining behavior for the problem can be overcome. Next, strategies are outlined to achieve a desired goal, however minimal that may be.

Q76: What do the various kinds of behavior therapy have in common?

A76: The many varieties of behavior therapy are commonly related to a behavioral learning model of psychopathology which focuses on "observable behavior" instead of on "hypothesized personality structures or presumptive subjective experiences" (Phillips and Kanfer, 1969). Speculation, appraisal, and interpretation are in terms of environmental stimuli and behavioral acts rather than in the wordage of inner conflicts and other "conjectural constructs." Modification of behavior is presumably bracketed to research findings and studies in experimental psychology laboratories. Being data-oriented, behavior therapy attempts to avoid speculative inferences about the meanings of events. This is not to deny the importance of such inferences or the usefulness of the reports of subjects about what is happening to them. But these concepts are not employed to explain behavior. The historical genesis of behaviors selected for modification is not considered material for diagnosis and treatment, even though there is recognition that abnormal behaviors have a historical origin. Rather, the circumstances that control and sustain these behaviors in the here-and-now are central targets.

Q77: According to behavior therapists, attitude change can be rapidly achieved by application of learning theory. As a psychoanalyst, I am unclear as to how this is brought about. Can you clarify this?

A77: Attitude change is a direct or indirect goal in many psychotherapies because inappropriate attitudes create destructive emotions and often express themselves in maladaptive behavior. Since attitudes are acquired through experience, it would therefore seem that they can be altered by experience—at least this is the assumption of those supporting learning theories. Consequently, what would be necessary for attitude change, according to some behavior therapists (Johnson, 1980), is: first, to get the person to describe his problems and to identify the patterns of thinking and behaving that promote the problems; second, to build trust in the patient, "reducing the person's defensiveness, egocentrism, and demoralization"; third, to apply "a theory (or combination of theories) of attitude change"; and, fourth, to stabilize the "new attitudes by building supports that will maintain them." The second proposition, of building trust, is fundamental and this is also more or less accepted by other theoretical schools as a means toward producing change in the patient. The response of the helper to the patient's disclosures is the key to trust building, with "expression of warmth, accurate understanding, and cooperative intentions" helping to achieve this objective. Some therapists, like Johnson (1980), believe that through cooperative interaction, expressed by the helper's reciprocal disclosures and information-giving, sharing "thoughts, feelings, attitudes and reactions relevant to the issue being discussed," defensive egocentrism and demoralization are reduced. Through role-playing and role reversal, it is assumed that the patient's understanding of another person's attitudes will be possible and his own misunderstandings clarified. Other behavior therapists utilize different tactics to achieve the same objectives, for example, methods that are more in line with cognitive theory.

Q78: Does the relationship with the therapist influence the course and outcome of behavior therapy?

A78: Definitely. Some behavior therapists minimize the effect of the relationship, but, in my opinion, the relationship is as important in behavior therapy as in any other form of treatment. A good relationship expedites the therapeutic process; a poor relationship inhibits or blocks it. Transference resistances are often at the bottom of failures in behavior therapy.

Q79: Doesn't behavior therapy avoid the important cognitive aspects of a problem?

A79: Modern behavior therapists consider internal (cognitive) aspects important if they are implicated in problem behaviors. After a systematic analysis of the problem (behavioral analysis), which considers the origins of the problem and the immediate reinforcing contingencies that keep it alive, careful consideration is given to both external (environmental) and internal (cognitive) factors that have to be modified. The actual techniques used here combine principles originally evolved by such pioneers as Pavlov, Skinner, and Hull, and elaborated by more contemporary authorities such as Wolpe, Bandura and Lazarus. Where cognitive elements are held responsible for some of the prevailing difficulties, an attempt is made to control or alter faulty patterns of thinking through methods of "cognitive behavior therapy" along lines developed by Ellis, Mahoney, Meichenbaum, Beck, Rush, and others.

Q80: How would you explain the drift of behavior therapists toward cognitive approaches?

A80: Recognizing that complex human behavior cannot be explained solely by conditioning paradigms, behaviorists since 1970 have turned to higher level processes, exploring what they have called "cognitive behavior therapy." As we might expect, different authorities have experimented with and developed innovative ways of implementing this new dimension. For example, some have focused on illogical thought patterns that in the past have forced the patient to draw false inferences from certain events, to overgeneralize from solitary incidents, and to fail to correct distortions even though life experience has pointed to the falsity of their assumptions (Beck, 1976). Others have advocated more active training procedures, working with patients toward employing positive, constructive self-statements along with practicing relaxation techniques (Meichenbaum, 1977). Still others continue to use Ellis' (1962) technique of actively presenting rational solutions to replace the patient's maladaptive ones.

Social learning precepts are prominently employed in training procedures with the object of rational restructuring of thought processes; of altering mental sets in line with optimistic rather than pessimistic expectations; of liberating oneself from the tyranny of conventional beliefs; of abandoning the notion that one has always to be right, loved, perfect, important and happy; and of relinquishing the idea that one's past indelibly stamps out one's destiny.

Patients are aided in acquiring coping skills by 1) putting themselves into challenging or upsetting situations in fantasy and verbalizing their feelings, and 2) role-playing constructive solutions. There is accumulating experimental evidence that these techniques help to reduce anxiety and to change attitudes that create pathologic feelings and behavior. Skill in problem-solving is encouraged by showing the patient that his attitudes, positive or negative, will definitely influence the outcomes; that it is essential to define and formulate the problem at hand for which a solution is needed; that alternative approaches should be designed in the event a chosen solution proves to be inadvisable; that a definite decision of a course of action must be made; and that verification of the validity of this choice in terms of achievement of set goals must finalize the process (Goldfried & Davison, 1976).

Q81: Psychotherapy is, as you have said, a relearning process where old useless patterns are unlearned and new adaptive ones learned. Isn't this no more than operant conditioning? Isn't all psychotherapy really a form of behavior modification?

A81: There is more to psychotherapy than simple operant conditioning, but I do believe that extinction of old patterns and reinforcement of constructive thoughts, ideas, attitudes and behavior are important. In other words, operant conditioning should take place as part of good therapeutic process. This does not qualify every therapy as behavior therapy any more than we would consider behavioral treatment which achieves cognitive alterations a form of psychoanalysis.

Q82: Can methods based on learning theory or cognitive theory reliably change pathological feelings? Can you give examples of this?

A82: John, age seven, does not like spinach. One can approach this negative attitude with learning theory methods, e.g., through classical or operant conditioning. Accordingly, one might encourage John to try to eat small quantities of spinach, sitting with him and rewarding him with supportive and approving statements, and perhaps with some material bounty like money, desserts, or other things John likes. Through such counterconditioning, John's feelings about spinach may be expected to change.

Harry, age 30, does not like himself. His depreciating feeling about himself are a longtime product of a devalued self-image. Here we might also try to reward him for anything good he says about himself or any act that indicates self-liking.

The first example illustrates a simple conditioning paradigm applied to a recently acquired feeling which will probably yield success in most cases. The second conditioning example falls into a different category. It involves deep-seated developmental difficulties and conflicts that in all probability will fail to be resolved with such learning theory methods.

Cognitive theory might also be recommended as a structure to change feelings. According to Johnson (1980), "One way to help a person who has a low evaluation of himself is to make his behavior so apparently and clearly of value that he will have little alternative but to change his self-attitudes if he is to achieve consonance or balance." This tactic, however, also will probably be ineffective in Harry's case. Logic and reason notoriously fail to alter basic feelings and assumptions rooted in developmental lacks. Thus, pointing out the inconsistencies of Harry's "bad" self-views, as contrasted with his actual "good" behavior and accomplishments, will undoubtedly fail miserably in changing his devalued self-image. Similarly, pointing out to Harry how his attitudes are unreasonable, how they fail to meet his needs, how they stir up anxiety, how they lead to self-defeat, how they destroy his capacities for adjustment, and how they create harmful emotions and actually enhance his behavioral difficulties may do no more than to supply him with ammunition to justify his hating himself even more.

Added to our difficulties in helping John and Harry with any methods is the contingency that they may *transfer* onto their therapist feelings of distrust and resistance that they harbored toward their parents. ("This person is acting like my mother who always tried to boss me around. I am not going to allow him to manipulate or change me.") Further, therapists may *countertransfer* over to their patients identifications with or feelings they had toward significant persons in their own past. ("This brat irritates me with his stubbornness. He deserves a kick in the pants.") Understanding and resolving these transference and countertransference resistances are fundamental in changing destructive and self-defeating attitudes.

In summary, behavioral methods based on learning theory and cognitive theory may mediate some pathological feelings, especially those that have been recently acquired and of which the individual is consciously aware. They are not so serviceable in altering feelings that date back to early childhood, especially those that are frozen in the personality structure and imbedded in unconscious conflict. A devalued self-image is usually difficult to change when it is bracketed to a masochistic need to punish oneself for guilt feelings. Even awareness of the extent of one's self-destructiveness is usually masked by denial and rationalizations. Awareness of these feelings and their origin is sometimes possible through psychoanalytic probings utilizing free association, dreams, and analysis of transference and resistance. But the surfacing of this material alone does not mean that the individual can or will alter his feelings. It is at this point that behavioral methods may help to translate insight into corrective attitudinal and behavioral change.

Q83: What are the minimal data that should be gathered during behavioral analysis in a short-term behavior modification program?

A83: It is necessary to examine 1) the situations where problem behaviors occur, i.e., which situations exaggerate and which ameliorate the behaviors; 2) the special ways the problem behaviors manifest themselves and the intensity of their manifestations; 3) the effect of the behaviors on the patient himself and on others, as well as the consequences to the patient, to others, and to the environment; 4) the personal assets and resources available to support anticipated changes, and the areas in the environment on which we may draw for help; and 5) the possible impact on the patient and on others of anticipated improvement or cure. The past life and conditionings that have acted as a seedbed for problem behaviors, and the past and present reinforcements that have initiated and are now sustaining the behavior are also examined. A hierarchy of problem behaviors is composed on paper with the object of establishing a priority regarding which problems to select for immediate focus and which for a possible later focus.

Q84: How do behavior therapists utilize behavioral assessment?

A84: A behavioral assessment focuses on the problem behaviors, their origins, manifestations, consequences, and reinforcements that keep them alive. Goals in therapy are discussed in terms of what the patient wants from therapy and what changes in behavior are necessary to achieve this. Some behavior therapists recommend a *Behavioral Self Rating Check List* (Cautela and Upper, 1975) which contains 73 kinds of behavior it is possible to change. The therapist must agree that the patient's goals are acceptable and not unreasonable. Next, a definition of the problem includes the situations in which problem behaviors occur, their frequency, the patient's thoughts and feelings that accompany them, the environmental consequences, and their effect on the behaviors. A clinical assessment, including history-taking, follows. Certain forms may be used, such as a *Reinforcement Survey Schedule* (Cautela and Kastenbaum, 1967) and the *Fear Survey Schedule* (Wolpe & Lang, 1964).

The patient may be asked to write down his reactions during an episode where problem behaviors occur (e.g., a phobic inspiring situation). He is also asked to quantify his reactions, to write down the number of times a day his symptoms occur and to note the circumstances that surround their appearance. What is searched for are the stimuli that set off problem behaviors and their reinforcements. In several interviews sufficient information should have been gained. After presenting the therapist's hypothesis of the patient's difficulty and gaining his acceptance of this, a treatment plan is devised and a contract with the patient drawn up. Therapy focuses on set goals. Should the individual fail to respond well in relation to the limited selected target, a wider range of targets, perhaps calling for different behavioral techniques, may be required.

Q85: What is "in vivo desensitization"? How is it related to implosive therapy and flooding? How does its effectiveness compare with systematic desensitization? And can you give an example of how it works?

A85: Exposure to a fear-provoking stimulus with no attempt to escape from it will tend to weaken the strength of the stimulus. The patient here is instructed to approach the phobic situation and, as long as possible, to tolerate it (by relaxing his muscles and by trying mentally to change the meaning of the danger he imagines invests the situation). The exposure time is gradually increased, being carried to the point where the patient feels moderately uncomfortable. Eventually it is hoped the fear will be extinguished. The therapist may himself model the proper approach behavior as an example of how controls can be established. Experience convinces that in vivo desensitization is superior to desensitization through imagery, as, for example, in systematic desensitization. However, desensitization through imagery may be used as a preliminary therapy in order to reduce the level of an intense anxiety reaction that can prevent the patient from even attempting to expose himself to a real situation. A trusting relationship with the therapist is of the greatest help to the patient whose terrors have kept him from facing the phobic situation by himself.

A massive form of in vivo desensititization is that of *implosive therapy or flooding,* during which the patient is exposed to fear-provoking stimuli, escape from which is not indulged. In some cases, induced exaggerated forms of fearful imagery related to the phobia precede actual immersion in the phobic situation, the therapist purposefully magnifying the sinister nature of the fantasy stimulus. After the patient learns to tolerate the imagery, the real stimulus in force is employed. Remaining in a fearsome position until the anxiety disappears may result in substantial improvement or cure. In obsessive-compulsive reactions the exposure is to the stimuli that produce the rituals and the patient is discouraged or blocked from engaging in them. For example, in hand-washing compulsions produced by touching dirt the therapist first models rubbing his hands on his shoes or the floor and then enjoins the patient to do the same. He thereafter sits with the patient, encouraging him not to go to the bathroom to scrub his hands. The results with this kind of therapy have been encouraging; however, "The therapist must not back away from the elicitation of anxiety, no matter how uncomfortable the patient becomes, and must not terminate the session before the extinction of anxiety is complete" (Seligman, 1979). Agreement must be reached with the patient in advance of using this technique that he will be willing to tolerate a certain amount of discomfort in overcoming his handicap, the advantages in time-saving being pointed out to him. It cannot be emphasized enough that the therapeutic alliance must be a firm one in order for the patient to trust himself to the massive exposure to flooding techniques. Time may have to be spent consolidating the relationship prior to suggesting the technique to the patient.

Q86: Would you describe the actual process of in vivo desensitization for phobias?

A86: Let us say an individual has a fear of dogs. The process is started by exposing him to closer and closer approximations to dogs. At first he is encouraged to look at a dog from a distance, then to move toward the animal, forcing himself to tolerate any anxiety that is set loose.

The therapist concurrently may model the approach behavior. Where reproduction of the fear stimulus is impossible or too frightening, visual imagery may be required as a preliminary. Positive reinforcements or contingency contracting may also concomitantly be used to accelerate desirable behaviors. Flooding (implosive) techniques are also often used, the patient being asked to imagine the fearful situation and to "ride" eventuating anxiety, or to expose himself to the actual fearful situation and stay in it until the anxiety leaves (extinction). Where the problem involves compulsive rituals, the patient is enjoined to expose himself to the stimuli that produce the rituals and to force himself to delay or avoid the ritualistic activity. Scenes are also presented to the patient that can provide the greatest anxiety through imagery (whether they involve aggression, sexuality, assertiveness, etc.) and they are continued until the patient fails to react to them. The therapist must be highly inventive and forceful and must have the endurance to stay with the patient until a positive result is scored. The therapist may continuously model desired behavior. Reinforcements may also be employed to reward the patient for executing restraints.

Q87: How is desensitization through imagery done?

A87: In desensitization through imagery it has been shown that the pairing of fear and relaxation responses reduces the intensity of phobic reactions. In Wolpe's method of systematic desensitization ("reciprocal inhibition") a hierarchy of fearful situations is constructed. The overcoming of lower level fear images encourages a progressive ascension in the hierarchial scale until the top level fearful situation is mastered in fantasy. A state of muscle relaxation is first produced, along with the image of a relaxing scene. The subject is then asked to visualize the lowest level fearful image. When this is tolerated with comfort, the next higher image is introduced. Should fear arise at any point, the scene is shifted away from the hierarchy to the relaxing image, and the relaxing muscle exercises are repeated. The scene prior to the one that produced fear is then reintroduced and progression up the scale continued. As fear reduction in imagery continues, the patient is encouraged to actually expose himself to graduations of the phobic situation that brought him to therapy. It is assumed, of course, that in the initial "behavioral assessment" a study has been made of the various reinforcement contingencies and that these are considered as part of the total treatment plan. Some patients are unable to learn relaxation procedures, or cannot use imagery successfully, or hesitate to report sensations of anxiety, or are unwilling to practice for weeks without immediate relief (which is sometimes what it takes for a proper response to develop) and hence will not be able to utilize this technique.

Q88: What does operant conditioning have to offer, how does it work, and is it successful?

A88: Operant behavioral approaches offer a prolific group of behavior change methodologies, as well as guidelines for their evaluation. A contingency relationship exists between operants and the environmental events that follow them. Thus, behavioral responses may be set up, accelerated and strengthened (reinforced) or diminished and eliminated (extinguished) by their succeeding environmental consequences. In applying operant methods, schedules of positive or aversive reinforcement are developed at fixed or variable intervals or ratios, which will gradually shape the desired behavior. This design has been utilized with variable success for overcoming of behavioral deficits, the elimination of maladaptive activities, and the continuance of therapeutic gains. Success is not always possible for the same reasons as in any other therapy: lack of skill in the therapist, secondary gains that reward illness, inner conflictual resistances that obstruct progress, a masochistic need that supports suffering, anxiety that accompanies achievement of health, and transference reactions that sidetrack therapeutic aims. Operant conditioning probably plays a part in all therapies, the therapist reinforcing certain verbal and behavioral responses that accord with his theoretical convictions and the goals toward which he is directing his treatment. A vast bibliography is available, but for a rapid review, I would recommend the article by Karoly (1980).

Q89: The matter of reinforcements in behavior therapy puzzles me. How is this done? And what is "contingency contracting"?

A89: One of the basic techniques in behavior therapy is *positive reinforcement* that rewards behaviors that are to be expanded. Among the ways of encouraging constructive responses are verbal approving comments, the therapist paying rapt attention to what the patient is saying, and nodding, smiling and making other commendatory gestures. On the other hand, discouraging responses by frowning, shaking the head or withdrawing attention may accompany self-punitive, masochistic, complaining and depressive opinions and behavior. In this way the therapist may shape tendencies toward constructive problem-solving.

Some behavior therapists try to direct the patient toward productive change through reinforcements in *contingency contracting*. It is agreed that the execution of desired behaviors (socialization, assertiveness, dietary abstinence, etc.) will result in certain positive rewards. The contract is drawn up between the patient and the therapist, or in couples therapy between the two partners. The selection of appropriate reinforcements may be aided by use of a *Reinforcement Survey Schedule* (Cautela and Kastenbaum, 1967). The contract is time-limited and specifies the behavior the patient is to perform (e.g., smoking control, weight loss, assertive behaviors, etc.) and the rewards he is to receive for such behavior. The patient collects data in writing on the daily frequency of such behaviors and his reactions to their execution. The rewards must be reasonable, but must be sufficiently intense and meaningful for the patient to compensate him for whatever deprivations he undergoes in performance of assigned tasks. The patient, for example, must feel that he is attaining a previously denied or absent prize and that he has earned it through his own efforts. If money is the reward, paid by a third party, this should not be accumulated but should be spent as soon as possible since saving may dilute the effort put into performance. Thus, a child who is rewarded with money for certain socializing behaviors should not be requested to save the money for college. Rewards to adults may consist of vacations, trips and various kinds of entertainment. Sometimes when a patient rewards himself with money, he deposits money with the therapist, who then distributes it in accordance with the patient's compliance with the contract. In contracts between couples (contingency or exchange contracts), the desired behaviors on the part of one member are rewarded with specified behaviors on the part of the other member.

Do sought-for behaviors continue after the contract ends? The claim made by behavior therapists is that in well-conducted therapies the patient begins to enjoy the behaviors for their own sake and for what they do to his self-image and self-respect.

Q90: What is the best way of conducting assertiveness training?

A90: Among the most annoying deficits are not being able to stand up for one's rights, rejecting criticism even of a constructive nature, acceding to being coerced or manipulated by others, expressing one's desires and preferences only with guilt or embarrassment, and countenancing rejection as a sign of being worthless and debased. These deficits are usually associated with a devalued self-image and a hypertrophied and punitive conscience. Related as they are to such basic personality distortions, it is difficult to see how they can be altered without self-understanding.

A way of facilitating self-understanding, important to enduring change, is to bring the patient to an awareness of his anxieties, evasions, and other defenses through plunging him into situations where he must assert himself. Whether thinking and acting in ways consonant with a positive self-concept can in themselves correct a devalued self-image is debatable, although some therapists assume "that if a patient behaves and thinks in a manner indicating a positive self concept, he has, in fact, acquired one" (Seligman, 1979, p. 169). In my opinion, some cognitive alteration is essential.

A format that is often used for assertiveness training is a time-limited group of eight to ten patients led by a man/woman therapist team. A questionnaire rating reactions to certain situations may be found helpful (Gambrill and Richey, 1975). Patients are taught to differentiate acting assertive (expressing one's rights) from acting aggressive (putting others down). Discussions involve self-assessment of assertiveness by the group members. Modest goals are then set for each at first. The actual training procedures include such techniques as behavior rehearsal, role-playing, imagery and cognitive behavior therapy (relabeling certain acts), etc. (Smith, 1975). Homework is assigned with the object of increasing assertive responses and lowering non-assertive ones. A diary is kept of experiences. Modeling by the therapist is often employed. Patients set up problem situations in which there is practice in asking for a favor, saying "no" to an unreasonable request, making a date with a person of the opposite sex, etc. The ability to accept rejection without anger, shame, or feelings of being inferior is developed by role-playing and discussion of feelings.

Coincident with such assertive performances there should preferably be an analysis, either in individual or in group therapy, of each individual's underlying conflicts that have been responsible for and that are sustaining the devalued self-image. This combination of behavioral and dynamic therapy offers the patient the best opportunity for correcting problems in assertiveness on a permanent level.

**Q91: Is there any danger in assigning self-help books on asser-
tiveness training?**

A91: This depends on the books assigned and on the readiness of the
patient to utilize assertive techniques. The greatest objection is confusion of aggressiveness with assertiveness, leading the patient to
make a nuisance of himself and exposing himself to rejection and retaliatory action. It is desirable, therefore, that a person be in therapy
during the period when he is experimenting with new assertive behaviors.

**Q92: Isn't assertiveness training by itself a superficial way of
dealing with problems that undoubtedly have their origin
in dynamic conflicts?**

A92: On the surface it would seem so. Experience, however, brings out
the practical utility of this behavioral approach, since it meets the
problem directly and challenges the patient's defenses head on. My
own conviction is that a combination of dynamic and behavioral approaches is the best way of dealing with difficulties involving shyness
and fear of asserting oneself. Of course, dynamic therapy alone over
a long-term period may get at the core of the responsible personality
distortions, but the treatment may bog down when, after insight is
gained, the patient resists putting his insights into action. Starting off
with assertive training, on the other hand, almost immediately puts
the patient in a position where he is confronted by his anxiety and the
defenses that prevent him from resolving his problem. He has to deal
with these as realities, not as theories.

It is interesting that in the face of this confrontation and in breaking
through the resistance by practicing assertive exercises, many patients
acquire insight into the dynamics of their problem. A dynamically
oriented therapist will be able to expedite insight by examining and
interpreting the patient's dreams, behavioral acting-out, and transference reactions. Past sources of trouble and early conflicts may surface; by working on these the therapist may connect them with the
patient's current personality problems and more pointedly with the
self-image pathology that expresses itself in symptoms. Thus, a reconstructive effect on the character structure may be scored. Incidentally,
even where the therapist is not dynamically oriented, some patients
will put the pieces together by themselves in a kind of unconscious

ing hospitalization and surgery; Csapo (1972) for correcting disturbed classroom behavior in withdrawn or disturbed children; Perry and Cerreto (1977) for training of living skills in mentally retarded persons; Hingtgen et al. (1967) for working with autistic children; Gutride et al. (1974) for helping psychotic patients reinstate adaptive behaviors; Sarason and Ganzer (1973) for rehabilitating juvenile delinquents; and Reeder and Kunce (1976) for preparing heroin addicts for adjustment following treatment. Modeling may also be used in professional training programs for counselors and therapists, for example, to develop greater capacities for empathy (Perry, 1975).

Q95: How successful is aversion therapy?

A95: Presenting an unpleasant stimulus in close temporal relationship to an undesirable behavior, with the object of extinguishing it, is not as popular or successful as other forms of therapy. The dedication to the behavior, conscious or unconscious, may be too great. Or a masochistic need for punishment may enable the subject to endure the painful consequences in order to appease a demanding sense of guilt. Moreover, for some patients aversive methods serve to reproduce the parental precedent of punishment for infractions; the patient will then rebel against the therapist or passively resist getting well. In certain cases, however, when nothing else seems to work, and an obnoxious habit or behavior must be controlled, aversive therapy may surprisingly be the only method to which a patient will respond.

There are several types of aversive schemes, principally those that follow the Pavlovian model and those that are patterned after the operant model. In the former group of therapies are the conditioning of alcoholics with nauseating drugs like emetine and Antabuse, and with electric shock. In self-injurious behavior like head-banging, self-biting and face-slapping in retarded children, and in self-induced vomiting, painful shock has also been used. Pavlovian aversive methods are employed far less often than operant techniques, which attempt to control behaviors largely with unpleasant consequences. Aversive or punishing sequelae are employed less often than withdrawing positive rewards or reinforcements, for example, shutting off a TV set during an argument of children regarding the choice of a program. A more severe disciplinary action is penalizing the individual for reprehensible behavior by levying a fine on him. More punitive is the delivery of an unpleasant stimulus like an electric shock from a small battery operated unit by the patient on himself whenever he indulges in certain behaviors he wishes to control. In hair-plucking and skin mutilation which have not responded to other methods, this painful stimulus may replace the masochistic need to torment oneself.

Rapid inhalation of cigarette smoke to a point where the mucous membrane hurts or burns, for the purpose of overcoming of the smoking habit, is another example of aversive control. The use of an alerting system to eliminate bedwetting and of delayed auditory feedback in stuttering has elements of both Pavlovian and operant methods. Compulsive overeating, gambling, and sexual deviations (fetishism, exhibitionism, voyeurism) have also been treated with aversive control methods with undocumented claims of success. A substantial literature has accumulated detailing aversive techniques for the reversal of homosexuality in cases eager to change to heterosexuality. While not strictly an aversive technique, the patient's use of a diary, simply charting the frequency of undesirable behaviors for which control is sought, appears to lessen the incidence of such behaviors.

Q96: What assessment procedures of progress should be used with behavioral methods?

A96: Keeping a diary, listing the problem behaviors, their intensity, frequency, and duration, can be helpful in assessment. Not all problems are equally recordable. For example, values, attitudes, and complex relationship constellations may be difficult to chart and monitor. Perhaps the greatest advantage of diary keeping is in the therapeutic effect on the patient as he observes progress or regression and gains reinforcements from this.

Q97: If your goal in treatment is problem-solving or symptom alleviation, why would you need a dynamic orientation for this?

A97: A dynamic orientation in behavioral and other problem-solving approaches is not for the purpose of expanding the goals of treatment beyond symptom cure or problem-solving, but to deal with some of the most powerful resistances that impede progress. These have to do with unconscious needs to perpetuate a childish dependent adaptation, to assuage guilt through masochistic self-punishment, and to project onto the therapist needs and attitudes originating in early relationships with important parental and sibling figures (transference). These drives can distract the patient from aims congenial with the objectives of treatment. They can make a shambles out of the most dedicated and skilled efforts of the therapist.

In part, behavioral therapists have come to recognize the importance of cognitive factors which operate as resistance as in some of the recent cognitive behavior therapy approaches. What is still lacking, however, is recognition of the importance of unconscious conflict as one of the significant determinants of behavior. Of course, a dynamic orientation is not always necessary, since there are considerable numbers of patients who do not resist behavioral and other symptom-oriented approaches. But for those who do not respond, the understanding of unconscious motivational deterrents, as well as application of this understanding toward their resolution, can spell the difference between success and failure.

V. Group Therapy

Group therapy enjoys a well deserved popularity, although there is no unanimity of opinion about its practices. Accordingly, a wide range of methods are promulgated by practitioners of psychoanalytic, psycho-dramatic, existential, transactional, client-centered, behavioral, gestalt, systems theory, and experiential schools. Controversy continues regarding a number of dimensions of group therapy such as: whether the dyadic model is doomed in favor of group models; whether true intrapsychic restructuring and cognitive alterations can be effectuated through group therapy; whether group dynamic phenomena when they appear should be considered constructive forces or elements of resistance; the actual value for different conditions of supportive, inspirational, and self-help groups; the indications for multiple therapists; the relative virtues of the regressive-reconstructive as opposed to the experiential-affect approaches; the ideal composition of a group; what facilitative techniques are best employed to expedite therapy and resolve resistance; and the advantage of combined group and individual therapy. In recent years there has been a tendency to organize groups around specific problems such as alcoholism, drug addiction, obesity, smoking, sexual problems, insomnia, phobias, cancer, depression, delinquency, criminality, marital discord, divorce, adolescent difficulties, and geriatric problems. There are those who contend that such homogeneity invites progress and that a heterogeneous group will accomplish less for the individual members, a point about which there is disagreement.

Q98: Is group therapy to be preferred to individual treatment?

A98: Some therapists believe it is the treatment of choice, with individual interviews as adjuncts (Grotjahn, 1980). Other therapists have the opposite viewpoint. Determining factors in the preference for group therapy are the therapist's training, style, experience, expertise, and faith in group processes. Important also is the patient's ability to relate to and utilize constructively the specific group constellation into which he is introduced. These factors will weight the preference toward either groups or individual treatment.

Q99: Is group therapy contraindicated in certain patients?

A99: Delusional, hallucinatory, severely paranoid individuals and those with bizarre sexual perversions usually do not do well in group therapy. Patients with good ego structures who develop strong transferences and for whom intensive psychoanalysis is decided on as the preferred therapy should also avoid or postpone group therapy, but for another reason. Dilution of the transference in the group may inhibit or prevent the development of a transference neurosis.

Q100: Are borderline patients, serious psychosomatic problems, and severe character problems (masochistic, schizoid, etc.) suitable patients for group psychotherapy?

A100: Yes, and sometimes this is the treatment of choice. Concomitant individual therapy may also be employed. One of the reasons group therapy is useful in these cases is that it tends to dilute the transference, which is spread out among several group members and not concentrated on the therapist with what may be an unsettling intensity.

Q101: Can group therapy resolve resistance? If so, are there any readings on this subject?

A101: In group therapy the participant members often easily detect resistances in each other and the continuing confrontations may have a significant effect on breaking them up. Among recommended readings are: Ormont, 1968; Redl, 1948; Rosenthal, 1976, 1980, and Spotnitz, 1969.

Q102: In a patient whose values and attitudes are twisted and need correction, could group therapy help change these?

A102: Peer pressure in a group setting may influence the individual in the direction of the group norm. Certain authoritative pressures that demand conformity with established rules of a society also have a powerful effect on individual values. Thus, a governmental group which is in political control may make laws that can revolutionize the individual's standards and modes of thinking and behaving—sometimes in weeks if not days. For example, a religious, peace-loving individual, who all his life has been taught to love his fellow men and to "turn the other cheek," may be drafted into the army, change into a heroic soldier, and in an astonishingly short time become a killer who gains plaudits for killing. It is surprising how often this kind of value change happens without inspiring guilt and remorse, simply because the individual feels he is obliged to obey orders. There are, of course, exceptions where draftees refuse to abandon their original precepts even at the expense of being considered unpatriotic pariahs, but this is the exception and not the rule.

I am citing this example merely to illustrate how injunctions imposed by an authoritative group can change principles that have dominated an individual's existence over a lifetime. We may conclude from this that group therapy can help alter some pathological values if the group is respected by the individual, the participant members pressure the individual in the direction of non-pathological values, and he feels forced to comply with the changes demanded of him in order to remain in the group and retain the goodwill of the members.

Q103: What facilitative techniques work best in group therapy?

A103: There are many techniques that therapists use to facilitate activity in a group. Their effectiveness depends on *how* they are used. For example, the "going around" technique of Wolf and Schwartz (1962), during which each member presents associations and fantasies about the other members of the group, results in stirring up emotion and breaking down defenses. Some therapists extend the length of sessions to the point where they approach marathons. In this way defenses weaken and dynamic material surfaces. Other therapists reconstitute a sluggish group by introducing new members while shifting some old members to a different group. Introducing a borderline patient whose anxiety level is high often stirs up the other members. Role-playing techniques, gestalt techniques and playing back videotapes of the group in action are also common ways of mobilizing interest and tension, breaking down resistance, and releasing material for discussion and working-through. Interpretation techniques, consisting of detecting repetitive patterns in each member and pointing out which stimuli in the group release these patterns and their ramifications to outside relationships, will often break up an impasse in the group (Aronson, 1972).

Q104: How does group therapy affect the individual's transference reactions?

A104: In several ways. First, it may dilute transference reactions to the therapist, scattering these among selected individuals in the group (multi-transferences). This can be an advantage in patients, like borderline cases, whose transference responses to the therapist become explosive and too upsetting. By widening the available opportunities for transference, the group functions as a new "family" for the patient, various members being identified with parents and siblings toward whom projections may precipitate. The handling of transference by the patient's peers in the group may be more effective than if done by the therapist, toward whom the patient is apt to be defensive. On the other hand, there are patients who need to build up strong transference feelings before they can become aware of them. Here individual therapy offers the advantage of concentrated reactions toward the therapist until they reach a "break-through" intensity. In many cases, combined therapy offers advantages of both situations.

Q105: Does combined group and individual therapy have any advantages?

A105: Definitely. Combined or conjoint group and individual therapy seem to catalyze one another. Naturally, we may expect some transference and countertransference buildup, but these complications may be further helpful in understanding the patient's problems and defenses and in their working-through.

VI. Family Therapy

Understandably, therapists have special ways of looking at family pathology and they organize their ideas around favorite systems, such as behavioral family therapy, structural family therapy, psychodynamically oriented family therapy, operationally oriented family therapy, and systems family therapy. Yet a therapist's clinical operations with families are influenced more by his individual styles of working with patients and by his own unresolved family problems than by the theories he espouses. This results in many different forms of practice which vary in such areas as selection of the unit of intervention (i.e., identified patient and parents, total immediate family including siblings, extended family, distant relatives, etc.); time allotted to sessions (one hour to several days [marathon family therapy]); duration of therapy (one session to many months); activity during sessions (listening, supporting, challenging, confronting, guiding, advising, censoring, praising, reassuring, etc.); relative emphasis on insight and behavioral alteration; and employment of adjunctive procedures (videotaping, use of one-way mirrors, role-playing, etc.).

How to manage resistance in family therapy is another area of discrepancy. Families struggle to maintain the homeostasis of a neurotic family system by preserving pathologic ways of relating. A great many of the current writings about family therapy specify contrasting ways of dealing with such resistance, and one is impressed with the lack of agreement for proper management of this disturbing phenomenon.

Q106: What is the basis for recommending family therapy?

A106: Family therapy is organized around the hypothesis that the focus of individual psychopathology is imbedded in the core of family relationships. If this is so it would seem essential to alter defects in family relationships before pathology in individual members can be corrected. Many methodological problems arise when we attempt to test this hypothesis, not the least of which is the fact that we are dealing with an extremely complex social unit in the family. It is difficult enough to try to sort out variables in individual adaptation. These difficulties are multiplied greatly when we deal with contingencies that govern group interactions. Nevertheless, a number of important research studies have emerged which cast light on the involved problems. Among the tested findings are the facts that in harmonious "normal" families 1) communication patterns are more explicit, permitting easier problem-solving; 2) there are fewer unresolved conflicts among the members and greater tolerance of alternative courses of action; 3) family members are less hostile, dependent, and immature than in "abnormal" families. The objective in family therapy then is primarily to change the family system of interaction in quest of a more perfectly functioning group. It is hoped that individual family members displaying psychopathology will then change as a result of living and operating in a new, more congenial matrix.

Q107: When is family therapy indicated?

A107: Family therapy is indicated where the interactions with other family members have initiated and/or are now reinforcing the identified patient's difficulty. This is usually the case in problems of children or adolescents. In adults problems necessitating crisis intervention are generally best handled with family therapy as the main or necessary treatment process. Where hospitalization of the identified patient is contemplated or has occurred, family sessions are indispensable for the gathering of anamnestic data, to discuss the role of the different members during treatment planning, and to secure their cooperation. Family therapy is also useful when both individual and group therapy have failed to help the patient.

Q108: What is the best approach in family therapy?

A108: There is no single preferred approach to family therapy. There are many approaches and it is becoming apparent that a range of eclectic approaches are essential since both systems, interactional dynamics and psychoanalytic dynamics play a part. Were we to select that dimension in family therapy that requires the greatest attention, it is the improvement of communication skills among the family members. This calls for mastery by the therapist of the dimensions of communication skill training. Not all therapists can do family therapy, certain personality difficulties producing an inability to work with families, which will tend to nullify all other positive factors. The same, of course, can be said for other therapies, like dynamic psychotherapy, behavior therapy, cognitive therapy, hypnosis, etc. Another important factor in doing family therapy is the need to search for and expand any positive elements that exist.

Healthy elements are present in all families that may not at first be apparent because the aggression between and withdrawal tendencies of the different members are so much on the surface. Family therapy may mobilize these healthy latent resources, which should be nurtured as a primary objective, irrespective of the techniques being used.

Q109: In research studies, how does family therapy compare to other forms of treatment?

A109: In reviewing 58 outcome studies of family therapy as compared to alternative treatments (i.e., individual therapy, group therapy, hospitalization, and drug therapy) Kniskern and Gurman (1980) found that 41 (i.e., 70 percent) of the family therapy outcomes were found to be superior, 15 (i.e., 25 percent) were found to be equal, and only two (i.e., 4 percent) were found to be inferior. Many of the primary patients in the studies complained of clinical problems (such as depressions) for which individual psychopathology traditionally is believed implicated. However, the authors, probably with good reason, state that interactional difficulties, such as marital problems, are the most likely conditions to respond best to family and conjoint marital therapy. Compared to such approaches, individual therapy, concurrent marital therapy (where one therapist sees each partner separately), and collaborative marital therapy (where each spouse is seen by different therapists) produce less impressive results. What is interesting, nevertheless, is that individual psychopathological difficulties, other than interactional problems, do respond well to good family therapy methods.

Q110: What are the preliminary steps to be taken in utilizing the behavioral model in family therapy?

A110: The first step is defining the problem. The patient's assessment of the situation and the desired goals in therapy are, of course, important. In itself patient assessment may be incomplete, because certain disclosures are often concealed out of guilt, anxiety, or nebulous unconscious resistances. For example, a woman justifies her hostility toward her husband on the basis of his steadfast premature ejaculations. She credits his sexual inadequacy to selfish lack of concern with her rights and needs. She neglects mentioning that for years prior to the birth of her child she shied away from intercourse except on a few occasions. The reason for this abstinence was dyspareunia and vaginospasm. Her demands and activities seldom went beyond mutual masturbation. After childbirth, her vaginospasm was relieved and she permitted penetration only to discover that her husband ejaculated before she could get excited enough to climax. This brought to a head her conviction that she needed to terminate her marriage. Only by persistent questioning was the therapist able to determine that the patient bore a good deal of the responsibility for the sexual incompatability.

Some therapists find a self-rating check list such as the one by Cautela and Upper (1975) useful as an assessment tool. An effort is made to identify the stimuli that activate symptoms and problem behaviors. Can these be controlled? How does the patient participate in bringing them on? Further information is occasionally obtained by the patient filling out certain standardized forms (Walsh, 1967, 1968). Observation of the patient in actual situations where problem behaviors occur (with family at home, in phobia mobilizing circumstances, etc.) may be helpful if this can be arranged. The use of visual imagery to identify cognitive elements associated with problem behaviors has been described by Meichenbaum (1971).

The next step is quantification of the problem. The frequency and duration of problem behaviors are charted, recording how often and under what circumstances difficulties occur (Homme, 1965). A man with headaches, for example, is given homework to report the days and times when his headaches appear, the immediate circumstances preceding the onset of headaches, the consequences of his headaches, to himself and others around him, and what if anything he does to relieve them.

The third step is examining the reinforcing contingencies. Are there any gains the patient derives from symptoms or problem behaviors, like sympathy from those around him, freedom from responsibility, etc. If so, can these reinforcers be supplied by altered activities less destructive to the patient? Is the patient aware of such gains? A woman with periodic fainting spells was brought to the realization that these episodes focused attention on her by her family. Assured regarding their functional nature by the family physician who had been summoned to several such emergencies, the therapist suggested the family show studied neglect after a spell. On the other hand, the members were to lavish attention and praise on the patient when she engaged in constructive family activities.

The fourth step is outlining the treatment plan. Once sufficient information is available, a hypothesis is presented to the patient, the treatment plan is formulated, agreement is reached on the focus and goals, and a contract is executed.

Q111: Isn't family therapy helpful in determining who within the family is really responsible for the existing problems?

A111: Family therapy is not utilized for the purpose of allocating responsibility for problems. Rather, it is employed as a means of giving the participants a different way of perceiving what is happening in their relationships with each other. Out of the ensuing interchanges, it is hoped that each member will derive an understanding of his or her specific role in creating and sustaining the problems for which help is being sought. The working-through of this understanding will hopefully enable the family to reorganize their relationships, with not only a resolution of the immediate difficulties but also a fostering of a healthier adjustment for each member.

Q112: In family therapy should you let the family interrelate freely without imposing restraints on their activity or should you structure their activity and be directive and educational, such as along the lines recommended by Minuchin?

A112: Passivity on the part of the therapist will bring few rewards. The idea of allowing a family to engage in a free-for-all squabble often accomplishes nothing more than to encourage greater antagonism between the members. Providing some structure in the session, on the other hand, can be most helpful. This is done by asking specific questions, directing the different members to explore certain areas of feeling, and suggesting what behavior changes should be undertaken. Minuchin (1974) and Minuchin and Fishman (1981) have written about "structural family therapy" along these lines. Goals for the family are set by the therapist, at the same time that the family members are encouraged to utilize their own resources in moving toward behavior change. For diagnostic purposes, if the therapist deems that it is appropriate to do so (and that he will not lose the family after the first session), it may be advisable to observe an undirected family in action in order to get a biopsy of the existing pathology and the distorted lines of communication. Once this is done, the therapist will be in a better position to structure, guide, direct, educate, and set goals.

Q113: How do you deal with the hostility among family members during family therapy?

A113: Hostility that emerges in family therapy often derails the therapeutic process. How to deal with it is an important technical question. Usually the hostility is directed at a selected member who may be the identified patient or a parent who may be blamed for the events leading to the crisis. Unless hostile interchanges are interrupted, the status quo will tend to remain. One method is to divert the hostility by asking questions related to nonpersonal areas: the housing situation, arrangement of rooms, daily routines, employment, certain historical events, etc. Some therapists, who feel they have a good relationship with the family, sometimes try to focus the hostility on themselves to take it away from the scapegoated member. This may be done by asking: "I wonder if there is something I have done or not done that upsets you. I am suggesting that you are really angry at me." Opening up areas of transference can be highly productive at times, but the therapist must be able to control his countertransference. The best way of dealing with hostility, of course, is to interpret it in terms of the personality, needs and defenses of the attacker. This is possible only after a therapeutic alliance has been established, the family pathology comprehended, and the dynamics of the individual family members understood.

Q114: What is the "interactional" approach in family therapy?

A114: There are various orientations in family therapy, but a common one conceives of problems in any individual as resulting from interaction of that individual with other persons in some system like the family. Since the actual difficulties are produced by the behavior of the individuals in the system, the resolution of such difficulties will necessitate changes in the behavior of the persons involved in the disorganizing interactions. Problems are not regarded as the tip of the iceberg, so to speak, emerging from buried inner manifestations, but as the iceberg itself. A good number of the therapeutic interventions are directed at the activities that are being used as "solutions" to control or eliminate undesired behavior. These activities usually sustain and reinforce the difficulty. Since such "solutions" often serve merely to aggravate the problem, therapy is concentrated on eliminating these futile "solutions." New problem-solving methods are encouraged, focused on behavioral alterations rather than intellectual insights. A behavioral change in any member of a system can produce a change in the entire system. Accordingly, treatment may concentrate on the member who is most responsible for bringing about difficulties in the system, although the family as a whole is taken into consideration.

Q115: What idea is behind the systems approach to family therapy?

A115: A problem involving a single member of a family is often one aspect, or let us say the surface manifestation, of ongoing family pathology. In the systems approach it is avowed that any change in one of the family members will upset the habitual interactional balances of the family as a whole, producing, if continued, alterations in the family system itself (Watzlawick et al., 1967). Accordingly, once a survey has been made of the interactional links and lines of communication, the family is helped to change aspects that have generated pathology in one or all of the members.

Q116: How about family therapy for schizophrenics? Is it desirable?

A116: Highly desirable, because the problems do not start or stop with the patient. The least that can be accomplished is the hope of better lines of family communication and a softening of scapegoating. Family therapy may be one of the most effective ways of reducing rehospitalization, in addition to safeguarding maintenance medication.

Q117: Has family therapy with schizophrenics been successful and are there any advantages with multiple family therapy?

A117: You cannot generalize about outcome in family therapy because this depends on who does it, on whom it is done, and how it is done. Understandably, schizophrenic families are difficult to work with. Many problems exist, the members sometimes being entangled in interpersonal difficulties that seem impossible to unravel. The untrained therapist is apt to encounter insuperable problems with these families. On the other hand, an effective family therapist may accomplish good results impossible to achieve by another method. Multiple family therapy has many advantages because, apart from the relationships established and opportunities presented for positive identification, the presence of individuals from the same cultural background allows for the mutual exploration of common problems and for the better understanding of the existing family code.

Q118: Would you recommend video recordings in family therapy?

A118: Very much so. Among the techniques is "cross-confrontation," during which a family unit is exposed to playback of tape-recorded excerpts demonstrating interactions. Video recording with playback is a strikingly useful tool.

Q119: Since countertransference is often a great problem in family therapy, isn't it important to have a cotherapist?

A119: A cotherapist may help neutralize countertransference as well as sharpen observations of what goes on in therapy. However, working with a cotherapist may bring on some complications for the primary therapist. He is apt to interpret ongoing interactions with the cotherapist in terms of his own family. Of necessity he must become actively involved and he cannot hide, as in individual therapy. Different anachronistic patterns may then emerge which the therapist will have to detect and overcome should they obtrude themselves on the family he is treating.

VII. Marital (Couples) Therapy

Marital therapy techniques draw from several fields, including psychoanalysis, behavior therapy, family therapy, group therapy, marriage counseling, child therapy, and family casework. Although the goal is productive alteration of the marital relationship, a hoped-for and usually serendipitous objective is intrapsychic change, which surprisingly may come about in those with readiness for such change and with relief from the distracting cross fire between the two spouses. The problems encountered by those doing marital therapy are compounded by lack of unity in the conceptual schemes recommended. The most successful approaches stress the importance of communication toward effecting changes in the transactional system. A system behavioral orientation is particularly helpful, while flexibility in the application of techniques calls for a good deal of experimentation as to which techniques work best for each therapist. Therapists must also determine through experience the relative advantages for their styles of operation of the different marital therapeutic formats (conjoint, collaborative, concurrent, combined, combined-collaborative, and marital group psychotherapy); how to utilize assessment aids; how to combine psychodynamic and behavioral approaches; methods of interpretation of offensive behaviors; and the management of countertransference.

Q120: Why are the marriages of persons with emotional problems so often disturbed?

A120: Marriage is a vehicle through which people constantly try to satisfy an assortment of needs and influences. It is often regarded by neurotic people as a way of overcoming defects in their own development and handicaps in their current life situation. The marital partner is therefore cajoled, seduced or terrorized to perform and is held responsible for any deficiency in projected assignments. This imposes an enormous burden on the healthier of the two spouses since the demands made are usually impossible to fulfill.

On top of it all, the habitual hostilities, anxieties, defenses and coping devices that have plagued the individual since childhood become transferred over to the most conveniently available recipient—the spouse. The expression of such improprieties is complicated by reactive guilt feelings, remorse, and attempts at reparation which in turn invite attack from the injured spouse, perpetuating the continuing chain of indignation, anger, and counterattack. Couples often get locked into this sadomasochistic circuit. It would seem that the battling partners need each other to act out mutual neurotic needs, which insidiously may keep the marriage together while serving as a platform for combat. A final neurotic gesture is the blaming of each other for personal shortcomings, mediocrities, failings, and even symptoms. Disillusionment is inevitable unless the spouses are willing to compromise. But where the needs of a marital partner are too insistent and the initial idealization and expectancies are too high, the explosive mixture gradually accumulates until detonated by some (perhaps minor) incident that will tend to blow the marriage apart. One severely neurotic member preying on a more healthy spouse is bad enough, but where both members are working on each other, the atomic stockpile builds up to frightening proportions.

Q121: Why is couples therapy sometimes to be preferred to individual therapy and can this be organized on a short-term problem-solving basis?

A121: Generally, one member of a distressed pair appears for treatment as a result of some crisis or because of disturbing symptoms. During the interviews the patient may reveal in greater or lesser degree troubles in the marital relationship. If it is possible to arrange for an interview with the spouse, the therapist may be able to determine how responsible the marriage is for initiating and sustaining the patient's complaints. Often each partner regards himself or herself as the victim of the other partner's personality peculiarities and denies responsibility for existing problems in the relationship.

Most couples come to therapy not really prepared to change. Each partner has a private agenda, usually organized around the premise that it is the spouse who is at fault. Or, if one individual admits to problems, these are usually justified as consequences of the other partner's negligence or derelictions. One of the most useful therapeutic strategies, even where difficulties are clearly weighted toward one member, is to involve both partners in the therapeutic situation. The mutual interaction and the opening up of communication can have a catalyzing effect on the working-through process of the identified patient, with the marital relationship benefitting as a welcome dividend. Another advantage of couples therapy over individual therapy is that the patient has a helpmate with whom new behaviors and coping skills can be practiced on an ongoing basis.

In marital therapy it is essential to start out with the assumption that it takes two people to make a problem. For treatment to register the greatest effect, therefore, it is essential for both partners mutually to collaborate on a solution. Treatment, which can be on a short-term problem-solving basis, involves therapeutic sessions with the couple together as well as individual sessions. Some therapists routinely see both members individually and also together. Other therapists utilize individual sessions only when necessary, as when progress is halted by periods of resistance. Homework assignments are given to accelerate treatment and, *after some improvement has occurred,* problem-solving sessions at home are prescribed. These sessions serve the purpose of helping the couple to generalize the lessons learned with the therapist to situations outside the therapy room. Unless such generalizations occur, deterioration effects will gradually obliterate gains scored in treatment and the couple will revert back to pretherapy behaviors. The sessions at home, moreover, provide opportunities for finding solutions to new problems as they develop, without answers being delivered by the therapist.

Termination of therapy is also expedited by homework practice sessions, the therapist gradually increasing the intervals between visits, say from a once a week to a bimonthly basis, then occasional booster sessions. Following therapy, couples are encouraged to continue their sessions at home on a weekly routine. Through such sessions couples learn to approach problems as collaborators rather than adversaries.

To expedite problem-solving sessions, some marital therapists provide their clients with a printed manual which details ground rules. An excellent example of this is contained in the behaviorally oriented book by Jacobson and Margolin (1979).

Q122: I have a feeling that marital problems are often due to communication failures. Are there approaches to expedite therapy for this area of trouble?

A122: Central to many of the problems of marital couples are difficulties in communication. Behavioral approaches to communication training contain a number of procedures geared toward acquisition of communication skills with provision for feedback instructions and behavioral rehearsal. Dynamically oriented therapists may use these as part of their treatment with marital problems.

During joint sessions the therapist will have observed patterns of communication issuing out of the interaction of the couple. He will be able to offer the couple information about their verbal and nonverbal exchanges (criticisms of one by the other, attacks, praise, protectiveness, etc.) in descriptive terms without interpreting the deeper meaning or motivations for such exchanges (which, of course, can be made in a dynamic approach). Immediate feedback to both partners of provocative and disturbed communication patterns may help break the chain reaction of attack, counterattack or retreat that is characteristic of the couple's verbal interactions. With adequate preparation, video feedback may also be used with some advantage. In employing feedback the therapist should not lose any opportunity to comment on *positive* communication patterns in the hope of reinforcing these. Thus when a partner praises his or her mate the therapist may say, "I liked the way you complimented (or praised) him/her."

Generally couples are not fully aware of their abrasive thrusts at each other or their corrosive answers to comments. Following an unjustified verbal blast, the therapist may ask a partner to reconsider what the spouse has said and then to give an alternative response. Sometimes the therapist may model a response, playing the roles of both the husband and the wife to avoid one's feeling discriminated against. Cotherapists, if this is the format, may each play the role of one of the spouses and model communication.

Behavior rehearsal is an important part of the relearning process, in that couples may practice in order to increase their skills of communication. Here the therapist provides instructions and modeling if necessary, giving continuing feedback. A valuable technique is *role reversal,* each spouse taking the role of the other in talking about a special situation. In this way, marital partners may teach each other problem-solving skills.

One of the most common difficulties is the insistent use of aversive control strategies by one or both partners ("If you do that again, I'm going to leave you"). Verbal threats and coercion increase until the only way left to deal with mutual intimidation is by detachment techniques, which cause estrangement from one another, further enhancing conflict. By arriving at some sort of agreement regarding areas of change through discussion, an avenue is opened for problem-solving which can be kept alive and expanded by proper reinforcements. Before changes in behavior can be proposed, however, there must be a clear definition of the problem (Jacobson and Margolin, 1979).

Q123: Are the first few family therapy sessions diagnostic or therapeutic?

A123: Obviously the first few family therapy sessions are diagnostic in the sense that we try to understand the structure of the family neurosis. Yet by bringing the family together and starting communication this can serve a therapeutic function. What we try to determine in the early interviews are the nature of the authority structure, the subgroup arrangements, the areas of responsibility assumed by different members, communication patterns, the varying defensive maneuvers, the character of role assumptions, and foci of pathology. Health zones of interaction are noted. We then try to formulate in our minds how the dynamics of the primary patient are related to the entire family structure. We ask ourselves what characteristics in the parents and other members reinforce the patient's symptoms and whether there is a collusion against any healthy strivings. There may be a tentative exploration of what essential roles are being abandoned, for example, a father's absence, lack of caring, etc. Out of this data an assay of the existing problems is made, the therapist outlining in his mind reasonable goals he wishes to achieve within the limitations of time, finances, willingness of family cooperation, extent of pathology in the individual members, and other aspects of the existing reality situation.

Q124: What are some of the pitfalls of marriage counseling?

A124: There are many. Among these is the unhappy fact that one or both clients may have already decided to split, and come to counseling merely to be told to do so. With this rigid attitude no strategem will work. Often one of the spouses is motivated only to get rid of the burdens of a distraught or hostile partner by turning the partner over to the counselor, washing one's hands of troubles at home. There may be no desire to participate in the counseling process other than this. The counselor is conceived of as a referee, not as a helper. Partners who have already separated are the most difficult ones to bring together through counseling. Usually one of the partners has already decided on an independent course of action and comes to sessions merely for the show of cooperativeness.

Q125: Can you mention alternative approaches to marital therapy and indicate some texts?

A125: A number of intervention strategies exist oriented principally around psychoanalysis (Ables and Brandsma, 1977; Sager, 1976), systems therapy (Haley, 1976; Minuchin, 1974), client centered approaches (Guerney, 1977), behavior therapy (Jacobson and Margolin, 1979), and combined therapies, (Paolino and McCrady, 1978). Formats include crisis counseling, collaborative therapy, concurrent therapy, conjoint marital therapy, conjoint family therapy, combined-collaborative therapy, and multiple group therapy (Wolberg, 1977, p. 734).

Q126: Are there any key questions one can ask a patient who comes for marital therapy?

A126: Among important questions are these:

1) In what ways would you want your spouse to change?
2) If your spouse did everything you wanted him/her to do, and was

everything you wanted him/her to be, do you believe you would still be angry at him/her?

3) Admitting that your spouse is at fault, could you be projecting on him/her some of the anger you carried over from your childhood that you had toward your mother, father, or other member of your family?

4) Do you believe *you* have any problems that could *not* be resolved if your spouse were willing to change?

5) As you may realize, change often occurs slowly. Would you be willing to accept small changes at first if you felt that progress was being made? Also, change is never always upward. Like the stock market, there are ups and downs. Would you be willing to accept this and not get too discouraged if your spouse didn't change immediately?

Replies to these questions, while important, should not be taken at their face value. The patient may harbor additional, perhaps contrary, opinions that will come out with continued therapy.

Q127: Are there any assessment aids in marital therapy?

A127: Some therapists find several assessment questionnaires helpful in therapeutic planning. These provide data regarding the degree of marital satisfaction and the stresses that exist in the relationship. Among the most commonly used questionnaires are the following:

1) The Locke-Wallace (1959) Marital Assessment Scale (MAS) is a way of assessing the degree of stress in a marital relationship, considering such areas as the level of marital satisfaction, the degree of disagreement of the partners in various areas (such as finances, recreation, etc.), the responsibility taken for decision-making by each partner, and estimates about the wisdom of the original marriage.

2) Revisions of the above have been made by Kimmel and van der Veen (1974) and Spanier (1976), the latter revision dealing with both married and cohabitating couples.

3) A lengthy questionnaire, the *Spouse Observation Checklist* (SOC), which details interaction patterns (i.e., pleasing and non-pleasing behaviors) is sometimes utilized by those following social-learning theory approaches (Weiss et al., 1973; Weiss, 1978; Patterson, 1976).

4) A list of *Pleasant Thoughts about the Spouse* (Patterson et al., 1972) focuses on positive aspects of the relationship.

Q128: Where it is obvious that both members of a couple need treatment and they do not wish to be seen together, what do you do?

A128: Sometimes it is advantageous for the same therapist to start individual therapy separately with both spouses, different appointments being given the two (*concurrent marital therapy*). They may not yet be ready for couples therapy, which can be instituted later. Where hostility between the partners is high, and appropriate communication is difficult, the therapist may be able to start a relationship individually with each partner, being careful that he does not fall into the trap of being used by either against the other. It takes a good deal of ingenuity to do this. The therapist may anticipate competitiveness for his attention, desires to be the preferred one, misinterpretations of what he says to support an importunate demand on the part of one spouse, and resentment at the partner and therapist for presumed collaboration. Where the spouse of the patient seeking help refuses to see the therapist, one may try a referral to another professional or suggest that there be a personal selection of a therapist. In such a case the different therapists sometimes may have conferences to exchange information and discuss developments and plans (*collaborative marital therapy*). Where the spouse absolutely refuses any kind of therapy, treatment may be started with the presenting patient alone (*individual marital therapy*), trying to influence the reluctant partner indirectly.

Q129: What do you think of a therapist and the therapist's spouse working together with a couple in marital therapy?

A129: Where both persons have been trained and themselves have a good marriage, this may be ideal. A therapeutic couple working with marital partners can advantageously serve as a model, demonstrating how two people with differing viewpoints can disagree and compromise. Because each member of the therapeutic couple will have a unique point of view, each can act as a check on the other, perhaps discussing transferential and other reactions later with each other.

Q130: Are there any directive strategies in marital therapy that can cut through the usual resistances?

A130: Obviously, it is difficult to pick out of the air activities to revitalize a disintegrating relationship. Partners must be motivated to engage in a mutually productive relationship and they must have the ability to carry them out. As a diagnostic gesture some marital therapists ask couples individually to write out privately (in the therapist's office) answers to the following questions (these are not shown to the other partner):

1) What activities or behaviors by your spouse do you find *very pleasing* to you?
2) What activities or behaviors by your spouse are *most displeasing* or *offensive* to you?
3) In your opinion what are the *most interesting* things that you and your spouse do together? Would you enjoy more of this?
4) In your opinion what activities on your part *that you are able to do* would please your partner greatly? Is it difficult for you to engage in any of such activities?

Utilizing these responses as guidelines, homework assignments are then made. Some of the formulas that have been proposed may sound foolish and even offensive. If so, they should not be pressed, especially when resistance is strong. Among the prescriptions are these:

1) Instruct each partner to engage in some activity daily that pleases the recipient. These should, with each succeeding day, be increased by small increments. (Jacobson and Margolin, 1979, p. 164.)
2. Establish "love days" once or twice during the week during which the designated person strives to be especially pleasing to the other member (Weiss et al., 1973).

Discussion of the results with the couple may reveal restraints to engaging in pleasing behaviors; an inability to recognize what gratifies the partner; hesitance or refusal to communicate what is desired in uncritical, non-demanding terms; clumsiness in accepting small demonstrations of desirable behaviors on the basis of a total expectance; anger on the part of the giver that too much is expected of him or her, etc.

A common snag is powerlessness of a person to articulate requests for certain kinds of pleasing behaviors on the part of a spouse. This may be due to guilt feelings about making such a request, or anger that the spouse has to be reminded of one's preferences. "By this time he/she should know what I like. The s.o.b. just doesn't care." The spouse's failure is then credited to negligence or malevolence, whether there is or is not a response, or to conformity out of duty, rather than inclination. These resistances will require working-through, perhaps in individual sessions, during which role-playing may be used to train a patient to express certain desires without guilt, anger or vulgarity. Saying, "I would really appreciate it if you would (the request is then made)" may be very difficult for some patients to voice at first. But with practice the statement may slide off more easily. Requests should be modest at the beginning so as not to sound too unreasonable. They should never consist of activities around which there has been argument or contention in the past. A man who insists on taking every Saturday off for golfing, fishing or baseball games cannot be expected to give up his weekly pleasure without some compensatory trade-off. Nor can a person enslaved by a stubborn habit abandon it readily to please an importunate spouse. The spouse will have to be taught patience and forebearance, settling for small concessions at the start.

During therapy with a couple, the therapist may encourage a member to express a request and then have the partner confirm whether or not it will be possible to carry it out during the week. If there is too great hesitancy, the request should be shelved and another substituted for it more in line with what the recipient believes is achievable. At the next visit how thoroughly the request was fulfilled may be discussed, as well as the mutual reactions. Some therapists encourage making out written "contingency contracts" which specifically outline requests made by each partner in order that there be no misunderstanding as to what exactly is to be done. Example:

> Jane promises to take care of John's clothes, to see that they are cleaned and pressed.
> John agrees to baby-sit Sunday afternoon while Jane goes out to play bridge.

It must be emphasized that these behavioral tactics will fail miserably where deep emotional conflicts nurture hostility, competitiveness, detachment and other traits and patterns that make for a difficult relationship. However, we may consider them in the light of a trial balloon, and occasionally we are pleasantly rewarded with rapid and substantial improvement.

Q131: Many couples coming for marital problems want some immediate help for their difficulties. They want action, not insight. How can you apply a dynamic approach to action-oriented techniques?

A131: There is no reason why we cannot utilize educational, behavioral and other short-term techniques if this is what the couple expects and wants. These may accomplish the objective of allowing the partners to function better with each other, at least temporarily. Where no serious personality problems exist, accommodation for the other's shortcomings may come about in this way. What concerns us, however, are the couples whose failure in adjustment is rooted in deep personality difficulties. Here a dynamic approach may be indispensable. Hopefully, our short-term action-oriented techniques will have accomplished a solidification of the working relationship with the therapist, around which we can construct our dynamic therapeutic techniques. Recognizing that exposure of unconscious motivations will be difficult, we may have to proceed with a compromise treatment plan.

A good initial interview with each partner separately will yield enough data to allow a hypothesis of the underlying dynamics. The information obtained is, of course, for the therapist's edification only, since even if the therapist is correct in his hypothesis, its revelation would undoubtedly be rejected and might inspire a negative therapeutic reaction. Later on, when the therapist has more information and has succeeded in establishing a therapeutic alliance, it may be possible to titrate interpretations to each partner's level of tolerance and capacity for understanding. Continued collection of data will give an idea of the geography of the terrain that has to be crossed, without knowledge of which the therapist would be wandering in a maze.

A practical way of proceeding, once the therapist has obtained a bird's-eye view of the fundamental problems, is to expose the marital partners to a number of assignments, more to discover how these are accepted and the resistances they inspire than to expect a solution for the presenting problems. The reactions of the couple to the stratagems (behavioral, cognitive, etc.) employed will bring into play the neurotic defenses and the personality distortions that constitute the basic dynamic underpinnings of the difficulties for which help is being sought. The surfacing of these reactions may give the therapist an opportunity, assuming that a therapeutic working relationship exists, carefully to interpret some of the unconscious needs and drives from which they arise. Of utmost importance is an understanding of dream symbolism, for while the couple may successfully mask offensive feelings and attitudes through accommodating gestures and pseudo-compliant behavior, dreams more directly signal what actually is going on. Insistence that dreams be reported should pay worthwhile dividends. Transference reactions and acting-out activities may also become apparent and will require proper interpretation and management should they operate to obstruct treatment.

Q132: In working with marital couples using a dynamic model of therapy, do you ever combine this with behavioral approaches? If so, how is this done?

A132: Yes, even though the theoretical base revolves around unconscious conflict, behavioral methods may play an important part in devising intervention strategies. These are focused on problem solving, communication training, negotiation of differences and other practical reality based modes of operation. An outline of how behavioral methods may supplement a dynamic scheme may be illustrated in the case of a couple in conflict. Mary and John are on the verge of divorce. Mary consults a therapist because of tension and anxiety. She complains to the therapist that her husband does not love her. He pays no attention to her. He makes no statements of an endearing nature. He makes insufficient physical gestures of affection. He does not consider her an equal. He does not spend enough time with her. With the wife's permission, the therapist arranges an interview with John. John complains that his wife is not considerate of his needs. She does not appreciate him. She nags too much. She minimizes the things he does for her. The therapist on the basis of these interviews, proceeds along these lines:

1) Delineation of the problem behaviors. Are they the product of unfulfilled expectations on the part of one or both members? Are these expectations reasonable? (In the above case expectations are unfulfilled and to an extent unreasonable. See 3b.)

2) Selection of target behaviors to be modified in treatment. (In the above case the behaviors chosen are excessive fighting and arguing.)

3) Definition of the variables that influence such behaviors. (In the above case anger on the part of the wife, withdrawal on the part of the husband.)

   a. Which stimuli (environmental antecedents) initiate target behaviors? (In the above case the couple is seen as spending too little time together, which is resented by the wife. There is also inadequate communication.)

   b. Designation of the forces within the individual which sensitize him or her to such behaviors. (In the above case, following a number of interviews, faulty cognitions are believed to exist on the part of the wife regarding the proper role of the husband in a marriage. Her expectations are patterned after the wife's desire for a man who is like her father. On the husband's part he is seen as characterologically dependent, with a good deal of associated hostility, masochism and detachment. Some understanding of these neurotic forces is deemed necessary prior to instituting definitive interventions. It is here that a dynamic approach can prove to be important. Even a small amount of insight induced by careful interpretation may spell the difference between success and failure.)

   c. Examination of the behavioral responses and the consequences of such responses. What forms do the fighting and quarreling take and what happens as a result? (In the above case the wife attacks the husband verbally and the latter withdraws. This produces a feedback exaggerating the responses.)

4) Treatment planning. Exploration of possible interventions that may control problem behaviors (individual dynamic therapy, family therapy, multiple family therapy, couples therapy, communication practice sessions, contingency contracting, etc. The therapist may ask himself: "Is it possible for the couple to look on their relationship in a different way? What forces block such new perceptions (excess dependency, masochism, etc.)?"

5) Getting the couple to agree to utilize specific interventions and to engage in data collecting to chart the incidence of problems and the effect of interventions.

6) Assessing the consequences of such interventions. Do they control the problem behaviors? (Both therapist and couple should monitor change.)

Q133: Can you give an example of how you would use interpretation in marital therapy?

A133: As an example we may cite the case of a man who resents assertive actions on the part of his wife and who becomes violent when she is in the least critical of him. A portion of an interview shows how careful interpretation may open a chink in a patient's defensive armor.

Pt: I can't stand it when she is bumptious and demanding.

Th: This creates very upsetting feelings in you.

Pt: Yes, and then we have a running battle. She calls me a dictator, says I'm dogmatic.

Th: Does this battle go on all the time?

Pt: Yes. It reminds me of what my dad used to go through with my mother.

Th: What kind of a person was your mother?

Pt: Bossy, like my wife. She was bigoted too, gave me a hard time.

Th: But your wife says that you are the one who is bossy and jumps down her throat when she opens her mouth.

Pt: Not true. But sometimes she talks too much.

Th: Bossy?

Pt: Yes.

Th: Well, you can't be blamed for not getting in a situation like you had with your mother. When a child has a domineering and hostile mother, he is bound to feel crushed and upset. Once he breaks away from home he tries to avoid new domineering and hostile mother substitutes. (*I am interpreting the transference elements here*).

Pt: Doctor, that is exactly how I feel when my wife starts criticizing. I feel like she is putting me down, regards me like a little boy.

Th: So you have to get the jump on her and put her down first.

Pt: (*Laughs*) Maybe I am too tough. I can see what you mean—that if I let her she'll treat me as if I was a little boy.

Th: A helpless little boy. You see, in a situation like yours, with a background like yours, you're likely to be overly sensitive to even mild criticism. After all, nobody can be perfect.

Pt: I can't help it if I'm the way I am.

Th: Yes, you can. You can gain strength and self-confidence so that you can cope with even strong criticism without attacking and without feeling crushed and put down.

Pt: I'd like that.

Role playing was then utilized with his wife in my presence. I also modeled responses to criticism.

Q134: Can you say something about countertransference in marital therapy?

A134: A therapist who steps into a marital melee will have more than he bargained for, particularly when each of the participants attempts to recruit him as an ally against the other partner. It is here that the therapist may become emotionally involved, being tempted to fulfill the roles of arbiter, judge and high priest, rendering verdicts, making decisions, establishing criteria and setting values. Personal standards and prejudices will unfailingly impose themselves and the therapist's own unresolved problems will vigorously come to the fore. A great deal has been written about countertransference in psychotherapy, but in no other area than marital therapy is it apt to be so pronounced, particularly in cases where the therapist's own marriage is a mess. No wiser words have been said than for the marital therapist to look at his own marital values before he can effectively deal with the marriages of others. Even though a therapist has some personal problems, an awareness of these and of how his judgment may be warped by certain offensive behaviors or attitudes on the part of his patients should permit him to exercise greater objectivity.

Q135: What are bad prognostic signs in marital therapy?

A135:

1) The patient never had a good relationship with any person in the past.
2) Many of the disturbed feelings and attitudes of the patient are projections from the past onto the spouse.
3) The most important feelings and attitudes are unconscious in nature and the patient is unwilling or unable to deal with these.
4) The patient is emotionally and sexually involved with a person other than the spouse.
5) One spouse has especially serious emotional problems.
6) One spouse is uncooperative with the treatment plan.

Q136: In designing objectives in marital therapy, don't you have to question whether it is possible even with good therapy for two people to live together who genuinely hate each other?

A136: The answer to this question is suggested by the fact that many hating couples do live together, sometimes for a lifetime. It may be that the ties are economic, or because religion proscribed divorce, or because young children are presumed to need a father and mother, or because one's family would feel disgraced, or because the partners require a scapegoat in each other for the discharge of mutual hostility in order to preserve their homeostasis. Often the tie is an inseverable sadomasochistic bond which makes marriage a lifelong term of imprisonment activated by periodic crises and emotional explosions. In marital therapy our objective would be to resolve the sources of hatred so that living together is motivated by more positive ties, and a good treatment process should often be able to do this.

Q137: What is contingency contracting in marital therapy and what are the limitations?

A137: Contingency contracting which operates on the basis of quid pro quo conciliations plays an important part in marital therapy, particularly in its behaviorally oriented forms. Here couples by negotiation come to a written agreement of what each member has to do in the relationship to produce changes with which both members are in harmony.

In contingency contracts each partner promises to alter some aspect of behavior the other partner finds disagreeable. Contingency contracting is for those in whom verbal resolutions alone are not sufficient to put a restraint on their impulsiveness. The presence of a legal-like document helps to promote compliance with prescribed behaviors. When carried out, positive actions produce reciprocal pleasing responses which act as reinforcers for mutually constructive behaviors. The contract should be specific, spelling out exactly the kind of activities to be executed; otherwise arguments may break out as to meanings of vague expressions. The behavioral changes of each should also be sufficiently equivalent so that both partners feel they are getting an equal share of benefits.

One must keep in mind that the very behaviors that a spouse grumbles about may subversively be reinforced by certain actions of the offended spouse because such behaviors satisfy unconscious needs or defenses in the latter. Thus, a woman complaining about infrequency of sexual relationships may during the sexual experience act in a disinterested, bored, or sarcastic manner. In this way, she punishes the very behavior she desires to increase. When we investigate why these ambivalent attitudes exist, we may find that, in spite of a surface interest, sexuality is laden with a great deal of fear, guilt, and shame. Or her anger at or disgust with her husband forbids carnal intimacy. Or perhaps there is a prohibitive incestuous barrier to sexual activity. Such dispositions, which have their origin in earlier conditionings, might cause us to anticipate that the wife would be unable to halt her punishing activities even though in the contingency contract she promised to do so. This may actually be the case in instances where underlying needs and defenses are intensely and urgently pressing. On the other hand, even where such tendencies act as negative reinforcers, experience teaches that people can exercise a considerable degree of willful control over inner impulses, and through self-discipline and continuing practice gradually master adverse predispositions. It is, of course, helpful to provide in the contract positive reinforcements of some kind for the control of repugnant reactions. In the case cited, the husband may reward his mate for refraining from her customary reactions with praise and some material or behavioral bounty that is significant to his wife. Where no improvement in the sexual situation occurs, however, it may be necessary to utilize a more psychoanalytically oriented approach aimed at expanding the couple's understanding of their motivations and behavior.

Q138: Considering that marriage counselors do a good job in many marital problems, wouldn't you consider extensive training in dynamic psychotherapy unnecessary in most cases where a counselor limits himself to marital problems?

A138: Couples in trouble often consult marriage counselors, ministers, lawyers, and even friendly people of goodwill to advise them on proper steps to straighten out their entanglements. Where the partners are not too seriously plagued by neurotic drives, where their defenses are flexible and reasonably intact, and where they essentially love and respect each other, they may at least temporarily be held together in marriage by such consultations. Usually, however, the sources of serious marital problems are rooted in inner conflicts and stem from the operation of personality disturbances that resist pressure, education, convention and the lessons of morality and proper decorum.

The prescription of tasks and exercises that are intended to influence couples to be less abrasive toward each other, to communicate more constructively, and to foster a balanced relationship will therefore not succeed in those couples whose behavior is intractably motivated by urgent unconscious needs and impelling inner conflicts. For example, if a wife transferentially relates to a husband as if he represents a hateful brother with whom she was in competition during early childhood, she may resent being nice to him and continuously fail in her therapeutic assignments. A husband who is struggling with a dependency need, idealizing his wife as a mother figure who must love, nurture and take care of him, may be unable to give up acting irresponsibly, resisting the independent role his wife insists he must assume as a condition for more fruitful living together.

We should not minimize the utility of the various persuasive, behavioral, and cognitive techniques practiced by counselors to expedite marital congeniality. They can be valuable, but they will miss their mark if one utilizes them while ignoring the enormously important developmentally inspired motivational forces that are constantly maneuvering marital partners to act against their best interests. These more insistently dictate the terms of conduct than any injunctions, maxims, precepts, recipes, prohibitions, and interpretations presented by the most skilled and dedicated marital counselors. In my opinion, training in dynamic psychotherapy is important for any professional who seeks to do good marital therapy.

VIII. Cognitive Therapy

Emphasis on cognitive processes represents a shift from stimulus-response and drive models to the dynamics of systems and subsystems of thought. Psychotherapy, following this paradigm, is organized around the direct influencing of thought systems and the interpretation of events. The questions that puzzle some therapists are what symptoms and syndromes are best attuned to cognitive methods; whether these methods are applicable to those patients who have little capacity for introspection or the making of proper inferences; whether serious distortions in thinking (e.g., paranoidal ideas) can be corrected through cognitive techniques; and how best to integrate cognitive theory with one's own accepted theoretical orientation.

Q139: What is the basic idea of cognitive therapy and how would you differentiate cognitive from dynamic therapy?

A139: In contrast to dynamic therapy that tends to alter cognitions through insight into how past conditionings mold attitudes and behavior, cognitive therapy deals directly with present-day thoughts, irrational assumptions, destructive self-statements and self-defeating ideas. Their influence on feelings and behavior is explored with the object of regulating a more harmonious adjustment and helping the patient reduce or eliminate anxiety, depression, anger, and accompanying physiological residues.

The original work in this field was done by Ellis (1962). Several elaborations of Ellis's ideas have occurred, for example, the work of Meichenbaum and Cameron (1974), who have concentrated on the determining effect of the patient's negative self-statements and other irrelevant cognitives on behavior. Beck (1976) and Rush (1978) have also contributed substantially to the field through their stress on faulty thinking patterns, particularly in depressive states.

Q140: What essentially is the purpose of cognitive therapy?

A140: Disturbed thoughts and ideas are believed capable of setting off chain reactions ranging from emotional outbursts to behavioral aberrations to physiological upheavals. Such thoughts and ideas, which we may call cognitions, are often the product of faulty belief systems acquired through improper upbringing and false cultural values. The end result is interference with a satisfactory personal and social adjustment. Therapeutic efforts are therefore directed toward the forthright and immediate correction of faulty belief systems through techniques of "cognitive therapy."

Q141: What, in your opinion, is the greatest value of cognitive therapy?

A141: Through recent cognitive approaches attempts have been made to improve problem-solving as well as to enhance social adjustment. Where rudiments of adaptive skills are present and where anxiety is not too paralyzing, in a relatively brief period the individual with proper therapy along cognitive lines may be able to reorganize his thinking skills and to find alternative, constructive solutions for difficulties in living. Intervention programs of this type have been designed for application in a variety of clinical and educational settings (see Spivack et al., 1976).

Q142: How is cognitive therapy historically related to the old time philosophical, persuasive, and advice-giving approaches?

A142: Originally developed by early Greek observers as far back as the sixth century B.C., philosophical concepts evolved as a revolt against religious ideas about the origin and nature of the universe. What the early philosophers sought to establish was the precept that ideas and values had to be supported not by faith but by reason and evidence. Human beings, it was recognized, must depend on powers of accurate cognition to substantiate certain facts and to discern differences between knowledge and opinion. Unfortunately, such powers were often subverted by aberrations in the way people were brought up, by spurious educational indoctrinations, and by distortions in logic enforced by political or religious authority.

To circumvent such errors in reasoning more modern philosophers such as John Locke and Immanuel Kant advocated conscious introspection and testing through experience as a way of eliminating unfounded dogma, particularly in relation to the popular concept of innate ideas. Despite opposition from the more traditional philosophers and those revolting against rationalism, such as the existentialists, this shift toward empiricism has more or less fashioned many of our present-day concepts about how people think and act. The development of psychology as a science was a natural outgrowth of the emerging empirical orientation. Recognition that erroneous thoughts, ideas and values were responsible for many of the symptoms of neuroses led to the evolvement of measures designed to influence cognitions through advice-giving, suggestion, coercive pressure and persuasion. For a considerable period, prestige suggestion and persuasion dominated the field of treatment. Through advice-giving and authoritative injunctions, an effort was made to guide and direct the person seeking help. In prestige suggestion, commands and exhortations were forcefully delivered. Results were dependent on the credibility of the agent giving the suggestions. In pressure and coercion, rewards and punishments were employed to reinforce fruitful actions. In persuasion, the therapist functioned as a mentor to convince the person to change attitudes and values by appeals to "common sense" and reason.

Many of the foregoing measures are still employed today, adorned with new titles and scientific terminology. And in certain cases they continue to prove effective, given a motivated patient and a therapist who has undaunted faith in what he is doing and communicates this faith to the patient. For the most part, however, these approaches have failed to produce expected results and different modes focused on correcting faulty belief systems have evolved among both behavioral and dynamically oriented schools.

Behaviorally oriented methods which have taken on a cognitive dimension have been classified under the label of "cognitive behavior therapy." The distinctive quality of these techniques is that they do not attempt to force ideas on the patient but rather seek cooperation by providing the patient with graded tasks and assignments calculated to instill new ways of thinking. Thus, through instruction and modeling patients are taught to replace negative thoughts with thoughts that are more relevant to a proper adjustment (Meichenbaum and Cameron, 1974). Messages may be written out and given the patient for study and reflection. The aim is to soften the projected consequences of worrisome or destructive ideas. Eventually, it is hoped, negative self-statements and irrelevant cognitives that provoke untoward behavior may be eliminated.

Psychoanalytically oriented schools have also increasingly recognized the prime importance of altering cognitions and many therapists have been mindful of the need to utilize methods other than psychoanalytic to achieve this aim. Thus, techniques derived from the field of cognitive therapy are increasingly being employed in concert with dynamic exploratory measures. For most people, an understanding that they are being manipulated by erroneous belief systems is helpful in motivating them to accept active reeducative efforts of the therapist designed to correct the false assumptions and noxious self-statements that provide the lifeblood of resistance. Alterations in faulty cognitions have thus helped to resolve some resistances to awareness of unconscious conflicts and to the utilization of insight in the direction of change.

Q143: Will the present-day interest in cognitive processes help unify the dynamic and behavioral schools?

A143: Contemporary interest in the mental health field has been shifting toward the primacy of cognitive processes. Important to this issue is the hypothesis that higher central activities govern motivation and behavior. There is a growing realization of the centrality of the role of thought and language, the achievement of meaning, and relevance of images as ways of organizing experience. In psychoanalysis we have witnessed a progression from the original concern with drives to ego defenses to the dynamics of systems of thought and their influence on the totality of behavior. In problem-solving forms of therapy, like behavior modification, we have also seen a movement from the stimulus-response paradigm to recognition of the extensive links that exist between cognition and affective-behavioral-visceral regulatory functioning. It is hoped that this commonality of focus will bring the dynamic and behavioral schools closer to each other.

Q144: What is "thought stopping"?

A144: Exercises in thought substitution (i.e., replacing nihilistic with constructive ideas) are reinforced by eliciting positive thoughts during the day at times when no irrational ruminations are present (Homme, 1965). Where infelicitous cognitions keep obtruding themselves persistently some therapists utilize the technique of "thought stopping" (Wolpe, 1958). Here the patient practices turning on worrisome thoughts by verbalizing them; then in the course of this the patient shouts "Stop!" in order to interrupt the verbalizing and to turn off the thoughts. The upsetting thoughts are then deliberately elicited without verbalizing them, and the word "Stop" is said subvocally. It is hoped that practice will cause a diminution and then disappearance of the problem.

Q145: Does cognitive therapy help depressions?

A145: Where the depression is not a too severe endogenous one and a relationship can be established with the patient, cognitive therapy *in the hands of a trained, skilled therapist* may rectify idiosyncratic thought patterns and faulty ideational premises that reflect themselves in a depressive mood. Other forms of therapy, especially antidepressant medications, may be needed concomitantly in the endogenous depressions.

Q146: Can you use cognitive therapy along reassurance lines to treat a person with an overwhelming sense of inferiority?

A146: Reassurance to try to convince a person he is not inferior does not work. All it does is anger the recipient because he is convinced he *is* inferior and that if you knew him as well as he knew himself you would agree. He may then believe you are insincere or stupid or that your standards are low. It takes a long while before one can solidify one's sense of identity and elevate one's self-esteem. This will require a considerable period of working-through, which in short-term therapy takes place slowly after treatment has ended and the patient has put into practice the learnings he has acquired during the active treatment period.

IX. Hypnosis

Even though hypnosis has been with us for many years, it continues to excite curiosity, awe, and skepticism, not only among the laity, but also among professionals in the mental health field. On the one hand, it still is tainted with misunderstanding as a lewd and decadent art; on the other hand, it continues to be lauded sky high as a magical essence and miracle monger. What it is, how it works, when it should be employed, the best modes of induction and application, its continuity with consciousness and sleep, its effect on the therapeutic relationship, the validity of the material it brings to the fore, the permanence of its cures, its contraindications and dangers, and many other questions perplex professionals who may refrain from employing it for fear of its effects and complications.

Q147: What is hypnosis?

A147: We are no closer to defining hypnosis than we are to defining consciousness or sleep. All we can say is that it is an altered state of awareness suspended like a hammock between waking and sleep. Alteration of awareness can be produced by other psychological and pharmacologic agencies (Ludwig, 1966). Among such agencies are yoga, Zen, Transcendental Meditation, biofeedback, autogenic training, "mind altering" (psychomimetic) drugs and hypnotic medications.

Q148: What is the value of hypnosis in psychotherapy and in what conditions is it most useful? Aren't there many drawbacks to using hypnosis in psychoanalytic therapy?

A148: Employed by reasonably trained professionals within the context of a structured therapeutic program, with proper awareness of limits of its application, hypnosis can make a contribution as an adjunct to any of the manifold branches of psychotherapy, whether these be supportive, reeducative, or psychoanalytic. Hypnosis also has value as an analgesic agent helping to compose apprehensive patients and, by suggestion, to lessen their pain. It has been used with effectiveness in obstetrics, minor surgery, plastic surgery, dentistry, and diagnostic examinations, such as bronchoscopy and sigmoidoscopy. Prior to administration of electroshock, it may be useful for its calming effect. The dangers inherent in its use are few or non-existent if it is skillfully employed by a responsible therapist.

Most professionals who are fearful of hypnosis as a therapeutic tool or who exaggerate its virtues either have never experimented with it for a time sufficient to test the method or are victims of superstition, prejudices, or naive magical expectancy. A number of spokesmen for hypnosis, some writing extensively, unfortunately help to discredit it by overdramatizing the process, by exaggerating its powers, by participating in and publishing results of poorly conceived experiments, by engaging in naively organized therapeutic schemes, by offering therapeutic formulations that violate the most elementary precepts of dynamic psychology, or by promulgating its presumed dangers for which there is little basis in fact.

Hypnosis as a relaxing agency has been employed in many physical and psychological disturbances that are characterized by stress and tension. Since stress may have a damaging effect on all bodily functions, its amelioration may constitute an important healing instrumentality. Tension relief may, on the basis of suggestion during the trance state, be supplemented by self-hypnosis or such techniques as autogenic training.

The use of suggestion for the short-term treatment of a number of emotional ailments may succeed in relieving symptoms rapidly, permitting the individual to return to his optimal level of functioning. Suggestive hypnosis is generally utilized in cases of emergency or where time limitations prevent a more extensive treatment endeavor. Thus in emergency situations it may be the treatment of choice, succeeding in returning the individual to his customary equilibrium without necessarily resolving basic conflicts. Where the symptom does not bind too much anxiety, or where its pleasure and masochistic values are not too intense, it may be possible to resolve or alleviate it without symptom substitution. Not only may relief initiate a better adjustment, but it may set off a chain reaction that, reverberating through the entire personality structure, influences its other dimensions. Suggestive hypnosis may also be of value in controlling the ruminations of chronic obsessive-compulsive patients whose preoccupations immerse them in interminable misery. By helping such victims to divert their thinking into more constructive channels, it may be possible to initiate abatement of anxiety and a better adaptation.

With caution, hypnosis may be adopted as a suggestive instrument in controlling certain habits, such as overeating, excessive smoking, and insomnia. The phrasing of suggestions here is all important. Rather than commanding a patient to abandon his symptoms or destructive practices, their release is made contingent on the suggestion that he will want increasingly to give them up. As his desire grows stronger, he will soon relinquish them on his own accord. Under these circumstances it may be possible to circumvent competitiveness with and defiance of authority which are registered in resistance to suggestions.

In behavior therapy, hypnosis is useful in various ways. First, it establishes in the mind of the patient the authority of the therapist who will act as the reinforcing agency. Under these circumstances, positive counterconditioning, aversive conditioning, extinction and other tactics will be catalyzed. Second, by promoting relaxation through hypnosis, a positive stimulus is supplied which becomes affiliated with the conditioned stimulus and helps to extinguish it. Thus, in the method of desensitization through reciprocal inhibition, anxiety-provoking cues are presented in a climate of relaxation in progressively stronger form. Third, on the basis of suggestion, the objectives of the therapist, once explicitly defined, may be more easily accepted. The patient is encouraged to behave in emotionally constructive ways in quest of reversing established patterns or correcting behavior deficits.

Questions which understandably concern the dynamically oriented therapist who contemplates using hypnosis are these: Will not hypnosis interfere with the non-interfering climate essential for undiluted transferential projections? Does not a technique which virtually puts the patient under the domination of the therapist tend to subjugate him and mobilize undue dependency? What about the fear expressed in the literature of precipitating a psychosis, particularly in a schizoid patient? Is there not an undue concern with the unconscious during hypnosis to the neglect of the important conscious ego elements? Will not hypnosis merely succeed in liberating strangulated emotion in a cathartic outflow without, in any definitive way, altering the repressive forces that conceal the conflictual core? How can hypnoanalysis, which deals with the inner repudiated aspects of experience, succeed in effectuating essential alterations in character structure necessary for lasting change? How can hypnosis reduce the severity of the superego when the hypnotist functions in the role of the commanding authority? These and other concerns would seem to cast a shadow on experimentation with hypnosis as a possibly serviceable technique in psychoanalytic therapy. The caveats inherent in these questions, however, do not necessarily restrict the pragmatic employment of hypnosis as a facilitating tool in psychoanalytically oriented psychotherapy when executed by a dynamically trained and experienced therapist who is skilled in the use of hypnosis. Indeed, study of the patient's reactions, including dreams, to induction, to the trance state itself, and to the therapist make excellent grist for the analytic mill. Resistance phenomena mobilized by hypnosis also lend themselves to productive exploration.

Q149: What is the best way of inducing hypnosis?

A149: Hypnosis is remarkably easy to induce and there is no one technique that is superior to others. The most advantageous way to find out which technique (eye fixation, relaxation suggestions, hand levitation etc.) is best suited to one's style and personality is to experiment with several methods, selecting the one with which the therapist feels most comfortable, and perfecting it with practice. Toward this end a number of books are available detailing different methods of induction (Brenman and Gill, 1964; Chertok, 1966; Edelstien, 1981; Weitzenhoffer, 1957; Wolberg, 1948).

Q150: My patients on whom I try to use hypnosis usually tell me they weren't in a trance after they come out of it. This discourages me. How can I make them believe they have been hypnotized? And are there any tests of depth I can use to establish the fact of hypnosis?

A150: Most patients at the start will deny being in a trance even when they have entered deep hypnosis. This is partly defensive and partly due to the expectation of unusual, arcane, or transcendental happenings brought about by hypnosis. Some patients equate hypnosis with sleep and since they are not asleep they do not feel as if they were hypnotized. One way of handling this situation is to tell patients in advance of the first induction that you do not want them to go to sleep, and to try to fight sleep off if they feel sleep coming on. You want them to experience no more than a light state of pleasant relaxation. But even this injunction often does no good, some patients still expressing disappointment about not being hypnotized. Should the patient then complain about not going deep enough, the therapist may counter that the patient followed suggestions in not allowing himself to go too deep. The next time hypnosis is induced you may say, "If you want to go a little deeper you may. But it doesn't matter. All we are aiming for is a state of pleasant relaxation." The patient will usually then concentrate on her experiences and your suggestions without considering the induction a challenge to her or your competence. It is unnecessary to conduct tests for depth of trance because if patients do not achieve success in any of the tests, this may give them the idea they are failing in hypnosis.

Q151: Can a patient's reactions to hypnosis give you leads as to his diagnosis or the best therapeutic methods to employ?

A151: Some interesting speculations may emerge in watching how patients respond to the induction of hypnosis, but these are not sufficiently reliable to pinpoint either the existing diagnosis or choices in therapeutic method.

Q152: Is there any correlation between personality structure and hypnotizability?

A152: Generally no. However, I have noticed that highly imaginative artists (such as actors who can readily assume roles) and deeply religious people or those who were in childhood immersed in religion often make excellent hypnotic subjects.

Q153: Can you by any method succeed in hypnotizing a person who is considered nonhypnotizable?

A153: The method of induction is not as important as the state of mind and the motivation of the subject, as well as the quality of the relationship with the operator. Your question brings up an important point of controversy. Is the degree of hypnotizability or non-hypnotizability a stable quality which cannot be changed? The problem here is that we never know whether a so-called "nonhypnotizable" subject latently possesses an aptitude for hypnosis which might display itself given the proper conditions. One variable is the existing degree of anxiety and sense of mastery. During World War II "shell shocked" soldiers showed a much higher degree of hypnotizability than when they recovered later on. Could we say that the shattering of defenses and the presence of anxiety motivated the soldier to trust and relate confidently with the operator and that this brought out the latent capacity? Yet there were some "shell shocked" soldiers who could not be hypnotized. Was this due to the absence of a latent ability for hypnosis or was it because this subgroup could not develop the proper motivation or trust?

In my own practice I have noticed that patients in a crisis are more readily hypnotizable than when the crisis has passed and their sense of mastery restored. The personality of the operator also has something to do with whether or not a subject is hypnotizable. I have been able to hypnotize patients referred to me by therapists who claimed they were nonhypnotizable, and I am sure the reverse is true also; that is, my failures could be reversed by others.

Another factor that must also be considered is the persistence of the operator. Too often a therapist gives up after the first minute or two have failed to put the patient in a trance. I remember one patient years ago, a youth in late adolescence with a severe obsessive-compulsive problem, whose doubts and challenges made him resistive to a number of approaches, including hypnosis. He had fruitlessly sought out the best-known therapists doing hypnosis in New York since he expressed confidence that hypnosis was the only approach that could possibly help him. Each therapist, including myself, gave up in frustration. Milton Erickson was visiting New York at the time and fortuitously arrived at my office at the hour I was seeing the patient. The thought occurred to me that Erickson might enjoy the challenge of trying to get a nonhypnotizable patient to enter a trance state. Erickson readily agreed to try his hand at induction and I set him up in a separate room with the dubious patient. Periodically I came into the room to observe what was happening, which for the first hour and a half was nothing. At the end of two hours, the patient entered what I would consider a deep trance, experiencing auditory and visual hallucinations, the ability to open his eyes and blot out certain objects in the room, and post-hypnotic suggestions and amnesia. I must admit that I was more astonished than the patient, who seemed confused rather than pleased by the experience.

Erickson's triumph, I believe, was due to a shattering of the patient's control and sense of mastery by use of his persistent confusional technique. There are few of us who have enough dedication, skill and fortitude to spend two hours trying to hypnotize a reluctant subject. The sequel to this episode was that for a while I had a very anxious and disturbed patient on my hands, but after a few weeks, we worked on his need for control and distrust of authority, during which real progress followed.

The point I am making is that had Erickson not been around I would have classified the patient as completely nonhypnotizable. But this merely illustrates the dilemma I previously pointed out. Could not all so-called nonhypnotizable subjects possess latent abilities for hypnosis that certain operators might be able to bring out under special conditions? And could not the depth of trance similarly be a variable in the same subject and with the same operator dependent on the state of cooperativeness and motivation, the anxiety level and transference existing at the time? I do not have the answer to these questions. Ordinarily I would have said you cannot make a silk purse out of a sow's ear—and you cannot make a somnambule out of a patient capable of entering only a light trance. But the experience with Erickson casts some doubts in my mind.

Q154: Do you subject your patients in hypnosis to a test to determine their depth of trance?

A154: In the early days when I started working with hypnosis I did, but I soon discovered that this was not necessary and often created discouragement in patients when they discovered they could not achieve certain phenomena. The only time I find it necessary to test the level of trance is when I am doing hypnoanalysis or the setting up of experimental conflicts, techniques which require a deep and preferably somnambulistic trance. Under these circumstances, I perform an innocuous test by giving the patient a posthypnotic suggestion of a casual nature and then see whether he is capable of executing it with amnesia for the trance events.

Q155: Do unconscious factors influence trance depth?

A155: Probably. If anxiety is present in contemplating entering a trance or during trance induction, i.e., if there is fear of attack, seduction, subjugation, etc., the subject, while seemingly motivated consciously and apparently trusting the hypnotist, may resist entering a trance state or may not go beyond a state of light relaxation. On the other hand, an unconscious masochistic desire for subjugation and seduction should hypothetically enhance cooperativeness and permit utilization of hypnotic suceptibility to the full.

Q156: How would you distinguish deep relaxation from hypnosis?

A156: This may be difficult because there are few reliable differential signs except in very deep hypnosis where hallucinations or regression and revivification can be evoked. In light or medium hypnosis one may have to rely on the subjective statements of the patient: "I felt not quite myself," or "My body felt disjointed," and other comments related to distortions of the body image. Some therapists gradually deepen relaxation by progressive suggestions starting with arm levitation. When the subject's hand touches his face they assume he is in hypnosis (Frankel and Zamansky, 1978). Actually there is a difference between relaxation and hypnosis insofar as the depth of alteration of consciousness is concerned. Whether suggestions are more effective in hypnosis than in relaxation will depend on how the patient interprets the suggestions and their meaning to him during both states. We might anticipate that suggestibility is increased with hypnosis and that the deeper the trance the more effective the suggestions. However, this rule does not always hold. In some patients, the anxiety of losing control as hypnosis develops and deepens may cause them to resist suggestions more during hypnosis than when they feel they are in better control of their faculties during relaxation.

Q157: Are suggestions given during mere relaxation less effective than if given during hypnosis?

A157: Suggestions given in the waking state can be highly effective in some persons. Yet in the same individual the identical suggestions during hypnosis may be more strongly acted on. Paradoxically, in some cases the reverse is true. The reason for this is that patients who have a powerful need for control may fear losing control during hypnosis and consequently they will act more oppositional as they enter the hypnotic state than when they are fully conscious. The crucial element is the *meaning* to the person of the proffered suggestions. If the subject has the motivation to execute a suggestion, she is likely to do so both in the waking or trance state. On the other hand, where a suggestion creates too much anxiety, it may not be effective. What helps a subject tolerate an anxiety-provoking suggestion is the protective relationship with the hypnotist. Where the subject trusts the therapist and has confidence in him, where she has a need to win the approval of the therapist, she may execute even anxiety-provoking suggestions like probing for past traumatic experiences and recalling anxiety dreams. There is a limit, of course, to the extent of tolerance of anxiety or the accepting of untoward, guilt-inspiring or criminal suggestions, even if there is trust in the hypnotist. One's critical judgment is never suspended and usually will neutralize such suggestions. On the other hand, where no warm relationship exists with the hypnotist and there is little trust and confidence in him, anxiety-provoking suggestions are likely to be vigorously resisted.

Q158: What about the manner of giving suggestions?

A158: What is important is that the therapist exude conviction in his manner and assurance in the giving of suggestions, radiating an expectation of success. Suggestions made in a halting, timorous, and spiritless way will tend to stimulate doubt and lack of enthusiasm leading to failure. The patient should not be imperiously ordered to comply. Rather, he is helped to see the importance of complying with a suggestion and invited to act on it when he is ready.

Q159: Can a lightly hypnotized subject experience hallucinations?

A159: Hallucinations related to touch and smell may sometimes be easily induced, but it is more difficult to produce auditory hallucinations and visual hallucinations. Hallucinations may under certain conditions be experienced in the waking state by suggestion or self-suggestion where the need for such a sensory experience is great. Thus during a seance a person wanting to hear the voice of a departed person may be able to do so.

Q160: Doesn't hypnosis make the patient more dependent on the therapist?

A160: Peculiarly enough it does not. A penchant for dependency is inherent more in the characterologic makeup of the individual and because of existing personality needs than in any techniques employed, including hypnosis. On the contrary, hypnosis, properly implemented, with the teaching of the individual of ways she can utilize self-hypnosis, will often lead to greater self-sufficiency. Some therapists dictate a cassette tape with relaxing suggestions that the patient may use by herself to promote relaxation and to reinforce ego-building suggestions (Wolberg, 1980, pp. 223-234). In follow-up studies with patients using such tapes, I have never discovered a single person who has become addicted to the tape. Indeed, the situation is the reverse. After feeling more relaxed and self-confident, the patient often forgets to play the tape or deliberately stops using it.

Q161: Doesn't hypnosis mobilize sexual feelings in patients which will interfere with the therapeutic relationship?

A161: An erotic transference is possible in any kind of psychotherapy where a strong relationship develops between patient and therapist.

If handled properly, it need not interfere with the therapeutic process. One is reminded of the experience of Freud in his first uses of hypnosis. In speaking about a patient with whom he had secured excellent results by tracing her attacks of pain back to their origin under hypnosis, he wrote: "As she woke up on one occasion, she threw her arms round my neck. The unexpected entrance of a servant relieved us from a painful discussion, but from that time onwards, there was a tacit understanding between us that the hypnotic treatment should be discontinued. . . . I felt that I had now grasped the nature of the mysterious element that was at work behind hypnotism. In order to exclude it, or at all events to isolate it, it was necessary to abandon hypnotism" (S.E. 22:27). Freud (S.E. 18:143) believed that hypnosis resembled the state of being in love and was "based entirely on sexual impulsions that are inhibited in their aims. . . ." This idea has long been repudiated. In my own experience with hypnosis, I never got the impression that the erotic transference was an especially prominent event, but I would assume it might come up with certain repressed hysterical patients. If it did arise, it could certainly be managed therapeutically.

Q162: When is hypnotic symptom intensification used? What is hypnotic age regression and revivification, and how is hypnotic time distortion used?

A162: Where a symptom, such as a functional physical ailment, has become dissociated from an affiliated emotion, intensification of the symptom in the trance state and the stimulation of imagery may enable the patient to see their relationship. Thus, hysterical symptoms like aphonia, paralysis, muscle spasms, etc. may lift when their linkage with hostility, fear, and guilt feelings becomes apparent. The symptom relief, while important, is complemented by the understanding the patient gains regarding dynamic personality operations provocative of the problems. With proper motivation, this insight may be helpful in resolving the conflictual base of a hysterical symptom.

In hypnotic age regression and revivification the patient is directed to remember and perhaps relive an important past memory or experience related in some way to a present symptom, or to anxiety in general. This is similar to the method originally utilized by Breuer and Freud.

In hypnotic time compression the patient is directed to abbreviate an experience so that it seems to pass very quickly. For example, in some cases of a pain syndrome the time of suffering is condensed so that the painful experience passes quickly. The same is true in living through in fantasy a disagreeable event or situation, or reviving memories of a traumatic experience. In time expansion, sensations of pleasure are stretched out so that moments seem like hours. These pleasurable interludes in a depressed patient are extended in the imagination to enhance acceptance of enjoyment and to dull the sodden mood.

Q163: How about pain relief through hypnosis as compared to a placebo given in the waking state?

A163: Studies show that there is a difference in the degree of analgesia achieved in favor of hypnosis.

Q164: What is the best way of producing anesthesia for pain relief?

A164: There are several good methods. One I have found effective is to produce a glove anesthesia by hypnosis, then lifting the anesthetic hand and placing it on the part to be rendered numb and relaxed. It is suggested that the numbness, warmth, or tingling sensation in the fingers and hand will surround the ailing part and cause any uncomfortable feeling to disappear. In migraine headaches the hand is directed to feel cool. Then the patient is instructed to transfer the cool feeling to the area of the head pain through touch. This, it is suggested, will send the blood from the head to the fingers. Self-hypnosis is taught and the patient enjoined to carry on by herself. The patient may also be told that any presence of pain will seem short in time and that the period of feeling relief through the exercises will seem to stretch out very much longer.

Q165: Can hypnosis accomplish anything that cannot be achieved in the waking state? In other words, can people be made to perform better—to write, paint and excel in abilities—by hypnosis?

A165: With proper motivation an individual may achieve in the waking state anything she could achieve in hypnosis. But hypnosis is an easier route to suggest proper motivation for certain tasks. People will perform beyond their usual capacities when they have a latent potential to excel, but never beyond this potential. Suggestions in hypnosis may stimulate a greater incentive to achieve one's potential, but this can also be done by properly motivating the subject in the waking state.

Q166: Are subjects in hypnosis susceptible to immoral or criminal suggestions?

A166: No more than they would be in the waking state. Very good somnambulistic subjects, however, can be tricked by a clever hypnotist to distort reality and unwittingly expose themselves to a hazardous situation. However, even here the subject never loses complete control and has the power to neutralize unscrupulous suggestions if she wishes to do so.

Q167: Can hypnosis be employed with groups of patients?

A167: Group hypnosis may be even more effective than individual sessions, where the goal is the giving of supportive and persuasive suggestions for purposes of tension relaxation, the overcoming of obnoxious habits like overeating and smoking, symptom control as in phobias, and assertive training for the building of self-confidence and promotion of self-esteem.

Q168: Is hypnosis useful in criminal investigations?

A168: Where a subject is likely to incriminate herself by confessions, she may resist revealing information. She may bring up false fantasies or deliberately lie, even in deep hypnosis. On the other hand, where the subject trusts and has confidence in the operator, she may decide to relieve herself of guilt and tell the truth, even revealing suppressed or forgotten experiences. Facts brought up during hypnosis have to be scrupulously tested because fantasies are more vivid in this state than in the waking state.

Q169: Why shouldn't hypnoanalysis be used routinely in psychoanalysis if it makes the unconscious more easily conscious?

A169: The routine use of hypnoanalysis is out of the question since most hypnoanalytic techniques require a somnambulistic trance. This restricts the use of techniques like regression and revivification, posthypnotic suggestion, and the induction of experimental conflicts to a little over 10 percent of subjects. Freud abandoned hypnosis for this very reason, since it was a limited instrument for evoking past memories of early traumatic experiences. However, hypnosis, even in light or medium trance states, may be employed to stimulate dreaming and to augment transference in patients who find it difficult to remember dreams or to relate intensely to the therapist. Since psychoanalysis requires technical neutrality, we might perhaps better label exploratory therapy which employs hypnosis "psychoanalytically oriented psychotherapy" rather than "psychoanalysis."

Q170: What are the problems in doing research on hypnosis?

A170: An important deterrent in doing research on hypnosis is the inability on the part of the operator to maintain objectivity. The hypnotist must involve himself intensely with the subject in order to produce the expectancies around which development of a trance evolves. This tends to distort the hypnotic phenomena being studied. Moreover, the expectancies of the subject and her needs to please the operator by fulfilling explicit or implied demands will produce reactions that have little to do with the hypnotic state itself. Almost inevitably some transference and resistance manifestations will arise, further contaminating the trance phenomena under investigation.

X. Somatic Therapy

There are some therapists who still denigrate the contributions of somatic therapy by insisting that proponents of drug and other biological treatments are deliberately attempting to reduce the importance of the cerebral cortex in favor of the mid-brain. Yet the results of somatic therapy speak for themselves. In some conditions the outcomes have been little short of spectacular. In other conditions the somatic therapies have failed miserably. The hypothesis that all emotional illness is rooted in disarrangements of the cellular or subcellular systems has never been proven, though it has many vocal advocates. How psychotropic drugs, ECT and other somatic therapies work has not yet been fully investigated, although existing empirical research and clinical studies have added a great deal to our knowledge.

Among the problems that vex the therapist are when drugs expedite or retard the psychotherapeutic process; which neuroleptics, antidepressants, and anxiolytics are most suitable for selected target symptoms; when to change from one drug to another; the prophylactic value of drugs; how to deal with "drug defaulters" who do not take their medications; how to avoid distressing side effects and complications; the safety of ECT; the uses of drugs with children and the elderly; whether nonmedical therapists should legally be able to prescribe drugs; and a variety of other concerns that are dealt with in this section.

Q171: When would you give the patient a tranquilizer during therapy? Also, when would you use maintenance tranquilization?

A171: When the intensity of anxiety is so great that the patient cannot attend to therapeutic tasks, she may be so concerned with defending herself against anxiety that constructive concerns are put aside. One consequence of too great anxiety is negative transference, which may then become a way of blaming the therapist for not being protective enough.

In chronic anxiety maintenance, tranquilization is sometimes employed, but in the case of neurotic and personality disorders this is not a good idea because of the likelihood of addiction. Psychotherapy, perhaps maintenance psychotherapy over a prolonged period, with spaced visits to control dependency, is to be preferred. Where anxiety continues in spite of psychotherapy, a mild tranquilizer like Valium may be given for a few weeks and then interrupted. In schizophrenia or borderline cases, neuroleptics like Thorazine or Mellaril are to be preferred and may be used as a maintenance medication in as small doses as will control the symptoms, with occasional drug holidays. Chances of addiction with neuroleptics are nil.

Q172: What are the best indications for antianxiety medications like Valium?

A172: Where a usually well-adjusted individual is temporarily upset, benzodiazepines may tide him over a rough period. During psychotherapy, they may be useful when anxiety is so strong that it interferes with treatment. Benzodiazepines should not be used routinely especially where anxiety is tolerable, since they may interfere with motivation to explore one's problems. There are some patients who have no desire for psychotherapy or cannot use it and who insist on pills. These patients tend to make a way of life out of benzodiazepines and they can become addicted. The therapist may try benzodiazepines for a short while in the hope of instituting and then substituting supportive or reeducative approaches. Some therapists give these patients small doses of neuroleptics like Mellaril (10mg.), which is less addicting than benzodiazepines and which acts principally as a placebo.

Q173: What are the disadvantages of anxiolytics?

A173: Long-term use can be habituating and abrupt cessation after high doses can cause convulsions. Combination of anxiolytics with barbiturates or alcohol may be lethal because of respiratory depression. Anxiolytics may interfere with coordination, posing some risk if a person must drive a car or do work that is hazardous like operating a machine. In older people side effects are especially annoying. But, all in all, their advantages exceed their disadvantages.

Q174: What are the most common anxiolytic agents? What is bromazepam?

A174: Perhaps the most common antianxiety substance is alcohol. While it is quite effective, its side effects and dangers of habituation eliminate it as a useful medication. The same can be said for opiate drugs (morphine, heroin, etc.). Barbiturates in the past were commonly used, but not so much now. Their danger lies in their toxicity and in their habituation potential.

The most useful of anxiolytics are the benzodiazepines (Valium, Librium, and Serax). Their advantage lies in their relatively high therapeutic level as compared to their toxicity. They function also as muscle relaxants, hypnotics, and anticonvulsants. New benzodiazepines are constantly being tested and in the near future will undoubtedly be approved. Bromazepam (Lexotan), for example, has been found to be effective for anxiety in phobic conditions and obsessional personalities, and it is said to have an added advantage in being less sedating and producing fewer side effects. A useful available anxiolytic is Ativan (lorazepam), which is rapidly absorbed and metabolized and has low toxicity.

Q175: Are benzodiazepines like Valium good once a panic attack has started? If not what helps?

A175: They are helpful to subdue anticipatory anxiety, but once panic breaks out they do not seem to help too much. Sometimes intravenous injections of sodium amytal do help to subdue an intractable panic.

Where a psychotic-like reaction exists or threatens, a parenteral neuroleptic like Haldol can be quieting.

Q176: Are beta adrenergic blocking agents like Inderal ever used in anxiety?

A176: Where cardiac arrhythmia, tachycardia, and heart palpitations create anxiety, Inderal may be effective in reducing panicky feelings and preventing attacks by blocking discharge from the sympathetic nervous system.

Q177: Can Tofranil help agoraphobia?

A177: In some cases panic attacks with palpitation, tachycardia, depersonalization and other symptoms in the syndrome of agoraphobia are helped greatly by Tofranil (imipramine). Psychotherapy should coordinately be employed. An average of 150 mg. of Tofranil is generally used and several weeks of medication may be required before definite relief is obtained.

Q178: When would you use antidepressant medications in depressive episodes?

A178: The more prominent the physical symptoms, the more indicated are antidepressants. Among such symptoms are psychomotor retardation or agitation, difficulties in thinking and concentrating, early morning awakening and insomnia, loss of appetite and sexual desire, and diurnal variation in symptoms. Where suicidal impulses are present, the patient must be carefully watched since a release of energy produced by the medications may give the patient the impetus toward making an attempt at suicide. Hospitalization and the administration of ECT should be considered seriously where a suicidal risk exists. Antidepressants will not correct existing personality difficulties, relationship problems, and distorted attitudes and values which are best approached with psychotherapy.

Q179: Doesn't the prescription of a psychotropic drug interfere with the psychotherapeutic situation?

A179: Not always. In the more severe emotional problems like schizophrenia, paranoia, mania, and deep depression, the use of drug therapy is indispensable for the conduct of psychotherapy. In conditions where anxiety is profound, an anxiolytic medication (Valium, Librium, Ativan) may actually expedite the therapeutic relationship. In other conditions, like the hyperkinetic syndromes of childhood, we may have to depend on medications to make the patient cooperate with our treatment efforts. In emergency situations, such as panic states, toxic drug and alcohol intoxications, psychotic outbreaks, and suicidal attempts, the use of neuroleptic and anxiolytic medications may be essential. During crisis intervention where our objective is to restore the patient to his previous emotional equilibrium, drug therapy may facilitate this objective. In the average case requiring psychotherapy, however, psychotropic drugs should be avoided so as not to introduce a palliative that can divert the patient from correcting behavioral or attitudinal patterns that are responsible for his symptoms. This does not mean that we may not occasionally prescribe a temporary mild tranquilizer during the course of treatment, should the level of anxiety necessitate this.

Q180: How would you treat anxiety associated with depression?

A180: Where depression is the primary condition, the basic therapy is the institution of tricyclic antidepressants like Elavil in adequate dosage. In atypical depression, where phobic states and hypochondriacal complaints occur, the monoamine oxidase inhibitors, like Parnate, may be effective. Results with these antidepressants may not be registered until after three or four weeks of drug intake.

Q181: Is it all right to use Valium in depression?

A181: Where anxiety and insomnia exist in a *mild* depression, the temporary use of a benzodiazepine like Valium may help. It should not be used for more than four to six weeks because of danger of habituation.

Q182: Is there any advantage in giving tricyclic antidepressant medication on a once-a-day basis rather than in multiple doses?

A182: Recent studies indicate some advantage with no increase in side effects (Weise et al., 1980).

Q183: What can you do with a severe depression that does not respond to either psychotherapy or tricyclic antidepressants? With the latter drug some severe side effects have occurred in my patient.

A183: It may be helpful to try an antidepressant medication of a different class. For example, atypical depressions may respond well to monoamine oxidase inhibitors like phenelzine (Nardil) or tranylcyromine (Parnate). These medications have to be prescribed by and supervised by a psychiatrist who understands the side effects and the essential precautions related to their use. Some new antidepressants that have been utilized recently have little anticholinergic effect and less influence on the heart and blood pressure. The best-known examples are the tetracylic drugs like Mianserin and maprotiline. These medications, if available, may be tried on a patient who is sensitive to tricyclics. Of course, if the patient is suicidally depressed, ECT should be considered as an emergency measure.

Q184: Is megavitamin therapy effective in schizophrenia?

A184: Evidence of its effectiveness has not been proven.

Q185: What about maintenance pharmacotherapy in depression?

A185: In cases where depression is recurrent, maintenance employment of an antidepressant drug may be necessary to help prevent depressive attacks.

Q186: How long do you continue giving antidepressant drugs after recovery from a depression?

A186: At least three or four months, but in many cases as long as nine to 15 months. Then the drug is gradually reduced in dosage and discontinued. In the event of a relapse the medication is reinstituted for three to six months, then again slowly withdrawn. Where there has been a history of a chronic depression over a long period, maintenance antidepressant drug therapy may be required.

Q187: Is trazodone a better antidepressant than the usual tricyclics?

A187: Trazodone is a new antidepressant chemically unrelated to tricyclics. It seems to have a lower cardiac toxicity and fewer anticholinergic effects. It is at least as effective an antidepressant as the tricyclics. Since it is sedating, the largest dose (which ranges from 50 to 800 mg. per day) is given at bedtime. Many new antidepressants are being tested and are not yet available in the United States. Eventually some will be released and undoubtedly used for their reduced side effects and greater rapidity of action.

Q188: Can phenothiazines be used in depression?

A188: Patients with psychotic depressions with great restlessness and delusions may respond well to thioridazine (Mellaril). Other phenothiazines work also and they may be combined with the tricyclic antidepressants. A common prescribed combination is Triavil or Etrafon.

Q189: Since depressions and schizophrenia are known to be caused by chemical imbalances, shouldn't the treatment be through psychotropic drugs?

A189: Your assumption of an exclusive biochemical focus is not justified at this point in time. The etiology of depression, of mood disorders in general, and of schizophrenia is still not entirely clear. Multifactorial elements enter into the picture, only one aspect being defects in neurotransmitter chemistry. As important as pharmacotherapy may be, neglecting developmental, conditioning, intrapsychic, interpersonal and social elements will leave the therapeutic process denuded and incomplete (see Wolberg, 1980, pp. 135-137).

Q190: Has the recovery rate of schizophrenia been bettered with the use of neuroleptics?

A190: The recovery rate of schizophrenia is the same as before, but the hospitalization rate is lower since patients can make a better social adjustment when on neuroleptics.

Q191: Isn't the recovery rate for schizophrenia improved by the introduction of neuroleptic drugs as compared to milieu therapy?

A191: When we compare the recovery rate under good milieu therapy with that of drug therapy, the difference is not dramatic. This may be because the drugs we now have, while controlling and eliminating some of the symptoms of schizophrenia, do not really cure the illness.

Q192: What are some rules to follow in prescribing neuroleptics in schizophrenia?

A192: The least amount of medication for the smallest amount of time is the best rule to follow. All drugs are to an extent toxic; therefore at some time the patient should experimentally be taken off all medications. If he decompensates, he can be put on medications again. Keeping a patient on neuroleptics continuously is dangerous. Drugs differ in their side-effect profiles, and if the patient shows disturbing side effects he should be shifted to a neuroleptic of another class because most patients will, away from the watching eye of the therapist, give up medications because of dizziness, drowsiness, constipation, etc. Insofar as the initial choice of a drug is concerned, the target symptoms one wants to control are important. Also, the history of prior drug use gives some leads. It is a good idea to ask if another member of the family has ever been on neuroleptics and the manner of the response since there is evidence that drug response runs in families.

Q193: Is there any preference in using one antipsychotic drug over others?

A193: Not a great deal although some, like Thorazine or Mellaril, have a sedating effect and are preferably used in excited reactions. Others like Haldol, Permitil, Prolixin and Navane are preferred where a sedating effect is not desirable, as in retarded reactions. The fact that there are many neuroleptic drugs available enables us to substitute medications if one type does not work satisfactorily.

Q194: Aren't antipsychotic drugs dangerous in their complications?

A194: Most complications are not serious and can be handled with antiparkinsonian drugs. Long-term therapy (over a period of years) with large doses can, however, cause bad physical and neurologic effects. Tardive dyskinesia is a serious complication occurring in patients who have been on high doses of neuroleptics for many years. The answer to this is proper drug supervision and regulation of dosage.

The most annoying extrapyramidal effect is dystonia with facial muscular contractures and difficulty in talking. It can be alarming but it is not serious. It will disappear in a few minutes with an intramuscular antiparkinsonian drug. Other side effects are Parkinsonianism and akathisia. Anticholinergic effects like urinary retention sometimes occur. It is best to tell patients about these side effects and what can be done about them if they occur.

Q195: When should you use neuroleptics intramuscularly?

A195: In an excited or dangerous patient where rapid sedation is essential, neuroleptics should be given in adequate dosage intramuscularly to quiet the patient down within 24 hours or so. Neuroleptics can be concomitantly administered orally, and the intramuscular neuroleptic given in smaller doses when symptoms subside. Injections can be withdrawn when the patient is getting ample oral medication. Prolixin enanthate or prolixin decanoate are long-acting neuroleptics whose effects on injection last two to four weeks and are given as a maintenance drug in patients loath to use oral medications.

Q196: What do you do if you suspect that a patient "cheeks" his neuroleptic medication? He pretends to swallow it but doesn't.

A196: The medication should be given in liquid form and someone should be with the patient when he takes it.

Q197: Should antiparkinsonian drugs be used routinely to prevent parkinsonism that may occur with neuroleptics?

A197: In most cases these medications should not be used prophylactically.

Q198: Is it advisable to reduce the dose of a neuroleptic drug if a schizophrenic patient is doing well on it? If you do, isn't there a possibility he will relapse?

A198: Drug dosage should be adjusted as low as possible without the return of symptoms. Sometimes even 2 mg. of Stelazine may suffice to keep a patient in balance. Going below a minimal amount may cause the patient to decompensate, at which point the dose must be increased. The lower the dosage, the less chance for destructive side effects.

Q199: Is rapid tranquilization advisable in patients who need quieting down?

A199: For the emergency patient rapid tranquilization may be helpful to protect him or others, but it is not necessary for chronic patients.

Q200: Should you delay giving neuroleptics in schizophrenia, hoping the patient will pull out of her attack by herself?

A200: Neuroleptics should be given early when there is hope of aborting a psychotic break. One can then deal better with existing stress and personality factors. I do not see the point of allowing a patient to go into a psychosis on the theory that she will learn something valuable from it. Actually the psychosis may leave her with an impairment.

Q201: How would you control schizophrenic or manic excitement and agitation?

A201: The best method is intramuscular injections of a neuroleptic like haloperidol (Haldol), which rapidly controls the psychosis. Injections of 5 to 10 mg. are given at intervals of 30 to 60 minutes until the patient quiets down. From one to four injections are usually needed to bring a patient out of an excitement, followed by oral Haldol (approximately double the total intramuscular dose that has been used in the first 24 hours is given, then gradually lowering it to half the intramuscular dose after symptoms have been controlled). The drug is relatively safe and well tolerated, the only complications being a lowering of blood pressure and extrapyramidal symptoms. Where the latter complication is annoying, 2 mg. of extramuscular benztropine mesylate (Cogentin), followed, if necessary by oral medication, will control it. In the case of manic excitement lithium may be given orally.

Q202: What do you do if you feel a patient needs a neuroleptic drug to control his violence and he refuses it?

A202: The therapist here is in a bind. If he does what is medically appropriate, he may be exposed to a lawsuit for interfering with the patient's rights. If he does not do what is medically appropriate, he is liable for neglect. Should a person close to the patient or a relative be available, one may try to get this person to convince the patient of the need for medication. Hospitalization may be required and appropriate personnel should be available to get the patient safely into a hospital. If the patient is considered dangerous to himself and others, a neuroleptic will have to be administered by injection without his consent. Above all, everything that is done and that happens should be documented.

Q203: What is the most common cause of drug failure in prescribing psychotropic medications?

A203: Inadequate dosage. Initial doses may have to be quite high, for example, the equivalent of 1000 and occasionally even 2000 mg. of Thorazine daily (Haldol and Permitel 1/50th of this dose) in acute psychotic upsets. With the resolution of the disturbing symptoms, dosage may be reduced. Once a maintenance dose is reached (e.g., 100 to 200 and as high as 400 mg. of Thorazine or the equivalent) the patient may require prolonged medication (with occasional drug holidays) to safeguard him against hospitalization and rehospitalization. The maintenance medication may be given as a single dose at bedtime. However, pharmacotherapy and psychosocial therapy are not incompatible since the latter deals more with the initiating sources of stress and the former with its consequences.

Q204: When would you use lithium in schizophrenia?

A204: In schizoaffective disorders or in patients where manic-like symptoms exist, it is empirically indicated to use lithium.

Q205: Would you give neuroleptics or lithium for a manic attack?

A205: Lithium works better but may take two to three weeks to be effective. One can start the patient on lithium and coordinately prescribe a neuroleptic which will calm the patient down rapidly. In two weeks the neuroleptic can gradually be withdrawn and the lithium continued. There is some dispute about the dangers of combining neuroleptics and lithium.

Q206: Can you use lithium on a regular basis over a prolonged period to prevent manic attacks?

A206: Lithium is a powerful drug with potentially toxic effects, especially on the kidneys and thyroid. It must be used carefully and preferably periodically to abort a manic attack. Its long-term use for prophylactic purposes poses a risk and must be accompanied by regular cardiac, kidney, and thyroid tests so that the drug can be stopped before toxic effects become prominent.

Q207: Is methadone maintenance therapy effective?

A207: Considering that it is not a cure for heroin addiction and has as its objective heroin abstinence and some degree of better social functioning, methadone maintenance therapy does serve a purpose. Where possible and indicated, other modalities should be coordinately employed, such as milieu therapy, psychotherapy, and family therapy.

Q208: What precautions do you follow in prescribing psychotropic drugs for older patients?

A208: Geriatric patients do not handle drugs as well or at least in the same way that younger patients do. Some of these patients have been taking pills and capsules for a long time and a number of their symptoms are due to over-medication. Taking them off the drug may clear up their symptoms. Or it may be necessary to reduce the dosage of essential medications. It is important therefore in dealing with the older population to ask questions about what drugs they have been using.

Q209: When would you prescribe amphetamines for patients? Are they ever used in depression?

A209: Amphetamines are being used much less frequently than in the past. Apart from occasional employment as a temporary measure in mild depressions, senile withdrawn behavior, and the behavioral syndrome in children, they are now rarely prescribed. Their potential for abuse is great and their employment in alcoholism, anxiety reactions, fatigue, and drug dependence is contraindicated. It is best not to prescribe amphetamines in depression because of the danger of habituation. There are better antidepressants available. Very temporary use of an amphetamine is occasionally prescribed in situational depressions, but even here caution is necessary.

Q210: What drugs are of value in alcoholism?

A210: Initially Antabuse can be of value, but in most cases it may not be required after abstinence has been established and the patient is participating in a good treatment program. Benzodiazepines, like Valium or Librium, should not be continued after their employment in detoxification because of the addiction propensity of the alcoholic. Antidepressant and antipsychotic medications are sometimes employed where depression and psychotic tendencies exist. Where the patient shows manic-like behavior, lithium may be tried empirically.

Q211: Does tryptophan sold in health food stores help insomnia or depression?

A211: There is evidence that the aminoacid l-tryptophan helps people who have trouble falling asleep, but it does not seem to increase the total sleep time. The dose ranges from 1 to 7 gm. It also has been found to have an antidepressant effect in certain depressive patients.

Q212: Is ECT (electroconvulsive therapy) still being used?

A212: Very much so, and in very severe suicidal depressions it is the treatment of choice. It is still used in dangerous drug, manic, or schizophrenic excitements that cannot be controlled by psychotropic drugs. Early overemployment of ECT has now fortunately given way to a judicious conservative application for situations that do not respond to other treatments.

Q213: What are good indications for ECT?

A213: Suicidal depressions, and manic and catatonic excitements. In such excitements no more than four or five ECTs may be required to quiet the patient.

Q214: Should ECT be used in schizophrenia?

A214: There is little indication for ECT in schizophrenia except for uncontrolled agitation that does not respond to medications. Some therapists believe first attack schizophrenia may respond well to ECT, but there is no uniformity of opinion about this.

Q215: What is the argument against ECT?

A215: The only real argument I know of is against the use of ECT for non-emergency conditions. Where a depression is deep and the possibility of suicide likely, ECT can prove to be a life-saving measure. Also, in intractable excitements where neuroleptics and tranquilizers fail, ECT may succeed. The one great disadvantage of ECT is memory impairment which in 30 percent of cases may persist in the form of gaps in recall of past events centered around the period of treatment. Unilateral ECT does result in a somewhat lesser impairment of cognitive functioning. In short, there is no real contraindication where an emergency condition threatens the life and well-being of a patient and his physician avows that he is in a satisfactory physical position.

Q216: What is the most serious side effect of ECT?

A216: Memory loss which usually resolves. But this has been cut down by modern ECT methods. Where it is anticipated that memory loss will be too disturbing, unilateral ECT may be used which has a minimal effect on memory.

Q217: Is ECT safe for endogenous depressions in the aged or medically infirm?

A217: There is obviously some risk with both drug therapy and ECT in all patients, including the infirm and aged. But there is compelling evidence that ECT is even safer than psychopharmacological medications in older people and it may be a life-saving measure in suicidal depressions.

XI. Short-term Therapy

The advantages of short-term over long-term therapy may be debated on various grounds. Financial savings, more efficient employment of psychotherapeutic resources, opportunities to reduce waiting lists—these and other expediencies are often presented as justification for short-term programs. Admitting that there may be pragmatic reasons for abbreviating treatment, we may ask some important questions: How truly effective are short-term approaches in modifying disturbed neurotic patterns? Are the changes brought about temporary or lasting? Can we empirically prove the effectiveness of dynamically based short-term therapy? Can brief methods duplicate the results of the traditional long-term procedures? Do the variant models of short-term therapy represent alternative styles of operation or are there fundamental differences among them? Do they approach best different classes of patients? Are there common principles that can be combined in a general format of operation? Are all patients potential candidates for short-term therapy or should it be avoided in certain cases? These and many other questions present themselves to the student, therapist and researcher seeking to explore the virtues of briefer treatment methods.

Q218: Short-term therapy implies that the treatment process stops once appointments with the therapist end. Yet you say good short-term therapy never really ends. What is the contradiction?

A218: The term "short-term therapy" may be a misnomer since the therapeutic process can be self-administered and continues throughout the life of the patient once formal psychotherapy has ended, however brief it may be. This ongoing movement is, of course, dependent on what impact has been made on the patient during treatment. Ideally, the patient should 1) have derived a notion of the sources of her problem, 2) have recognized how she is perpetuating some of her own difficulties, 3) have learned self-investigatory methods of how to go about working on her own, and 4) have accepted an adaptive goal toward which she will point her efforts. Under these circumstances, psychotherapy, though restricted to relatively few formal sessions, may register a more than limited impact on the patient by motivating continuing self-help.

Q219: Can brief therapy help depression?

A219: Brief interpersonal therapy can definitely help depressive symptoms and the associated social malfunctioning in patients who are not too severely depressed. However, it cannot do much in changing personality attributes that contribute to depressive overreactions to losses and stresses. Antidepressant medications are not contraindicated here and can be coordinately used with brief psychotherapy.

Q220: What is the shortcoming of brief directive approaches in marital therapy?

A220: Serious personality problems will not be influenced by the use of educational, persuasive, behavioral, and cognitive therapeutic stratagems, and little change may occur in the marital complaints themselves unless a pathological character structure is altered through extensive, perhaps prolonged, dynamic therapy. Those patients who do not respond to short-term methods will then have to be treated or referred for individual long-term therapy, assuming they are motivated to receive it. But the majority of marital difficulties fortunately can be helped, sometimes significantly, by less ambitious procedures. Where depth therapy is impractical, as in older couples, or in those unable to afford the cost or make the time for extensive treatment, or in those who are completely unmotivated for such treatment, something can still be done in teaching couples alternative ways of behaving and problem-solving and more congenial styles of living together, while making a try at offering them some idea of the unconscious maneuvers they employ in their interactions.

Q221: Doesn't short-term therapy avoid the ideal goal of personality reconstruction?

A221: Expediency is a harsh mistress, but compromises are often inescapable when one has to deal with groups of patients, third-party payments, cost accounting and community approaches to mental health which demand rapid and effective therapeutic intervention. Economics and the shortage of trained personnel may make mandatory a limiting of the time span devoted to individual psychotherapy, particularly in outpatient clinics. This may sometimes necessitate abbreviating goals in treatment to symptom relief and the bringing of the patient to a reasonably optimal level of functioning.

It is expected that termination with such moderate goals will be resisted by therapists who traditionally are committed to intensive long-term psychotherapy, and by patients who resent giving up a comfortable dependent niche in the therapeutic relationship. In private practice there is a temptation to hold on to patients for an extended period, not only for economic reasons but for the utopian and often unrealistic objective of complete personality reconstruction.

The sober reality we must face in psychotherapy is that at our present state of knowledge we do not possess any definite techniques that can guarantee a completely reconstructive cure, even in patients who are motivated for change and who are willing to spend a long time in treatment. This is particularly true in those so damaged through inimical early life experiences that resources for reconstructive change are minimal. Indeed, insistence on long-term dynamic therapy may serve merely to feed the patient's dependency needs, which will cripple him even further. Our emphasis on depth-oriented insight therapy tends to denigrate as second best short-term active methods that for a good number of patients can bring substantial relief from symptoms and suffering—goals that are as far as the patients want to go or are capable of achieving.

Institution of active measures scaled to the current needs of patients with periodic review of their progress, and shifting into different methods where no positive response occurs after a reasonable period certainly would seem indicated in the majority of cases. Group, family and rehabilitative approaches serve here as helpful adjuncts.

Employment of short-term methods does not mean that subtantial personality changes cannot be obtained where a patient has the incentive for such changes, where he is willing to apply himself to prolonged homework after the formal period of treatment has ended, and where the therapist is skilled in doing short-term therapy (Budman, 1981; Mann, 1981; Malan, 1963; Sifneos, 1972; Wolberg, 1980).

XII. Miscellaneous Therapies

Palpable testimony to humankind's reluctance to yield its emotional miseries is the large number of therapies that crop up annually. At the very time that Cassandras are bemoaning the death of psychoanalysis and other traditional therapies, these "new" treatments dip into the pool of mortal credulity to exploit anomalous "cures" for all imaginable ailments. It is almost impossible to chronicle the myriad systems of helping that have appeared on the psychotherapeutic horizon. Many of these are revivals of old and discarded recipes; others are more novel and innovative. Still others are products of the counterculture which spawns a variety of egregious approaches reflecting the anti-intellectualism of the day. All inspire expectations of success, especially when promoted by charismatic leaders who seek to etch a lasting profile on posterity. Most of these approaches, following a spectacular rise in popularity, fizzle out like a Fourth of July pinwheel. Among the surviving systems are some that, blending with the personalities and working styles of certain therapists, actually enhance therapeutic outcomes. They then acquire conventional respectability and become part of an eclectic schema.

Q222: To what would you credit the great profusion of innovative therapies like "health models," "delusion models," "stroking models," "feeling therapy models," "body therapy models," and so forth, and why do they all claim credit as the best therapy?

A222: I believe that innovative therapies come about largely as a revolt against the semantics and rigidities of the traditional therapies. Some of our present-day theories and methods are coached in language that is confusing not only to patients but also to professionals trying to make sense out of them. However, when we examine critically what the "new" therapies introduce, we usually find nothing essentially original. Rather they take a small section of the familiar ideas long in use and merely explicate this area in terms that may be more comprehensible and hence acceptable to patients. The great dedication and enthusiasm of the innovators come through to enhance the placebo effect and to enliven other nonspecific elements.

Because therapists practicing innovative therapies are so intensely convinced of the validity of what they do, they will score greater triumphs than if they were to use traditional methods about which they feel lukewarm. The results of innovative therapies show that about two-thirds of the patients "improve," irrespective of the models used. This compares favorably with the traditional therapies, which probably means that the theories and even the methods we employ are not the basic things that account for success in psychotherapy. Rather, the constructive use the patient makes out of the relationship with the therapist toward acquisition of a sense of mastery and more adaptive modes of coping is probably what counts most. This does not mean that all therapies are the same, because there are differences in the dimensions and permanence of improvement with different therapies. We cannot expect that short-term treatment with supportive or educational methods will influence the personality structure in as great depth as will properly conducted techniques aimed at the intrapsychic structure and dynamic interpersonal operations. But irrespective of the kinds of therapy done, their alignment with the personality and style of the therapist and coordination with the essential learning capacities of the patient are fundamental ingredients of success (see also Abroms, 1969; Dolliver, 1981; Halleck, 1974; Marmor, 1974, 1980; Wolberg, 1977, pp. 245-255).

Q223: What is the basis for the use of biofeedback? What conditions are treated with it? Is its use proven, and what is a good text you can recommend on the subject?

A223: Arising from research on the instrumental conditioning of autonomic activities, biofeedback has recently come into prominence as a way of mediating functions that in the past were considered uncontrollable. Utilizing electronic devices, feedback from visceral organs, the central nervous system and the muscular system provide the individual with information that can be used in the shaping of autonomically mediated responses. Such symptoms as migraine, tension headaches, high blood pressure, arrhythmia, anxiety, phobias, muscular dysfunctions, localized pain reactions, epileptic seizures, and sexual dysfunction are the most common difficulties for which biofeedback has been recommended. It has also been employed for purposes of stress management. What is most commonly measured is muscle activity, especially the frontalis muscle, through an electromyographic (EMG) machine. This is a way of assessing tension, and the individual learns to reduce or eliminate the muscle signals of tension by physical relaxation and the thinking of quieting thoughts. The galvanic skin response (GSR) gives data as to emotional arousal, and its control may help lessen tension. The blood volume may also be assessed by special machines, especially through temperature measurements, in this way redirecting the blood flow from one area of the body where blood engorgement causes symptoms (e.g., the brain in migraine attacks) to other areas (e.g., the hand). A blood pressure apparatus and an electrocardiographic (EKG) machine are also employed to control blood pressure and the heart rate. The electroencephalogram (EEG) is occasionally used in epileptic patients to teach them to increase the sensorimotor density rhythm in order to reduce the frequency of seizures. There is some evidence that penile tumescence, the operation of sphincters, respiratory activities, optic and stomach functions may be mediated through special instruments in this way, helping impotence, fecal incontinence, excess gastric acidity, asthma, and myopia. The work in these areas is still incomplete.

Practically no scientifically controlled studies exist which truly establish the effectiveness of biofeedback, but the clinical reports are optimistic—perhaps overly optimistic. There is danger in this overoptimism of misuse of the method, and of arousing false hopes that biofeedback is a panacea. Should this happen, we may expect a backlash reaction leading to the denigration and premature elimination of biofeedback as a viable technique. What is needed are carefully designed studies with adequate controls.

A good text is the one by Gaarder and Montgomery (1977).

Q224: Does relaxation training with biofeedback for relief of psychosomatic problems have a prolonged effect on a patient's condition even beyond the treatment period?

A224: This would be the only rationale for its use. There is evidence that the relaxation effects do last. An example is the lowering of hypertension in a study reported by Agras et al. (1980).

Q225: Among the relaxation methods, would you see any advantage in using biofeedback?

A225: Personally, I do not. I find verbal relaxation methods equally effective and less expensive. However, some therapists feel more comfortable with and some patients are impressed by the mystique of biofeedback equipment, thus enhancing the placebo influence.

Q226: What are the uses if any of biofeedback during psychotherapy?

A226: In biofeedback one may accomplish not only tension relief (similar to that obtained in hypnosis, relaxation exercises, autogenic training, or meditation) but also some voluntary control over certain autonomic functions. Most commonly used are muscle tension indicators, which may help control such conditions as hypertension, arrhythmia, tension headaches, and Raynaud's disease, and temperature indicators for amelioration of migraine. Biofeedback only indirectly is an aid in some forms of psychotherapy, relieving anxiety in supportive approaches and accelerating hypnogogic imagery during insight therapy.

Q227: What is meant by a humanistic-phenomenological approach?

A227: In a humanistic-phenomenological approach therapists posit the core psychopathological problem in terms of a failure in self-growth. The goal in therapy is therefore not to explore unconscious conflict with the object of promoting insight, as in dynamically oriented therapies, or to achieve symptom resolution or cure, as in behavioral therapies, but to liberate the frozen assets of the individual ("self-actualization") by various means, such as providing an empathic, accepting relationship (Rogers), or understanding the existential meaning of life (Frankl), or focusing on perceptions of oneself and the world ("the phenomenal field") in order to reorganize disarrayed self-concepts.

Improvement in the patient's condition is ascribed to the experience in growth achieved through the immediate therapist-patient relationship which is said to help rectify the distortions in the self-image, leading to a more harmonious expression of thoughts and feelings.

Q228: Is gestalt therapy effective?

A228: Like any other therapy, it is only as effective as the therapist who implements it. Not every therapist can manage the intense, active, direct, confrontative manner required. The many techniques embraced under this format also offer themselves for selective use in other forms of treatment, including psychoanalytically oriented psychotherapy. Whether they can be effective for a therapist can be determined only by experiment.

Q229: How do gestalt therapists operate?

A229: Gestalt therapists have different ways of operating. Many follow the precepts of Fritz Perls (1969), particularly in working in the here and now, eschewing the "why" in favor of the "how." Since review of the past cannot change what has happened, the past is avoided, the focus being on the immediate I-Thou therapeutic relationship. There is insistence on the patient taking full responsibility for the choices and decisions she makes. Only by self-acceptance can meaningful contact be made with others. Closely observing ambiguous nonverbal behaviors and confronting the patient with these without analysis or interpretation may open up channels of repressed ideations and feelings. The patient may be asked to repeat or exaggerate unusual movements and amplify or adopt opposing modes of verbalization. "The whisperer experiments with yelling, the yeller experiments with whispering, the intellectual explainer who drowns everyone with words experiments with babbling sounds, enabling new awareness of sharing and holding back" (Kriegsfeld, 1979). An important objective is restoration to one's total being of split-off and dissociated aspects of the self. The person is consequently exposed to a group of "therapeutic experiments" in order to come to grips with repressed and repressing aspects of himself. A patient may be requested to hold conversations with various parts of her body that feel tense or painful, or with people and objects in her dreams. One may project these parts, people, or objects onto an empty chair and engage in a dialogue with these. A number of texts are available detailing gestalt techniques (Perls, 1969; Smith, 1976).

Q230: Are gestalt methods employed in groups and can you describe a typical gestalt group intervention?

A230: Gestalt techniques are often executed in a group setting. Family and couples therapy are also sometimes administered in a gestalt format. Among the varied techniques is that of the "hot seat." A patient here may be enjoined to meditate and then to reveal fantasies in a chosen chair. The therapist or another group member in a second chair then engages the patient in confrontation and encounter challenges. A third empty chair is for role-playing, with one's projections extended to imagined persons in this chair. Another technique is "going around," with each member reporting his or her feelings and experiences evoked by the hot-seat patient's verbalizations. The technique serves as an opportunity for exploring personal feelings, but interpretations of these feelings and experiences are not encouraged.

Q231: Isn't a therapeutic encounter such as offered by the experiential or existential schools sufficient to produce growth and the elimination of a neurosis without analyzing conflicts and stirring up transference reactions?

A231: In experiential therapy, a basic assumption is that man possesses unlimited potentialities that may be liberated in an empathic, nonjudgmental, understanding therapeutic relationship. But no matter how empathic and humane the therapist may be, the development of a relationship is apt willy-nilly to inspire transference which can, unless it is detected and resolved, act as a resistance to the liberation of self-actualizing forces. Existential philosophy adds a dimension to a dynamic understanding of man, but it does not substitute for a solid recognition of the role of unconscious conflict in creating neurotic illness.

Q232: When would one use role-playing?

A232: Role-playing may be valuable for the learning of behaviors in which the patient is deficient. It is ideal for assertiveness training, for the acquisition of social and job interview skills, and for the working out of marital problems. It may be employed also to expedite attitude change. It can be exploited as an adjunct in many therapies, including dynamic and behavioral therapies. Its application in groups and with modeling and video feedback adds to their value and effect.

Q233: Can role reversal help change attitudes?

A233: Inducing a patient to take the role of an individual with whom she is in conflict and to playact the position and behavior of this person, espousing the latter's attitudes and ideas, results in greater modification of the patient's attitudes than exposing her to persuasive logic. Role reversal is often a good technique to use in marital therapy where reciprocal changes in attitude are a fundamental objective of the treatment plan. One technique in role reversal used in group therapy is physically to change chairs with the person in the group who is taking the part of the antagonist. Or in individual therapy the patient first may present her point of view and complaints to an imagined antagonist in an empty chair and then assume the role of that person by sitting in this chair. The patient may then argue her own points by changing her position to her previous chair, moving back and forth between chairs as the dialogue goes on.

Q234: Could you describe the use of paradox as an intervention strategy?

A234: The encouragement by the therapist of the very symptoms and behavior that constitute the targets to be eliminated lend a paradoxical complexion to the treatment effort. The rationale behind this contradiction is that some patients, for both conscious and unconscious reasons, will resist getting well and may consider the therapist's goal-directed maneuvers an intrusion on their rights of self-determination. They will therefore fight for control of the relationship with the therapist by a stubborn insistence on failing. By presenting the patient with paradoxical directions to exaggerate her symptoms or promote her own failure, the therapist puts the patient in a bind. If she fights the therapist by refusing to experience her symptoms or untoward behaviors, she will in essence yield her symptoms and behave more normally. If she accedes to the therapist's request, she is relinquishing control and accepting the therapist's authority. Later she will hopefully be more amenable to suggestions and directions that are pointed toward improving her condition. A number of writings have appeared which have detailed the rationale and methodology of this approach (Frankl, 1960, 1975; Haley, 1963, 1973; Raskin, 1976; Watzlawick et al., 1974). Several approaches have been offered utilizing these principles but are labeled by different designations like "reframing," "massed practice," "negative practice," "paradoxical intention," "implosive stimulus satiation," and "symptom scheduling."

Q235: Do paradoxical methods of treatment really have a utility and how can they be introduced to a patient so he can better accept their rationale?

A235: Paradoxical methods occasionally are used in short-term therapy. Some patients who insist that their symptoms are involuntary may be helped through these methods to realize that they themselves create and exaggerate difficulties for which they have disclaimed responsibility.

A rationale must be given the patient for paradoxical instruction, such as that the therapist needs to have more information about the symptoms or the behavioral difficulty for its proper evaluation. The use of an easygoing humorous attitude can be helpful to reassure the patient that the assignment is going to be difficult but that nothing terrible will happen.

A fighting marital couple may be enjoined to engage in constructive fighting at regular intervals and even to exaggerate the conditions over which battles habitually rage. Here the therapist may insist that it is difficult for him to understand what is going on unless he witnesses an altercation. He may then ask them to select a situation about which there is controversy and then to engage in a verbal struggle in the office. He may interrupt the exchanges should they be too mild and insist that the couple put their heart into their argument, scream louder, pound the sides of the chair, swing into the air—in other words, create a battle royal out of the skirmish. The therapist may then assign regular periods at home for the dogfights, and perhaps ask that the fray be recorded on a cassette which they are to bring to the office.

A patient with enuresis may be requested to urinate in bed for a week straight instead of going to the bathroom, even when he has the ability to delay emptying the bladder. A man with premature ejaculation may be enjoined to ejaculate as rapidly as possible, timing himself with a stopwatch; a man with impotence to inhibit an erection when it starts; a woman with frigidity to block any sensuous feeling should it begin. A man with insomnia may be asked not to try to force himself to sleep. Rather he is instructed to try to stay awake as long as possible and fight off going to sleep. A patient with a phobia may be enjoined to try to increase her anxiety when she is in an anxiety-provoking situation. An individual with tics may be requested to produce a set number of tics voluntarily within a determined special time period.

Q236: What is the basic idea in systems therapy?

A236: Systems therapy considers any one patient as part of a complex aggregate of forces attempting to achieve a homeostatic balance. The general environment and particularly the individuals with whom one is in constant contact must be considered in the treatment plan. A number of types of systems therapy exist, including family therapy.

Q237: In doing sex therapy, are there any drugs that a male patient may be taking that should be eliminated because of their inhibiting effect on potency?

A237: Any drugs that act on the autonomic nervous system, such as major tranquilizers (especially thioridazine) and antihypertensive drugs, may impair sexual functioning in from one-third to one-half of cases. It would obviously be inadvisable to cut out these drugs when needed. One may ask the patient to check the dosage with his physician to make sure excessive amounts of drug are not being taken. Where indicated, sex therapy should be instituted irrespective of the coordinate use of essential medications.

Q238: Are telephone contacts with chronically sick mental patients useful at all?

A238: Very useful, even if done once monthly. One can obtain a great deal of help through contact with a therapist with whom a relationship exists, even on an auditory level.

Q239: Is psychosurgery still being used and, if so, what are its indications?

A239: In the past, psychosurgery was performed in much greater frequency than today for various conditions including pain, depression, anorexia nervosa, aggression, hyperactivity in children, seizures, sex offenses, and Parkinson's disease. Among the surgical procedures employed were prefrontal lobotomy, hypothalamotomy, amygdalotomy and cingulotomy. Largely because of a public outcry deploring the use of psychosurgery without reliable research regarding its effects and dangers, and the recommendations by a special commission that elaborate safeguards be employed, the number of operations has fallen to 200 to 300 annually, largely cingulotomies. Added to the existing restraints is the fact that informed consent has generally been required.

Where cases of intractable pain associated with terminal cancer, "catastrophic rage" in temporal lobe epilepsy, and severe chronic depression are not amenable to all known somatic and psychosocial treatments, psychosurgery done by a skilled neurosurgeon may offer some help. Selection of cases must be scrupulously made.

Q240: Can environmental manipulation effectively alter basic values and attitudes?

A240: Certain attitudes may be altered by changing the environment in which the individual functions, such as his habitat, place and type of work, marital partner, etc. Values and attitudes that are linked to basic personality needs and defenses, however, stubbornly pursue the person and carry on an existence in their original or slightly modified form in any kind of environment. These attitudes, if the individual senses they are obnoxious to others or disastrously harmful to himself, may be controlled to some extent. However, they are apt to break through and reveal themselves when guards are down. For example, hostile attitudes may be concealed by a gracious, smiling, obsequious manner, which may rapidly disappear with frustration, tension, loss of control, or the imbibing of alcohol. Environmental manipulation should, if possible, be supplemented by other techniques that potentially can bring about cognitive changes.

Q241: What about different kinds of residential care for the deinstitutionalized patient?

A241: This is a neglected area and such neglect can make a shambles out of a planned treatment program. Among the resources to be considered if available are communal group living arrangements, supervised hotels and apartments, hostels, ex-patient self-help clubs, foster homes and family care. Supervision is vital to see it that the residence is suitable and continues to be suitable.

Q242: Is acupuncture of any value in the treatment of emotional problems?

A242: In some cases acupuncture acts as a placebo and abates tension and anxiety. Theoretically, through the release of brain neurotransmitters (endorphins), it aids in pain control. It has very limited use in emotional problems per se.

Q243: Is Rosen's "direct analysis" method a good technique to use in schizophrenia?

A243: This method of confrontation of the patient with primary-process material, utilizing reward and punishment and continuous pressure, has not been shown to be as effective as originally hoped for. Very few therapists are able to play the many roles demanded of them in this technique and very few patients or families can afford the costs of the program. When used, the results are apt to be short-lived after therapy ends unless bolstered by a continuous care program.

Q244: What would you say about the values of counseling and educational approaches as distinguished from psychotherapy?

A244: First, we must distinguish between counseling, educational approaches, and psychotherapeutic interventions. Many of the schemes employed in facilitating psychotherapy are rooted in counseling and educationally oriented techniques, although they are labeled with hybrid designations. Guiding, directing, advising, information-giving, applying pressure and coercion, reinforcing, instructing, providing feedback, and behavioral rehearsing are methods targeted on problem-solving. Some of these stratagems have traditionally been employed by caseworkers and psychological counselors in helping their clients toward a better adaptation. Psychotherapeutic techniques, on the other hand, are aimed more at distorted intrapsychic processes and deal with faulty motivations, misdirected developmentally acquired needs and impulses, maladaptive defenses, and self-defeating coping measures. These techniques require special psychotherapeutic training beyond counseling and education.

Educational and behavioral techniques may be employed exclusively as principal helping agencies or they may be used adjunctively with psychotherapeutically oriented procedures. Psychotherapeutic interventions are geared toward clients who are adequately motivated to accept treatment and who ideally do not have uncontrollable unconscious needs to act out too destructively in their relationships. Should the latter situation prevail, psychotherapy is best grounded in psychoanalytic principles and may require in some cases long-term treatment. But even here counseling, behavioral, and other active interventions may adjunctively be employed as facilitating stratagems. Indeed, the use of such interventions helps release transference and resistance that are parcels of nuclear and derivative conflicts and that present themselves to a trained observer for exploration, discussion and interpretation.

In short-term therapeutic programs we may start therapy with an accent on counseling and educational tactics and with the hope that the patient will respond rapidly to such active, directive methods, alerting ourselves to subversive resistances, which, if they appear, are dealt with through the usual interpretive tactics. Should the patient fail to respond to this kind of program, longer-term psychotherapeutic procedures may then be implemented.

XIII. Emergencies

Although emergencies are not common in the practice of the average therapist, preparation for their proper management, should any occur, makes good sense, since mishandling can be destructive to the patient and ruinous to one's reputation, apart from the medico-legal complications that can ensue. Not only will the therapist have to palliate the patient's turmoil, but he will also have to cope with the concerns of the patient's family, as well as the anxieties within himself. To retain objectivity and composure in the face of ominous happenings will tax the resources of the most stable therapist. Responsibility should therefore be shared with a skilled consultant psychiatrist, especially if the therapist is a nonmedical person.

Crucial decisions are essential in emergencies. Knowing when to pacify, when to confront, when to enjoin, when to direct, when to order, when to notify relatives or friends, when to hospitalize, when to prescribe medications, how to evaluate existing stress situations, how to appraise useful support systems, how to gauge available ego strengths, how to bring the patient to an awareness of factors that keep the crisis alive, when to involve the family in the treatment plan, and the solution to other troublesome points requires expertise in crisis intervention practiced in the medium of an empathic relationship.

Q245: What are the chief emergencies you are likely to see in psychotherapeutic practice?

A245: Many crises are apt to come up that are not really emergencies. The true emergencies are episodes of violence, acute psychotic states, suicidal attempts, acute drug intoxication, acute alcoholism, reactions to rape and incest, organic and hysterical confusional states, acute stress responses, and problems involving runaway children. (Helpful readings are those of Glick et al., 1976; Resnik & Ruben, 1975; and Wolberg, 1980, pp. 208-222.)

Q246: Should you treat a dangerously disturbed or assaultive patient in your office?

A246: Common sense dictates that the therapist should be reasonably protected, which means that where a patient is potentially dangerous to himself or others he should be treated in a hospital or where adequate help will be available if necessary. In emergency units in general hospitals, sufficient personnel should be available to restrain the patient (at best four accessory persons are needed, one for each limb) should restraint be essential. The attitude of the therapist is a most important factor, an easygoing, calm manner being reassuring for a patient. Since most violence is a consequence of fear, a quiet, secure atmosphere surrounding the consulting room is desirable. Angry threats directed at a disturbed patient merely aggravate his fear and create further violence. More can be accomplished with calming demeanor than with drugs, which, of course, also should be administered where necessary. Once communication is established with the patient and the patient has confidence that he will not be hurt, psychotherapy may be possible under the usual office conditions.

Q247: What do you do to abort a threatened psychotic break in one of your patients?

A247: This can occur during intensive psychotherapy, especially in borderline or schizophrenic patients. The first step is to identify the immediate stress factor that is upsetting the patient. Is it in the current life situation? If so, the patient should be helped to resolve the problem or to extricate herself from it. Is it a consequence of what is happening in therapy? Transference reactions are extremely common and in one with weak ego strength can send a patient overboard. Such reactions may be concealed and evidence of them may be manifested only in acting-out or in dreams. Getting the patient to talk about her feelings in regard to the therapist, with proper clarification and interpretation, may restore the patient's equilibrium. It may be necessary to increase the patient's visits during a period of emotional turmoil.

Second, if the precipitating factor cannot be identified, an attempt should be made to get the patient to speculate as to some cause for her troubles. Her theory may then be used as a focus around which one may pursue further probing with the object of either supporting the patient's suppositions or of discovering more cogent etiologic factors.

Third, where the support offered through psychotherapy does not restore the patient to an equilibrium in a short time, one should prescribe a neuroleptic drug, like Thorazine (chlorpromazine), Haldol (haloperidol), Stelazine (trifluoperazine) or Permitil (fluphenazine), in proper dosage. Too frequently, inadequate doses of medication are used. A non-medical therapist will have to bring a psychiatrist who knows drug therapy into the picture.

Fourth, a precaution is not amiss. In moving from an exploratory to a supportive relationship with the patient, the therapist should appreciate that the patient's dependency needs may enjoin her to become overdependent and to make therapy an interminable process. Therapy should have as its ultimate objective a strengthening of the patient so that she may eventually function on her own with only occasional visits to the therapist. Otherwise the patient will remain locked into an interminable infantilizing relationship.

Fifth, group therapy, marital and family therapy are useful adjuncts and may help along with the other measures above to defuse an impending psychotic break.

Sixth, as a preventive measure, after termination of therapy the patient should have the feeling that written or personal contact is permissible and even desirable when and if the patient is not able to work through by himself any difficult problems or upsets that arise. (See also Qs 201 and 202.)

Q248: How do you keep your countertransference with a violent patient under control and what is the best way to quiet the patient?

A248: It is natural to react emotionally when a patient becomes violent, particularly when part of this violence is directed toward you. Counter-violence will only stir the patient up more. Recognize your own fear of violence, as well as the pot of anger you yourself may be trying to control that always seeks some kind of release. Try to get the patient to verbalize her anger and outrage without your being judgmental and without trying to justify the conditions against which the patient is rebelling. If the patient's reaction is an aspect of negative transference, try to interpret this, but do not make the patient feel guilty for her acting-out. If the patient is responding to some outside stimulus, ask yourself: "How would I feel if I were in the patient's situation?" Since the other side of violence is fear, try to find out what frightens or upsets the patient and act empathic, supportive and reassuring. A simple statement such as, "I don't blame you for being upset," may do much to quiet the patient.

By acting composed you may be able to calm the patient. If you show fear this will engender more fear and violence in the patient. If the patient continues to be disturbed after you have attempted to pacify her, you may suggest a "tranquilizer" to calm her down. Here a neuroleptic like Haldol (haloperidol) (2 1/2 to 10 mg. intramuscularly) can be helpful. Should the patient be considered dangerous to herself or others, hospitalization may be necessary. It goes without saying that where violence against you is a possibility, the availability of protective personnel, who are briefed on what might be expected, should be assured. (See also Qs 201 and 202.)

XIV. Psychotherapeutic Practices

Many therapeutic systems take into account such concepts as predisposing factors in emotional illness, the effect of early experience on personality development, the relationship between personality structure and maladjustment, the primacy of environmental versus inner conflictual sources of problems, the meaning and function of anxiety, and the mechanisms of defense. The actual implementation of therapy, however, varies greatly even among members of the same theoretical school, differing in such areas as the way a working relationship is set up, the degree of activity or passivity displayed, the amount of guidance and support, the manner of expressing empathy, the interview focus, the extent of history taking, the frequency of visits, the use of psychological testing, management of transference, employment of dream material, adjuncts utilized during treatment, projected goals, and duration of therapy. Experience continues to suggest the virtue of flexibility in method toward a reasoned technical eclecticism. This does not presuppose a disordered conglomeration of disparate devices thrown together in an expedient therapeutic potpourri. Rather, the conjoint employment of selected techniques has been proven to be clinically most effective. Such combined usage has corroded some of the traditional ossified concepts of practice that have operated to the detriment of good therapeutic results. In this section, questions about a number of treatment interventions are reviewed.

Q249: What do you do with a patient who breaks or cancels appointments consistently?

A249: This can be a disturbing problem since consistency in attendance is vital to good therapy. Should confrontation and discussion fail to resolve this problem, the therapist may suggest discontinuance of therapy. Where, as in a clinic, the therapist is obliged to see the patient irrespective of the latter's motivation, the therapist may insist on the patient's calling for an appointment when he wants to be seen. In this way the burden of stopping therapy is put on the patient, and if there is any motivation at all the patient may "shape up."

Q250: How can you redeem a mistake that you make that upsets a patient, like forgetting her first name or calling her by a name that doesn't belong to her?

A250: Mistakes can happen and forgetting names and important incidents can occur. One way to handle an embarrassing situation such as you cite is to apologize to the patient and say you were temporarily distracted. If the patient has a characteristic like the person whose name was used, the therapist may mention this and, if the characteristic is important, then try to analyze its significance. Minor mistakes are readily forgiven and forgotten by a patient with whom you have a good relationship.

Q251: Is there any consistency about the therapeutic focus on the part of different therapists appraising the same patient?

A251: A therapist's judgment concerning existing core problems involves speculations that are not always consistent with what another therapist may hypothesize. Given the same data, different therapists will vary in choosing what is significant. In a small experiment I conducted, three experienced therapists trained in the same analytic school witnessed the first two sessions conducted by a fourth colleague through a one-way mirror. Each therapist, including myself, had a somewhat different idea of what meaningful topic was best on which to focus. But such differences, in my opinion, are not significant. Even where one strikes the patient's core difficulties tangentially, one may still register a significant impact and spur the patient on toward a better adaptation. After all, a reasonably intelligent patient is capable of making connections and even of correcting the misperceptions of a therapist where a good working relationship exists and the therapist does not respond too drastically with wounded narcissim when challenged or corrected.

Q252: In interviewing the patient, should a therapist disclose intimate facts about herself as a way of positively influencing the therapeutic relationship?

A252: Studies of the effects of self-disclosure on the part of the therapist are inconclusive insofar as their influence on the relationship is concerned. The results cannot be predicted in advance. Depending on their personalities, patients may respond to a therapist's revelations positively ("My therapist is marvelously human," "He does not present himself as a flawless god," "She trusts me by revealing these intimacies") or negatively ("This person has such weaknesses that I'm not sure she can help me," "If he can't help himself, how can he help me?").

Some research studies do indicate that therapist self-disclosure facilitates patient self-disclosure and greater therapist trustworthiness (Bierman, 1969; Sermat and Smyth, 1973). My personal view is to utilize self-disclosure very sparingly and only when it does not point to severe neurotic problems in the therapist. It may, for example, be employed to show how a therapist handled a problem or situation akin to that confronting the patient, thus enhancing modeling.

Q253: Isn't it unethical to trick a patient into giving up her symptoms? I am talking about certain strategies that are used to gain control over the patient and that force her to do things she ordinarily would resist if she were fully aware of what was happening.

A253: We assume that when a patient voluntarily comes for therapy at least part of her conscious self wants to get well. She still ethically has the privilege of deciding whether or not she wants to retain her symptoms.

This freedom of choice is a noble ideal, but when we examine from what it is compounded, we usually find that the individual really does not have a true freedom of choice. In many cases, anxiety or the threat of anxiety, the sources of which are unconscious, forces her to avoid the steps that would make her well. Were no anxiety involved, we could say that she has a chance of making an unprejudiced choice.

Some of the stratagems that are considered "tricks" are actually ways of dulling or circumventing anxiety and forcing her then to develop different, more adaptive ways of coping. To yield to the patient's need to avoid anxiety on the basis of her democratic right to a free choice is to avoid dealing with her real problems. The stratagems I am talking about generally are used in short-term therapy. They are demonstrated in the techniques of Milton Erickson (Erickson and Rossi, 1980).

In many cases, it is possible to bring a patient to an awareness of her resistances, the working-through of which helps her to make a conscious and deliberate choice to do what is necessary to get well without the need for subterfuges. But when subterfuges are necessary to counteract a neurotic enemy that subversively blackmails the patient through anxiety, we may consider any reasonable expediency justifiable.

Q254: Isn't it a waste of time to have acting-out patients verbalize their problems?

A254: If the content of their verbalizations is to rationalize their problems, blame the world and their parents for their deviations, and chide themselves for their guilt feelings and lack of control, this is a waste of time. Even though patients may be quite disturbed in their symptomatology, and their ego strength seems not able to tolerate further regression, it is important that they be encouraged to verbalize as freely as possible, the therapist directing the content by accenting and questioning in order to put them in touch with their innermost feelings and conflicts. A nonjudgmental attitude is mandatory to try to solidify a therapeutic alliance. Repetition of important phrases by the therapist, even without interpretation, tends to focus on selected pathogenic areas. Often patients will become defensive, try to engage the therapist in an argument, and even seek solace for guilt feelings by having the therapist criticize or castigate them. The therapist may be tempted to become a chiding superego for the patient, which will put the therapist in the very punitive role such patients have always battled against. This will tend to destroy the therapeutic alliance.

Especially in sexual perversions, alcoholism and drug addiction, the patients' need for their symptoms will usually triumph over any moralistic or overtly retaliatory responses on the part of authority. A much better tactic is working toward establishing a good relationship with the patient and then utilizing the relationship to encourage constructive behaviors which are reinforced. Verbalization at first may seem to do little good, but if continued along focused lines ultimately may help the patient recognize his dodges and resistances. The therapist may not be able to prevent the eruption of transference, which must be handled as soon as detected because it can easily get out of hand, sometimes in sicker patients becoming psychotic in quality and intensity.

Q255: How can you tell when a patient with violent tendencies will become dangerous, and isn't notifying parties threatened by the patient a violation of confidentiality?

A255: There are no known scientific tests that ascertain whether or not a dangerous tendency will be acted out. The therapist must rely on hunches, on information regarding a designed plan to harm or kill, and on the availability to the patient of a lethal weapon. Obviously the therapist will utilize his relationship with and influence on the patient to restrain him. But if there is a likelihood of an attack, the welfare of society and of the patient have a priority over abiding by the rule of confidentiality. The intended victim should be notified to safeguard himself, and the person closest to the patient should be enjoined to help in the situation. Hospitalization and the administration of proper neuroleptic medications are safeguards that may be essential in protecting the patient and his targets.

Q256: Is jogging useful in emotional problems?

A256: There is some evidence that it is helpful in some cases of mild depression. It may act as an outlet for aggression and a way of diverting the patient from ruminating about his troubles. Understandably it is a palliative, not a real therapeutic device.

Q257: Do simulation games or exercises have a use in psychotherapy?

A257: Simulation games are sometimes used as an educational technique when dealing with a large group of patients, as in a partial hospital or rehabilitation center, for the purpose of teaching a broad range of skills. For example, there is one game that is organized around the planning by the group of the daily activities and ultimate career of a fictitious individual, in order to teach the patients the organization of daily routines and future prospects. There are simulated "fight" games that permit patients to express aggression without hurting each other; games to enhance self-confidence; games to illustrate to the participants the virtues of honesty; games to be employed in group therapy, etc. Description of such games are detailed in the article by Flowers and Booraem (1980) and in the handbooks of Pfeiffer and Jones (1970), and Morris and Cinnamon (1974).

Q258: How would you handle a situation where you cannot understand a patient's confused communication, for instance, psychotic talk?

A258: One way is to ask the patient to help you understand better what he means: "I'm sorry but I wonder if you will help me understand better what you are saying. Could you repeat it in different words?"

Q259: Can you cite some readings on ways to acquire and display empathy?

A259: Some of the readings I have found useful are the following: Greenson (1960), Katz (1963), Schafer (1959), Scheidlinger (1966), Shapiro (1974), and Szalita (1976).

Q260: In using techniques that are calculated to facilitate psychotherapy, like hypnosis, for example, what should we look out for?

A260: What we must strive to do in all cases is to expose any resistance factors that sabotage the implementation of our facilitating stratagems. Unless the patient is brought to some awareness of oppositional influences, our treatment efforts will fail to register an optimal effect. This does not mean one will have to go through years of psychoanalytic probings to fish out resistances. Resistances will impudently announce themselves without invitation the moment one tries to impose on the patient tasks he considers distasteful. We may, once we have conducted the initial interview and gathered sufficient historical data, want experimentally to utilize suitable techniques, alerting ourselves to negative, defiant, or perverse reactions in the patient's attitudes or manner. More vividly, resistances will appear both in transference responses in relation to the therapist and in acting-out derelictions outside. They will also mask themselves symbolically in dreams. In spite of this, there will be considerable numbers of patients who have sufficient readiness for change to respond cooperatively to facilitating methods with little or no resistance. It is a delight to work with such patients, because we do not have to hack through thickets of opposition and contrariness.

Q261: Can a well adjusted therapist have sexual fantasies or feelings about a patient?

A261: It can happen, but this is not fatal if the therapist works on such fantasies to insure that they do not distort the way he behaves with the patient, for example acting seductive, overprotective, rejecting, punitive, etc. The therapist's reaction may be a countertransferential one mobilized by the seductiveness of the patient. Interpreting the patient's behavior often opens up areas for exploration, such as unresolved oedipal problems. Acting-out with the patient, even in an attenuated way, can create problems for both participants.

Q262: Since emotional catharsis is helpful, shouldn't you purposefully try to stimulate it?

A262: Provoking or encouraging emotional outbursts, screaming and carrying on may do nothing more than temporarily relieve tension in the patient. Indeed, the acting-out behavior may become a source of resistance, the patient believing that little else will be necessary for her to get well. Emotional catharsis occurring spontaneously, however, does serve a therapeutic function by opening the door to further exploration and understanding of repressed aspects of experience. It often relieves pathogenic conflicts of their destructive emotional charge sufficiently to permit the individual to challenge the hold they have on her. Moreover, the therapist's non-condemning attitude may influence the patient's attitudes toward the repressed material and make it more possible for her to work it through.

Q263: Isn't a stand of neutrality such as practiced by classical analysts outmoded?

A263: In many instances it is, for example where a patient acts out in a destructive way despite repeated interpretation. In some cases, however, neutrality serves as the best way, as Kernberg (1976) has pointed out, of resolving transferences. Neutrality has to be a studied stance that is abandoned at certain times during analysis to promote activity. Such abandonment will obviously produce reactions (transferences and other responses) in the patient, which can serve as grist for the analytic mill.

Q264: Isn't neutrality on the part of the therapist the best way to stimulate transference?

A264: Transference comes about not because the therapist has functioned like a blank mirror who is removed and anonymous, but because the patient may interpret the therapist's "neutrality" as a neglectful, unconcerned, derelict omission, as well as a disregard of her and her welfare. Neutrality is, of course, often a planned frustration on the part of the classical psychoanalyst to stir up emotions and to foster regression. But this is not the only way to stimulate transference, which will also come about through the use of confronting techniques as a product of the patient's particular needs for and resistances to authority. The idea that therapist neutrality is the only way to evoke transference is therefore incorrect. Incorrect also is the idea that transference in the face of active techniques is more difficult to work through.

Q265: Once the unconscious is made conscious, shouldn't this produce cure?

A265: Not necessarily. There are reasons why the individual prefers to retain attitudes and impulses even though he is aware of their origin and the mischief they produce. Perhaps the greatest part of dynamic therapy is spent in working through insights and resolving resistance to adaptive change. The greatest value of achieving as thorough an understanding of one's unconscious as possible is to motivate the individual to take active steps essential for change.

Q266: Can you ever achieve the ideal goal of making all of the unconscious conscious?

A266: I am not sure this *is* an ideal goal in all cases, even if it were possible, which it isn't. Most people tote around a considerable load of unconscious troubles and still manage to make a tolerable adaptation through defenses and characterologic façades. Even thoroughly psychoanalyzed individuals never can achieve what you call an "ideal goal" and retain some unconscious conflicts. In persons who are not suitable candidates for psychoanalysis, we accept the limitations imposed on us and we may actually try to bolster their defenses and strengthen their repressive processes. Moreover, not all emotional problems are caused by unconscious saboteurs. Most difficulties, even where analysis is possible, do not justify the investment of resources that such therapy entails. The patient may be able to live with unconscious irritants quite successfully after more conscious problems are resolved. And in well conducted therapy she may even have gotten sufficient awareness of some of her unconscious troubles to work them through by herself under favorable environmental circumstances, that is, if they really need resolution.

Q267: What do you think of the analytic technique that directly interprets the patient's unconscious on the basis of the therapist's intuition alone?

A267: Here the patient's productions act like a Rorschach test stimulating associations in the therapist which are presented with a greater or lesser degree of forcefulness. The therapist obviously can be wrong, but he may by suggestion and coercion force the patient to accept his interpretations. Should the patient have sufficient faith in the therapist, he may believe he has finally found an answer to his problems. This may reduce his tension, restore his equilibrium and eliminate anxiety. On the other hand, the patient may become very upset by such premature interpretations, even if they are right. Freud labeled this technique "wild analysis" and the designation, in my opinion, is still correct.

Q268: How can one shorten the working-through process? Does hypnoanalysis help?

A268: Neurosis is a hydra-headed monster: We chop off one of its heads and another appears to take its place. To cauterize the wound and interrupt its survival, we employ the working-through process. This requires time because the individual, as uncomfortable as she is with her neurosis, is usually reluctant to give it up. Her hesitancy appears in the form of resistance. Some of her symptoms bind anxiety; some bring secondary gains or yield other subversive rewards. The needs to perpetuate a regressive dependency, to maintain masochistic self-punishment for rampant guilt feelings, or to suffer fear of the responsibilities of normality are among the resistances that have to be exposed, unraveled, and worked through. As they are progressively introduced to awareness, the underlying drives and needs against which they defend are brought to light. The patient gradually comes to realize her own responsibility in creating the difficulties of which she complains, as well as their historical origin and purpose. This admission occurs only after a hundred and one evasions, each of which is uncovered and interpreted in terms of its defensive purpose.

Experimenting with new patterns of coping brings a fresh crop of fears, retreats and other dodges which progressively, under the aegis of a good working relationship, are aired, analyzed, and, with tempering of anxiety, slowly put to rest. All of this requires time, interpretations being repeated and repeated as defenses take new forms. This grinding process is especially prolonged where ego-syntonic maladaptive personality patterns require change. The therapist's fortitude and forebearance are challenged by the seeming impotence of his interpretations and this may stimulate countertransference, which will also require some working-through by the therapist.

In my opinion, the best way of shortening the working-through process is to give the patient homework so that the therapeutic process does not cease after leaving the therapist's office (Wolberg, 1980, pp. 235-242). In short-term therapy, the working-through must be carried on by the patient herself and must continue over a period after treatment has ended in order to approach substantial and enduring results. Dramatic techniques, like hypnoanalysis, that open up the unconscious and expose primitive conflicts, cannot bypass the need for a process that filters insights through various layers of resistance and ultimately wears them down. Only then can change be integrated on all levels of the personality structure, promoting more adaptive behaviors which hopefully will become permanently reinforced.

Q269: Is free association still used?

A269: In classical psychoanalysis it is the main source of communication with the object of stimulating transference, being utilized in concert with the couch position, focusing on the past and encouraging the reporting of dreams. In psychoanalytically oriented psychotherapy it is utilized intermittently with focused interviewing. In other forms of therapy, it is rarely or never employed.

Q270: Isn't interpretation the most effective operation in psychoanalysis?

A270: It sometimes is alluded to as such, but as Strachey (1969) pointed out, "The fact that the mutative interpretation is the ultimate operative factor in the therapeutic action of psychoanalysis does not imply the exclusion of many other procedures (such as suggestion, reassurance, abreaction, etc.) as elements in the treatment." Insofar as resistance is concerned, its interpretation is a most important tactic, since resistance can block the effectiveness of any other technical procedures that are being employed at the time. Through interpretation of the neurotic transference, both the transference and infantile neurosis are believed to have an opportunity for resolution.

Q271: At what phase in psychoanalysis should interpretations be made?

A271: Ideally interpretations should be made when the patient has an inkling of awareness of an unconscious trend which will enable him to grasp its full significance. To interpret repressed and repudiated aspects of himself before the patient is prepared may merely increase his resistance. Both confrontation and clarification of resistances and defenses are preliminary steps that help bring a patient to a readiness for interpretation.

Q272: Should making interpretations be the task of the therapist or should the patient be encouraged to make his own interpretations?

A272: In my opinion, interpretive activities should be a collaborative activity. Understandably, resistance is apt to be greater when the therapist makes interpretations. It is especially pronounced where the patient has problems with authority. On the other hand, even self-interpretations may be resisted where the patient has a stake in maintaining the status quo that would be threatened by insightful admissions. Here, while encouraging a patient to arrive at cogent judgments, the therapist will have to interpolate comments about meanings and motivations, sometimes with authoritative emphasis (see Wolberg, 1977, pp. 588-605).

Q273: What do you do if your patient has reached an impasse in psychoanalytic psychotherapy and you cannot get him out of his stalemate?

A273: First, ask yourself whether a transference problem is responsible for the impasse and get the patient to talk about his feelings toward you. Second, examine your own feelings about the patient in search of countertransference. Third, if the stalemate continues, get a supervisory session with an experienced colleague. Fourth, try another technique like behavior therapy or hypnosis to catalyze the treatment process. Fifth, put the patient in a group, which often can activate him. Sixth, if nothing helps, transfer the patient to another therapist.

Q274: Can you describe what is meant by projective techniques in psychotherapy?

A274: Where the patient cannot tolerate the effect of direct confrontation, i.e., where his ego is too weak to accept the implication of responsibility, the therapist interprets what is happening by attaching the impulse, attitude or feeling to a person other than the patient. Thus a borderline patient who has responded to a rebuff or insult by becoming very depressed may be told: "Most people who were handled the way you were would feel like killing the bastard," or "If this happened to me, I'd feel like kicking this rude person down the stairs. Of course you are not designed to respond this way, but if you did it would be understandable." By this roundabout method the anger underlying the depression is presented and the patient may accept it or reject it. If the patient identifies with it, stronger confrontation is possible.

Q275: Do you ever use the couch in dynamically oriented psychotherapy?

A275: This depends on the objective. If you are attempting to arrive at repressed content, free association is an excellent vehicle to encourage this and here the couch may find a use. Thus, in classical analysis the couch is a preferred position. In dynamically oriented psychotherapy the couch is used only occasionally, if at all. This does not mean that we cannot reach repressed content in other ways than free association, for example, dream analysis and the examination of nonverbal behavior, acting-out activities and transference. Some therapists may still want to use the couch to encourage free association during dynamically oriented psychotherapy, but this is a matter of therapist preference.

Q276: Is regression a helpful objective in dynamic psychotherapy?

A276: Regression may sometimes liberate deeply unconscious fragments and enable us to detect repressed nuclear conflicts. On the other hand, it can revive anachronistic promptings which are harmful to a realistic adjustment, especially in borderline or pre-psychotic conditions where it may shatter defenses and sponsor a breakdown. It should therefore be employed cautiously and only in those patients with good ego strength.

XV. Psychotherapy in Special Conditions

A common matrix of good psychotherapy is the working relationship that develops between the patient and therapist. Within this matrix, events are anticipated that will register themselves beneficially on the psyche of the patient. There are those who believe that the most important happenings in treatment are of nonspecific nature, parcels of the placebo effect, emotional catharsis, idealized conception of authority, suggestion, and dyadic group dynamics. There are others who, while not denying the impact of nonspecific elements, consider that they serve mainly to restore the patient to a habitual emotional equilibrium. What is even more important is the implementation of techniques which wrest the patient from self-defeating patterns of thinking, feeling, and behaving that constitute the bonds of the neurotic illness. The singular characteristics of each problem and syndrome require that special interventions be employed that have been shown to be effective through extensive clinical experience. In this section questions dealing with therapy for the most common diagnostic categories encountered in practice are reviewed.

A. Depression

Q277: Is the incidence of depression greater in women than in men?

A277: Statistics indicate that women are twice as likely to develop depression as men. The reason for this is not clear but it probably has something to do with environmental and status problems rather than genetic susceptibility.

Q278: Is depression caused by biochemical or psychological factors?

A278: There is an intimate interrelationship between the two. Some forms of depression, i.e., the endogenous depressions, are associated with disruptions in the hypothalamic, pituitary and adrenal systems, perhaps of genetic origin. The antidepressant medications are helpful here. Other forms of depression, i.e., the "reactive" depressions, seem to be environmentally inspired and biochemical disruptions are less apparent. Psychosocial treatment is especially useful in such cases. Nevertheless, we cannot eliminate multifactorial elements in all types of depression.

Q279: What are the distinctive differences among the different depressive states and are antidepressants or ECT ever used in neurotic depressions or in any other than endogenous depressions?

A279: Depression is a mood reaction that normally is related to situations of loss, separation, and bereavement. Its continuance after a period of time has elapsed, or its appearance when there is no adequate stimulus to account for it, can have a pathological significance and may require clinical intervention. The depressive mood in some cases is accompanied by motor and vegetative symptoms such as motor retardation, dulling of appetite, weight loss, sexual disinterest, insomnia, early morning awakening and diurnal shifts in the level of depression. It is in such cases that a diagnosis of "endogenous depression" or "primary affective disorder" is made, particularly when there has been no precipitating cause or previous history of depression.

However, some aspects of the symptom pattern just described are not unique to so-called "endogenous depressions," occurring sometimes in secondary depressions, in depressions following alcohol detoxification, in those associated with medical conditions like endocrine disorders, and with the intake of drugs such as the antihypertensive medications. The use of antidepressant substances such as the tricyclics or tetracyclics is consequently indicated irrespective of whether a depression has a psychosocial, "endogenous," or drug origin, in cases where symptoms are sufficiently profound and debilitating. Psychotherapy is also helpful, especially where a premorbid or neurotic personality had existed. ECT is usually restricted to suicidal depressions or to those serious depressions unresponsive to adequate drug and psychotherapeutic treatments. Bipolar depressions, where the depressive attack is followed by an overreactive manic state, may be initially approached with carefully regulated lithium medication, preferably during the manic phase of the illness.

Q280: Does loss of a parent during childhood predispose a person to a depressive illness in adult life?

A280: Bereavement during childhood increases the risk of depression in later life. However, depression is not inevitable. Among important factors are 1) a genetic predisposition sensitizing the individual to an "endogenous depression," and 2) precipitating stressful events that violently damage security and undermine self-esteem. While such events may lead to a "reactive depression" in most persons, early parental loss may intensify the depression to severely pathological proportions.

Q281: Are there certain personality types that are predisposed to reacting to losses or stresses with depression?

A281: I believe so. While most people respond to loss of a love object or a person close to them with grief and mourning, this is eventually worked through. The individual who goes on to an unresolved depression probably has a special biological makeup or has in childhood experienced a highly traumatic loss that makes the present trauma a difficult situation to resolve. Marital stress particularly is a potent source of depressive reactions. Those individuals who do not possess an intimate relationship with a person in whom they can confide are particularly vulnerable to losses and stresses of one kind or another, but I believe a biological or personality predisposition must be present for a pathological depression to establish its roots.

Q282: How would you describe the psychodynamics of depression?

A282: Depression has been variously characterized as

1) an improverishment of the ego;
2) a reaction to the loss of love object;
3) a response to an incapacity to love;
4) a subjective psychological experience related to biochemical disturbances in the brain;
5) a projection onto oneself of anger at the originally depriving internalized parental figure;
6) a generalized turning of hostility onto the self;
7) a masochistic maneuver;
8) regression to a fixation at the oral level of development constitutionally or experientially derived;
9) a defect in self-esteem created by frustration of narcissistic gratification or deprivation of external supplies;
10) a manipulative parental-invoking device;
11) absence of a properly cathected image of oneself with impairment of identity;
12) a failure to live up to one's idealized self-image;
13) possession of an overly critical superego resulting in pathological guilt feelings;

14) a grandiose and unrealistic ego ideal with expectations of oneself that are impossible to fulfill; and
15) a faulty fusion of self and object representations.

It is obvious that there is no uniformity of opinion about the psychodynamics of depression. Partly responsible for this is the fact the term "depression" covers a multiplicity of affective problems, research on which has produced conflicting findings among competent observers. We are probably dealing with a wide array of different *kinds* of depression for which there are different psychodynamic explanations.

Q283: Couldn't all of the psychological manifestations of depression be a product of biochemical derangements in the brain?

A283: The reverse may also be true, namely that the biochemical imbalances may be a product of psychological disturbances. Thus, a severe psychological disturbance may upset the biochemical balances in the body and produce physiological symptoms. On the other hand, a biochemical imbalance has its psychological corelates. Both contingencies are therefore probably correct.

Q284: When would you use drug therapy and when psychotherapy in depression?

A284: These are not alternative choices; rather, they supplement each other. Drug therapy (Ludiomil, imipramine, amitriptyline, doxepin, etc.) manages the biochemical and neurophysical components of depression and is useful where the patient is suffering from severe depressive physical and psychological symptoms. Psychotherapy deals with interpersonal and intrapsychic issues and works with developmental aspects and the consequences of faulty conditioning. Psychotherapy of some kind should ideally be employed in all cases, and drug therapy coordinately utilized where needed. In some cases, such as the "endogenous" depressions, drug therapy is the principal therapeutic agency; in other cases, such as the "neurotic" or "reactive" depressions, psychotherapy is the primary treatment.

Q285: Should antidepressant drugs always be used in severe depression?

A285: No. The therapist may try psychotherapy first to see if a working relationship can be established. Where there are disturbing physical symptoms such as loss of appetite, insomnia, and general motor retardation, there should be no hesitancy about prescribing medications since the symptoms will interfere with the setting up of a good relationship.

Q286: Can Dexedrine or Ritalin be given to a depressed patient on major antidepressants for purposes of stimulation?

A286: Where a patient is extremely withdrawn, temporary use (no more than three weeks) of amphetamine (Dexedrine) and methylphenidate (Ritalin) may be helpful.

Q287: Can sleeping pills be given to a depressed patient on antidepressants?

A287: Yes, cautiously and as infrequently as possible. But a hypnotic should be administered, one pill at a time, at night, by another person who keeps the hypnotic pills under guard to prevent the patient from acquiring them in bulk. Should hypnotics not work, a sedative phenothiazine like Thorazine (100-500 mg.) may be tried. A psychiatrist should always be in charge of an antidepressant drug program, monitoring any changes that are required.

Q288: If a depressed patient is getting antidepressant medication and still has a good deal of anxiety, can you add an anxiolytic?

A288: A psychiatrist should decide this. An anxiolytic like Valium may be added temporarily to the regime, adjusting the dosage to what controls the anxiety; a sedative phenothiazine like Thorazine may do the trick, should Valium not work.

Q289: Would you consider different antidepressants for different symptom pictures?

A289: Yes, the side effects of the drugs may be employed beneficially. For example, imipramine (Tofranil), which is stimulating, may be given in inhibited depressions; amitriptyline or doxepin (Sinequan) is, on the other hand, sedating and may be used in the agitated depressions. Monoamine oxidase (MAO) inhibitors, like tranylcypromine (Parnate) and phenelzine (Nardil), are sometimes preferably used in neurotic or hysterical depressions. These medications require constant regulation by a psychiatrist skilled in their use since they can be dangerous when unsupervised. (See also Q 290.)

Q290: Can you add phenothiazine drugs to an antidepressant?

A290: Where psychotic symptoms like paranoidal delusions exist and the patient is markedly agitated, chlorpromazine (Thorazine) or thioridazine (Mellaril) may be added to the drug regime; if the patient is withdrawn, trifluoperazine (Stelazine), fluphenazine (Permitil) or perphenazine (Trilafon) may be used. If improvement occurs, the combination of drugs in half dosage should be continued for six to eight weeks and after that the antidepressant drug should be stopped and the antipsychotic medication continued, substituting, if desired, haloperidol (Haldol) or thiothixene (Navane). After eight weeks with still no improvement, ECT (6-10 doses) may be given.

Q291: What about tricyclic antidepressants in the depressions of children and adolescents?

A291: They may be quite effective here. Individual and family therapy are, of course, conjunctively indicated in children and early adolescents.

Q292: Are there any tests to tell if a patient is getting enough of a tricyclic antidepressant drug?

A292: If a patient is taking a tricyclic drug in adequate dosage (e.g.,

300 mg.) and responds only partially, the blood level of the drug should be tested. If it is below 180 mg/ml, the dose of drug may be increased to 450 mg/ml, provided the patient does not have a cardiac or circulatory disturbance.

Q293: Once a patient has responded well to an antidepressant drug, what dosage do you continue?

A293: In case of a tricyclic, two-thirds of the dose should be continued for at least four months. In case of a MAO inhibitor, one-half of the effective dose is adequate. In some cases, antidepressants in lower dosage may have to be continued for as long as a year or two.

Q294: Should a depressed patient on drugs get concurrent psychotherapy?

A294: Psychotherapy (individual, family, groups) is definitely indicated at least on a short-term basis (twice weekly for 10 weeks, then once weekly for eight weeks, then monthly for six months). The relationship must be empathic and supportive rather than confronting and challenging. As improvement occurs, the therapist should insist on the patient's becoming more self-reliant to discourage dependency.

Q295: In depressions occuring in older people, should antidepressants be used? What about dosage?

A295: Antidepressants like Elavil can be effective, but the dose after the age of 60 must be cut down to 25-100 mg. daily. Individual, group or family therapy should be concomitantly employed. Tetracyclic antidepressants are useful in this group because of the minor anticholinergic and cardiovascular effects. Maprotiline, for example, may be started with 25 mg. to 50 mg. daily, increasing by 25 mg. every third day until 75 to 100 mg. is reached, which can then be given in a single evening dose.

Q296: What can you do with a severe depression that does not respond to both psychotherapy and tricyclic antidepressants? With the latter drug some severe side effects have occurred.

A296: It may be helpful to try an antidepressant medication of a different class. For example, atypical depressions may respond well to MAO inhibitors like phenelzine (Nardil) or tranylcypromine (Parnate). These medications have to be prescribed and supervised by a psychiatrist who knows about the side effects and the essential precautions related to their use. Some new antidepressants have been utilized in Europe that have little anticholinergic effect and less influence on the heart and blood pressure. The best known examples are the tetracyclic drugs, like trazodone (Desyrel) and maprotiline (Ludiomil), the latter of which is now available in the U.S. These medications, if available, may be tried in a patient who is sensitive to tricyclics. Of course, if the patient is suicidally depressed, ECT should be considered as an emergency measure.

Q297: What alternative therapies are there for depression besides pharmacotherapy?

A297: Many therapies are utilized, depending on the experience and training of the therapist. These include psychoanalytically oriented psychotherapy, cognitive therapy, emotive release therapy to discharge anger, marital therapy or family therapy where indicated, and even partial sleep deprivation. In my opinion, a deep depression is best helped by drug therapy and a suicidal depression by ECT. The other alternative therapies are useful, of course, especially as ways of helping to prevent future depressions.

Q298: Are cognitive and behavioral approaches more effective for depression than dynamically oriented psychotherapy or pharmacological approaches?

A298: If the therapists who execute these approaches are well trained, skilled and capable of relating well to their patients, and the patients are motivated for and cooperative with the interventions prescribed for such treatments, we may make a number of assumptions:

1) Severe, psychotic bipolar depressions do best with pharmacotherapy or ECT treatments.
2) Severe and moderate unipolar depressions can respond to pharmacotherapy but can do well also, and sometimes better, with well conducted behavioral and cognitive approaches. A combination of these modalities may be the preferred method. Psychoanalytically oriented therapy may be helpful here, but is probably less effective than the foregoing interventions.
3) Moderate or light depressions rooted in personality problems and accentuated by environmental traumas are best approached with dynamic or cognitive psychotherapy, combined, if desired, with any good pharmacotherapeutic appraoch.

In using any of the methods cited above, the therapeutic alliance may hold the key to whether the techniques themselves will or will not be effective.

Q299: Is there a special quality to the transference in depressive reactions?

A299: In depressions that have followed in the wake of actual or fantasied loss of a love object we may expect a rapid, positive transference as a means of object replacement. The substitution, however, is often rooted in magical expectations with desires for a giving, loving, nurturing and omnipotent object reincarnation. The immediate reaction to this may be a temporary lifting of one's spirits, an over-idealization of the therapist, and a stimulation of hope and anticipation that all will be well.

Inevitably, as the relationship with the therapist develops, the patient becomes aware of some failings in the therapist, a realization that the therapist is not the all-giving, all-powerful figure he imagined. What will emerge then is hostility and a feeling that the therapist has failed in anticipated obligations. The patient may try to vanquish his hopelessness by repressing his doubts about the therapist, passively submitting to the therapist with a sadomasochistic dependency. The hostility is usually suppressed by guilt feelings or in response to disapproving or attacking maneuvers on the part of the therapist. Depression may then return in full force or even become greater than before. Yet the patient will cling desperately to the therapist out of fear of undergoing another object loss.

The countertransference of the therapist will determine the fate of these transferential shifts, the proper handling of which will enable the patient to work through the termination phase of therapy. This involves resolution of the separation and grief reactions associated with loss of the love object that had initiated the depression. Some impact may also be scored on the original separation traumas sustained during the developmental years that sensitized the patient to later object loss.

Q300: How can you reassure a depressed patient that matters are not hopeless and that it is useless to worry?

A300: Reassurance rarely helps truly depressed patients. But telling the person that the depression is self-limited and that he will overcome it after a while may create a tiny spark of trustful expectation. The therapist should anticipate acting as a dependent prop for the patient where depression follows loss of a person close to the patient. Transferentially this may serve to neutralize the object loss. Countertransference is common and the therapist must control discouragement and anger that are being stimulated by the patient's constant complaints.

Q301: Is psychotherapy always helpful in depression?

A301: Not always, particularly where depth interpretation is done, many patients utilizing insight for purposes of further self-recrimination. The therapist must gauge the patient's readiness for psychotherapy, and utilize support and counseling until the patient shows a capacity to engage in psychotherapeutic treatment.

Q302: When should depressed patients be hospitalized?

A302: Hospitalization is needed: where suicide is a possibility; when no person is available to be at home with the patient to help him and to monitor the intake of medications; where the reality orientation is low and impulsivity high; where ECT is needed and no good outside support system is available.

Q303: Is there any way of telling if a person is on the verge of suicide?

A303: A therapist's feeling that the patient will not be coming back for the next session is a good index of whether or not suicide is a possibility. An intuitive hunch should be respected by trying to convince the patient to go to a hospital to protect himself. If the patient is unconvinced, a responsible member of his family should be notified.

B. Phobias

Q304: What is the best treatment for a phobia?

A304: Therapy must be tailor-made for the specific kind of phobia with which we are confronted. In spontaneous panic anxiety, which often initiates agoraphobia, tricyclic antidepressants are useful in blocking anxiety and controlling the panic reaction. A smaller dose than is utilized in depression is generally employed. One may start with 25 mg daily, slowly increasing the dose if necessary until the phobia disappears. The patient on tricyclic medications should be encouraged to expose himself to the phobic situation repeatedly in order to master it.

Where the phobic reaction is a conditioned one, for example, an airplane phobia produced by a bad experience in flying, behavioral desensitization, followed if necessary by flooding (implosive therapy), in which the patient immerses himself in the phobic situation massively and repeatedly for a prolonged period, can be effective. Group behavioral desensitization may be as good as or better than individual treatment and is much less expensive.

In anticipation anxieties, where an individual is beset with fearsome thoughts about the *possibility* of being unexpectedly confronted by a phobic situation, tricyclic antidepressants do not help. Here an anxiolytic like the benzodiazepines (Valium, Librium, etc.) may be helpful, along with in-vivo desensitization and flooding.

In phobias which are the symbolic expression of unconscious fears or repudiated impulses, for instance repressed anger which initiates the defense of avoidance of knives and other potentially lethal objects, dynamic psychotherapy is the treatment of choice.

Family and couples therapy are useful in many phobias where relationships with family members are disturbed, for example, excessive dependency of a man on his wife, with associated agoraphobia. Here, as the phobia resolves, the family homeostasis will be upset and other members of the family may exhibit neurotic reactions which must be handled therapeutically to prevent reactive disturbance in the patient.

Social phobias, such as fear of shaking while dining or terror of speaking to a group of people (stage fright), have been resolved through behavioral assertive training, role playing and psychodrama.

Thus the therapist must keep his options open. He may have to utilize a combination of techniques since many phobias are mixed, deriving from several sources and hence necessitating an eclectic approach to rectify the responsible determinants.

Q305: Is hypnosis of any value in the treatment of phobias?

A305: Hypnosis is sometimes employed as an adjunct to other therapies, i.e., to help the patient lower his tension level, and to fortify his resolve by hypnotic suggestion, so that he will cooperate better with techniques of systematic and in-vivo desensitization. Where a phobia has its origin in posttraumatic experiences, hypnoanalysis (Wolberg, 1964) may be able to eradicate it by exploring its roots and encouraging emotional catharsis. A technique that is helpful here is to regress the patient to a time prior to the traumatic incident and then slowly to reorient him to the period when the phobia developed. Repetition of these tactics may be necessary where the phobia has been operative over a long period.

C. Anxiety Reactions

Q306: How would you treat anxiety that is caused by environmental stress?

A306: A diagnostic evaluation of anxiety is necessary in order to prescribe the most effective treatment. If a person has habitually been well adjusted and manifests anxiety as a result of some crisis that has imposed itself, an antianxiety medication (anxiolytic) may be of help in bringing the person back to his or her customary equilibrium. A non-psychiatric physician usually prescribes this and generally referral to a psychotherapist is not made. If the crisis continues or the person does not resolve the anxiety rapidly, referral to a psychotherapist will be necessary. Recurrent bouts of anxiety indicate an adjustment problem and will in all likelihood require psychotherapeutic help, particularly where the precipitating stress factor does not seem sufficient to have caused the patient's anxiety reactions.

Q307: Is anxiety always a sign of an emotional problem?

A307: Pathological anxiety is generally a psychological problem, although there are a few physical conditions that can bring it on. These include hyperthyroidism, hypoglycemia, severe cardiac dysrhythmias and pheochromocytoma. Certain medications, such as amphetamines and other sympathomimetic substances, may stimulate anxiety, as may excess caffeine consumed in coffee, tea or cola soft drinks. Once we have eliminated organic disease, pharmacologic agents and dietary culprits, the sources of anxiety in the current life situation or in inner conflict require assessment. A certain degree of anxiety is normal in all people, serving as a signal to ward off impending danger. Where anxiety is too strong, however, it may shatter constructive defenses and encourage neurotic and in some cases psychotic defenses.

D. Alcoholism

Q308: Is there a gentic factor in alcoholism?

A308: Some therapists believe a genetic predisposition is present. About 50 percent of parents and siblings of alcoholics have themselves been heavy drinkers. Other developmental and environmental factors are obviously implicated also.

Q309: Are children of alcoholic parents at greater risk for developing alcoholism than children of non-alcoholic parents?

A309: Definitely. The defect is probably a genetic one since adoption by non-alcoholic foster parents does not seem to play a part in preventing alcohol dependence in many of these adoptees. Moreover, offspring of non-alcoholic parents are not duly influenced toward alcoholism by alcoholic foster parents (Cadoret et al., 1980). While we cannot entirely eliminate the environmental influence, the genetic component seems to be by far the most important etiological factor (Goodwin, 1979).

Q310: Can alcoholics learn to drink normally?

A310: This is a cherished hope of most alcoholics. Unfortunately, it does not work out in ninety plus percent of cases. Absolute abstinence is mandatory.

Q311: What about the recent finding that alcohol is good for the heart?

A311: While a small amount of alcohol has been found to lower the incidence of heart disease, more than moderate drinking in the normal person, and certainly in the alcoholic, can seriously damage physical health. Liver disease, greater risk of acquiring certain cancers, toxic interactions with a number of drugs, nutritional deficiencies, birth defects in the offspring of pregnant women, depression of the cardiac musculature, interference with hypothalamic and pituitary hormones and various other calamities shadow the indiscreet drinker. On top of this are the abundant psychological ravages that interfere with adaptive functioning.

Q312: What is the best way to detoxify an alcoholic who has gone on a drinking binge?

A312: Abrupt withdrawal may be followed by such alarming symptoms as convulsions and hallucinosis. More ominous is delirium tremens, which may appear in three to four days. It is consequently best, as a preventive measure, to put the patient on a quieting medication like Valium or Librium and then slowly to withdraw these medications over a period of a week. Patients with cardiac or pulmonary disease, or those who cannot be treated at home, should be hospitalized during the detoxification period. The withdrawal phase is often utilized by the therapist to administer supportive treatment as an initial step in establishing a relationship with the patient in the hope of rendering further therapy and achieving permanent abstinence.

Q313: What are some of the crucial roadblocks in the treatment of alcoholics?

A313: Among the difficulties encountered are the patient's tendencies to denial, the masked dependency and grandiosity, the frustration intolerance, the masochistic need for self-punishment, the rationalizations, the underlying depression, the need for tranquilization and release from inhibitions that have habitually been supplied by alcohol, and the inevitable frustration and countertransference on the part of the therapist.

Q314: Can alcoholics ever be cured? Can you recommend a good book on the subject?

A314: There is a saying that the best that can be done for an alcoholic is to make him a non-drinking alcoholic. Implied is the fact that it is difficult to alter the basic personality structure and the biochemical vulnerability that will always put the alcoholic at risk. Nevertheless, *if* the treatment program is especially designed for the patient's needs and flexibly arranged in stages (moving from supportive to educational to reconstructive goals), and *if* therapy is eclectic, including, if necessary, Antabuse, family therapy, marital therapy, counseling and psychosocial treatment, and *if* the patient can be persuaded to join an Alcoholics Anonymous group, and his family, if possible, convinced to affiliate with Al-Anon, the patient will have the best chance of overcoming the alcoholic habit. These are complicated "ifs" and the therapist's skill and dedication to the patient will undoubtedly be strained in the process. The most notable successes are with patients selecting a suitable Alcoholics Anonymous group in which they are congenial with other members who constitute for them a new family. A good book to read on the treatment of alcoholics is *Practical Approaches to Alcoholism Psychotherapy* (Zimberg, Wallace, and Blume, 1978).

Q315: Are community alcoholic programs of value?

A315: Some communities have excellent alcoholic treatment facilities to which a patient may be referred for detoxification, arrangements for hospitalization, and expert counseling and further support. The therapist should have a list of these facilities and the admission requirements. He also should visit these to observe their suitability as referral resources.

Q316: In view of the vast damage of alcoholism, can any measure of a preventive nature be exploited?

A316: At least 10 million Americans are directly handicapped by alcoholism and through them 40 million family members are adversely influenced. Alcohol abuse accounts for half the nation's homicides, half the driving fatalities, and one-third of the suicides. As important as therapeutic services are for alcoholics, preventive services are equally important for family members. The children of alcoholic parents, particularly, both the troubled and seemingly well adjusted, should get counseling and, where needed, therapy since they are at high risk and probably make up the bulk of future alcoholics. Education, especially while in training, of professionals (physicians, ministers, social workers, etc.) to whom alcoholics and their families come for advice or help when in trouble, also is important.

E. Schizophrenia

Q317: What are the criteria for the diagnosis of schizophrenia?

A317: Criteria for the diagnosis of schizophrenia in the United States have for many years been questionable; schizoid, narcissistic, borderline and paranoid personalities, as well as atypical psychoses, have often been falsely classified as schizophrenia. An attempt has been made in the Third Edition of the Diagnostic and Statistical Manual of Mental Disorders (DSM-III) to tighten the diagnosis and to restrict it to overt psychotic conditions that develop before mid-adult life, and that have a minimum duration of six months. Usually there is also a deterioration in behavior or adjustment following recovery as time goes on. A thinking disorder is more or less manifest, characterized by associational disorganization, ideas of reference and delusions. Perceptual distortions may occur with hallucinations. There is a singular flattening of affect, which may be inappropriate in relation to the thought content. Identity problems are frequently present and ego boundaries are blurred. Functioning may be impaired by disorganized ways of behaving, by withdrawal from the outside world into the self, and by preoccupation with delusional ideas. In severe cases motor excitement, inactivity, stupor, bizarre posturing, mannerisms and grimacing may occur (catatonia). Often there is a prodromal period prior to the outbreak of psychosis characterized by social withdrawal and peculiar behavior. Following the acute psychotic break some stabilization may develop, but there is generally a residual mood disturbance, such as flattening or inappropriateness of affect, which impedes social and work activities.

Schizophrenia should be distinguished from schizoid, schizotypal, paranoid, and borderline personality disorders, from identity problems in adolescence, from paranoidal states, from atypical psychosis, from brief reactive psychosis, and from schizophreniform disorders. In the latter condition the duration of the illness is less than six months; there is a rapid onset, a high degree of confusion and emotional turmoil, and a good likelihood of recovery to premorbid functioning. A *brief reactive psychosis* must be differentiated from schizophrenia. Here the psychosis follows a strong stressful environmental stimulus and there is recovery within two weeks. Where no such psychological stress has occurred and there is still a psychosis (disturbed behavior, hallucinations, delusions, associational disorganization, etc.) that disappears in less than two weeks, the diagnosis of *atypical psychosis* is often given. The diagnosis of *schizoaffective disorder* is more difficult to make since it is a wastebasket for combinations of affective and schizophrenic symptomatology in the form of mood incongruent psychotic features that do not fit into any of the other categories.

Q318: Can you make a diagnosis of schizophrenia on the basis of hallucinations and delusions?

A318: No, because these symptoms can occur in other conditions like drug-induced pyschosis (like amphetamine, LSD or Mescaline), affective disorders, organic brain disease, and transient stress-inspired psychoses. Other symptoms are more diagnostic like autism, emotional dullness, and lack of integrative activities.

Q319: What is the prevalence of schizophrenia? What are the risk factors? Why does schizophrenia affect the lower social classes in greater proportions than other classes? Are data on recovery of schizophrenia reliable?

A319: Approximately one percent of the population will develop schizophrenia. A genetic factor is prominent, offspring of schizophrenic parents being at least 13 times more likely to develop schizophrenia than the general population (Slater and Cowie, 1971). However, what is significant is that the majority of children from schizophrenic parents do *not* develop schizophrenia. A certain kind of family dysfunction, as well as the presence of immediate stress factors in social relationships, appears implicated in activating the genetic predisposition. Many authorities believe that without a genetic predisposition family and stress factors will not evoke schizophrenia (Gottesman, 1979). The exact reasons why lower social classes are in greater risk are not clear but probably involve the greater stresses suffered by this population and fewer available resources for stress control.

Data on recovery rates of schizophrenia are not entirely clear. We must qualify what we mean, first, by schizophrenia, and, second, by recovery. If we utilize the definition of schizophrenia to include the vast number of conditions subsumed under this title prior to DSM-III, the recovery rate may go as high as 70 percent. If we exclude transient psychoses with schizophrenic features (schizophreniform psychoses) and borderline cases, which is done in DSM-III, the rate falls to as low as 15 percent. Next, how do we describe "recovery"? If we mean restoration to a prepsychotic level, the rate will be considerably higher than if we consider recovery to be the elimination of defensive prepsychotic personality distortions.

Q320: Is it certain that schizophrenia is a disease caused by an excess of the neurotransmitter dopamine?

A320: This is oversimplifying a very complex disease. The dopamine hypothesis is still a hypothesis, even though the evidence is strong for a disturbance in dopamine transmission. This could be because excess dopamine exists in the body of the schizophrenic, or because the patient is unduly sensitive to dopamine, or because there is an excess of receptors for dopamine in the limbic system, the caudate and putamen. But the dopamine disturbance (whether the cause or effect of schizophrenia) is merely one aspect of the problem in this disease. Developmental conditioning, intrapsychic and interpersonal problems also exist, contributing to the development and symptomatology of schizophrenia.

Q321: What are some of the present-day ideas about the etiology and pathology of schizophrenia?

A321: While we do not have a complete picture regarding the etiology and pathology of schizophrenia, it is reasonable to assume from all the available evidence that a genetic factor exists in schizophrenia. For one thing, the fact that the concordance ratio for schizophrenia is three times greater in monozygotic than in dizygotic twins suggests a hereditary component. But the finding that in 50 to 75 percent of monozygotic twins one member *does not* become schizophrenic when the other twin develops the disease indicates that a genetic deficit is not enough to produce schizophrenia. Non-genetic constitutional factors must also be considered, for example, flaws through damage to the brain during intrauterine life or as a result of birth trauma. In short, while schizophrenia appears to be a genetically determined disease, its phenotypical expression is, at least in part, influenced by life experience.

Among the life experiences that have a destructive impact is the use of the child by the parents as a foil for their own neuroses. Where parents are themselves emotionally unstable and mentally confused, they are unable to provide sensible and temperate learnings. The child thus receives training in irrationality, as Lidz has remarked. Communication patterns are distorted and the child is exposed to contradictory messages. There is defective gender identity and a crushing of the child's efforts at autonomy. The parents offer poor role models for the child. The consequence of the personality deficits that eventuate out of these conditionings is a deficiency in ways of interpreting reality and of handling and resolving stressful life events.

Of all speculations advanced to account for the outbreak of schizophrenia, the stress hypothesis seems to me to be the most feasible. Postulated here is the idea that stress activates in the schizophrenic individual anomalous biochemical and neurophysiological mechanisms as a result of faulty enzyme action. It is likely that the end product of this action is hyperactivity of catecholamines, especially dopamine, as well as the release of pathological psychotogenic metabolites such as dimethyltryptamine (DMT), resulting in a disorganization of brain function. Some authorities have also conjectured the existence of increased numbers of dopamine brain receptors to account for dopamine hyperactivity.

As to the cause of the stress reaction, this is often an environmental event that has a special traumatic meaning for the individual. Perhaps the most powerful sources of stress are disturbed family interactions and there is ample evidence of difficulties in families of schizophrenic patients. But, we may ask, why are not all members within a family where there is a schizophrenic member affected with schizophrenia? The answer to this is that there is no such thing as the same environment for all family members, even for identical twins. Some are more protected than others; some are chosen for projective identification by a mother or father; some are scapegoated, or subjected to contradictory demands, or exposed to discriminatively defective communication signals. The consequence is an interference in the character organization making for conflicts that in themselves become sources of tension. The stresses that impose themselves on the individual therefore are environmental difficulties from without and irreconcilable conflicts from within and such stresses may become critical at certain periods in the developmental cycle (as during adolescence) and when pressures and demands both from without and within exceed the individual's coping capacities.

Q322: What is the nature of the family pathology and faulty upbringing of the child who becomes schizophrenic and how does this upbringing influence him?

A322: The schizophrenic patient has in early development often been exposed to *selective illogic* which makes for irrational thinking around specific areas. The consequence is that the patient can think seriously about certain subjects and disjointedly about other subjects. He can deal better with selected stresses and be completely unable to manage other stresses to which he is singularly sensitive.

Among the deficits that emerge from a difficult childhood are an overwhelming sense of helplessness, a defective self-image, and overpowering hostilities. These impulses are handled by defenses organized around different levels of reasonableness. Helplessness may be managed by either a dependent clinging to some magical protective figure or movement or by denial manifested in compulsive independence. Ambivalence toward objects will make for varied responses to people and be so disturbing to the individual that he will become apathetic and detached from people to avoid being rejected, hurt or completely engulfed in a relationship. A defective self-image gives rise to a host of coping devices, ranging from inferiority feelings on one end to grandiosity on the other. The hostility may be turned outward in sadistic attitudes and aggression, or turned inward in the form of masochistic self-punishment. Because of existing pockets of irrationality, the manifestations of these impulses and the defenses that control them may become highly and even psychotically symbolized and distorted. Thus dependency may be expressed by feelings of being influenced and manipulated by powerful or protective or malevolent agencies or machines. A devalued self-image may take the form of being accused by voices of emitting a foul odor or the idea of changing into an animal. Or it may be neutralized by the defense of a grandiose delusion. Hostility may be acted out directly in terms of paranoidal delusions and of violence toward persecutory enemies. Periods of rationality may alternate with those of irrationality and the nature of the symbols may vary. When emotional stability is restored, pathological manifestations may temporarily vanish, only to reappear under the impact of stress.

Most people who are able physiologically to deal with stress are threatened with periodic irrationalities, but they are able to process these cognitively and to control them without distorting reality. Yet psychotic-like impulses may appear in fantasy or in dreams. Other persons maintain their stability by circumscribing and isolating areas of psychotic or psychotic-like thinking or behavior, for example, by paranoidal ideation which serves as an outlet for hostility. This defense permits them to function and to maintain some adaptive capacity. Still other persons decompensate temporarily under the impact of stress and show overt psychotic behavior from which they rapidly recover (schizophreniform psychosis). Where there is a specific genetic vulnerability, however, the cognitive distortion may be extensive and prolonged, resulting in the syndrome of schizophrenia.

Q323: Is there a common denominator among parents of schizophrenics?

A323: There is controversy about the importance of familial conditions, some doubt being cast on Frieda Fromm-Reichmann's idea of the schizophrenogenic mother. Nevertheless one cannot dismiss the fact that in many schizophrenics one does come across families who are unable to fulfill the child's needs, who convey contradictory messages to the child, who do not provide good models for identification, who utilize the child as a scapegoat or as a means of satisfying their own neurotic designs. The genetic predisposition that sensitizes the child is probably fundamental, but familial mischief can play a significant role, and certainly must be considered a primary factor in any continuing treatment plan, especially with young schizophrenics who are attempting to individuate. Family consultation and therapy are vital to enable the family to tolerate the patient's individuation and growth.

Q324: What do you think of Laing's idea that schizophrenia is less a manifestation of disease than an expression of his state of being or existence, and a rational reaction against a disturbed society?

A324: I believe firmly that schizophrenia is a pathological state and not merely an expression of one's existence. It is true that the schizophrenic does experience himself in a different way with an altered identity, as more unreal than real, more dead than alive so to speak, and, as Laing puts it, "He may feel his self as partially divorced from his body." Laing (1960, 1967) describes the inner experiences of the schizoid individual well, and his indictment against a disturbed society has important points. However, his idea about schizophrenia as "a successful attempt not to adapt to pseudo-social realities" and that "there is no such condition as schizophrenia, but the label is a social fact and the social fact a political event" is one that cannot be endorsed. To call schizophrenia an *adaptive* response to a disordered society is little short of fanciful. There is no question in my mind that schizophrenia is a disease that affects behavior adversely and that it is maladjustive rather than adaptive. To put this in another way, the kind of adaptation achieved in schizophrenia is at the expense of optimal functioning.

Q325: What are the main points in organizing a good treatment program for schizophrenia?

A325: It would seem that what we are dealing with mainly in schizophrenia are three entities: 1) a genetically determined defective biochemical derangement that sponsors the kind of symptoms on which we base our diagnosis of schizophrenia; 2) initiating sources of stress which set into motion the biochemical upset; and 3) a personality organization with developmental arrests and inadequate defenses that sponsors illogical thinking and that makes it difficult or impossible for the individual to mediate stress appropriately. In designing therapy for schizophrenia it is expedient to consider all of these entities. We must remember, however, that while broad generalizations are possible regarding an ideal treatment plan, each individual will require specific measures unique to himself or herself that take into account such factors as susceptibility or intolerance to special antipsychotic drugs; degree of the patient's resistance to conforming with a prescribed treatment plan; the willingness to extricate oneself from current sources of stress; the presence or absence of sufficient ego strength to explore and deal with inner conflict; the kinds of family problems and strains to which the patient is exposed; the available resources in the community that can serve as a support system for the patient, etc. With these precautions in mind we may proceed with the following outline of a treatment program.

1) *Pharmacotherapy.* Where the psychotic disorder is so pronounced as to interfere with the patient's judgment and reasoning powers, or where excited or bizarre behavior is present, or a thinking disturbance

exists with delusions and hallucinations, neuroleptics *in adequate dosage* are in order. The object here is to rectify biochemical imbalances, to palliate symptoms, and to enable the patient to cooperate better with the treatment plan. But neuroleptics alone will not resolve sources of stress that activate continuing biochemical turbulence.

2) *Tension reduction.* A supportive relationship with an empathic person who is interested in helping the patient may reassure and calm a tense patient. When such a relationship develops, relaxation exercises or meditation may be taught a patient who is cooperative. In some cases relaxing hypnosis or biofeedback may be used for purposes of tension reduction.

3) *Resolution of external stress.* A careful assay of environmental stressors should be undertaken and the patient removed from them if possible. This includes finding new residential quarters with an accepting family when the patient is living at home and is subject to overemotionality, criticism and hostility, and when it is obvious that the patient's family will not change. But where the family is amenable to change, family counseling may enable the patient to continue living at home. Casework, counseling, and milieu therapy may be helpful in instances of financial distress, medical problems, work difficulties and other situations where environmental manipulation and the utilization of community resources is needed. A day hospital, rehabilitation unit or social therapy club will often serve a useful purpose. Our object is to lower external pressures on the individual and to create an environment in which the person can function with as little turmoil as possible.

4) *Reduction of internal stress.* Of greater difficulty is the task of promoting logical thinking and resolving inner conflict which acts as a potent fountainhead of continuing stress. While schizophrenics are flooded with upsurges of the unconscious which come through in direct or symbolized form, a peculiar splitting and detachment insulate what remains of the reality sense from doing much about unconscious manifestations. Indeed, reality and fantasy are intermingled and confused and the therapist will usually struggle in vain with appeals to reason. It is necessary then to approach the task of lowering conflict indirectly by strengthening the self-image and sense of independence, and by reducing the towering dependency level with its accompanying hostility through living skills training. A reassuring empathic counselor or skilled paraprofessional is extremely important as an aid in implementing this task. Family therapy is also helpful by encouraging better communication among the participant members.

Individual psychotherapy is, of course, a propitous means of helping to resolve conflict, but its use is contingent on the therapist's gaining the patient's confidence and establishing a working relationship with the patient. This is a difficult accomplishment with the schizophrenic because of the evasions and detachment that will for a long time hold the therapist at bay. Other deterrents to be controlled are hostile countertransferences and overinvolvement with the patient on the part of the therapist. Working psychotherapeutically with a schizophrenic patient is an art. Although our goal is more modest than in neurotic or character disorders, in that we are not looking for notable reconstructive changes, enough may be accomplished with good psychotherapy to justify its employment. Through properly conducted psychotherapy, buttressed by such modalities as behavior therapy, group and family therapy, we have the best opportunity to raise the patient's level of stress tolerance and to help him deal more appropriately with people as well as with himself toward an improved life adaptation.

Q326: Do chronic schizophrenics ever truly recover?

A326: Given a favorable environment with a reduction of stress factors and an occasional but continuous contact with a sympathetic therapist, a patient whose affect is not significantly frozen can make a good adaptation. The schizophrenic predisposition under these conditions remains under satisfactory control, even though complete recovery is doubtful. The most that many therapists expect is that the patient will return to the prepsychotic mode of adjustment with a minimum of impairment. (See also Qs 319, 356.)

Q327: How can you tell when schizophrenia is first breaking out so that treatment can be started early, and what are the first therapeutic steps with the patient? Also, can schizophrenia be prevented in an individual at high risk, that is, where parents are schizophrenic and the patient is brought up in a schizophrenic family?

A327: The onset of schizophrenia varies. Often it is insidious, becoming apparent only in late adolescence or in early adult life. The individual shows behavioral changes like isolation, withdrawal, and a dropping out of school or work. Emotionally he may be unstable and depressed, resorting to drugs or alcohol for relief. Unhappy at home, he may run away, seeking out groups of other isolated children or young adults with whom he establishes an unstable affinity. Affiliations are shallow, ideation more or less fragmented, the self-image devalued, and the boundaries between reality and fantasy blurred. The expression of needs is chaotic, and often fulfilled only in fantasy. Omnipotent, grandiose and paranoidal ideas prevail. There is constant moving about, seeking some refuge in relationships which eventually are distrusted and abandoned. There is repeated experimenting with disorganized ways of regaining control, solving problems, bolstering security and enhancing self-esteem.

The big problem for the therapist at this stage is that the patient has little or no motivation for treatment, distrusting people and resisting any kind of a close relationship, which is the vehicle through which psychotherapy is done. It will take all the tact and resourcefulness a therapist can muster to keep a patient coming for his sessions in the face of his detachment, suspiciousness, fear and hostility. The therapist should try to avoid giving commands and orders because the patient will resist these. Nor should any mention be made of the need for or direction of change. Clues as to focus are gathered from what the patient is interested in and wants to deal with. No judgments should be expressed about the patient's behavior or his dynamics except when the patient asks for these. Even then interpretation must be carefully and reassuringly made. Attempts to alter the patient's attitudes, to plan goals for him, and to tell him how he may best manage his affairs will usually be resisted. Breaking of and lateness in coming for appointments call for great flexibility in time arrangements. The therapist concentrates on ways of solidifying his relationship with the patient and on introducing some reality into the patient's perceptions of what is happening to him.

Once a genetic vulnerability exists, the individual always is at high-risk. The avoidance, removal or palliation of environmental situations that have a stress potential for the person, the identification and mediation of inner conflict through psychotherapy, the building of self-esteem through positive achievements and productive work, the presence of accepting role models with whom the patient can identify, the utilization of support systems where necessary, and the administration of neuroleptics when a breakdown threatens may bring the individual back to his customary equilibrium.

Q328: Is it possible to make sense out of the bizarre symptoms of the schizophrenic patient?

A328: The experience of therapists who have been working with schizophrenic patients for years leads them to conclude that schizophrenic symptoms, bizarre as they may seem, do make sense to the patient, even though they may be unintelligible to others. Otto Will (1967) pointedly states that ". . . schizophrenic behavior has a purpose and is a product of learning, and inferences regarding past learning experiences can be drawn from observations of current interpersonal involvements."

The basic needs and impulses of the schizophrenic are probably no different than those in any other person, but their expression is bizarre because they are not fettered by the restraints of reality. They are so highly symbolized and distorted that they become difficult to decode. In part this is due to "training in irrationality" sponsored by contradictory parental communications during the developmental years. In part it is the product of a massive biochemical upset set off by stressful stimuli with which the individual cannot cope. Impulses are fed through neurophysiological channels disorganized by these biochemical alterations. This produces changes in the transmission messages in the subcortex, ultimately influencing thought processes.

Previously dissociated and repressed memories, impulses and ideas become intermingled with immediate perceptions. Added to this is a tendency toward loss of continuity between the self and others, a blurring of the boundaries of fantasy and reality, a deterioration of the processes of organization and integration. Communication in sicker patients becomes jumbled and difficult to understand in conventional terms. For example, omnipotent and grandiose desires, which in the average person are held in check and expressed only in dreams or fantasies (e.g. like in the movie "The Secret Life of Walter Mitty") come through in some schizophrenics as "I am Jesus Christ" or similar pretentious identifications. Identity problems may find a projective outlet in hallucinations of being talked about and accused of homosexuality or grotesqueness. Repudiated sexual sensations may be credited to malignant electrical forces or cosmic rays being directed at one's sexual organs. Hostility toward maternal figures may find expression in the idea of an oral assault through poisoned food or in cannibalistic fantasies.

There are some sensitive and talented therapists who are able to recognize what strivings the patient is trying to express out of the patient's idiosyncratic symptoms and in this way to establish communicative contact with the patient. The capacity of the therapist to convey an understanding of the underlying needs and anxieties calls for an uncommon perceptiveness and an ability to endure ambiguity. This skill can be developed once we accept the principle that the patient's productions are not haphazard outpourings but rather his unique way of looking at reality. They do have a significant meaning once they are translated.

Q329: In treating schizophrenia we are confronted with the premorbid personality precursors which initiated the disorder in the first place. Is there a specific personality type susceptible to schizophrenia and shouldn't treatment deal with this basic personality constellation?

A329: The question is a difficult one to answer. First, there is no specific personality typology that antedates the psychotic break. One characteristically finds various personality problems and neurotic defensive operations (anxiety, phobic reactions, obsessive-compulsive reactions, depressive reactions, etc.) before the individual decompensates in a psychosis. A number of individuals, but not all, do manifest early detachment and signs of autism, and in them this may be an initial indication of schizophrenia. Certainly if the premorbid personality has interfered with adaptive coping, a rectification of this, with strengthening of defenses to manage stress better, should be an aim of psychotherapy. Understandably such an aim is an ambitious one and often difficult to achieve.

Q330: Is there research or other evidence that psychotherapy has any effect in schizophrenia?

A330: The literature is contradictory. For example, May's 1968 research indicates that psychotherapy had little to offer schizophrenics in comparison with medication. The Massachusetts Mental Health Center study by Grinspoon, Ewalt and Shader (1972) also cast doubts on the value of psychotherapy. The studies by Rogers et al. (1967) and case reports of Vaillant, Semrad and Ewalt (1964), Kayton (1975), and Rubins (1976) are more optimistic. However, May's research was flawed by the use of only inexperienced therapists and supervisors who were dubious about the use of psychotherapy with schizophrenics. The other studies could also be criticized for faulty design and controls.

My own opinion, bolstered by work with schizophrenics over many years and by observation of the results of experienced therapists, is that psychotherapy can be both a success or a failure, depending on who does it and how well it is done. Properly employed, it offers a good number of schizophrenic patients an opportunity to remain symptom-free and better able to manage stress in daily living.

This does not detract from the value of medication or of other modalities, like social rehabilitation, family therapy and behavior therapy, which are best employed conjunctively with psychotherapy. The most important ingredient in therapy is a good relationship. An empathic therapist who is really interested in working with and helping a schizophrenic patient will get better results, even when relatively inexperienced, than a highly trained, experienced professional who is only casually involved with the patient or convinced that not much can be done for him. Psychoanalysis is relatively valueless, but once a working relationship exists, a psychodynamically oriented eclectic approach has the potential of reaching some patients. Short-term therapy does not accomplish much with most schizophrenic patients, who will usually require years of treatment.

There are many pitfalls in working psychotherapeutically with a schizophrenic, not the least of which is provoking and nurturing a hostile dependency that cannot be resolved. Transference is frequently a problem and if not dealt with in the early stages may evolve into a disturbing transference neurosis or transference psychosis. No less troublesome are the therapist's irritation and anger at the patient, which is understandable considering the vexations inherent in dealing with the patient's obstinacy, querulousness, uncooperativeness, contentiousness, belligerence and detachment. Such emotions on the part of the therapist must be controlled. Countertransference mismanaged can interfere with the therapist's objectivity and ability to provide an empathic relationship.

Q331: Have there been any studies on the long-term course of schizophrenia in patients who did not receive any neuroleptic or other pharmacologic treatment?

A331: A relatively recent one is by Manfred Bleuler (1976) who studied more than 2,000 such schizophrenics from many countries over a 40-

year period. Among these were 208 of his own patients at the Burghölzli Clinic whom he followed personally "until death, or for at least 22 years, together with the destiny of their parents, siblings, marital partners and children." At least 25 percent of such schizophrenics recovered completely and remained recovered with no psychotic signs, a normal social integration, and the ability to work. Approximately 10 percent required permanent hospitalization.

Q332: What do you think of the many different psychotherapeutic approaches to schizophrenia such as those of Sechehaye, Sullivan, Weil, Laing, Frankl, Binswanger, Bellak, Semrad, Rosenfeld, Searles, and the therapists who use the body ego nonverbal approaches? Do they have anything in common?

A332: I believe they do. They constitute unique ways the authors have of establishing a relationship with their patients and then of utilizing the relationship to bring the patient back to reality. The methods coordinate with particular styles of relating. They will work for some therapists and not for others. Experimentation with any methods that seem reasonable is in order, however, to see whether they fit in with one's own style of making contact and opening a dialogue with these sicker patients.

Q333: Can you hope to achieve any reconstructive changes in personality in schizophrenia through psychotherapy?

A333: This is always our hope but its achievement may be possible in only a selected group of patients, assuming of course that the therapist possesses the personality, training and skill to work toward this goal. Among the characteristics one looks for in proper candidates are:

1) concern about oneself and motivation to do something about this;
2) the capacity to understand that there are emotional forces operating within oneself that are creating problems (psychological mindedness);
3) a relative absence of fixed paranoidal projections that act as rigid resistances to insight;
4) existence of affect along with one's symptoms;
5) presence of at least one good relationship in the past;

6) successful past achievements in education, work, sexual and social adjustment;
7) average or above average intelligence;
8) ability to make a relationship with the therapist.

At the start of therapy these positive signs may be concealed under a host of symptoms, but once the patient has calmed down and a relationship with the therapist crystalizes, some positive signs may appear under which circumstances more intensive therapy can begin.

Q334: Freud originally felt one could not produce transference in schizophrenia. Do we still believe this?

A334: Transference can be intense at times in schizophrenia, sometimes reaching psychotic proportions. Because the patient may assume that the therapist has unlimited powers, he may make demands on him that are impossible to fulfill. The therapist is caught in a bind here because the patient will feel let down and angry should the therapist refuse requests or say he cannot satisfy them. The therapist may declare that he will do his best but that he is not in complete control of everything. Should a hostile transference develop, the therapist will have to control his feelings, interpreting the patient's reaction if possible and showing the patient calm consideration in the hope that the transference will eventually burn itself out.

Q335: Which schizophrenic patients are most likely to respond to psychotherapy? What characteristics in the therapist are best suited to work with these patients?

A335: The best candidates are young, normally intelligent persons who in the past achieved success in their studies, work, interpersonal and sexual relationships, and who are now motivated for therapy. These qualifications obviously are present in only a small fraction of the schizophrenic patients who come for help. The bulk of patients will possess handicaps with which the therapist will have to cope, and which will tend to challenge his effectiveness. The burden of responsibility, in my opinion, is on the therapist and not the patient and will reside in setting goals for each patient that are achievable within the range of the patient's potentialities and environmental limitations.

A number of therapist characteristics are helpful, perhaps the most important one being an ability to control countertransference, since work with chronic mental patients is bound to be frustrating. Genuine sincerity and dedication are important since patients, especially schizophrenic patients, will see through simulation and hypocrisy. One must be interested in working with these patients and in establishing communication with them. Other important qualities are enthusiasm, optimism, and ability to handle frustration and to persevere in the face of lack of progress. Some authorities humorously say that a bit of masochism doesn't hurt.

Q336: Isn't the treatment of choice in schizophrenia drug therapy and, if so, isn't psychotherapy superfluous?

A336: Drug therapy with neuroleptics is the treatment of choice where the objective is to bring the patient back to a prepsychotic level rapidly. The goal is therefore a limited one. Any attempt made to correct intrapsychic distortions or to strengthen the personality structure will call for psychotherapy. Where the patient is in good contact with the therapist, it may not be necessary to utilize neuroleptics during psychotherapy. There are many authorities who believe that drugs in schizophrenia are overused and that patients should be given an opportunity to work through their problems with psychotherapy alone. Personally, I believe this is an optimistic point of view. Where there is a thinking or attention disorder, neuroleptics may be necessary to establish satisfactory communication.

Q337: Is drug therapy in schizophrenia ever contraindicated?

A337: There is a subgroup of patients in whom natural restitutive powers exist in overcoming an acute schizophrenic attack (Marder et al., 1979; May and Goldberg 1978) some of whom (with the aid of psychotherapy) gain important insights from it. This subgroup has not yet been precisely identified, but I should estimate that it contains adolescents who are going through developmental crises, in whom the working-through of a psychotic attack may serve as a positive growth experience. There are also young adults with first-break schizophrenia who have made a good premorbid adjustment and have a favorable prognosis. Apart from these groups, most schizophrenics require drug therapy as an essential part of treatment where the symptoms of the patient require amelioration.

Q338: I know there are different stages in the therapeutic process with a schizophrenic patient. Which is the most important one?

A338: The first stage, namely establishing a relationship with the patient, is most important. This can be a formidable task with a schizophrenic since he feels so misunderstood and vulnerable. His primary defense is detachment and withdrawal. Any attempt to break through this defense is considered by the patient to be a real threat to his integrity. There may be a strong yearning for nurturance. Yet the distrust is so great that the patient will not allow himself to get close. Paradoxically, as he begins to relate he may respond with anxiety and rage and even try to attack the therapist for causing him to come out of his shell. These vicissitudes can tax the endurance of any therapist, but persistence should ultimately triumph.

Q339: How do you establish a relationship with a difficult schizophrenic patient who refuses to make a relationship with anyone?

A339: Establishing a relationship with a nonmotivated, paranoidal, severely detached, or withdrawn patient is an arduous and trying job. Where such patients have been hospitalized it is difficult enough, but where the patient has been shepherded into one's office by a concerned relative the task is doubly challenging. The patient will usually be silent, sulky, or casually unconcerned. Questioning him about his past history or about whether he hears voices or believes that people are talking about him will merely heighten his defenses. His reactions are generally motivated by distrust, feelings of being misunderstood, and a heightened vulnerability that insulates him from any potential threat in his contact with people.

The best tactic is to try to engage his interest by searching for clues in his manner or verbalizations and engaging in conversations that are not too personal in reference. Often the patient may mention an unsatisfied need, as for food, clothing or a luxury that is within the therapist's capacity to supply. Sometimes asking the patient if he would like some coffee or a soft drink and joining him in the refreshment may be all the relationship the patient can tolerate. Playing checkers, chess, or cards with the patient is another activity that can be tried. If the patient prefers to be silent, this should be respected and the patient should not be subjected to a grilling. Sitting quietly with him and making casual nonpersonal remarks may eventually be rewarded.

If the patient demands that the therapist release him from the hospital, it is best not to promise that this will be done. As withdrawn as the patient may seem, the chances are that he will remember the broken promise. The therapist may say that he will do his best to help the patient feel better and will help the patient solve any problems that prevent his leaving the hospital. The therapist may state that he has no control over discharging the patient but will do what he can to help, with the patient's cooperation.

Even though the patient offers a gold mine of rich symbolic material in his hallucinations and delusions, it is quite premature to interpret these before a good relationship exists. The therapist can file these data in his mind or enter notes in the case history for future reference.

For a fuller account of working psychotherapeutically with the schizophrenic patient, see Wolberg, 1977, pp. 915-923.

Q340: Are there any rules that can be helpful in establishing contact with a schizophrenic patient?

A340: A few general rules may be helpful:

1) The initial task is to establish a relationship and not to collect information. Asking the patient if he hears voices or believes someone is against him is a poor tactic. Nor should he be grilled about previous attacks or hospitalizations. The therapist should act attentive and reassuring. Sitting behind a desk is not as good as facing the patient directly. Walking with the patient, having coffee with him, and touching him occasionally are not contraindicated.
2) Do not argue, cajole or try to reason with a delusional or hallucinating patient, no matter how absurd his ideas or fantasies may seem. Not only will the effort be useless, but it may also convince the patient that you are aligned with the forces of evil against him. Listen respectfully to what he has to say. If he complains about something and if you must make a comment, simply say reassuringly, "This must be upsetting to you."

3) If the patient is perturbed or agitated, one may say: "I certainly understand how upset you must feel. If such a thing happened to other people they'd be upset too."

4) If the patient prefers to remain silent, accept this, and do not try to bully or shame the patient into talking.

5) If an upset patient asks you for help in allaying his tension or anxiety, you may reassure him that you will do everything you can. If he is not taking medications, ask him if he would like to have some medicine to quiet his restlessness. You also may suggest teaching him how to relax his tensions. If he responds positively, utilize relaxing exercises or relaxing hypnosis. This may rapidly expedite the relationship.

6) Give the patient regular sessions, and be sure you keep the appointment times. If you will be late for a session, notify the patient in advance if possible and tell him you will make up the lost time. Anticipate the patient's breaking appointments and being tardy. If this happens do not chide him—merely say you missed him.

7) Bizarre behavior or attitudes may strike the therapist as humorous. To succumb to ridicule or laughter may shatter the chances of a relationship.

Q341: Are there any tips on how to work with a psychotic person psychotherapeutically once a relationship is established?

A341: I will cite 20 tips I have found useful in work with schizophrenics:

1) Any activity that can bolster the patient's self-esteem should be supported. This includes the patient's grooming and clothing habits, and positive achievements of any kind. These should be talked about and encouraged; the patient should be praised for even slight accomplishments in work, hobbies and creative activities.

2) The best way to handle delusional or hallucinatory material is to listen respectfully and never ridicule nor make light of them. One may even act as if uninterested in the hope of discouraging the frequency of these pathological responses. On the other hand, reasonable talk should command alert attention and active responses in an effort to reinforce rationality. If the patient is disturbed by what he brings up, the therapist may agree that if matters were as the patient reported, anybody would be disturbed. Then the therapist may gently offer an alternative explanation as a possibility, not pressing his point if the patient does not agree.

3) No matter how truculent, neglectful, disrespectful, or hostile the patient acts toward the therapist (even if the patient throws a tantrum), punitive, scolding, or rejecting responses should never be indulged. The patient may be merely testing the therapist. Nor should the therapist encourage any regressive behavior, avoiding talking to or treating the patient as if he were a child. In other words, irrespective of how "crazy" the patient acts, he should be treated with dignity and respect as an adult. After their recovery, many patients talk about how they appreciated the therapist's manner.

4) For a long time direct interpretation may have to be delayed, projective techniques being used instead. The therapist may by illustration make comments such as: (to a patient in despair at being rejected) "*Most* people feel hurt if people neglect them"; (to a patient with fantasies of death and killing) "It often happens that when a person feels angry he may imagine the person he is angry at will hurt him, or will die"; (to a woman who felt her looks repelled men) "I knew a woman once who felt she was so ugly, no man would want her and she would get furious if a man wanted to date her because she believed he was taunting her." These comments illustrate how one does not directly confront the patient with his actions, but uses other individuals as examples. The patient may or may not then pick up the implications. If he applies what is being said to himself, the interpretations can be made more directly.

5) With paranoidal patients who have fixed delusions, disagreeing with these delusions will put the therapist in the class of all other persons who have tried to argue the patient out of what he believes to be true. Thus, a therapeutic relationship may never get started. Yet, to support the patient's delusion completely may not be wise. Here the therapist may give credence to the patient's right to believe what he knows to be true and express an interest in all the facts that have led to the patient's conclusions. One should not directly support the patient's conclusions, but merely state: "I can understand how facts like these lead you to feel the way you do." For example, a patient felt he was being pursued by the Mafia, who wanted to steal his business away from him. As evidence he cited seeing an automobile with New Jersey license plates in the area of his apartment. He was sure he was being watched and followed by New Jersey gangsters who were out to kill him. His complaints to the police and District Attorney were greeted with amused disdain. Instead of challenging the patient I asked him to be sure to keep a diary of all of his daily observations that pointed to his persecutions. At every visit he would bring many sheets

of written matter containing detailed rambling "observations," which I would greet as interesting and important and which I promised I would later read in studied detail after our visit. I would then put the material aside and we would talk about his other interests and daily activities, avoiding the psychotic area as much as possible. The volume of the reports gradually dwindled to a single sheet and then stopped altogether, the patient apologizing for his neglect in bringing in this material. With the cessation of his reports he began to concern himself with immediate problems in his daily life and work and soon lost interest in the Mafia delusion. His dreams during this working-through phase brought out the homosexual dynamics in rather clear focus, which I interpreted casually in a projective way. Years have past since we terminated therapy with no return of his delusion.

6) The management of transference reactions will call for fortitude on the part of the therapist. The range of how the patient regards the therapist is great: God, mother, father, sibling, the devil, seducer, lover, persecutor, friend. Dependency reactions must be expected and these release other impulses and defenses like sexuality, hostility, masochism, devalued self-esteem, and detachment. Different phases of these reactions express themselves at varying times and the patient will try to involve the therapist in his schemes. The therapist must resist acting out with the patient and becoming countertransferentially rejecting, seductive, overprotective, or punitive. Yielding to the patient's importunate transferential demands will breed more irrationality. Yet, an honest careful explanation of why it is impossible to fulfill the patient's demands must be given so that the patient does not feel rejected as a person.

Expressed hostility will be especially difficult to handle, since it can be like a never-ending spring issuing out of depths that have no bottom. So long as it remains on a verbal level, the therapist may be able to tolerate it, realizing that some of the rage is in the way of a test, some a means of warding off a threatened close relationship with the therapist, some a belated effort to resolve a needed breaking away from the maternal figure, some a rebellious desire to assert and be oneself. We may suspect that the patient retains a ray of hope that the therapist will handle the patient's anger and not respond in an expected retaliating way that would justify a continued withdrawal. If the therapist can stand this test, feelings of unthreatened love and closeness may bubble through. On the other hand, should rage take the form of expressed violence which does not cease when met by a calm and self-assured manner on the part of the therapist, and by statements that the patient does not want to lose control, it will require firm but kindly and considerate action or physical restraint to protect the patient, the therapist, and others, an explanation later being given the patient for the preventive action. The therapist here must act in a composed but determined way without giving the impression of retaliating for the patient's behavior. One way of diluting transference reactions is by involving the patient in some group activity—a hobby, social group, or therapeutic group.

7) Where there is no desire to work analytically with the patient (which will happen in a majority of psychotic patients), visits are gradually lessened in frequency once improvement is stabilized, but then never discontinued completely in that the patient is given the option of seeing the therapist once in two weeks, then once a month, and then at longer intervals.

8) False promises should never be made to a patient because they will inevitably be broken and with this the therapeutic relationship may terminate. Nor should deception be utilized as a way of escaping a difficult situation because here too the patient somehow will divine the deceit. Sometimes it is necessary to withhold the true facts temporarily from the patient since the patient may not be prepared to deal with them in the state he is in, but he may later be able to handle them when his ego gets stronger. Whatever explanations or interpretations are given the patient, these should be coached in frank but reassuringly optimistic terms.

9) Whether to engage in deeper analytic therapy is a decision one must reach after working with the patient for a long period, seeing how he handles interpretations and observing the buildup of ego strengths. Schizophrenics live close to their unconscious and they are often first in arriving at insights themselves. Whether such insights can help the patient is another matter. When stress becomes too strong, the patient will collapse, insight or no insight.

10) The greatest use of therapy is to increase the patient's stress tolerance and this means a careful assay of current and future stressors, preparing and helping the patient to cope with them.

11) Avoid language the patient cannot understand. If possible, utilize the dialect of the patient.

12) Point out in a non-accusatory and nonjudgmental way patterns the patient indulges that are hurtful to him and tend to make others withdraw. The message should be given in as reassuring a manner as possible, reflecting the therapist's confidence in the patient's ability to change.

13) Avoid interpreting the dynamics of the patient's symptoms. Without a firm working relationship with the patient and evidences of his trust, this will be counterproductive. Do not belittle or ridicule the patient's delusions, no matter how foolish they may seem.

14) Do not take notes while with the patient. This will enhance his suspiciousness, especially if there is some paranoidal tendency. Notes can be made after the patient leaves.

15) Credit the patient's disturbed behavior, if he shows it, to the fact that he is being frightened and upset and not to the fact that he is a difficult violent person. The patient may be responding to his environment as dangerous and he will need reassurance and support, not condemnation.

16) Before prescribing medications, explain why drugs are useful in quieting a person down, helping one sleep, etc.

17) As soon as the patient's symptoms subside, reduce medications to as low a level as will control symptoms. When the relationship becomes firm, the medications may even be discontinued. If symptoms reappear, drug dosage may be increased.

18) Start family therapy as soon as the patient quiets down, building a relationship with the family and counseling them as to steps each member can take to improve communication. Establish a contact with the most stable family member, who will act as a liaison. Instruct this member when to increase medications. Invite this member to telephone you if problems occur.

19) There is no reason why the patient cannot be taught to medicate himself when he feels his equilibrium threatened. Having Mellaril or Permitil on hand and utilizing such medications to quiet and stabilize oneself can often nip a psychotic break in the bud.

20) Flexibility in approach is the keynote of good therapy with schizophrenics.

General rules such as I have cited here are useful but they will have to be adapted to each patient and modified according to individual reactions. Similarly, the use of aftercare services will depend on what special needs each patient has and the availability of services in the community in which the patient lives.

Q342: Should you delay giving neuroleptics in schizophrenia, hoping the patient will pull out of his attack by himself?

A 342: Neuroleptics should be given early when there is hope of aborting a psychotic break. One can then deal better with existing stress and personality factors. I do not see the point of allowing a patient to go into a psychosis on the theory that he will learn something valuable from it. Actually, the psychosis may leave him with an impairment.

Q343: What is the greatest handicap to the therapist in working with schizophrenia?

A343: Countertransference is common among therapists working with schizophrenia, and failing to understand and control it can make a shambles out of any therapeutic endeavor. Working with a schizophrenic is often a frustrating experience. The therapist may feel startled, repulsed, upset, angered, rejected, and abused by his patient, whose resistant, unconventional, and antagonistic behavior can unbalance the most stable reserve of the therapist. If the therapist interprets antics of the patient as offensive to him, he will have difficulty helping his patient. Recognition that the behavior of the patient is not as haphazard as it seems, and that its design is not necessarily to frustrate the therapeutic effort, may enable the therapist to empathize with the patient and to prevent countertransference from interfering with the relationship. As an antidote to countertransference and even as a preventive measure, I suggest consultation with one's colleagues where one is dealing with a large caseload of schizophrenic patients. (See also Q 364.)

Q344: How friendly should you become with a schizophrenic patient?

A344: Showing friendship and caring are important, but one must remember that the patient may not be able to enter into a real friendship relationship. His need for distancing has to be respected. There is also a danger of becoming too involved and overprotective, which will enhance the patient's dependency with accompanying hostility. Sufficient friendship, however, must exist so that the caretaking person or therapist can serve as a role model in such matters as dress, comportment with people, management of fear or anxiety, impulse control, and dealing with difficult life situations. The object is to alter those attitudes, values, and behaviors that interfere with adaptation to the environment in which the patient will function.

Q345: How would you handle a schizophrenic's jumbled communication in the course of trying to establish a relationship with him?

A345: This is a difficult task because the patient will interpret almost any response as a challenge, confrontation or indication of disapproval which may cause a further withdrawal. One way I have found useful is to tell the patient: "I hope you will excuse me, but I sometimes find it difficult to understand some things. I wonder if you can help me understand what you were just saying. Maybe we can say it in a little different way so it will be a little clearer for me."

Q346: If a schizophrenic patient asks you if his diagnosis is schizophrenia, what do you say?

A346: The question is whether you should be honest and say "yes" or sidestep the question with an enigmatic answer. Since your answer can make the difference between keeping the patient in therapy or his leaving therapy, it is important to get an idea as to why the patient is asking this question. Your reply will have to be organized around the meaning of the word "schizophrenia" to the patient. The patient may be assured that he has no illness that cannot be helped with treatment and that his cooperation can hasten his getting better.

Q347: Should you allow a schizophrenic patient to become dependent on you?

A347: You may have no alternative at first, since this may be the only way the patient can relate. Once a relationship crystalizes, however, more and more responsibility should be put on the patient so that the dependency begins to resolve. Where dependency is allowed to continue unabated, the patient will become increasingly helpless, demanding, and hostile.

Q348: How do you handle a silent, uncooperative schizophrenic patient?

A348: Where the patient is completely silent and unresponsive, the therapist's frustration is understandable. One way of handling frustration is for the therapist to assume that what the patient is displaying is a defensive, protective mask to avoid hurting or being hurt. Behind this weird, hostile, and unfeeling mask is a suffering human being who needs help, love, and understanding. A more wholesome part will ultimately reveal itself if the therapist can avoid responding punitively.

What the therapist can say to a silent patient is something like this: "I realize it's hard for you to talk, but I know you have feelings. I am not sure what they are, but what I believe is that you feel hurt and upset. I want you to know that I'd like to help you and when you believe you can trust me you can tell me what you think. In the meantime, it's OK to be quiet and I'll sit with you for a little while." The therapist may then sit near the patient refraining from trying to goad him on to talk. However, every few minutes the therapist may make a casual comment about an idea or feeling that has come to him. The therapist may perhaps say: "Some time you may want to tell me how you happened to come to the hospital." "I'll bet things get upsetting." "Of course, I don't know how you feel, but I wouldn't blame you if you got angry." "If there is anything I can do to help you, I hope you will tell me about it."

After a period of several weeks with nothing happening, the therapist may speculate on what the patient is feeling: "You look so upset. I know something is bothering you. You must feel hopeless," or "You probably feel hurt by the people you were close to." If the patient blurts out, "I don't want to see you again, go away," one might say, "I know you don't want to see me. I won't stay long." One may then stay a few minutes and then leave, but making sure that the next appointment is kept on time.

Touching the patient on the shoulder, or inviting him to have coffee or a soda, or to play cards may sometimes draw a response. The response may be a positive one or it may be rejection. Instead of quieting him down, contact with a patient may serve only to stir him up. The very fact that someone is interested in him may be upsetting because it threatens the patient's defense. In the latter case, the therapist will have to handle his own feelings of irritation. If one realizes that the patient feels threatened by some positive emotions that are coming through and dares not hope that he has found someone who understands him, the rejection will be treated as a sign of activity in the patient. One may say to the patient: "I guess you are angry at me for bothering you. I believe I can help you if you'd let me. It's not necessary to run away. I won't hurt you."

If the patient refuses to come to the office, the therapist may go to the patient and sit with him briefly. I have found that once the patient asks for help it may be possible to solidify one's contact by teaching him how to relax utilizing a hypnotic induction technique. Giving the patient relaxing suggestions often stirs up feelings of greater security and puts the therapist in a benevolent role. This can cut through the patient's detachment.

Sooner or later the patient will begin to talk more spontaneously to the therapist, perhaps flooding him with complaints about what is going on, about being incarcerated, etc. The therapist will welcome this opening-up and will use the opportunity to get the patient to talk about himself. The therapist should at all times try to sense transference and should interpret the patient's untoward emotional feelings in a calm and understanding way. Sometimes the therapist may advantageously say: "It bothers me that I am not helping you as much as I would like," or "I don't blame you for being mad at me and for feeling let down by me. I, too, feel bad that I am not helping you as much as I would like. But it is important for you to do things that will be helpful to you." Some positive activities may then be suggested, fulfillment of which should be rewarded.

When a working relationship develops and the patient seems interested in understanding more about himself and what has happened to him, one may start working dynamically with the patient, utilizing a projective method of interpretation.

Q349: How do you manage a schizophrenic's great dependency and how do you get a chronic schizophrenic to be less dependent?

A349: There are some isolated, detached individuals who stablize themselves around a rigid paranoidal defense and who have skills that enable them to earn a living and take care of themselves, in this way covering up their dependency. But the majority of chronic mentally ill persons will have to maintain a contact with some empathic overseeing and nurturing person or a supportive group the remainder of their lives because of a continuing dependency need. The inherent ambivalence of the patient and his distrust of people is such that, even though he needs a dependent, supportive relationship as a lifeline, he finds it difficult to accept. For a long time the helping individual will be on probation, the butt of misunderstanding and subject to rigorous testing. Confidence in him is never complete because of periodic eruptions of transference. When the patient feels himself getting too close, he is apt to burst out in anger, which may occasionally assume psychotic proportions. It is as if the patient is trying to provoke his host to act in a retaliatory way so as to confirm his idea that authority is not to be trusted. It is here that control of one's countertransference can make the difference between success and failure. On the other hand, the patient may shower the therapist with unjustified praise and even test the therapist by saying he is cured and should stop therapy. Should the therapist agree, this will constitute for the patient a rejection.

The best tactic for the therapist is to accept the patient's dependency need as basic, but not to get involved so intimately that the patient projects all his dependency demands on the therapist. This means that even though therapy may go on for an indefinite time the therapist should dilute the dependency by distributing it among a number of available resources, such as a stable member of the family; a professional "caretaker" who coordinates the patient's living arrangements, medical needs, financial requirements, etc., if such a person is available; or a staff member of a day care, social or rehabilitation center where the patient receives aftercare. Group therapy can be extremely helpful here because transferences usually develop with a number of people and this softens the transferential intensity. Often a supportive group in itself satisfies the patient's dependency needs, the patient selecting one or more members as an emotionally sustaining prop. A hobby group or a job where the patient relates to other people, and where demands are not made on him that are beyond his capacity, can supplement the supportive network.

Gradually the patient will loosen his hold on the therapist by finding resources outside the therapeutic situation. In my opinion, once a good relationship is established, the therapist should never entirely bow out of the picture. He may increase the interval between visits and even shorten them. He may invite the patient to attend one of his large groups (Wolberg, 1980, pp. 13-14). All some patients may need is the security of knowing that an afternoon, morning or evening once weekly or bimonthly is open indefinitely for a visit if the need arises to use it. This knowledge may satisfy the patient even though he may not show up regularly. The idea that he will have someone to consult or socialize with when he requires advice or support will go a long way toward stabilizing him. When the patient does appear, a brief individual interview with a professional person should focus on how the patient is adapting and whether medication adjustment is necessary should the patient be on drug maintenance therapy.

As the patient strengthens his contacts in the community, he may need contact with the therapist and aftercare therapeutic groups less frequently. I believe it is a mistake to eliminate such therapy altogether for a patient. Rather, the simple tactic of giving the patient an appointment card with the therapist's name, address and telephone number, and a date as far off as three to six months in advance may be extremely reassuring to the patient. Some patients will stabilize and not show up for this appointment and a new appointment should be mailed to them. The therapist who deals with chronic mentally ill persons may set aside a one- or two-hour slot weekly or bimonthly for a supportive or social group session with a number of patients, while managing individually to interview briefly, if only for a few minutes, each patient who shows up. Some patients prefer to maintain mail or telephone contact with the therapist and this should not be denied to them. To repeat, some connection with the therapist, however tenuous, may in itself be the only therapy some patients want and need, and may help prevent rehospitalization.

Q350: Does behavior therapy have a place in the management of schizophrenia?

A350: Definitely, especially with withdrawn and uncooperative ward patients whom a token economy rewards for active, useful, social activities. It can be helpful also in some adolescent schizophrenics where it is possible to identify reinforcers for suitable behaviors. In certain cases it is sometimes employed in conjunction with psychotherapy.

Q351: Should group therapy or a group approach be prescribed for all schizophrenic patients?

A351: If possible the patient should become part of some group at some time during the treatment process, although it will be necessary to gauge the patient's readiness for this. The choice of the right kind of group is important because transferences do develop and the patient may become the target of abuse from disturbed patients. The projections of manic and paranoidal patients are particularly difficult to control.

Q352: Don't all schizophrenic patients do well in a good therapeutic community with active milieu therapy?

A352: Paradoxically no. Reactions have to be watched because some patients do better in an authoritarian setting which is run more or less along custodial lines. Certain patients are overstimulated by the many activities offered in busy programs and need to withdraw. A good unit should make provision for this. Provision should also be made for continuing drug maintenance therapy, which is still the most important modality in schizophrenia in terms of protection against relapse.

Q353: How important is the home environment in preventing a relapse in schizophrenic children or young adults?

A353: Fundamentally important. Where family disturbances are severe or the living environment disruptive, a relapse is probably inevitable.

Q354: Is the self-image of a schizophrenic the true reflection of how he was viewed by his parents?

A354: There is no evidence that the devaluated and damaged self-image of the schizophrenic is always an actual carryover of parental attitudes or convictions. Rather, it is the product of a host of personal experiences, assumptions, fantasies, needs, and defenses acquired by the individual from early childhood on, the relationship with the parents playing some part. On the whole, parents have been accused too freely and without justification for promoting schizophrenia in a child who develops this illness. This does not absolve some families for providing the soil in which the schizophrenic pathology can germinate. It points out the need to consider a multiplicity of biochemical, neurophysiological, developmental-conditioning, interpersonal, intrapsychic, and sociological variables that are implicated in the disease.

Q355: Which therapies would you consider of not too great value, as far as we know, in schizophrenia? What is the disadvantage of drugs in schizophrenia?

A355: Insulin, psychosurgery, renal dialysis, megavitamin therapy and acupuncture are therapies whose positive effects on schizophrenia have not been proven. The disadvantages of drugs is that they tend to dampen emotions and interfere with perceptiveness and proper responses to stimuli. Side effects are common and are the chief reason for patients going off drugs. In some cases, especially where given over long periods, they may cause irreversible neurologic sequelae (tardive dyskinesia). Unfortunately drugs are sometimes employed as a chemical straitjacket with patients who might better benefit from psychosocial treatments. This does not detract from the tremendous importance of neuroleptics as an integral part of a treatment plan. Why are they being overused? Some factors are personnel shortages, lack of proper staff training in psychosocial methods, and costliness of the latter as compared to the administration of drugs.

Q356: Can a schizophrenic condition be completely cured?

A356: Insofar as symptoms and social functioning are concerned, the individual may return to his usual prepsychotic "normal" state. The genetic predisposition will still be there, however, which will sensitize the individual to overreacting to certain stress situations. There may also be a residual emotional impairment. With good psychotherapy the patient's stress tolerance will be improved. (See also Qs 319, 326.)

Q357: Does unemployment influence the recovery rate of schizophrenia?

A357: Let us say that a schizophrenic who is allowed to work at a stress-free job and to function at the optimal level of his capacity has a better chance of recovering than one who is not given a chance to assume a role in which his self-esteem can rise and where he has an opportunity to relate productively to others. We would expect then that unemployment affects recovery adversely. Naturally, this is only one of the variables involved in outcome.

Q358: How do you control anxiety in schizophrenia?

A358: Neuroleptics (phenothiazines, butyrophenones, etc.) are the best drugs to use in schizophrenic anxieties. Benzodiazepines are relatively ineffective.

Q359: Is ECT useful in schizophrenia?

A359: In patients with early schizophrenia who have affective or catatonic symptoms, ECT may be of some help. In acute schizophrenic upsets lasting less than one year, complete remission is possible in some cases. Pharmacotherapy is superior to ECT in chronic patients.

Q360: What proportion of schizophrenics get well, that is, are cured?

A360: This depends on the basis of our diagnosis. Where transient psychoses with schizophrenic features are classified as schizophrenia (and not called schizophreniform psychosis), the recovery rate is as high as 70 or 80 percent. Where only patients who retain their symptoms for over six months and who show a continued impairment in certain areas of functioning are classified as schizophrenia, the rate of full recovery may be as low as 15 percent, and social recovery about 30 percent. (See also Qs 319, 326, 356.)

Q361: What can we expect regarding the future psychiatric morbidity of patients with schizophrenia?

A361: A number of studies show that 50 percent of such patients will continue to have serious problems. About 20 percent will show an excellent social recovery, and 30 percent will have only sporadic episodes of trouble. It is difficult to prognosticate which cases will do well because so much depends on the stresses to which individual patients are exposed and the therapeutic and other programs that they receive.

Q362: Do patients with an acute schizophrenic break do better hospitalized or treated while remaining at home? In the latter case are there any guidelines?

A362: A good deal depends on the situation at home, the motivation of the patient for help, and the resistances that interfere with therapy. Should the patient's condition be dangerous to himself or others (assaultiveness, suicidal tendencies, etc.) hospitalization is urgent. Where the family members are hostile and unsympathetic to the patient, and where they are unwilling to enter into family therapy, it will be difficult for the patient to resolve his upset readily in his home environment. He will do better in the calmer atmosphere of a hospital. If drug therapy is urgently needed to protect the patient or others, and the patient resists medication, being totally uncooperative with the treatment plan, a short period of hospitalization can also be of great help. Under other circumstances, and especially where family therapy is possible, there is no reason why the patient cannot be treated on an outpatient basis. There are advantages in outpatient treatment, since the patient will not have to make the adjustment of having to return to his usual milieu. Moreover, it is easier to involve the family in the treatment plan while the patient is at home.

The therapist must establish a relationship with the most responsible member of the patient's family, who will look after the patient and take responsibility for administration of medication and for reporting to the therapist any important changes in the patient's condition. In some cases a patient who resides at home may during therapy become sufficiently disturbed to necessitate brief hospitalization. It is therefore wise to have a hospital available, either a psychiatric unit in a general hospital or a private mental hospital, where the patient may receive care and, if possible, be visited by the therapist. Exploration and utilization of the available support systems (halfway houses, rehabilitation units, social therapy centers, partial hospitals for day care, therapeutic workshops, etc.) is more easily accomplished when the patient is being treated outside of a hospital. These supplementary aids are especially important after the acute phase of the illness has receded and the patient needs aftercare services. Where the patient's home condition is upsetting to him, and when other family members are disturbed and upsetting to the patient, arrangements should be made for housing outside the home (with other relatives, friends, or day and night care centers) in order to avoid stress and insure proper living conditions.

Q363: How do you deal with attitudes and behavior in a schizophrenic that are bizarre and can result in rejection or other kinds of punitive retaliation?

A363: If you have a relationship with the patient you can point out the fact, in a considerate and non-punitive way, that his or her attitude or behavior is apt to be considered unusual or awkward by some people and result in withdrawal or rejection. It is better then to substitute other activities. The therapist may act as a role model to show how this can be done.

Q364: How do you handle your own anger or frustration in working with a disturbed, hostile or unresponsive patient?

A364: Reacting with anger or retaliatory rejection or indignation will get you nowhere. Attempting to understand what there is in yourself that sensitizes you to the patient's behavior may help. You may also need to vent your anger or frustration at a team conference, or to a colleague or supervisor. (See also Q 343.)

Q365: What is the most effective way of forestalling rehospitalization of a schizophrenic patient?

A365: There is no one effective way since every case is unique and requires a selection of modalities tailored to the patient's needs. However, most studies confirm the value of maintenance neuroleptic therapy combined with psychosocial and rehabilitation therapy. Patients on placebos alone or placebos plus psychosocial and rehabilitative therapy tend to relapse at a greater rate than when medications, with proper precaution that they are not overused or underused, are added to the treatment regime. Good aftercare services are also an indispensable means of helping these patients make an adjustment outside of hospital and we may be able to keep many patients in equilibrium without drugs through such services.

Q366: Do nonprofessionals have a role to play in the treatment of schizophrenia?

A366: Definitely. Trained nonprofessionals can be of great help both with hospitalized patients and with chronic deinstitutionalized patients. In the latter case they may take patients into their own homes or supervise their activities in other quarters.

F. Chronic Mentally Ill

Q367: Is there a model program for the chronic mentally disabled that has proven effective?

A367: Model programs have been developed (Bachrach, 1980; Mendel et al., 1980; Stein and Test, 1978; Talbott, 1981) on an experimental basis, but they lack practical value in that most existing service delivery systems are unable to operate fully for financial reasons, insufficient community interest, and lack of trained personnel. The models are important, however, in providing guidelines for the development of care systems in the future—with one important caveat. Innovative as they are, they have not yet been properly evaluated, nor is it certain that because they have worked in one setting and with one demographically designated group of patients, they will work in others. In the main, they provide designs for seeking out patients who are in need of help, for the designation of adequate residential quarters where patients will be safe and under minimal stress, for cooperation with available community resources and support systems, for training in living and coping skills, for individualized treatment programs organized around the patient's needs, for adequate crisis intervention and emergency help, for the best kind of hospital connection should rehospitalization be necessary, and for the training of staff who have the motivation and forebearance to work with this difficult population. Some of the ideas advanced by the authors of these model programs may be adapted to other settings with their unique cultural and political characteristics. (See also Qs 368, 373, 374.)

Q368: Where can one refer a chronically mentally ill person for further care after seeing him in consultation?

A368: An adequate support system for the chronically mentally ill is one of the current lacks in our present-day community mental health program. By and large the community mental health centers have not been able to provide adequate care for the chronically disabled. These patients respond less to traditional psychotherapeutic methods than to practical approaches that deal with everyday problems in daily living. What is required is a long-term relationship with an empathic person who oversees housing, medical care, and educational, occupational and recreational activities. This requires knowledge as well as coordination of the available community resources and sufficient interest and motivation on the part of the overseeing person to maintain contact with the patient and the agencies to whom the patient is referred. Home visits may be required, particularly where broken appointments persist.

Well-run partial hospitals, social rehabilitation centers, and therapeutic workshops can supply a number of important needs toward providing support, group relationships, recreation, and work activities. Input from a psychiatrist will certainly be needed, both for staff consultations and for direct work with a patient who requires crisis management, drug therapy and the handling of emergencies. A professional, trained in psychotherapy and adequately motivated to work with chronically ill patients, will over a long-term period, dealing individually and/or in groups, become an invaluable part of the program. In a rehabilitation unit where a changing staff cannot be avoided, there should be at least one person (preferably the supervising or overseeing individual or the psychotherapist) who consistently works with the patient over a prolonged time span. Should the patient live with or be in close contact with his family, family counseling and therapy can play a vital role.

These varied requirements for a good support system are obviously complex and cannot be satisfied in some communities. The consequence is constant rehospitalization of the chronically mentally ill. This is a costly proposition (apart from any wage loss and the impact on the family and community), considering that in some areas the rehospitalization rate is 60 percent, with most patients being readmitted more than once during the year. The development of an adequate support system can be cost-effective and hopefully future governmental fiscal planning will take this into account. (See also Qs 367, 373, and 374.)

Q369: Why should we bother with hopeless chronic mental patients when there are so many others that will respond better to treatment and who need help?

A369: Your assumption that chronic mental patients are hopeless can be challenged. Apart from a humanistic goal in helping a shamefully neglected section of the population, these patients constitute a great problem for their families and the community, especially since the process of deinstitutionalization has been set into motion. With proper care and the right kind of support, many of these so-called "hopeless" individuals can be rehabilitated.

Q370: Shouldn't the care of deinstitutionalized mental patients be a responsibility of community mental health centers?

A370: Unfortunately, most community mental health centers are not taking this responsibility and are concerning themselves primarily with better adjusted and less disabled patients. Other ways of handling this problem on a community level must be found.

Q371: Why are the chronically ill not receiving the high level of care that their condition calls for?

A371: There are many reasons for this.

1) It is not considered cost-effective to have psychiatrists spend their time and energy on this population, even if there were sufficient numbers of psychiatrists available.
2) Facilities for the adequate care of these patients are not being provided, probably because of financial reasons.
3) Most available private practice psychiatrists are not willing to work with more than a handful of these patients. The financial payments by Medicaid or Medicare are not as great and the responsibilities and problems are greater than with less sick patients.
4) There is a current shortage of psychiatrists in the public sector, which provides the bulk of care, namely because (a) work in institutions pays less than in private practice; (b) the status level of working in the public sector ranks low in the minds of some doctors; (c) private practice is more gratifying and less risky.

5) The public does not place as high a priority on social welfare concerns for the mentally disadvantaged as for drug addiction, alcoholism, delinquency, and criminality.
6) Financial outlays for care would put a heavy drain on public resources, threatening existing priorities.

Q372: When would you employ psychotherapy with deinstitutionalized, chronically ill mental patients?

A372: A chief objective in working with chronic mentally ill patients is providing them with coping skills. This is not done too well in the average institution, where staffing problems and the capabilities of personnel are geared more toward custodial care than toward corrective change. While psychotropic drugs are helpful in overcoming thinking disorders, they do not prepare the patient to manage problems in living. Psychotherapy would be of help but it is generally impractical in these patients because verbal interchanges are resisted, resented, or misinterpreted, and a working relationship is difficult to establish.

On the other hand a structured program in a partial hospital day care center, rehabilitative unit, or social therapy club staffed by empathic and trained workers is more attuned to the needs of the chronic patient. At the Social Rehabilitation Clinic of the Postgraduate Center for Mental Health in New York City, for example, a number of activities are employed, including arts and crafts, meditation, poetry therapy, play reading, sports and music therapy, and even cooking. Patients can choose their own pace and time in pursuing these activities and then entering into assertiveness training groups, dance therapy, game activities, horticulture groups, living skills groups, social issues groups, and drama and human relations groups. In this way patients gradually overcome their shyness and fear and gain some interpersonal and basic living skills. Relationships with the counselors and therapists develop and become the basis for ongoing psychotherapy. It was found best to assign each patient to a staff member who coordinates the program and becomes for the patient a parental surrogate who can help with various services and welfare problems. The program is sufficiently stabilizing and elastic so that many role models become available for identification. Multiple transferences also develop and when troublesome must be dealt with in a supportive, reassuring, or interpretive way.

As patients become stabilized and a relationship with the assigned therapist develops, psychotherapy then may be possible, the intensity being adapted to the patient's needs. The idea that chronic patients cannot utilize psychotherapy is not a correct one. Failures are due to its premature employment and to a lack of skill and training on the part of the therapist. Obviously we will not be able to employ classical analytic techniques, but a dynamic orientation may be combined with whatever eclectic techniques (behavior modification, relaxation, group therapy, family therapy, etc.) are suitable under the circumstances.

Part of the rehabilitation process is getting the patient to do some productive and possibly remunerative work. Here psychotherapy may prepare and sustain the patient to tolerate training in a therapeutic workshop with a vocational objective in mind. Obviously, chronic patients will not be able to compete with more normal individuals or tolerate average degrees of stress.

Q373: What is the best way of managing in your office chronically mentally ill patients who have been released from a hospital and whose relatives want them to get professional help?

A373: The traditional tactic was to keep these patients on antipsychotic drugs over a long haul, allotting 10 or 15 minutes periodically to check on the medications. The object was to produce a chemical tranquilizing straitjacket so that behaviorally the patients would create as few problems as possible for their caretakers. Disregarding the side effects, especially tardive dyskinesia, and the refusal of some patients to follow a drug schedule regularly, the writing off of these patients as hopeless is unfair to the patients, to their families, and to society. Rehabilitation of the chronically mentally ill not only is a humane gesture, but may rescue a number of abandoned souls who can become more self-sufficient and less of a burden on society.

The first step in rehabilitation is establishing an ongoing supportive relationship with the patient. This means that a therapist will have to spend a session with the patient at regular intervals over a period of months, if not years. Because of the patient's detachment and loss of interpersonal skills, it will take a therapist a considerable period to establish contact. This cannot be done where there is a rotation of therapists or where five or 10 minutes are allotted to a session. The therapist should be the key person to coordinate all of the therapeutic and rehabilitative measures that will be employed. An assay must be made of the true requirement for medications to establish that they are not being used needlessly or in excess, or that, if truly indicated, they are accomplishing their purpose and are being taken as prescribed. Drug holidays will have to be judiciously arranged to try to reduce unfortunate sequelae. The best guarantee that drugs are properly employed is to get the patient's cooperation. Once a relationship exists, the therapist will have to educate the patient as to why medications are needed and get him to realize that in spite of the fact that they may slow him down and perhaps make him feel sleepy they do clear his thinking and help reduce his anxiety, irritability, detachment, and discomfort. When the patient recognizes the purpose drugs serve and the ways he can benefit from them, the hazards in drug use will be reduced.

Work with the family of the patient is essential, especially where the patient shares his residence with them. Here the therapist may productively spend some time with key family members, educating them regarding the nature of the patient's problem, the purpose of drug therapy and how to recognize when drugs should be reduced or the dosage increased. Important also is the search for ways of lowering stress within the family, since this is the principal reason for acute relapses. Family therapy may be a prime requirement, particularly where the identified patient is an adolescent or young adult. It may also be necessary to educate the family to respect the patient's need for autonomy and for some isolation when he seeks it. Occasionally, patients will feel emotionally overcharged and need to separate themselves from the people with whom they are intimate to restore their reserve. This means allowing the patient more privacy and not goading him to be active socially if he has no desire for this. A reliable member of the family should be used by the therapist as a liaison to see to it that the treatment recommendations are carried out.

In beginning to work with the chronic patient, a complete physical and psychiatric workup is important, provided the patient can stand the intensity of contact that this entails. It may be necessary to delay this until a relationship has been established and a discussion with the patient secures his cooperation. We are particularly interested in existing physical and psychological assets we can draw on for help when needed, and deficits that will interfere. We also want data on available support systems in the community.

A primary goal in a patient whose sense of reality is blunted is to bring him back to at least a functional level. This may mean teaching him simple living skills that involve taking care of himself, and establishing good eating, grooming and hygienic habits. Some patients at first may seem hopeless, since they have literally been out of circulation for a long time and their coping skills, let alone social capacities, are practically nil. Moreover, they may have little motivation for therapy, with no desire to do anything about themselves. To work with such patients calls for a high degree of dedication and the making of strenuous efforts that might seem unprofitable. Yet the gratification can be great in witnessing the return to relatedness of an abandoned mortal after the therapist has made a consistent effort to extend friendly, supportive, and loving gestures. Nothing more may be needed at first than to sit with the patient, perhaps offering and sharing some food, soft drinks or coffee, or playing cards or checkers if there is any interest in these activities. Sooner or later, if countertransference reactions can be controlled, a penetration of the patient's resistive protective armor may occur.

Once a relationship starts, the patient may be referred to a rehabilitative unit, day care center, or social club. At first, some diversions, such as simple games or listening to music with others, are useful. As soon as there is some interpersonal communication, role training and community living training may be approached.

In preparing the patient for psychotherapy no attempt is made to probe for conflicts, or to challenge defenses, or to make interpretations. The patient is not ready for this and it may be a long time (if ever) before such psychotherapeutic maneuvers can be started. We must content ourselves with teaching some patients coping skills to enable them to deal with the sheer needs of daily living and to permit some gainful work. We may never be able to get the patient to enter the competitive job market or even to manage noncompetitive work of any kind of complexity. But successful achievement of some tasks is important for self-esteem. Here a sheltered workshop may be useful.

It is necessary to reemphasize the factor of getting for the patient the kind of residence that is best suited for his needs. Is he better off with his family, even if some of the members are disturbed, than living alone? Since family stress is principally responsible for relapses, family therapy, as has been mentioned before, may be an essential aspect of treatment. Where the patient is expected to live at home, where family members are too demanding or too hostile, and where they refuse counseling or therapy, living arrangements away from home will have to be considered. (See also Qs 367, 368, and 374.)

Q374: In treating a chronic mentally ill patient recently released from a hospital, what are some of the problems that come up and what do you do about them?

A374: First, I would consider the matter of housing and living arrangements for those who cannot, should not, or will not live with their families. The movement toward deinstitutionalization of patients is a humane but idealistic one. Communities are still not prepared to receive and accept mentally ill persons, and resist having such persons in their neighborhoods. Patients, consequently, have been released from hospitals to wander about the streets or to dwell in single occupancy rooms under squalid unsupervised conditions. Many of them would have been better off remaining in state hospitals, inadequate as the staffing and treatment services may have been. Quality treatment is impossible in situations where living arrangements are bad. A good many chronically ill patients are incapable of looking after themselves and require some person to oversee their activities so that they are cared for properly. All this costs money, and not enough money has been available to provide for housing and adequate physical care.

Second, the patient should be seen regularly by a good psychiatrist who manages the overall treatment program and sees to it that the patient taking drugs is neither overmedicated or undermedicated. Since the care of not a few of these patients will come under the jurisdiction of the community, assigned psychiatrists will have to relate to the public sector. There is resistance among some psychiatrists, as well as other professionals, to working in the public sector or in agencies supported by public funds, not only because the monetary and status rewards do not compare favorably with other areas of practice, but because of the risk of exposing themselves to attack and harassment by eager politicians, investigators, and newspaper reporters bent on uncovering scandal and gaining publicity for themselves. For these and other reasons there has been a shortage of good psychiatric personnel for work with chronic patients, and the turnover of staff in clinics and agencies causes lack of continuity of care. Patients must go through the travail of periodically forming new relationships with strange professionals.

Third, community aftercare services should be fully utilized for day care, social therapy, occupational therapy, recreation and rehabilitation. The use of a sheltered workshop can be a helpful asset in suitable patients, with the realization that some patients will probably never be able completely to return to a normal competitive work role.

Fourth, a hospital resource should be available for short-term hospitalization should this be necessary. The psychiatric unit in a general hospital is adequate for this purpose.

Fifth, psychotherapy on some level, ranging from supportive to behavioral to dynamically oriented therapy, will be most effective where the above priorities are adequately fulfilled. (See also Qs 367, 368, and 373.)

Q375: What about work therapy for the chronic mentally ill person?

A375: A good rehabilitation unit should have vocational rehabilitation as part of its program. Job training, vocational counseling, sheltered workshops, and careful protected job placement are important. If possible, some compensation should be given the patient for work done while learning. This can contribute greatly to the patient's self-esteem. Maintenance drug therapy should be continued during job placement because stresses are inevitable and the relapse rate is high when the patient is withdrawn from medication.

Q376: How can you make sure chronic mentally ill patients take their medications?

A376: This constitutes a great problem and some provision has to be made to monitor drug compliance and to check that the patient is not overmedicated. Where the patient is seen regularly in an outpatient clinic or private office there are some safeguards, although this is not guaranteed. An occasional visit by a social worker or psychiatric nurse is often fruitful in maintaining contact with the patient and family and checking on the medication schedule.

G. *Personality Disorders*

Q377: How would you distinguish between a personality trait and a personality disorder?

A377: We all "normally" have personality traits which spread along a broad band of reactions some of which might be considered egregious. Their differentiation from an actual personality disorder is their *degree* of pathogenicity. If they impede the individual's happiness, relationships with others, capacities for self-fulfillment, work, creativity, and social adaptation, we would consider the diagnosis a personality disorder.

Q378: How would you handle pathological character traits when you perceive them in a patient?

A378: Interpreting character drives in a way that will be therapeutic is an art. Generally, characterologic traits are so ego-syntonic that the individual accepts them as much a part of himself as the skin. If he acknowledges any unusual traits, and admits they are self-defeating, they are indulged in a self-punitive way as part of his masochistic defensive system, or they are relished as unique signs of distinction. Reactions to interpretations of anger, offensiveness, denial, disbelief or detachment can have a negative effect on the therapeutic alliance.

One way of softening the negative impact of interpretations is to couch them in terms of universals. In this way, one hopes to avoid a disintegration of the therapeutic relationship. For example, the following statements were offered patients:

> (Strong dependency traits in a man) "Many people come through a difficult childhood with scars that burden them. Because of an unfulfilled early life they try to make up for satisfactions they

failed to get by looking for and getting dependent on a better, more idealized parent figure. Could it be that you are reaching for a more fulfilling relationship which you believe your wife is not supplying?"

(Masochistic tendency) "There is really nothing so unusual in the way you are reacting. People who are angry at what has happened to them often are very guilty and may seek to punish themselves for even feeling angry."

(Detachment) "It is only natural that when a person feels hurt he seeks to protect himself from his feelings. Sometimes not feeling emotions or physically getting away from people is an effective defensive maneuver. But there are penalities one pays for detachment."

(Perfectionism) "Doing things perfectionistically is one way people have of protecting themselves. The only trouble is that nobody can ever be perfect, and if perfection is a goal one always has to suffer."

By avoiding confronting the patient directly with a character defect one may obliquely be able to penetrate defenses. Once the patient acknowledges a problem openly, confrontation can then be more direct and personal. The therapist should watch the patient's reactions to interpretations to see whether the patient is strong enough to tolerate and make use of them. Initial reactions should not be taken at face value. As long as there is evidence that confirm the assumptions of the therapist, interpretations should carefully be woven into questions, continuously presenting these to the patient in the hope that the patient will eventually make the proper connections.

Q379: How would you view Kohut's ideas of the idealizing and mirror transference in narcissistic patients?

A379: Some therapists believe that the narcissistic personality disorder is a product of deficits acquired in the developmental years related to the archaic idealized self-object and to fixation on certain aspects of archaic objects. They search for and usually find evidences of this in the transference relationships the patient develops with them in therapy. The patient will appear to project his needs for a grandiose self onto the therapist in the form of what Kohut calls an "idealizing transference." He will also project his needs for exhibitionism and greatness in the "mirror transference." The proper handling of any transference reactions with empathy and without rejection or retaliating counter-transference will determine the fate of the analysis. While there are other ways of explicating the dynamics of narcissistic personality disorders, Kohut (1971) does provide guidelines for management that may be helpful to therapists who accept his formulations.

Q380: What is the best treatment for narcissistic personality disorders?

A380: There is no one best treatment since each therapeutic program must be tailored to the patient's needs. However, combined individual and group therapy, in my opinion, gets the best results. The confrontations by the patient's peers in the group cut through characterologic defenses rapidly. Multiple transferences permit the patient to experience feelings and conflicts that have been repressed since childhood. The family as a whole as constituted by the group provides support when the patient's defenses are low. Individual therapy, I believe, is also indispensable to work through the primitive transferences, the faulty perception of early objects, and the conflicts and feelings stirred up in the group. It serves also to provide support in the face of attacks by the group.

Q381: Are there personality typologies that correlate with hysterical or obsessive symptoms?

A381: The so-called hysterical personality, i.e., one disposed to narcissistic self-indulgence, histrionic displays, needs to sexualize relationships, etc., has traditionally been credited with a predisposition to hysterical symptomatology. While this may be true, other personality typologies also may demonstrate conversion and dissociative symptoms. Indeed, most people, given the appropriate stressful circumstances, may display on occasion at least minor and temporary hysterical symptoms. Such terms as "paralyzed with fear," "struck dumb with astonishment," "blind with fury" have not crept into the lexicon of everyday phraseology by accident. Insofar as obsessive-compulsive neurosis is concerned, there is a definite correlation with personality traits of over-intellectualizing, meticulousness, scrupulousness, attentiveness to details, etc. Both the hysterical and obsessive personality types have distinctive cognitive modes of learning, which, it is claimed, may advantageously be taken into account in therapy (Horowitz, 1976, 1977).

Q382: What is the difference between borderline, narcissistic, and schizoid personality disorders?

A382: The characteristic feature of the *borderline personality disorder* is instability of interpersonal relationships and emotions. This instability sponsors continuous problems in dealings with people and in expectations and demands made of others. Moods fluctuate, with outbursts of inappropriate anger and difficulty in controlling it when it erupts. Identity problems are also present, punctuated by periods of intense loneliness and boredom. When the stress level becomes sufficiently high, the symptoms may spill over into the psychotic sphere, but unlike the schizophrenic upset there is usually a rapid recovery. Because of the inherent instability, borderline personalities find their marital, social, and work relationships in turmoil ("I can't depend on his moods or behavior from one minute to the next"). Decisions may be made on the basis of momentary anger that may shape the individual's life adversely for some time thereafter.

The *schizoid personality disorder* is organized around the defense of detachment. The individual is often referred to as a "loner" or "isolate" with whom it is difficult to establish a relationship. There is a consuming flatness of mood with an inability to resonate through the spectrum of normal feelings from happiness to sorrow to anger. People who seek to establish contacts with schizoid personalities complain that they are withdrawn, isolated and "standoffish" ("I'd like to shake him into reacting and feeling"). Daydreaming and living in fantasy are common. The schizoid personality disorder must be differentiated from the schizotypal personality disorder which is closer to schizophrenia and in which there are distortions in thinking (ideas of reference and influence, depersonalization, peculiar fantasies and paranoidal notions), odd manner of speaking, and episodes of eccentric behavior.

The *narcissistic personality disorder* is centered around a self-oriented core of grandiosity, a need to constantly promote oneself, insatiable exhibitionism, preoccupations with one's personal self-importance, and selfish demands on others with reluctant reciprocation. On the surface the individual may radiate promises of warmth, charm, and "givingness" but these are proffered only as means of displaying oneself or inviting bounties of praise and admiration. Emotions may be explosive with periods of depression and anger. This personality type often is fused with a *histrionic personality* disorder given to excitability, manipulativeness, self-dramatization, and acting-out.

Since there are no hard lines of demarcation that separate these personality disorders from each other, some confusion in diagnosis may occur. It may be necessary to obtain information from sources other than the patient, if this is possible, to get data which will aid in assigning the patient to a special category.

There are some authorities who are convinced that the type of personality disorder that emerges is the product of genetic and constitutional factors. Others believe that personality problems reflect the stage of development at which arrested growth (fixation) occurred due to environmental traumas and serious deprivation in essential needs. Therapy therefore is directed at uncovering and resolving the fixation by transference analysis and working-through the developmental blocks in the more congenial atmosphere of the therapeutic relationship. Some therapists focus on reinforcing constructive traits through behavioral approaches and reinforcement, while others firmly believe that developmental deficits are best fulfilled by supplying the unsatisfied needs through empathy, genuineness, encouragement, and respect for the individual's right to make choices. Whichever viewpoints prevail, personality disorders are difficult to treat because the distortions they engender are ego-syntonic.

Q383: What criteria do you use for a diagnosis of borderline personality disorder? I find it difficult to make a proper diagnosis.

A383: I believe that the basic symptoms of the borderline are great impulsiveness, difficulties in self-control, emotional instability, tendencies to act out, vulnerability to selective stresses, fragility of defenses, pervasive anger, inability to sustain good interpersonal relationships while needing such relationships, a somewhat impaired reality sense, tendencies toward projection, a defective sense of identity, periodic bouts of depression with proclivities for suicide, transient psychotic episodes with rapid recoverability, and likelihood of abuse of alcohol and drugs. Superimposed on these core symptoms are wide variations in character traits and neurotic defenses which tend to obscure the

diagnosis. If one considers the core symptoms as primary and the existing neurotic symptoms as secondary, there should be less difficulty
in making a proper diagnosis.

**Q384: What do you think of present-day concepts about the bor-
derline patient organized around object relations theory?**

A384: People have a penchant for jumping on bandwagons and psychotherapists are no exception. In their eagerness to find a theory that
explains the many contradictions of human behavior, therapists have
shown a relatively noncritical acceptance of the ideas and formulations
of authorities who present their concepts with firmness and conviction.

The dynamics and treatment of the borderline patient have occupied
a good deal of contemporary interest. Some therapists consider the
contributions of object relations theorists advanced and brilliant. On
the other hand, a gathering group of dissenters, while admitting the
ingeniousness of the developmental theories, question their validity.
Perhaps the most extensive criticisms have come from Heimann (1966)
and Calef and Weinshel (1979), the latter expressing reservations
about the clarity of the theoretical conceptualizations and the usefulness of the advocated technical procedures. Others have branded current ideas about object relations pejoratively as a jerry-built structure
of metaphor upon metaphor compounded out of a pseudo-synthesis of
Kleinian, Bionian, ego-psychological, object relations, and other theories. These criticisms, it seems to me, are altogether harsh, for if the
authors under criticism have done nothing else, they have challenged
the sanctity of some existing metapsychological credendas and opened
the way to a reassessment of their value. This does not certify concepts
which modern researchers on development would consider questionable, such as some ideas about infantile development and ideation. Object relations theory is perhaps more tenable then tripartite structural
theory in accounting for some phenomena of the borderline state, but
it still does not embrace the multiple variables that enter into borderline personality formation.

**Q385: In treating borderline patients some analysts claim that
classical analysis can be used to develop and then resolve
a transference neurosis through interpretation. Others
claim that a transference neurosis should be assiduously**

avoided while utilizing analytic techniques, including interpretation, in an expressive psychoanalytically oriented format. Still others recommend a supportive type of
psychotherapy and discourage the use of analysis altogether. In your opinion, what *is* the best treatment for borderline conditions?

A385: There is no such thing as a unitary borderline condition. Rather,
there is a wide spectrum of borderline states which possess a varying
pathology. Some borderlines possess less fragile defenses than others.
Some are so poorly defended that they shatter easily. It is consequently
necessary to design therapy to "where the patient is," to what he can
best utilize at the time he is being seen.

There are borderline patients, though admittedly few, who may be
able to tolerate the technical neutrality and anonymity of the classical
analyst, and who can utilize the therapist's interpretations of an evolving transference neurosis in a beneficial way. There are other borderlines who will fall apart with such an approach and who require more
of a "here-and-now" kind of handling, away from a focus on historical
material. In some of the latter patients, ego strengthening may occur
after a prolonged period and they may then be able to tolerate analytic
techniques that lead to regression and that can productively be interpreted by the therapist. Generally, the approaches of different therapists accord with their concept of the dynamics of the borderline case,
their skill and experience in working with borderlines, and their management of countertransference. If one studies the methods of Kernberg, Frosch, Eissler, Knight, Stern, Bion, Rosenfeld, Winnicott, A.
Wolberg, Zetzel, Grinker, Masterson and others, one can see how
Freudian, object relations, and other developmental and ego psychological models fashion methods that vary widely in design and objectives. Yet, according to the published reports, they work effectively for
every author who writes about them.

A large number of therapists prefer a psychoanalytically based exploratory therapy utilizing eclectic techniques, e.g., pharmacotherapy,
group therapy, family therapy, etc. suited to their patient's immediate
needs. Some therapists find their preferred modus operandi psychoanalytic object relations theory, which they believe allows them better
to understand and to deal with the primitive defensive systems of the
borderline, the incessant conflict between self and object representations, the lack of unification of the psychic apparatus, and the disturbing emergence in these patients of contradictory ego stages that

are dealt with by dissociation and splitting rather than repression. Primitive transferences and defenses are consistently interpreted in an atmosphere of technical neutrality "and this requires a purely expressive, meticulously analytic approach, although not psychoanalysis proper" (Kernberg, 1980B) Not all therapists nor all patients can work with every method proposed by different authorities. It is generally important, therefore, for a therapist to experiment with a number of recommended methods and then to concentrate on the one that is best suited to his temperament, philosophy, and skill.

Q386: Are there any pointers on techniques to use with a borderline patient who has already failed to benefit from treatment?

A386: The therapeutic focus in borderline patients should be organized around the here-and-now rather than the past, genetic reconstructions being delayed until the patient is well along in therapy, and after the therapist is assured that the patient can adequately reality-test. Since acting-out is so frequent and so destructive to the treatment process, the therapist should try to interrupt it as soon as its presence is perceived. The environmental situation should be structured so that it imposes as few temptations to act out as possible. Where a positive relationship exists, the setting of limits to destructive behavior may be urgent. Negative transference should not be permitted to build up and the defensive operations it stimulates will require interpretation whenever they first appear in order to prevent their interfering with the therapeutic alliance. Interpretations should be carefully constructed so as to support and enhance and not to undermine the already fragile self-esteem of the patient. Projective techniques are useful and include "the use of the other" to preserve the projective defenses of the patient, recognizing that when he speaks of others he may be talking about himself. Roundabout, indirect interpretations are made to attitudes, dreams, fantasies, impulses and behavior to circumvent denial tendencies.

Visits should be no more frequent than once or twice weekly to reduce the likelihood of a transference neurosis or transference psychosis. Probing for psychotic material should be avoided and the focus should be on reality-oriented areas. Active reassurance, advice giving and environmental manipulation are freely employed at first and a challenging of the patient's distorted ideas is delayed until the therapeutic relationship can be depended on. Role-playing, pharmacotherapy, and other adjuncts may be useful at certain phases. Group therapy is especially of value since it dilutes the transference and helps the patient keep reality-oriented. The patient may need prolonged therapy, which in the more serious cases can go on for years. (For further ideas about therapy see Wolberg, 1977, pp. 901-906).

Q387: Are the transferences of borderline patients different from those of neurotic patients?

A387: The transferences of borderline patients are more chaotic than those of neurotic patients, reflecting many primitive self and object representations. These are especially imbedded in sadomasochistic impulses and they stimulate archaic defenses, such as dissociation, splitting, omnipotence, denial and projective identification akin to those that had originally weakened the ego during the developmental years. At the same time the patient tries to hold onto and control the relationship with the therapist by appeasing maneuvers, even though the therapist is feared and distrusted. Often the patient attempts to justify his embitterment by experiencing the therapist as a hostile, arbitrary, and conniving person. These maneuvers are bound to stimulate countertransference in the therapist, which, if uncontrolled, will cause the patient to consider his paranoia justified. By reacting to the therapist as a hostile object, the patient may then try to break up the therapeutic alliance. Because reality-testing is strained, interpretations of the therapist fall on deaf ears. What makes the situation even more difficult is acting-out within and outside of the therapeutic situation through which the patient derives a direct gratification for his sadomasochistic impulses. Even though the patient may sometimes mouth what seems like insight, unlike the neurotic he rarely integrates it as a corrective force.

H. Miscellaneous Problems

Q388: Have any methods been successful in anorexia nervosa? Is ECT ever done here? Is there a cure on its own without treatment? Can you cite a regime one can follow?

A388: Anorexia nervosa is a difficult condition to treat. No single method has proven universally successful, including psychoanalytic, behavioral and pharmacological treatment. An interesting regime is described by Anderson (1979) who recommends an empirical, team-oriented, *inpatient* program with eclectic methods. Most important in the first stage of therapy is nutritional rehabilitation administered by a trained nursing staff at the same time that issues of growing up and psychological conflict are dealt with. The patient is diverted from concentrating on calories and weight even though these are the concern of the treatment staff. Once 80 to 90 percent of the ideal weight has been restored, therapy changes from supportive to insight-oriented sessions several times weekly. Common issues explored are the fear of losing control, and problems of separation-individuation, devalued self-esteem and perfectionism. Group and family therapy may also be employed. Finally, nutritional and exercise controls are returned to the patient who orders a personal diet with the aid of nutritional counseling. Where depression exists, a tricyclic antidepressant may be given. Follow-up is vital with guidance and reinforcements for social readaptation. Approximately 25 percent of anorexic patients remain severely ill and a certain number show some residual disability. Continued psychotherapy may be necessary. ECT is of little or no value. The outlook without therapy is extremely poor.

Q389: What recommended readings on anorexia nervosa would you advise?

A389: This disturbing illness has been refractory to most treatments including psychoanalysis, psychotherapy, ECT, psychotropic drugs, desensitization, operant conditioning and group methods. A combination of psychoanalytically oriented therapy and family therapy have yielded encouraging results (Liebman et al., 1974; Rosman et al., 1975). An interesting review article is that of Bemis (1978). The book by Bruch (1973) and her article (1975) on the subject can be recommended.

Q390: Aren't hysterical problems among the easiest to treat?

A390: Conversion and dissociative symptoms may rapidly resolve with suggestion, hypnosis, or narcosynthesis. Hysterical personality problems are another matter. They can be among the most difficult to manage. The patient makes a rapid and intense transference, becomes demanding of attention and nurturing, tends to sexualize the relationship, often reacting with rage at the therapist's refusal to respond, feels trapped by the ensuing dependency on the therapist, and fails to correlate feelings with ideas, thus circumventing insight. Resistance to true therapeutic involvement is great, even though on the surface there is play-acting of a good relationship. Powerful repressive defenses shield unconscious conflicts from awareness. Under these circumstances countertransference can scarcely be avoided, the acting-out of which will further complicate the situation and lead to a therapeutic impasse. On the other hand, because transference can become strong, intensive psychoanalysis with evolvement and resolution of a transference neurosis may produce depth changes not possible with any other method. Not all hysterical patients, however, lend themselves to formal analysis. Short-term therapy and psychoanalytically oriented psychotherapy with the analysis of immediate interpersonal relationships may bring the patient to a satisfactory adaptive equilibrium.

Q391: What is the best approach for obesity? Are there any good readings on the subject?

A391: Many designs for obesity have been devised but no one program is universally successful with all patients. Among the most common programs are

1) those that rely on group methods and peer pressure like Weight Watchers;
2) self-regulating methods oriented around behavioral techniques with self-monitoring, contingency contracting, and self-rewarding (Malcolm et al., 1977; Mann, 1972);
3) operant methods that deal with the contingencies that initiate and maintain overeating (Stuart and Davis, 1972);
4) aversive procedures (Janda and Rimm, 1972);
5) hypnosis (Stanton, 1975);
6) anorexant medications (Dykes, 1974); and
7) dietary regulation (Tullis, 1973).

With varying success psychotherapy and psychoanalysis (Bruch, 1973) have also been employed, as have surgical bypass operations in life-threatening obesity (Solow et al., 1974). Since each individual's problem is unique, treatment must be tailor-made for one's personality and needs. Generally a combination of methods including behavioral techniques works best.

Q392: What do you think of self-help programs for obesity?

A392: Unless the individual is very highly motivated, self-help programs, whether they are dietary in nature or related to a comprehensive behavioral self-control design or to other devices, are either ineffective or only of temporary help.

Q393: Can hypnosis control or eliminate the smoking habit?

A393: Success in smoking control has been modest with all treatments, including behavioral methods, stimulus satiation, group methods, pharmacological aids, psychotherapy, and hypnosis. Hypnosis may be employed to reduce tension (Spiegel and Spiegel, 1978) and to enhance the patient's resolve to overcome the habit; some therapists find an ego-building tape useful for this purpose (Wolberg, 1980, pp. 223-234; 1977, pp. 931-932). Operant methods, contingency contracting and behavioral self-control procedures have also been employed with varying success (Bernstein, 1969; Lichtenstein and Keutzer, 1971). What is probably best is a multidimensional approach tailored to the patient's needs.

Q394: Can you treat organic mental disorders with psychotherapy?

A394: Organic mental disorders cover a variety of conditions chiefly caused by neurological problems (e.g. tumors), the ravages of deteriorating effects on the brain of aging, and the unscrupulous imbibing of toxic substances like alcohol. Some of the ensuing changes, like those caused by toxic substances, may be reversible. Other changes are permanent, as where actual tissue destruction has occurred. The impact of brain disturbance on the well-being of the person and on adjustment will depend on the areas of the brain that are damaged and the functions they mediate. Even more important are the psychological effects on the individual. People react differently to functional impairments. For example, memory loss in an obsessional personality is apt to create great anxiety and feelings of intolerable self-devaluation. In other personalities deep depression may result; in still others consuming rage or paranoidal projections are seen. These psychological symptoms are definitely amenable to psychotherapy if a working relationship can be established and if motivation toward change is developed.

Q395: Disability problems have been increasing. How do these evolve and why are they so hard to treat? Can any preventive measures be used to avoid prolonged disability?

A395: Disability problems must be distinguished from malingering in that symptoms in disability are real; in malingering they are faked.
    As a result of an accident the following events are likely to occur.:

1) There is first a shock reaction during which there may be displayed detachment, a dazed response, and a tendency to deny.
2) As the implications of the accident or injury sink in, there develops a shattering of the sense of mastery and a weakening of customary defenses.
3) An elaboration of secondary defenses develops which if unsuccessful stimulates regressive defenses such as dependency and phobic re-

actions. Masochistic maneuvers are also common, in part as a device to promote rescue responses from authority.

4) Activation of latent neurotic and psychotic tendencies can occur as anxiety heightens.

5) There is development of revenge motives against the world, the company, the employer, or the individual's supervisor, with the childish aim of punishing them by remaining ill. Transference reactions are common here with projection of feelings of anger toward surrogate parental or sibling figures or a turning of hostility on the self with depression and psychosomatic symptoms.

6) Problems develop at home because of the disabled individual's boredom, incessant demands for attention and sympathy, and the reversal of roles, as where a wife, for example, becomes the dominant breadwinner.

7) Secondary gains sustain the disability in the form of compensation benefits, freedom from work responsibility, and a feeling of importance as the individual seeks the center of the stage through dramatic accounts of his accident and the atrocities he claims he has encountered in medical care.

8) There is a gradual crippling of effective functioning as dependency deepens, and as a fear of performance increases in the event a return to work becomes threatening. This aggravates symptoms, which are used to protect against being forced to return to work.

Governmental laws and company policies unfortunately support this chain of events and create a class of "crippled beggars" (Ross, 1977). What has been recommended are new laws and policies that would put a time limit on disability benefits, keeping these considerably below what the individual ordinarily earned. Instead, a liberal allowance should be made for financing rehabilitation and psychological therapy.

Q396: Are there any guidelines for the proper management of disability cases?

A396: Many problems invest efforts to work therapeutically with disability cases. In the first place the disabled person usually resents being considered a psychiatric casualty. His suffering and pain are real, not imaginary. Motivation for psychiatric help is usually lacking, even though tension, pain, discomfort, and depression exist along with anger and guilt feelings. On the surface the individual seems cooperative with the initial interviewer, but it is readily apparent that he is on his guard. In spite of this the interviewer must try to establish some kind of relationship with the patient. With the aim of establishing a diagnosis, a good history is important. If possible, an interview with a person who has known the disabled individual before the accident or injury may be helpful. What problems, physical and psychological, preceded the incident? Did the individual's personality change after the incident? Where they are available, medical and personnel records may be important. During the initial interview no intimation should be made that disability payments will stop if symptoms disappear. The attitude toward the physical complaints should more or less be that they understandably are disturbing and create a good deal of tension and pain for the individual. In treatment the therapist may be able to help control pain and tension since this will relieve suffering. An offer may be made to demonstrate how this may be done and toward this end relaxation methods may be taught the person. Once a relationship is established, it may be possible to refer the individual to a sheltered workshop to help restore confidence in himself. Other modalities may be employed, such as marital counseling where marital problems exist, or behavior therapy and tricyclic antidepressants for phobias, depression and pain. Psychotherapy should be started, preferably on a group level.

Q397: Have therapeutic communities proven helpful in drug dependence programs?

A397: Yes, but results are good only where the patient stays in the therapeutic community for more than two months. A lesser stay yields no greater improvement than where simple detoxification is done. Apparently it takes a period of time before the patient integrates himself into the community.

Q398: Is there any evidence that drug abuse programs are truly effective?

A398: A number of studies bear out their effectiveness. A good follow-up study is that of Simpson and Savage (1980), who report impressive behavioral improvements associated with treatment.

Q399: Does PCP, which is gaining popularity among drug-experimenting adolescents, have a damaging effect on brain function?

A399: Studies have shown the chronic use of PCP (phencyclidine), apart from inducing aggressive and belligerent personality reactions, can impair memory and judgment, probably aspects of an organic brain disorder.

Q400: Does oral maintenance methadone really render a heroin addict free from the need for further heroin?

A400: In some cases, yes, particularly where auxiliary aids like a therapeutic environment and counseling are employed. In a considerable number of addicts, however, illegal sources of heroin supply are still utilized supplementarily whenever the addict can find the money to acquire the drug.

Q401: Can you do heroin detoxification on an outpatient basis?

A401: Yes, but the results are hazardous. Inpatient detoxification is far more successful.

Q402: In dealing with a sex offender, namely a rapist remanded by the courts, what would you focus on in therapy?

A402: Once some kind of working relationship is established, the focus in most rapists may be on the devalued self-image that makes them feel unacceptable by women on whom they have to force themselves. Coordinate themes are fear of and compensatory hatred of women (stemming from early resentments toward parenting figures) and deficient feelings of masculinity which incite a "macho" kind of violence to prove themselves. Sex in the rapist is an act of violence rather than expression of love, and correcting this distortion will involve a good deal of therapeutic work on the character structure over a period of time.

Q403: In treating hyperactive children, are there any drugs that are effective and have less addictive potential than Ritalin or amphetamines?

A403: Pemoline (Cylert) has been used with some advantage including its once-a-day administration and longer action. The usual dose is 2.25 milligrams per kilogram of weight or an average of 60 mg. per day.

Q404: What is the preferred way of working with an acting-out adolescent?

A404: Acting-out behavior, such as drug abuse, is often a symptom of family pathology. Family therapy is consequently the most important modality, especially in working through problems of separation-individuation, hostility, etc. A peer group is also a helpful activity for the adolescent. While a restructuring of relationships and lines of communication is fundamental and calls for a dynamic psychotherapeutic approach, certain adjunctive measures along behavioral and recreational lines can also be coordinately useful.

Q405: How would you manage a school phobia in a child?

A405: A school phobia is really a family problem and usually involves an immature, indulgent, or highly controlling mother who has been unwilling to separate herself from the child. A prephobic conditioning occurs prior to the school years. A child who has been reared with the idea that the world is an unsafe place, and that a mother is necessary to protect one and make things safe, is particularly vulnerable when thrust into the strange environment of a school. Often the mother is unaware of her own dependent needs and of her ambivalence to her own mother, which she is projecting onto the child.

Once we have ruled out reality causes for fear, such as stressful situations within the school itself, juvenile terrorists who threaten or attack the child, a disturbed teacher, identifiable handicaps like reading disabilities and other cognitive dysfunctions, or childhood depression, we may apply ourselves to treatment. The first step is to insist that the parents be firm with the child to the effect that school must be attended. Sometimes the child will have developed a host of somatic complaints (headaches, "stomach trouble," intestinal cramps, etc.) to reinforce the stay-at-home position. After a physical examination has revealed no organic problem, the parents will have to handle their fear that they will damage the child by insisting on school attendance. They must be indoctrinated with the fact that the longer the child stays away from class the more difficult it will be for the child to return. The school personnel may have to be brought into treatment planning to bolster the parent's resolve that the child must go to school even if the child complains and acts ill in class.

Some family therapy with the parents is usually necessary to apprise them of their own involvement in the situation (in terms of their personal history and problems) and to give them support in the handling of the child's recalcitrance. The father or mother may physically have to bring the child to school at first and the therapist should be available on the telephone to render assistance to the flagging parent who is wilting under the child's intransigence. Occasionally, behavioral desensitization is helpful as an adjunct (Eysenck, 1960a).

If the child's fear is associated with another child who terrorizes or threatens, this will have to be handled with the school authorities. Should the problem be the child's classroom teacher who is disturbed, the child may do better in another class. Coordinately, psychotherapy may be needed for the child, as well as the parents, and sometimes they may all be seen together. If the child has a serious emotional problem, such as a depression, intensive therapy may be required and perhaps some antidepressant medications. The mother may have to continue in long-term therapy after the child's symptoms have come under control to work through her own dependency problem.

Q406: What is the best approach to use in a violent teenager who is difficult to control, beats his parents, and has even been arrested once?

A406: Where there has been a serious breach of the law, responsibility for the treatment should be shared with the juvenile justice system. Responsibility should also be shared with an internist and neurologist in terms of a good physical and neurological examination to rule out neurological disease (e.g., brain tumor, epilepsy, vascular abnormalities, limbic system dysfunction, etc.) in which violence may be a prominent symptom. It is important furthermore to rule out minimum brain damage, acute schizophrenia or a manic attack.

In the actual management of the case the therapist will need to handle his own anxieties and his countertransferences. The problem, of course, once a diagnosis is made, is not only getting the patient into therapy, but keeping him there. Dealing with poor motivation for help, with resistance to establishing a relationship, and other obstructions calls for specialized help such as an experienced child therapist who works with adolescents. I would recommend listening to audio cassette recordings by Miller (1980), Dince (1981), and Marohn (1977).

Q407: Should group therapy be employed with adolescents?

A407: A peer group can be the treatment of choice. One should nevertheless not minimize the need for coordinate individual therapy with a therapist who can act as a role model. The therapist-leader of an adolescent group requires training and experience in working with adolescents.

Q408: Is depth therapy or psychoanalysis suitable for adolescents?

A408: Usually no. Adolescents going through developmental crises should not be stirred up with depth therapy. Once the adolescent has stabilized in early adult life, he may not need therapy or, should he require help, he might then be evaluated for depth therapy. Adolescents in crisis who need help may benefit from counseling or psychotherapy focused on symptom relief or behavioral alterations.

Q409: Has the suicide rate among young people increased?

A409: Drastically so. As many as 10 percent of the adolescents at school are at risk. The suicidal attempt may be a manifestation of deep depression, an attempt at communication to invoke sympathy from or to punish caretaking persons, the consequences of a life crisis with which the adolescent is unable to cope, or a psychotic act.

Q410: I get the impression that many old people assigned to nursing homes are really psychiatric cases. Can anything psychotherapeutically be done for them?

A410: People in nursing homes are often oldsters who, while they may have been given a physical diagnosis, actually have organic brain problems and have not been able to be cared for elsewhere. State hospitals tend to shirk responsibility for these patients and nursing homes are not really equipped to deal with these aged psychiatric patients. Facilities for care of this group are woefully lacking. Nosologically the patients usually fall into the diagnostic category of Senile Dementia and Arteriosclerotic Brain Disease. What these people require are better housing and total care facilities, as well as counseling, medical services, and supportive therapy. This becomes an expensive proposition that few communities are capable of affording, and that nevertheless should be a high-level priority. Psychotherapy is considered one of their lesser requirements compared to other urgent medical and physical care needs.

Q411: Can psychiatric symptoms be caused or exacerbated by medical illness?

A411: Definitely—and the reverse is also true. There is always feedback between psychological, physical, and environmental factors and sometimes it is difficult to know which is the primary etiological agent. A thorough physical examination is apt to reveal previously unrecognized and undiagnosed medical problems in a sizable number of cases. Included are hyperthyroidism, hypothyroidism, liver disease, diabetes, neurologic illness (e.g. Wilson's disease), dietary deficiencies (e.g. folic acid defects), syphilis, blood dyscrasias (e.g. severe anemia), temporal lobe epilepsy, circulatory disorders, and endocrine disease. Treatment of underlying medical problems may bring about improvement in the psychological status. This is not to say that psychological difficulties cannot occur independent of a coexisting medical problem. In such cases, we would expect an exaggeration of such difficulties as a consequence of organic illness. It is essential to rule out medical conditions in all psychiatric problems and to treat them where they exist without prejudicing the employment of psychotherapy.

Q412: Are there any special problems in working with patients who come from poverty levels?

A412: There are, of course, individual differences, but, in general, such patients are apt to be somewhat handicapped in capacities for self-observation and in their ability to communicate inner feelings. This does not mean one cannot train such patients in these areas. The biggest problem is the therapist's ability to relate to patients who come from a different social class, to empathize with them while avoiding a patronizing attitude, to accept their projections which at times may assume a paranoid-like quality, to understand and operate within the framework of the cultural background that molds value systems differing from one's own, and to refrain from utilizing language and concepts that are beyond the patient's comprehension.

Once a conformity of language is established, there is no reason why a dynamic frame of reference cannot be utilized. In the main, one has to focus on practical problems in the life situation and to assign tasks that the patient agrees are important. The patient may then be enjoined to examine his feelings regarding these zones of interest. Where competence in dealing with life's difficulties has always been lacking, a scaling down of goals may be essential, striving to adapt the patient to as high a level of functioning as is within his potential. Family therapy with role-playing may be helpful as a principal technique because neurotic family interaction commonly exaggerates the patient's problems. Among obstacles blocking treatment is the tendency on the part of the patient to break appointments, to come late for sessions, to distrust authority, and to anticipate rejection of himself and his demands. At the beginning of treatment, a working relationship is facilitated by the therapist taking a counseling, advocacy role and rendering some active help in a current problem. The economically disadvantaged individual has a long history of being dependent on agencies, institutions and other persons to meet his basic needs, and he cannot be expected to assume significant responsibility, at least at the start of treatment. Gradually a trusting relationship will come about as the patient dissociates the therapist from his image of arbitrary and punitive authority. When this happens one may begin to approach inner feelings and conflicts and then to talk about their origin in the past. It is essential to accept modest goals in treatment, such as symptom relief or crisis resolution, realizing that the disadvantaged individual who survives on welfare may not be employed or even willing to consider job training and the accepting of a job. Considering his relative lack of skills, work is apt to pay him little more than he gets from welfare. Helpful readings include: Haggstrom, 1964; Minuchin, 1968; Goldensohn, 1981; Goldensohn and Haar, 1974; and J. Spiegel, 1976.

XVI. Transference and Countertransference

Transference, perhaps the most important of Freud's discoveries, is considered by many to be the cornerstone of psychoanalytic treatment. Its universal appearance during psychotherapy and the fact that it can both expedite and retard progress make its proper handling essential. What constitutes proper handling, however, is a topic for disputation. What are the forms through which transference displays itself? Should it be encouraged as a means of dredging up from the unconscious the sour curds of one's past? If so, is it best exploded in concentrated form, or should its power be attenuated to bring it out under restraint? Need it be exposed or manifested at all? In what ways does transference act as resistance and how does one deal with its interferences? Is countertransference inevitable in all cases or does it selectively show itself? Can countertransference serve a useful purpose in therapy? Are negative feelings in the therapist always evidence of countertransference? These are a few of the questions puzzling students which are taken up in some detail in this section.

Q413: Aren't "transference," "relationship," and "corrective emotional experience" interchangeable terms?

A413: Transference has become a water-downed expression that is sometimes confused with other forms of the patient-therapist relationship. At different times in this relationship the patient will play different roles, depending on the special needs that exist at the time. One of the roles is transference, whose meaning should be restricted to the feelings and reactions that the patient harbors toward significant persons in the past that are now being projected into the present. To a large extent such feelings are repressed and relegated to the oblivion of the unconscious. When they do surface during therapy they give us insight into infantile conflicts. They also tend to distort the immediate reality situation and divert the patient from engaging in goal-directed therapeutic tasks. Because transference can in this way act as a resistance to therapy, an attempt is often made to work it through or resolve it by interpretation whenever traces of archaic stereotyped negative or eroticized reactions manifest themselves. There are circumstances, however, when the allocation and deliberate buildup of transference is encouraged in order to examine its dimensions, origins and effects, and especially how it engenders the present neurosis or character disturbance.

Analysis of transference is the major task in classical analysis and to elicit transference techniques are utilized to encourage regression and the acting out in the therapeutic relationship of repressed feelings and memories. When the buildup becomes so intense that the patient actually confuses the therapist with past important persons the phenomenon is sometimes termed a "transference neurosis." In certain patients, like borderline cases, the behavior may be explosive and psychotic-like (transference psychosis). Utilizing the leverage of the therapeutic alliance that has been built up, and appealing to the patient's "reasonable ego," the therapist actively interprets the patient's transferential responses, with the goals of bringing reality into the picture and of inculcating insight.

"Positive transference" is rooted in the patient's ever-present longing for an idealized parental figure who will love, protect, and lead the patient on to happy security and creative self-fulfillment. "Positive transference" thus is deliberately employed as a catalyzing force to promote supportive and reeducative therapy. It is only when it becomes unreasonable, the patient reaching out for magic in the hope of fulfilling infantile dreams and archaic sexual needs, that the transference must be neutralized by interpretation since its indulgence will interfere with or destroy therapeutic progress.

"Positive transference" should be distinguished from the working alliance in which the patient cooperatively relates to the therapist with expected trust. Experiencing understanding and empathy, the patient is encouraged to distinguish between punitive and nonpunitive authority, and to dissociate the therapist from the judgmental, punitive agencies in his past as well as from their precipitates in his superego. It is this unique kind of relationship that facilitates restoration of morale, alleviation of tension, the ability to divulge and face repudiated impulses and hurtful past experiences, tolerance of confrontations, absorption of constructive suggestions, identification with the value system of the therapist, utilization of reinforcements toward more adaptive modes of coping, and acceptance of clarification and interpretations that will lead to better understanding and a working-through of one's basic problems. The relationship itself then acts as a "corrective emotional experience."

These varying dimensions of the relationship do not operate exclusive of each other, but may shift from one to the other at different phases of the therapeutic process. It is important for the therapist to recognize what is happening to the relationship to avoid a bad impasse, which, should it happen, will eliminate perhaps the most potent corrective force in treatment.

Q414: We know that the patient's reactions to the therapist are important. How do you present this to the patient so he will cooperate in reporting his feelings about the therapist, which in my experience he too often conceals out of embarrassment, anxiety, and so on?

A414: One can say to the patient: "I am constantly going to look for the manner in which you react to me and how you feel about me. The reason for this is that in these reactions we can learn about how you have reacted to your parents and other people better than in wringing it out of your memories, many of which have been forgotten. So no matter how embarrassing it may seem, or how anxious you get, tell me about your feelings and ideas about me so we can both learn about you."

Q415: It is paradoxical to me that transference, which is the central issue in psychoanalysis, is not considered to be of importance in many other forms of therapy like behavior modification. How would you account for this?

A415: I believe that this dilemma can be explained. In classical analysis there is a deliberate creation of transference through frequent visits (four to five sessions weekly), studied anonymity, free association, and other devices for the purpose of activating unconscious and repudiated aspects of early experience. The surfacing of this material is often in the form of projection onto the therapist of the incorporated parental introjects. The working-through of unresolved past needs and conflicts in the more congenial atmosphere of the therapeutic alliance is for the purpose of resolving unconscious conflict, which is what analysts believe to be the pathogenic core of the neurosis.

In other less intensive forms of therapy no attempt is made to liberate unconscious ideation, the focus of therapy being on the more conscious and here-and-now aspects of experience. Repressive defenses are either unaltered or are approached obliquely, with the consequence that transferential projections do not occur with the intensity that they take on in classical analysis, where they may take the form of a stormy transference neurosis or frenzied transference psychosis.

This does not mean that transference is absent in symptom-oriented or problem-solving types of therapy like behavior modification. Transference may appear in attenuated forms as in dreams, in restrained acting-out, or in other highly disguised kinds of behavior. Under such circumstances therapy may still not be interfered with and may proceed satisfactorily with achievement of sought-for goals of problem-solving and symptom alleviation. Sometimes, however, especially where defenses are not too strong, transference may break through in force and act as resistance, under which circumstance its resolution may be required to expedite therapeutic progress.

Q416: Cannot reconstructions of the past from the history of the patient, dreams, and recollections serve as well as activating the past through transference?

A416: Not at all. Such reconstructions may have some effect, but only an attenuated one compared to the insight gained through living the past through in some dramatic situation in the present such as a transference neurosis.

Q417: What is the true value of transference in psychotherapy?

A417: Transference reactions enable us to penetrate into the past of the patient and to see how early experiences with important persons, usually parents and siblings, have produced a paradigm around which the individual fashions many of his present reactions. This knowledge is especially important in patients whose symptoms and behavioral difficulties and problems in their relationships with others are repetitively sustained through the insidious operations of transference. More importantly, the therapist often becomes the target of transference projections and, when this happens, the therapeutic process may get derailed because of resistance to the therapist and to the treatment techniques. Resolution of this resistance (generally through interpretation of what is happening) puts the treatment process back on the rails, so to speak. At the same time, the patient's new insight gives him an opportunity to appraise his behavior from a causative perspective, and, if he is motivated to do so, correct his unrealistic patterns and attitudes so that they are not contaminated by past experiences, traumas, and fantasies. In this way, the therapeutic relationship can act as a corrective emotional experience.

Q418: Are all positive reactions to the therapist manifestations of neurotic transference?

A418: There are genuine positive feelings in human relationships that do not have to be considered neurotic or transferential. These must be differentiated from distorted overvaluations and ideas of the therapist's magical powers, undaunted givingness and benevolence that are manifestations of neurotic transference. The former feelings are productive aids in the psychotherapeutic process; the latter are sooner or later destructive to the process.

Q419: When does transference act as resistance?

A419: Transference acts as resistance when the patient tries to live through with the therapist early ungratified needs and impulses at the expense of getting involved with therapeutic work. For example, needs to gratify oedipal wishes through sexualizing the relationship with the therapist (by fantasies, overt behavior during the session, or acting-out away from the treatment) may become an obsession with the patient. Also, needs and impulses, or mere awareness of these, may create anxiety and mobilize resistance to the therapist and to his interventions. Another and not uncommon form of transference resistance involves fighting off the influence of the therapist the way the individual fought off an authoritarian and interfering parental figure during the developmental separation-individuation struggle.

Q420: Can transference occur toward persons other than the analyst?

A420: Of course this can happen, but we must always alert ourselves to the possibility that such a reaction is a displacement from transference on the analyst which is being repudiated and expressed through displacement. Thus, infantile sexual wishes which ordinarily would be projected onto the analyst may be denied and then expressed through the body of another person outside of therapy. This type of indirect transference is complemented by true transference that is manifested toward persons in the environment, apart from the analyst, with whom the individual is in intimate and intense contact.

Q421: Should you try to regard a patient's outside emotional reactions as manifestations in some way of the transference?

A421: If possible, yes. Often what may be helpful is questioning whether in responding to outside happenings the patient had or now has thoughts, feelings, or fantasies about the therapist. If the patient denies this, one may casually accept this but should search in the nonverbal behavior, slips of speech, etc., for evidences of transference and confront the patient with such evidences.

Q422: Can one take transference reactions at their face value?

A422: It is always essential to search for latent content behind manifest behavior. For example, one of my patients experienced anxiety in one session and hesitatingly revealed a rape dream in which she was the victim and I the rapist. Thoughts of my having sexual designs on her had occupied her for several days. I interpreted her reaction as concealing a desire to be seduced by me. This interpretation started a series of memories related to lascivious fantasies about her father that accompanied her early masturbatory activities. Our focus on her oedipal fears and feelings had a most constructive effect on her relationship with me and resulted in a good deal of progress in her treatment.

Q423: Are there different kinds of transference interpretations, and if so, which are most effective? Also, is it better to relate transference to the here-and-now or to the past?

A423: Transference traditionally has connoted a concentration on the therapist of the patient's involvements with early objects. Accordingly, the therapist is conceived of as a repository of archaic needs and impulses, as well as a vehicle for defenses against them. This common concept of transference, namely that it acts like a bridge between the past and the present, has been expanded to include reactions related to here-and-now relationships between patients and therapists, as well as between patients and other authority figures. Defenses against such reactions have also been considered aspects of the transferential spectrum. The transference interpretation, while not neglecting exposure of origins in the past, may productively include how the past is influencing present reactions. Some analysts also search for manifestations of the self that are being expressed through transference.

Consequently, when we talk about transference interpretations, we are alluding to a range of activities, such as:

1) relating the patient's reactions to those he originally had toward his parents or siblings;
2) differentiating the patient's distorted attitudes and feelings toward the therapist from the actual reality of what the analyst is like;
3) pointing out how the manifest behavior toward the therapist shrouds latent intentions;
4) indicating how the patient's feelings and behavior toward the therapist reflect important incidents that have happened to him in the past; and
5) depicting how drives embodied in his character structure operate to create pathology.

Transference interpretations may also embrace displacements from the self onto the therapist.

Q424: Does interpretation of the transference always lead to insight?

A424: No, the patient may not be ready for the interpretation or he may resist the interpretation. The best results in transference interpretation will be obtained where the patient is immersed in strong emotions and the interpretation links these emotions to the transference situation. Similarly, a current conflict that can be connected with transference may make the impact of the interpretation greater.

Q425: Some authorities contend that only transference interpretations are important. Do you agree?

A425: There are many analysts who affirm Brenner's (1969) contention that "every interpretation must be a transference interpretation if it is to be effective." This implies that true insight can be achieved only through interpretation of the transference. Any analyst who has utilized and witnessed the effectiveness of interpreting the transference once it has developed to full intensity cannot argue with the sentiment behind these statements, but the implication that other kinds of interpretations are ineffective may certainly be challenged.

When we observe the resistance encountered in analyzing neurotic symptoms and character traits directly, we must credit transference interpretation with making the greatest impact on the patient. But to restrict ourselves to this single activity limits the therapist's flexibility. Indeed, attempting to wedge all events and reactions into a transference formulation may do no more for the patient than to mobilize resistance. Non-transference interpretations can be extremely important in their own right, apart from reinforcing the impact of transference interpretations.

Q426: How does free association relate to transference?

A426: Free association loosens past memories, which liberate emotions, which in turn tend to activate transference.

Q427: What is behind a patient's inability during analysis to gain insight into her immediate distorted relationships with important people?

A427: One important cause of this can be the patient's incapacity, reluctance, or refusal to analyze her transference with the analyst. Other causes can exist, such as absent motivation or strong secondary gains contingent on maintaining a contorted interpersonal role.

Q428: How truly essential is a transference neurosis for successful analysis?

A428: Most analysts believe it to be indispensable. Some do not. Thus, Gill and Muslin (1976) have pointed to Glover's assertion that "there may be successful analysis . . . where no transference neurosis develops." Of course we are dealing here with the definition of a "successful analysis." If it means the surfacing and interpretation of the unconscious repressed aspects of childhood, a transference neurosis provides the patient with the best opportunity for the working-through of these residues. If it means the achievement of reconstruction of the personality, there is no guarantee that a transference neurosis will accomplish this objective in every case. Nor is there validity in the idea that it is only through a transference neurosis that one can achieve personality reconstruction. Admitting these exceptions, the majority opinion still is heavily on the side of a working-through of a transference neurosis as a most helpful vehicle for a successful analysis.

Q429: Is acting-out always a manifestation of transference?

A429: Where a patient is in therapy, it should be regarded as such unless proven otherwise. But, factually, acting-out can occur exclusive of transference.

Q430: Why, if transference acts as a resistance to dynamic therapy, do dynamic therapists try deliberately to produce it in their patients?

A430: Transference embodies some of the core infantile conflicts that operate unconsciously to produce neurotic illness. Its elicitation allows the therapist to confront, interpret, and clarify the meaning and purpose of the patient's illness. It may, however, create resistance as it develops; a chief therapeutic task is the resolution of this resistance, the working-through of which becomes an important part of the cure. The purposeful encouragement of transference is an aspect of psychoanalytic treatment, particularly in its classical form. In other forms of dynamic therapy no effort is made to mobilize transference, but it still is dealt with by interpretation and clarification where it operates as resistance to therapy.

Q431: When would you consider it unwise to encourage transference as a therapeutic technique?

A431: Transference should not be encouraged:

1) When the patient already has a problem in reality-testing (as in psychoses, unstable borderline cases, and paranoidal personalities);
2) when there is not enough time to work through transferential dependencies (as in short-term therapy);
3) when the therapeutic alliance has not been firmly established to sustain the rigors of transference;
4) when the defenses of the patient are so fragile that he cannot handle anxiety or tolerate frustration (which is inevitable in the transference experience);
5) when the objective in therapy is not deep conflict resolution but, rather, a more harmonious adjustment to the current reality situation.

From a practical standpoint this limits the number of candidates for transference mobilization to a highly selected group. It must be remembered, however, that, as sincere as our attempts may be to limit transference, it may still appear spontaneously, and it will then require careful resolution should it interfere with the therapeutic process.

Q432: Should positive transference be analyzed?

A432: It should not be analyzed in short-term therapies, where it is utilized as a catalyzing force. Positive transference requires analysis in longer-term therapy where, because of the inherent magical expectations it invokes, the dependency it inspires, and the erotic interest stimulated, it can be a deterrent to progress. Incidentally, when a positive transference is resolved, a hidden negative transference may surface which will, of course, have to be worked through.

Q433: How soon will transference reactions begin?

A433: They can occur in the first session and even before the first session with fantasies about the therapist and anticipation of what will happen in treatment. Manifestations of transference may be more easily controlled early in therapy than later on when intensity increases. Transference may exhibit itself only in dreams, slips of speech and nonverbal behavior.

Q434: There is a form of transference during therapy that we call "falling in love" with one's therapist. Isn't this really a help in treatment?

A434: On the contrary, I would consider it as a resistance. It often comes when the patient is working on especially difficult phases of a problem. This transference is usually not a mere verbalization to appease the therapist, but stems from archaic eroticized needs that have been deeply repressed and have little to do with the real person of the therapist. The patient will urgently and persistently demand gratification, if not in an actual sexual experience, then in intimacies that have symbolic sexual values. The therapist's refusal to abide by the patient's wishes is extremely frustrating to the patient and the patient may seek external outlets for gratification in the form of acting-out with potentially disturbing and even dangerous consequences. So long as this transference need exists, the patient will resist the real aims of treatment. It is urgent, therefore, to resolve the transference. The best way to do this is to continue refusing to abide by the erotic transference need (gratification of which can be extremely destructive to the patient and the therapist) and to handle it through interpretation both as a form of resistance and as a means of understanding some of the deepest needs, conflicts, and defenses of the patient, certain manifestations of which are reflected in the symptoms for which therapy is now being sought. Interpretation of transference is an art and will call for astuteness and objectivity, as well as awareness and management of the therapist's own countertransference. Analysis of transference provides a way of metamorphosing archaic sexual fantasies and impulses into mature, fulfilling sexuality and constructive sublimations.

Q435: In dynamic psychotherapy how do you keep a balance of an empathic working relationship and the transferences that you want to come through to give you an idea of the patient's innermost conflicts?

A435: While you are interested in finding out the nature of the patient's infantile conflicts, you try to keep the lid on transference material that will act as too great resistance to you and your techniques. You do not have to use special tricks to bring out these transference manifestations. They will come through, if not in direct behavior toward you then in acting-out away from therapy. You will generally get clues about transference from nonverbal behavior and especially from dreams. If there are evidences of hostility, fear, sexual interest, detachment, or paralyzing dependency, deal with these through open discussion before they germinate into full-blown patterns that may be more difficult to handle.

Even though these manifestations will give you inklings about some of the most urgent conflicts, your first task is to see to it that transference does not interfere with the working relationship, at the same time that you utilize it to give the patient some insight into the origin and nature of some of his conflicts. In psychoanalytically oriented therapy one may want to encourage some transference, but, as I mentioned before, transferences will probably not need encouragement, emerging spontaneously in some form as defenses are challenged. Where controls are rigid, some therapists utilize techniques to encourage transference (more passivity on the part of the therapist, increasing the frequency of sessions, focusing on the past and on early relationships, encouraging dreams, etc.), although too great regression should be avoided. Where one wants to deal with present-day adaptations, transference is discouraged (by its early exposure and interpretation, by decreasing session frequency, by activity in the relationship and by focusing on real events rather than the past and dreams).

Q436: How can you tell when a patient is in transference or is going into transference?

A436: Generally, the therapist will be able to discern in the patient a manner that is different from his usual behavior. At the start of therapy the patient is generally highly defended and he plays the conventional role of patient with helping authority. After a while, and particularly where his defenses are challenged, a change in demeanor becomes manifest. The patient may engage in periods of silence, or complain of having nothing on his mind or having little to talk about, or cancel or break appointments, or come late, or keep looking at his watch if time is passing too slowly, or forget to pay the therapist's bills. On the other hand, the patient may verbally or nonverbally show an extraordinary interest in the therapist's private life, or become competitive with the therapist or with the therapist's other patients, or display dependency on the therapist, hanging onto every word, or openly or covertly make sexual advances toward the therapist. More difficult to detect are acting-out tendencies that the patient conceals from the therapist, in which feelings that are related to the therapist are projected to outside persons or situations. One way the patient has of concealing acting-out is by talking almost exclusively about the past, or speculating on his dynamics, or bringing in involved dreams that are extremely difficult to decode.

Often the first intimations of transference are in dreams in which certain behaviors are exhibited toward symbolized versions of the therapist. The way such intimations are handled will depend upon whether the therapist wants to let transference build up until it reaches a crescendo, as in psychoanalysis, or to dissipate it by exploration and interpretation before it acts as resistance, as in nonanalytic treatment.

Q437: What are some of the countertransference reactions of the therapist when a patient fails to respond to therapy? Also, is countertransference always bad?

A437: When a patient fails to get well, the therapist may become belittling, sarcastic, annoyed, bored, attacking, disinterested, or detached. He may be riddled with feelings of self-doubt, impotence, and defeat and he may find himself dreading sessions with his patient, watching the clock and hoping that the hour goes quickly, wiggling his toes, yawning, and fighting off falling asleep. Another consequence is a questioning of the value of psychotherapy and a shattering of faith in the theoretical premises he has hitherto held sacrosanct. There is then a reaching for new and dramatic cures which are readily available in the therapeutic marketplace as old ones are relegated to the trash heap.

Countertransference is not always bad. It may signal arousal in the therapist of unconscious needs and designs of the patient that are being communicated to the therapist and that can be interpreted productively. (See also p. 370.)

Q438: Are all angry feelings toward a patient manifestations of countertransference?

A438: Not necessarily. It is sometimes important to verbalize one's angry feelings toward a patient who is behaving in a self-defeating and provocative manner, especially when there is no need to build up a transference neurosis. Such verbalization is not done in a punitive way, but rather as a means of bringing the patient to an awareness of how he comes through with people and why reactions toward him are less than congenial. Where the patient is in a negative transference toward the therapist or the transference is acting as resistance to therapy, the therapist must control angry feelings and work on the interpretation of the transference to get therapy "back on the tracks."

XVII. Theoretical Aspects

The value of a theory is determined by its ability to encompass within its premises a vast number of observations, by the parsimoniousness of its assumptions, by its internal consistency and logic, and by its empirical validity, usefulness and testability. From a pragmatic standpoint, scientific theories in psychotherapy should constitute a structure through which clinical method is evolved. Coordinately, clinical procedures are an important means of corroborating the practicality of a theory. Ideally, theories should be fabricated not from the gossamer threads of speculation but from the sturdy fibers of clinical experience. We are handicapped in this pursuit by the fact that the state of mental healing still lacks substance as an empirical science. Present-day hypothetical assumptions about therapy have not as yet yielded significant validations. Yet the practicing psychotherapist, in utilizing his techniques, still must operate from the platform of some theory, as conjectural as it may be. It is here that many questions confound the therapist who is seeking firm footing in the marshy paths of practice. Some of these questions are contained in the present section.

Q439: How vital is possessing a definite theory in designing what we do in treatment?

A439: Theoretical concepts are important so long as they do not put the therapist into a straightjacket. They can provide a framework around which goals are formulated and therapeutic interventions designed. For one thing, they help stabilize the therapist in the shaky sea of the treatment process. But any theory loses its serviceability if it becomes so sacrosanct that it cannot be altered or discarded when clinical realities disprove its merit or validity. No two patients are alike any more than any two thumbprints, and no two patients will react similarly to the same interventions. We may thus have to reorganize our original ideas founded on our theories as we move along in treatment and as changing clinical conditions necessitate conceptual reorganization. Problems occur when theories become converted into dogmas and are then wedged into the narrow confines of fixed precepts and rigid imperatives that paralyze operative flexibility.

Q440: How would you account for so many different theories among psychoanalysts?

A440: Behavior is an extremely complex phenomenon and embraces many ingredients: biochemical, neurophysiological, developmental-conditioning, intrapsychic, interpersonal, social, and "spiritual." Therapists, because of their own personal predelictions and personality needs, may focus on fragments of the behavioral gestalt and organize their theories around a tiny vector that seems to them basic and fundamental. In this way they may attempt to subsume the world of psychopathology into a limited and perhaps biased axis. Psychoanalysts are particularly disposed to generalize from subjective beliefs, and many splits in the analytic movement have occurred around minor differences in focus. For example, we find schools of thought organized around such areas as the primacy of pregenital conditionings, oedipal strivings, separation-individuation, sexuality, aggression, masochism, narcissism, splitting, etc. Varying ideas about the role of insight, transference, activity, directiveness, demonstrativeness, confrontation, session frequency, areas of interpretation and preferred intervention strategies have pointed out the diversity of opinion as to what is considered important in psychoanalysis. Until we have more scientific evidence regarding the greater validity of any theory over others and proof of which techniques are most serviceable, we may anticipate continuing controversy. This hopefully will lead to experimentation with innovative ideas and methods, which is, of course, the essence of empiricism.

Q441: What would you consider the most important fallacies about our modern psychological theories?

A441: One of the fallacies in the construction of some of our modern theories, both psychodynamic and behavioral, has been the tendency to compare psychological processes in the human being with those of lower animals and to posit similar structures. There is, of course, some similarity in biochemical and neurophysiological dimensions, but when we consider behavior, and especially social behavior, the differences are so profound as to cast doubt on prevailing theories that are rooted in animal models. A phobia in a dog, for instance, is not the same as a phobia in a child, even though a conditioning process has taken place in both. In human beings the phobic entity is complicated by special symbolic meanings that are imparted to symptoms which change at progressive stages of the individual's growth and the impact of social factors. While genetic, biochemical, neurophysiological, ethological and other studies help us to understand some of the complexities of the interaction of heredity and environment, they do not go far enough in explaining human behavior, which is definitively influenced by social forces and belief systems that are uniquely human. Insects and animals may have to rely on instincts as a prime basis for their adaptation. Man, while possessing instincts, rapidly modifies them through social learning. Using instincts in explaining social adaptations is little short of farcical. To think of war, for example, in terms of an aggressive fighting instinct inherent in man merely serves to rationalize war and avoids the dominant and determining economic and political foundations for conflict.

Another fallacy in modern theory-building is the tendency to make assumptions about infantile and child development from observations of adult behavior and from fantasies and memories about one's childhood. Generalizations about normal development from the material gathered during psychoanalysis of emotionally ill patients are especially suspect. Some of these assumptions, of course, may be correct, but to generalize to childhood from adult ideas, fantasies and dreams is, to say the least, hazardous. Freud emphasized this in his conclusions about "cover memories," which he proved had little basis in fact. From the standpoint of treatment such "cover memories" and other fantasies can nevertheless be significant, since the individual will react to them with as great or greater intensity as to true incidents. But when we are constructing theories about sources of problems, our hypothetical formulations have to deal with validated facts. Statements about parents, their behavior toward the patient as a child, and their pathology presumed responsible for the patient's problems must be considered in the light that children often do misinterpret parental motives and that parents are not always as bad as depicted. The upshot of what I am trying to say is that theories should be based on scientifically validated data and not on opinions or speculations.

The problem with most theory-builders is not so much that they are wrong, but that they tend to generalize their assumptions to the world at large. Their ideas may actually be quite valid for a circumscribed area of behavior. However, human behavior is extremely reticular and is constantly being influenced by biochemical, neurophysiological, intrapsychic, interpersonal, social, and other factors. These elements all require different concepts and language forms that cannot be extrapolated and applied unequivocally to the entire spectrum of living activity. Accordingly, when we try to transfer intrapsychic formulations to neurophysiological, social, and other aspects of behavior, we are apt to run into problems. Even if we restrict ourselves to intrapsychic areas, the inherent complexities cannot be explained by any prevailing theory. Freud's drive theory, for example, sounds reasonable only when dealing with a tiny dimension of the intrapsychic process, and his structural theory, while explicating some sources of inner conflict, fails miserably to explain interpersonal and social phenomena. It would seem that multiple theories alone could resolve our prevailing dilemma, but we have no way yet of integrating these diverse theories into a cohesive body of knowledge, and to try to do so at present would involve a muddle of theoretical eclecticism that would leave us even more confused than we are now.

Q442: A great deal of discussion has been going on related to metapsychology. How do you feel about this?

A442: Classical metapsychology does not answer vital problems we encounter in clinical practice. That a revision has been long delayed and is necessary is obvious. But so far, any revisions proposed do not provide an adequate substitute. Some challenging ideas have been put forth, such as changing the language of psychoanalysis so it is more action-oriented, proposed by Schafer (1959), and centralizing the representational world of the individual in a psychoanalytic phenomenology, as described by Stolorow and Atwood (1979). Imaginative, creative concepts may in the future lead to greater clarification. What is important is that we continue working on revisions and testing their utility in the laboratory of our clinical work.

Q443: There is a current criticism of Freudian metapsychology and of the idea of metapsychology altogether. Is this justified?

A443: Freudian metapsychology, especially drive theory and structural theory, have been subjected to a great deal of criticism. Drive theory deals with the vicissitudes of the instincts as they strive to discharge energy. The consequences of the discharge are presumed to contribute to normal and pathological personality development. This formulation, which constituted Freud's "economic" point of view, has been rigorously challenged as being completely inconsistent with present-day findings in neurophysiology (Rubinstein, 1967) and "so riddled with philosophical and factual errors and fallacies that nothing less than discarding the concept of drive or instinct will do" (Holt, 1976). Criticisms have also been levied at the tripartite id, ego, superego structural theory as inconsistent with clinical realities. There are those who would replace the classical metapsychology with modern concepts derived from neurophysiology, systems theory, information processing, and present-day machine models (Kubie, 1975; Peterfreund, 1975; Rubinstein, 1967). Others seek to discard metapsychological speculations altogether (Gill, 1976; Stolorow and Atwood, 1979) on the basis that they are insubstantial and metaphorical, with tendencies toward mechanistic reification. To replace metapsychology there have been proposals to substitute concepts from clinical theory (Klein, 1976) that deal with the meaning of subjective experiences and their developmental origins.

My personal feeling is that some aspects of the structural theory have a certain utility in conceptualizing certain limited bits of psychopathology, for example, the conflicts that derive from impulses (id) clashing with moral prohibitions (superego) resulting in defenses elaborated by the ego. By the "id" I do not mean to support the idea of unverified libidinal and death instincts. Rather, under the term I would include any unconscious impulse (sexuality, aggression, assertiveness, hostility, etc.). The "superego" would embrace the standards and prohibitions imposed by the incorporated parental introjects, as well as society. The "ego" would incorporate the elaborated defensive systems which establish compromises between impulses and prohibitions. The problem as I see it comes from a tendency to extend the structural theory to embrace all of psychopathology, which it cannot do.

Q444: If metapsychological theories do not serve a useful purpose, are there concepts from clinical theory more serviceable?

A444: To an extent, yes. To replace metapsychology there have been proposals to substitute for them concepts from clinical theory (Klein, 1976) that deal with the meaning of subjective experiences and their developmental origins. In their book, Stolorow and Atwood (1979) attempt to illustrate how this can be done. Discarding metapsychology as a reasonable vehicle for examining behavior, these authors advocate a focus on the individual's own representational world, which emerges from the developmental history. Such subjective representations of self and object eventually become stabilized and the individual is said then to "assimilate his subsequent experiences into its structure," his representational world being characterized by "recurrent themes and leitmotifs which dominate his existence." These become embodied in his habitual character structure. The individual is motivated to express a number of needs through representational configurations which serve various functions. Among these are wish-fulfillment (as in dreams and symptoms), demand for self-punishment (masochistic behavior for desires or actions that are morally repugnant), adaptive activities (to resolve unresolved crises, as in repetition compulsion), restitution-reparation (to mend damaged aspects of self or object), and defensive operations (to overcome anticipated danger). In a process the authors call "psychoanalytic phenomenology," there is an attempt to determine the functional significance of the representational configurations and their developmental origins. The clinician seeks to determine the motivational or functional priority of the existing representational configuration to establish the appropriate clinical interventions.

In utilizing this type of approach, an attempt is made to determine the meaning of the symptom. Is it a defense that goes back to a previous developmental level (projection, incorporation, splitting) or is it a manifestation of a fixation (what the authors call "a pre-stage of defensive development")? In case the symptom is a defense, the therapist must interpret what is being excluded from awareness and being defended against. On the other hand, if it represents an arrest of a pre-stage of defense (fixation), the therapist conveys an empathic understanding of what has happened to the patient and encourages him "to achieve adequate representational differentiation or integration." How this diagnostic distinction is made the authors do not say. Moreover, the utilization of this idea presupposes acceptance of the concepts of fixation and regression which not all therapists are willing to do. In the first place, the idea of a person being *irreparably* blockaded from development beyond a certain early level due to the imposition on him of severe traumas or deprivations is no longer widely accepted (Thomas and Chess, 1980). Moreover, while regression to an earlier defense can be clinically demonstrated, it is never exactly the same as the original defense, being contaminated by accretions of more mature defensive operations.

Q445: Do present-day revisions of classical theory bring us closer to clinical realities? I am referring to the school of ego psychology which claims original and effective theories and methods.

A445: Many of the modern revisions of classical theory are nothing more than a rephrasing of Freudian formulations which are then presented as original discoveries. The "innovator" may extract from the vast corpus of Freudian ideas a small selected area around which a whole "new" ideology is erected. I suspect that some of the concepts emerging from the school of ego psychology fall into this category. This is not to denigrate the contributions of ego psychologists, some of which in my opinion are clinically helpful. Rather, it is necessary to examine them carefully so as not to be deceived into believing that they are the last word in solving the riddles of psychotherapeutic theory and practice.

Q446: Do theories really influence the therapist's choice of techniques?

A446: In some cases, yes, as among classical behaviorists and classical psychoanalysts. In other instances a diversity of eclectic techniques are practiced even though the theoretical denomination of the therapist is monolithic. Thus, a psychoanalyst may espouse classical theories and yet, in the same patient, utilize, in addition to dream analysis and transference analysis, pharmacotherapy, milieu therapy, group therapy and family therapy, doing what can be called "psychoanalytically oriented psychotherapy."

Q447: How does object relations theory look on basic conflict, and does this viewpoint have a validity in treatment?

A447: Disciples of object relations theory contend that essential intrapsychic conflicts deal with warring self and object representations. Defenses that are evolved keep these antagonistic components from awareness, often taking the form of character drives that are in expression completely opposite to the impulses they conceal. During normal development the unification of the ego-id-superego system produces an integration of internalized object relations and repression of irreconcilable aspects of self and object representations.

Neurosis involves a conflict between unified aspects of the psychic apparatus (ego-id-superego). Where there has been no unification of the constituents of the psychic apparatus, as in borderline cases, repression of self and object representations is incomplete, with the emergence of contradictory ego states that are dealt with by dissociation, splitting, denial, projective identification, omnipotence, and archaic idealization rather than by repression. Primitive intrapsychic conflicts may become manifest under certain conditions as in the transference during psychotherapy, and can act as resistances to therapy. Object relations theory credibly explicates some but not all clinical phenomena—but neither does any other theory completely elucidate all clinical phenomena.

A number of psychoanalysts believe that object relations theory is the best paradigm around which one may organize treatment in borderline conditions. Utilizing object relations theory, intensive treatment (three to five times weekly) is organized around the working-through of primitive split transferences involving self and object representations, with the goal of achieving reactions of a more integrated nature. Because technical neutrality is so difficult to preserve with these patients, the analyst who wishes to work on a depth level will require special training and supervised experience. Even here negative therapeutic reactions are common and in certain patients outcome results are disappointing.

XVIII. Development

Dynamic approaches draw heavily on data from the field of development. But objective appraisal of this data is handicapped by a number of obstacles, not the least of which is the practice of fitting the data mercilessly into a set theoretical frame. Despite such obstacles, a number of useful propositions have evolved from developmental studies that help clarify many aspects of personality pathology. Among these propositions is the contention that personality strength or weakness is more or less determined by experiences during childhood. Where essential personality qualities are not evolved, the individual will be burdened by residual childhood needs, attitudes, and ways of handling stress that tend to cripple adult modes of coping. There is less uniformity of opinion about the stages of growth, as they evolve in a time dimension, as well as their manifestations in different cultural settings. Disputed also is the exact way childhood developmental distortions produce adult psychopathology. But most of the controversy centers around the usefulness of developmental information in psychotherapy, some therapists depreciating the healing force of insight into inimical early experiences. There is, nevertheless, a tacit acceptance among dynamically oriented therapists that the past survives in the present and that its distortions must be rectified irrespective of whether it is remembered or not.

Q448: What important factors influence mastery of the various stages of development and what are some of the early outcomes?

A448: An infinite number of variables come into play as the child moves along to master the developmental challenges confronting him. The way the various stages of development are managed will thus depend on many factors and especially the individual's temperament and cognitive style. These are to a considerable degree a product of interaction of the hereditary makeup, intrauterine influences, and early postnatal experiences. A sensitive, active, emotionally robust baby will respond to the environment with curiosity, alertness, demandingness, and persistence. A phlegmatic inactive baby, on the other hand, is apt to show inattentiveness, distractibility and withdrawal tendencies. Capacities for learning and modes of adaptation will differ in these two groupings of babies.

The child's temperament probably influences his susceptibility to behavior disorders. Thomas and Chess (1980), in a longitudinal study of a large group of children with diverse national, cultural and class backgrounds, describe nine categories of temperament. These are 1) activity level, 2) regularity (rhythmicity) of biological function, 3) approach and withdrawal tendencies, 4) adaptability to new or altered situations, 5) sensory thresholds of responsiveness to stimuli, 6) reactive intensity, 7) quality of mood, 8) distractibility, 9) attention span and persistence. The authors stress that while children with negative temperamental qualities are liable to behavior disorders, difficulties can occur in children with any temperamental patterns "if demands for change and adaptation are dissonant with the particular child's capacities." The child's cognitive style is another dimension that can modulate his passage through the various stages of development. Moreover the kind of environment in which he is reared, its available gratifications and its deprivations will affect task mastery.

The urge for the development of social competencies that will help overcome progressively new and complicated challenges is present from birth on. Where the individual's competencies fail to master an essential challenge, the impact on him may threaten his security and damage his self-esteem. An eventuating set of defenses will then tend to circumvent the challenge (as by withdrawal), to deny its validity (as by paranoidal distortion), to reduce its intensity (as by graded attempts to deal with manageable aspects), and to indulge a variety of other coping devices ranging from aggressive attack to clinging dependency

in an effort to reduce tension and to preserve the self-image. Compli-
cating matters is the fact that the defenses themselves, by imposing
urgent needs on the individual for gratification, may then become
prime sources of action. Thus, perfectionism evolved to bolster the self-
image may become a way of life relegating more fundamental urges
to a secondary place. Defenses, nevertheless, may also be protective.
Their usefulness can be judged by whether they enhance or interfere
with adaptation. A phobia may insulate a man from anxiety, but it
may maladaptively also interfere with his social functioning. Sensitivity to discrimination may help a woman adaptively avoid being
taken advantage of, downgraded, or humiliated, but may foster un-
warranted withdrawal reactions.

What has been emerging from longitudinal studies of child development is that the infant himself plays a determining role in regulating
the processes of his own growth. He is neither a puppet manipulated
by the immutable hand of heredity nor an innocent victim of his environment, even though he is influenced by both.

**Q449: How do developmental difficulties operate to create ad-
justment difficulties in adult life?**

A449: It is generally accepted that developmental difficulties in early
childhood, if not corrected by later constructive experiences, will burden the individual the remainder of life with residues of unmet needs,
inadequate defenses, and defective coping mechanisms. Among the
distortions of personality generated by deficiencies in development are
incomplete separation-individuation, confused identity, and a blem-
ished self-image. These aberrations promote faulty cognitions and
characterologic complications that are bound to interfere with problem-
solving and wholesome relationships with people. A good deal of the
individual's time is spent in trying to make up deficits in upbringing
by forcing people to deliver what parents failed to supply, and to win
the love, admiration, and respect of almost everyone with whom there
is any kind of intimacy. Among the tactics pressed into service are
efforts to impress the world with one's cleverness and importance,
masochistic maneuvers to punish oneself and to win sympathy and
compassion, and punitive manipulations to intimidate and bludgeon
others to yield to personal demands. At the same time an unworthy
feeling prevents any conviction that full approval is merited. A constant performance to gain acceptance tends to frenzy the individual

and to alienate others around him. The performer is in the position of a gourmet cook who has to prove himself at every meal. Moreover, because needs are usually exorbitant and insatiable, disappointment, anger and depression become inevitable. Existing defenses and coping mechanisms are usually more suitable for a child than an adult, and these constantly stir up problems for the individual and the people around him. There is growing evidence that many early developmental distortions are not indelible and that they can later be resolved in a suitable environment.

Q450: In reconstructing the past during dynamic therapy, we often concern ourselves with distortions in the sense of self. At what age does the child's sense of self appear?

A450: Even though an identifiable "self" can be detected in the child at the age of nine months, its origin has defied proper timing. Opinions vary. According to Mahler (Mahler and Furer, 1968), the infant is in a state of "normal autism" the first month of life characterized by "primitive hallucinatory disorientation." During the second month there is "normal symbiosis" where the child and mother function as "an omnipotent system—a dual entity with one common boundary." There is no differentiation of the "I" from the "not I." At four to five months, according to this hypothesis, the second symbiotic phase occurs with the beginning of the development of the self and by the end of the first year there is beginning of separation-individuation. Anna Freud, Melanie Klein, Erik Erikson, and other authorities have contributed their ideas about self-differentiation which follows a period of chaotic selflessness. Thomas and Chess (1980), on the other hand, believe that individuation and self-differentiation begin at birth.

Q451: What is the effect on the individual of depriving experiences during the very early years?

A451: Research findings indicate that, during the first six months of life, the more the mother plays with, talks to and stimulates the infant, the more socially responsive, happier and less fretful the baby will be. Up to three years of age, a depriving institutional environment which does not provide good verbal and other kinds of interaction can result in cognitive, motor, social, and language retardation. These effects, however, are reversible with appropriate interventions.

Q452: At what age would you consider an individual's patterns stabilized?

A452: By the time a child has reached the age of six or seven the sense of identity and basic reactions and defenses become firmed up and, given a consistent environment, are more or less stabilized. A somewhat quieter period follows then in our culture (latency period), although there is continued development unless the environment imposes untoward pressures on the child. During puberty and adolescence the pressures from within and without are in most children great and "stabilized" patterns are apt to undergo at least a temporary disruption.

Q453: I know that childish patterns sometimes display themselves in mature people. Do they serve any real function?

A453: In my opinion, they serve only a neurotic function. They are maladaptive and usually come about during a temporary breakdown in adaptation. Even well-adjusted people may, during severe accidents or disasters, or when under the influence of alcohol, show tendencies more appropriate for a child than for an adult. During my medical externship, I was for three months assigned to ambulance duty. It was not unusual to rush to the site of a bad automobile accident and find a severely injured adult moaning for his mother who had been dead for years. Many married people whose mates die go into a severe and sometimes intractable separation reaction or experience a severe depression that may result in suicide or a fatal physical illness. A residual need for mothering and protection is latent to some extent in all persons. It becomes importunate in those who have never achieved adequate separation-individuation whenever their security needs are seriously threatened. Sometimes childish patterns may deliberately be employed to serve some immediate gain. For instance, a wife may throw a childish temper tantrum to force a miserly husband to loosen his purse strings. As she succeeds in terrorizing her mate to yield to her demands, the reaction becomes reinforced into an established pattern.

Q454: Do the newer contributions to psychoanalytic theory drawn from Kleinian and object relations theory deal better with the facts of infantile development than the older theories?

A454: Recent additions to developmental theory are ideas related to representational differentiation and integration of self and external objects. Here it is presumed that the neonate cannot differentiate himself from others nor discriminate between his own and his object's sensations. The first task of development, according to this idea, is to distinguish and separate self from object representations (usually the mother). This common notion is believed by certain authorities to be speculative and not in keeping with their opinions of child development substantiated by modern developmental research (Kagan, 1971; Kagan et al., 1978). They point out that object relations theory comes from observations of psychotics and of patients in deep regression (as during a transference psychosis) who are *presumed* to be repeating what the normal person goes through in infancy. Studies of development, they contend, indicate that the neonate is highly capable of differentiating himself from objects. They downgrade the notion that infants are unable to integrate contrasting emotions as related to object representations (i.e., positive affects associated with the "all good mother" and negative affects associated with the "bad mother") or that infants are at first unable to synthesize "good" and "bad" affects into a combined representation of the total mother figure.

The second developmental task, according to object relations theorists, is to effect synthesis of the "good" and "bad" mother, as well as the self-representations that issue from the developmental incorporation of the mother figure (the maternal introject). Under favorable conditions, this synthesis occurs with the evolvement of "object constancy" and the valuing of other persons for their true positive and negative qualities. This makes for consolidation of the self-image, acceptance of "good-bad" qualities within oneself, and a solid sense of identity and positive self-esteem. Failure in such integration is presumed to result in "splitting," an absence of self-object differentiation and delusional merging of self and object images predisposing to psychosis (Kernberg, 1975; Kohut, 1971; Searles, 1966). Causes of such failure are variantly attributed to constitutional predisposition, severe maternal deprivation, inconsistencies in care, mishandling, and cruelty. Milder difficulties in self-representation other than psychosis are said to occur where the damage is not so serious, resulting in 1) narcissistic personality disorders, who will require special kinds of management therapeutically (Kohut, 1971), and 2) borderline personality disorders (Kernberg, 1975) in whom "all-good" and "all-bad" self and object representations alternate and who also need special techniques. Again, these concepts derive from work on borderline and psychotic adults and have not been substantiated by modern researchers in child development (Bower, 1977; Condon and Sander, 1974; Dunn, 1977; Kagan et al., 1978; Lewin, 1975; Thomas and Chess, 1980).

Alternative explanations have been offered founded on empirical studies. For instance, detailed observations of infants have shown the presence of a need for investigation and exploration as a means to task mastery. The urge for social relationships seems also to be basic and this is satisfied by mutual interactions of the infant and mothering figures, not as a fused image, but as separate and individually functioning beings. This does not detract from the ingenuity of the object relations formulations and even their usefulness in giving the therapist some model around which to organize his interventions and to enhance his confidence in what he is doing. However, attempts that have been made to explicate these ideas in "metapsychological verifications of psychic structures, cathectic shifts, or fusions and defusions of drive-energies" (Stolorow and Atwood, 1979) are extremely confusing. To answer this question simply, Kleinian and other object relations theories have not brought us closer to understanding the dilemmas of development.

Q455: The stages of narcissism and omnipotence are emphasized in the recent literature as stations at which borderline cases are arrested or to which the severely anxiety driven individual may retreat. Is there any experimental evidence to validate this?

A455: First, we must remember that infantile narcissism and omnipotence are theoretic concepts whose existence has not been scientifically proven. Since they are subjective experiences that the neurotic cannot adequately describe, they may not even be provable. From all the experimental data we do have on child development, the assumption that during the first weeks of life the neonate is "in a state of primitive hallucinatory disorientation, in which need satisfaction belongs to his own omnipotent autistic orbit" (Mahler and Furer, 1968), is stretching the imagination quite far.

Many of the presuppositions about infantile development have been derived from data gathered during the psychoanalysis of adults. We are not at all certain that phenomena we describe as "egocentric" or "omnipotent" or "narcissistic" and that are present in some neurotic or psychotic adults can be projected into what goes on in infantile life. Nor can we say that psychotic adults truly regress to an infantile state, which is a pejorative way of looking at infantile behavior.

Such speculations about infantile functioning and theories that these speculations have given rise to are considered by many researchers to be a tissue of distortions derived from adultomorphic prejudices. They certainly cannot be confirmed by present-day studies, which have contributed greatly to our knowledge of neonatal behavior. These have exploded the old concepts of the infant as a withdrawn, inert, hallucinating, omnipotent blob of flesh (Dunn, 1977; Frantz and Nevis, 1967; Kagan et al., 1978; Lewin, 1975). Indeed, a newborn is quite reality-oriented, beginning life "as an extremely competent learning organism, an extremely competent perceiving organism" (Bower, 1977). There is increasing evidence that the brain is extraordinarily active at birth, manifesting properties of control and responsiveness. Both classical and operant conditioning are present and *within the first week of life* learning through imitation occurs along with discriminative recognition and social communication. One can see this in the remarkable films of Condon and Sander (1974). "With the first fondling, the first feeding, the first perception of the human face and human voice, the newborn responds to and integrates inputs from the environment which have both cultural and sensorimotor significances" (Thomas and Chess, 1980). These findings have convinced many authorities that the so-called "hallucinatory disoriented" phases of development do not exist.

Q456: In working on the psychodynamics would you endorse the idea that the relationship with the mother actually seals the destiny of the individual and influences one the rest of one's life?

A456: This is a conventional idea and predominates in our thinking about development. According to this conception, the person, whether suckling, weanling, yearling, toddler or stripling, establishes a liaison with the mothering figure which becomes the paradigm of future relationships, fashioning needs and defenses that act as permanent foundations of the personality structure. Paternal and other interpersonal influences presumably act on the child to reinforce or neutralize to some extent the maternal impact. The imprint of the mother-child experience is believed indelibly etched in character formation, and in studying its effects some investigators are only too vividly impressed with its enduring powers. Such a conception would credit to all experiences other than the mother-child relationship a secondary role, and would consider the individual permanently damaged as a consequence of a bad relationship with the mothering person.

Longitudinal studies do not confirm this pessimistic outlook. Indeed, it becomes apparent from these studies that there is little continuity between the adaptations of childhood, including the mother-child relationship, and the adjustments made in adult life (Thomas and Chess, 1980). The average individual exhibits a surprisingly flexible capacity to overcome deficiencies during the developing years, given a reasonable opportunity to compensate for these or resources to fulfill needs that have undergone deprivation. Thus, children who are orphaned or abandoned will readily develop relationships with surrogate parental figures if there is a reasonable opportunity to do so. It is likely that only where there is constancy in the destructiveness and insufficiency of an environment throughout the developing years will maladaptive coping patterns become stabilized and perpetuate themselves in adult life. The conventional conception about the indelibility of the mother-child relationship has evolved largely as a consequence of studies on neurotic, borderline, and psychotic adults. This is a special subgroup who have been severely traumatized, or whose environments have never offered them opportunities for change. The larger group of healthier individuals who have overcome damaging impacts in their early life is less commonly the subject for study and hence our findings become prejudiced by a non-representative sample. Yet we cannot eliminate the fact that where no means of correcting lacks or distortions in early childhood exist, the individual will be at the mercy of anachronistically regressive needs and coping measures, some of which burden a healthy adjustment.

Q457: Are the various stages of growth firmly fixed and invariantly sequential?

A457: In some areas like cognitive functioning and motor skills there are consistent sequences. Piaget described the successive periods of cognitive development (sensorimotor, preoperational, concrete and formal operations) as occurring at flexible age periods. However, his formulations have been challenged (Flavell, 1972). Erikson (1963) evolved a developmental chart positing sequential stages of basic trust, autonomy, initiative, industry, identity, intimacy, generativity, and ego integrity which has also been criticized by some observers. A few other attempts have been made including those of myself and Kildahl (1970). In most areas within a given culture there is an orderly, although uneven, sequence at flexible age levels, the reactions varying widely depending on individual differences and the nature of the environment.

What seems to be emerging from studies on child development is the great variability in capacities for reaction. Individual differences are enormous. While we may be able to define certain broad stages of growth that exist among all of humanity (which are probably genetically determined), the styles and patterns through which the stages exhibit themselves vary greatly. We need merely to observe the differences among identical twins in reactions to different stages of development to realize the inherent plasticity that exists in people.

We can say then that the individual enters the various phases with his or her unique combination of temperamental traits and cognitive styles, being blocked by some events, creatively overcoming some impediments, compensating for environmental lacks, and, even when arrested by unfortunate interferences, having the potential for overcoming these later. It has, for example, been shown that when mothers die or abandon a child, the child has reparative capacities for social bonds to other adults or to older siblings if they are available to him. Development is characterized by flexible interactions of neurophysiology and behavior, each influencing the other so that the organic and psychological become intertwined. This intimate organismic-interactional process has been emphasized by current research and longitudinal studies (Eisenberg, 1977; Kagan, 1971; Thomas and Chess, 1980; Vaillant, 1977). Where the environment accords with the child's capacities and sensitivities, development will be optimal in a progressive direction.

In summary, we are unable to delineate the same course of development, or the same patterns and outcomes, even though the stages of growth are most likely similar for all individuals. The combinations of heredity, constitution, and environment are so capricious as to put a stamp of uniqueness on every human being. We all have thumbs but our thumbprints are different and personality variables are much more numerous and convoluted than the ridges and whirls of thumbprints. Nor can we predict from childhood behavior the way the adult personality will finally crystalize out. In my own experience, I have seen children and adolescents in whom I would have predicted life imprisonment if not hanging who settled down as adults to become average law-abiding and decent citizens, as well as good parents.

Q458: What is sociobiology and does it have a place in explaining behavior?

A458: Sociobiology is a new discipline that credits social behavior to inherited forces, deriving its data essentially from primate studies. Genetically determined social behavior in man probably does exist to some degree, especially during infancy. The neonate is genetically programmed to respond to social learning from the moment of birth on. However, inherited traits are rapidly modified by experience. The complex patterns of behavior that evolve are principally products of such social learning and impositions of culture. In other words, while some lower animals manifest elaborate inherited social patterns, man does not do so. At this stage we might say that sociobiology does not explain behavior in man.

XIX. Psychodynamics

Authorities with varying orientations have different ways of looking at dynamic phenomena. Irrespective of orientation, one can always find data that seem to substantiate one's particular point of view. The same interview material may thus be variously interpreted by observers even of the same school. Some regard the available data as confirming their theory that neurosis is essentially a clash between instinctual strivings and the environment. Others enthusiastically castigate cultural forces as the primary provocative agent. Still others may find in the material evidence that neurosis is fostered by disturbances in the integrative functioning of the ego. Such divergence of ideas is not too serious; it is to be regarded as the inevitable forerunner of a real science of mind. In the study of the uncharted psyche, theories in abundance are bound to emerge, supporting many rifts and controversies. Fortunately, we are witnessing the beginnings of attempts of amalgamation—an honest effort to blend the findings of the various schools into a body of knowledge shorn of prejudice and bias.

Q459: Isn't rivalry for the mother's love a main source of anger and guilt feelings?

A459: The universal experience of jealousy and anger at sharing the mother with a competing sibling or parent is a powerful source of conflict. Fantasies and dreams of eliminating or vanquishing the competitor, or actual violent behavior toward the competitor, along with rage at the mother for divided allegiance, disloyalty and betrayal produce enduring traits whose contours may continue into adult life and become projected toward surrogate mother and competitor figures.

Understandably, such reactions can raise havoc with a proper adaptation. I have not uncommonly observed both men and women who, while otherwise well adjusted, were unable to succeed in their studies or work because of anachronistically inspired ambivalence toward authorities like teachers or employers. They accused these persons of disliking them, discriminating against them, neglecting them, and conspiring against them by favoring others in the classroom or on the job. The intensity of emotions in some individuals was so extreme that they left school or quit their jobs. Among some extreme reactions were writing poison pen letters to the presumably perfidious authorities or treacherous competitors, institution of legal proceedings, assaultive behavior, paralyzing guilt and in several instances suicidal attempts.

When in the developing years illness, divorce or death occurs in the family involving the mother or competitive sibling, the child may become unreasonably convinced that he or she is in some way responsible and guilt feelings thereafter hang over the person like a smothering cloud. Even where the individual conceals anger and guilt, a suffusion of hopelessness, despair and hate tend to poison his existence. In therapy, the anger and jealousy often appear in transference reactions toward the therapist, thus qualifying as a productive focus.

When we add to the copious angers that accompany the mothering experience the multitudinous misfortunes encumbering social disciplining, as well as the complications investing the acquisition of a proper sexual identity, we may wonder how any individual emerges into adult life unblemished. The fact is that none does. Fortunately, sufficient defensive resilience and flexibility are maintained in the average person to permit operation of a considerable degree of inner turmoil and environmental battering without destroying a reasonable adjustment. Use may, nevertheless, be made of aberrant interpersonal stratagems and devices that complicate one's life, to say the least, as well as create abundant difficulties with others.

Q460: How does guilt function as resistance to therapy?

A460: Among the most insidious of contrivances used to maintain psychological equilibrium are guilt feelings with self-condemnation and other masochistic maneuvers. These self-punishing techniques, exploited to gain forgiveness for one's offensive behavior, thoughts and feelings, are evolved early in development. Such devices are amply enriched later on by some religions which put the stamp of divine approval on repentance and self-abnegation, glorifying them as expediencies for the gaining of forgiveness and grace. Indemnification for one's transgressions is paid off in currencies of contrition, self-reproach, self-humiliation, and self-castigation, which are expressed through tormenting symptoms, torturing thoughts and even physical pain. The eventuating hysterical, obsessive, and hypochondriacal syndromes often resist resolution in the face of this masochistic onslaught, and the therapist may be at his wit's end in dealing with patients who obstinately cling to the very troubles for which they seek help. A prime focus in therapy may therefore be such feelings and the obstructive masochistic maneuvers they sponsor which, to the consternation of both patient and therapist, are preventing the patient from benefitting from treatment.

Q461: Will a truly adjusted adult ever exhibit the neurotic patterns that existed during the person's childhood?

A461: No adult person ever sheds completely the residues of his or her past. Traumatic happenings, unfulfilled needs, and childish modes of coping are deeply etched into the personality, and some manifestations of these can filter into one's present-day existence, especially when mobilized by current psychological demands. During crises compensating mechanisms that hold childhood promptings in check may crumble and early unsatisfied needs and impulses may be revivified, making a shambles out of harmonious adjustment. Childish patterns are not duplicated exactly in the original form, being altered by fantasies and the accretions of defense that have accumulated over the years. Even where regression and revivification are induced in somnambulistic subjects during hypnosis, or when powerful psychotomimetic drugs activate the tracings of the past, the manifestations, while drawing from previous imprints, are distorted, to some extent at least, by later experiences. (See also Qs 456 and 471.)

Q462: What are the most common sources of conflict?

A462: Among sources of conflict are the following:

1) Clash between impulses (needs, personality traits, etc.) and moral prohibitions.
2) Clash between opposing character traits. For example:
   (a) Dependency vs. independency strivings (union vs. separation).
   (b) Aggressive vs. passive strivings (masculine vs. feminine; self-punishment vs. aggression).
   (c) Grandiosity vs. self-depreciation (superiority vs. inferiority feelings).
   (d) Relatedness vs. detachment (sociability vs. isolation).
   (e) Assertiveness vs. timidity (approach vs. withdrawal behavior).
3) Unfulfilled needs or personality drives.
4) Recent traumatic environmental happenings which threaten security and damage self-esteem.
5) Anger, fear, or guilt feelings about past experiences and memories.
6) Forebodings about the future.

Q463: Classical analysts still focus on sexual repression and the oedipus complex as the core problem in psychopathology. Isn't this a narrow view of psychopathology?

A463: We deal here with murky semantics. The terms "sexual" and "oedipal" actually cover many aspects of development other than genital, and lack of clarity in definition has created a great deal of misunderstanding in our field. The goal of psychoanalytic therapy is much more extensive than merely overcoming sexual repressions and resolving a desire for exclusive sexual possession of the parent of the opposite sex. Most classical analysts acknowledge this.

Q464: Why in resolving anxiety do you sometimes precipitate hostility?

A464: Usually this is because the hostility has been suppressed by the anxiety reaction and the patient has barricaded it from awareness. Removing the anxiety block will then liberate the hostility.

Q465: What effect do memories of the past have on current conflict situations?

A465: Current conflicts or the mobilization of transference may stir up old memories and emotions which bear a relation to the feelings immediately being experienced. The effect of this revival of the past can be an illumination of present conflicts and of the transference situation, leading to gratifying insights. Resolution of a conflict may in turn produce a better understanding of the past. In this way a feedback occurs between the past and the present.

Q466: Is it possible to reconstruct the individual's past conditionings and traumas from material the patient brings into therapy, like memories?

A466: Sometimes, but one can be wrong. Rather than to be concerned with dead circumstances and mummified personalities (Strachey, 1969, p. 277), the best way is to observe how the past is distorting what is going on in the relationship with the therapist. Here a transference neurosis during psychoanalysis operates as an excellent revelatory screen. Talking about the past from one's recollections does not have the same therapeutic impact as feeling it operate in the present (in transference) and realizing its power in distorting reality. However, many current conflicts and present-day dreams may stir up feelings and memories that have a connection with the past and that revive the recall of authentic past experiences. There is nevertheless no question that transference opens up the earlier forgotten or repudiated events.

Q467: With the emphasis on ego psychology, I would imagine one would look for evidences of the self-system in dreams. How does the manifest content of dreams give one clues about the self?

A467: The dream is a highly personal piece of narrative in which the self is represented in both manifest or indirect forms. Even though the manifest content of the dream is highly symbolized, it contains clues to the latent meanings regarding feelings about oneself, one's relationship to objects, defensive operations, unfulfilled needs, etc., that can be fruitfully used for interpretations (Spangaard, 1969). An experienced analyst who knows his patient well and has already identified the patient's disturbing nuclear conflicts can derive a good deal of data from the manifest content and interpret it, sometimes without associations.

Q468: Are there any general rules for the interpretation of dreams?

A468: Franz Alexander (1950, p. 62) wrote that rules for interpreting a dream were no more applicable than rules for solving a crossword puzzle. Each therapist evolves rules for himself and each in a different way focuses on the manifest content as a way of exploring and interpreting the latent meaning. Once one has obtained from the patient his associations to the dream and has appraised the associations against the backdrop of what one knows about the patient from the sessions one has had with him, one may match this with the manifest content of the dream. The immediate conflict that has set off the dream, the latent wish and the defense, will then become more apparent and will offer themselves for interpretation.

XX. Prognosis

In textbooks of psychiatry there are many pages of index in closely packed fine print. Amidst the profusion of items there is, in most indexes, not a single entry under "prognosis." A search for synonyms of prognosis which would subsume similar predictive aspects also yields nothing. This absence is probably not fortuitous; it undoubtedly indicates that the complexity of the problem is formidable and that reliable facts cannot be readily collated. A few bold authors have ventured opinions about prognosis, but on the whole little is available in the literature on this very important subject. The question may be asked: "Do we have enough of an understanding of factors that enter in the cause and cure of emotional problems to prognosticate what will happen with any degree of accuracy?" Three subsidiary questions impose themselves before we can prognosticate the destiny of any emotional ailment: What? How? and Who?

The What: Obviously, we must qualify prognostic signs in terms of the ultimate treatment goals. What are we trying to achieve (stabilization, optimal functioning, reconstructive change)? Are the objectives we have in mind realistic in terms of (a) the potentials of the patient; (b) existing motivations; (c) the reality situation; (d) the available therapeutic facilities and support systems? *The How:* What techniques will we employ and have these proven successful in other cases? *The Who:* What about the competence of the therapist? Is the therapist experienced in working with cases similar to that of the patient? Can the therapist relate to the kind of person the patient is, managing the emerging transference and other resistances, as well as one's own countertransference?

Q469: If an agency refers a patient to you for a consultation as to whether psychotherapy would be effective in his case, what signs indicate that there will be a good response?

A469: There are very few signs that will give you this information because of the tremendous number of variables that are involved in the treatment process. An extensive study (the Penn Psychotherapy Research Project of Luborsky et al., 1980) found that not a single psychometric measure, demographic characteristic, symptom, psychological test or interpersonal inventory was related to outcome. Among the crucial variables are the skill of the therapist and the nature of the evolving therapeutic relationship. These are merely a few of the factors that will affect outcome. The actual happenings in therapy cannot be predicted in advance. We might roughly say, however, recognizing that there are many hidden caveats, that if a patient is highly motivated for therapy, has functioned well in the past, has had at least one good relationship previously, is uncomfortable with his symptoms or situation, seems to be able to relate well with the interviewer, has a curiosity about psychological forces operating in himself (psychological mindedness), and is reasonably intelligent, he has a chance of doing well in therapy with a good therapist.

Q470: Can psychological tests give you a definite idea of the prognosis?

A470: No. The patient's behavior and responses during the test may bear little resemblance to his behavior and responses to the specific kind of therapist treating him and the special kind of relationship that will develop during treatment. Tests may nevertheless be interesting as a source of some data about the patient's personality characteristics.

Q471: In estimating prognosis how important is early life experience in determining what happens to the individual as an adult?

A471: Both behaviorists and psychoanalysts agree on the decisive role of early childhood in molding and establishing the patterns of adulthood, both good and bad. Some therapists have a fatalistic attitude about this, as if all that matters is a salubrious early life for the creation of a happy, adjusted adult. On the other hand, a disturbed childhood presumably predisposes to an inevitable destiny of doom. These concepts have in recent years undergone some revision, as it has been proven that children are sufficiently resilient in their reactions so that, given a reasonably constructive milieu following a deprived and destructive upbringing, surprising reparative changes are possible (Clarke and Clarke, 1976; Rutter, 1972; Thomas and Chess, 1980). The degree of change will depend on the severity of early damage and the opportunities for growth offered to the child. An impressive number of studies has also cast doubt on "critical periods" of learning and even the so-called irreversible effects of imprinting in animals, whatever implications these have for humans.

Longitudinal studies indicate that it is impossible to predict the degree of competence and maturity in adults from the severity of confusion and disturbance during the childhood and adolescent years. Growth is possible at every stage of the life cycle from infancy to maturity. Yet we cannot guarantee that memory traces of a cruel and destructive early existence can be entirely eradicated by a propitious later environment, nor that these do not surface in dreams and in certain emergency reactions. Nor can we be assured that crisis situations where mature modes of coping are shattered will not sponsor some catastrophic reactions reminiscent of an earlier state of disorganization.

The fact that an individual disrupted in growth during early development *can* change in later life sufficiently to overcome early handicaps does not guarantee that he *will* change. Among the reasons for this inability are the continued existence of inimical environmental circumstances, and the confounding situation of the individual himself creating stressful conditions that resemble the traumatic happenings of his childhood, even though the milieu itself could be favorable in supporting constructive relearnings. We must remember that clinicians see a special subgroup of patients who have failed to change and that consequently false assumptions about capacities for change may be generalized to the population at large. On the other hand, most surveys and research studies have dealt with an unselected population and are more apt to present a more accurate picture of what happens. This may account for the discrepancy in ideas between clinicians and researchers.

In summary we must recognize that the individual does not need to be a victim of his early childhood and that his capacities for growth and change transcend any damages inflicted on him by negligent, thoughtless and irresponsible parenting. This is not to condone such behavior, but to remove from parents the onus of guilt about some of their activities, such as mothers absenting themselves from their preschool children part of the day to pursue work or independent careers. (See also Qs 456, 461, and 472.)

Q472: Can we predict from a preadolescent's symptoms and disordered behavior the kind or degree of disturbance he will have when he grows up?

A472: Surprisingly, neurotic and conduct disorders in early childhood or adolescence are not correlated with a greater incidence of psychopathology in adult life than where the child does not exhibit such early disorders (Thomas and Chess, 1980). This attests to the spontaneous healing potentialities in human beings, particularly where constructive environmental changes happen or are brought about that support a healthier adaptation. The only exception is extremely violent behavior or criminal activities during childhood; under these circumstances the incidence of psychopathology and sociopathy is greater than normal (Robins, 1966). (See also Qs 456, 461, and 471.)

Q473: Can we assume that a patient who has had good personality functioning prior to his present upset has a good prognosis?

A473: Good adaptation in the past is a positive prognostic factor, but it may be neutralized by other negative factors, such as a coexisting physical or neurological condition, a severe and irremediable stressful environment, defective motivation for treatment, or the misfortune of possessing a therapist who is incapable of establishing a good working relationship.

Q474: Can one estimate a bad or guarded prognosis from the kind of symptoms a patient has?

A474: This is possible to some degree, insofar as total cure is concerned. For example, drug dependence, alcoholism, severe sexual perversions, paranoidal tendencies, chronic schizophrenia, manic-depressive disorders, organic brain disorders, chronic obsessive-compulsive reactions, and intensive psychophysiological symptoms like hypochondriasis have a guarded prognosis insofar as cure is concerned. Yet they may be symptomatically helped and behaviorally ameliorated by treatment.

Q475: Can we predict the prognosis from any characteristics the patient shows?

A475: Not always, but occasionally we may be able to make educated guesses. A few studies have indicated some correlation between negative outcomes and chronicity of an emotional problem, maladjustment since early childhood, failure in previous therapies, low IQ, severe disturbances in interpersonal relationships, absent motivation, high secondary gain from symptoms, unreasonable expectations of what therapy can do, and faulty ego strength. Conditions like schizophrenia, obsessive-compulsive neurosis, alcoholism, drug addiction, paranoidal states, hypochondriasis, organic brain syndromes, and certain somatic conditions of psychological origin like severe ulcerative colitis usually have a bad prognosis for cure. The research in the field unfortunately is spotty and not of a high level of scientific virtue.

Q476: Can you estimate the prognosis of a case from good data obtained in the initial interview?

A476: The more complete the data, the better the capacity to predict the outcome. I remember one case of a beautiful, poised female writer of 32 who was referred to me for hypnosis by a friend of mine after many attempts to stop smoking by herself, and after several unsuccessful tries at psychotherapy. While there were no serious emotional problems that I could detect, and her present work adjustment, relationships with people and sexual life seemed fairly satisfactory, one piece of data that she gave me put doubts in my mind as to how successful I would be in getting her off tobacco. She confessed to me, somewhat shamefacedly, that she still used a baby pacifier that she stuck into her mouth alone at home (she was single) at times when a cigarette wasn't between her lips. Often she went to sleep with it in her mouth. I asked her if she knew what this meant. "After all, doctor," she replied, "I'm no fool. I'm just a plain oral character." Under the circumstances, I confessed to her that the chances of success with a symptom-oriented approach like suggestive hypnosis were poor, and that she had better get herself into analysis without wasting any more time or money. "God forbid," she retorted. Since I had promised to hypnotize her, I induced a trance with less than ardent enthusiasm, and went through my usual paces, hoping to demonstrate that my predictions of failure would surely come to pass. Two days later she telephoned me to tell me she had quit smoking, and she asked if I would make a hypnotic tape for her. We had three visits in all, and while she retained her discrete pacifier habit, she fooled me by staying off tobacco completely. A year went by and she still had not resumed smoking, nor were there any substitute symptoms. This abstinence was confirmed by several reliable friends who knew her well.

Now I have no idea of the dynamics of the symptomatic cure but it is possible that my pessimistic attitude was just the right tactic to use with her. She may have decided to accept the challenge and to show me that I was wrong concerning my estimate of her. Or perhaps the idea she would have to get into long-term analysis was more distasteful to her than giving up smoking. Frankly, I was delighted that I was such a poor prognosticator, even though I still am convinced that a good analysis would have been a worthwhile investment.

The point I am trying to stress is that as thorough as we believe our initial interviewing may be as a way of estimating outcome, we still do not have all the variables at our fingertips. We still can be right in our estimate, but sometimes, as in this case, we can be wrong, and to the patient's benefit. (See also Q 496.)

Q477: Can you predict the prognosis of a mentally ill patient by the severity of the initial symptoms?

A477: Not necessarily. Some of the most violent reactions have the best prognosis. On the other hand, what seems like a mild personality disorder may go on interminably and the pathology may progressively increase. There are many variables involved in prognosis, including the latent resources (ego strength) and defenses of the patient, which are balanced off against the demands and stresses the environment imposes on the person.

XXI. Outcome

Skepticism about the true value of psychotherapy has promoted increasing interest in outcome studies. Such studies have been conducted against the backdrop of recognition that present-day propositions in the field of psychotherapy are not of a high order of empirically tested probability, and that it is difficult to demonstrate the consequences of treatment by any concrete methods and operations. Evidence from statistics has been misleading since we have few criteria upon which to gauge the quality of improvement or the specific parameters of personality that are being influenced by psychotherapy. For one thing it has been found that, irrespective of the methods employed in treatment, approximately the same proportion of patients will experience "cure" or improvement. Were we to believe some of the published data, we would have to admit that there is little documentation that psychotherapy or psychoanalysis is any more effective than the spontaneous cure or counseling, or that trained, experienced therapists get any better results than dedicated paraprofessionals. Must we credit these confounding conclusions to the fact that present-day research in psychotherapy is insufficiently advanced to make possible the reliable application of experimental control studies to the evaluation of outcome? There is evidence that, with the recognition of the complexity of variables involved and the vitality and sophistication currently being manifested by researchers in the field, the outlook for definitive studies on outlook in the future is a bright one.

Q478: Governmental officials are concerned with the efficacy and safety of the different psychiatric treatment modalities. Aren't safety and efficacy difficult things to establish?

A478: Research data are contradictory. One important reason for this is that the studies concern themselves with the modalities themselves and not with *how* they are implemented and the qualities and training of the practitioners who are utilizing the different methods. After all a scalpel is no better than the surgeon who uses it. An untrained or inexperienced therapist or one with an unsuitable personality will not be able to do good work with therapies that require skill or the building up of a good relationship with the patient. Many studies do not even consider the therapist variable. Apart from this factor, controlled studies have been few. But we still have some good data to indicate that psychotherapy in the hands of a good therapist is safe and effective.

Q479: I don't see why we cannot compare the relative values of different therapies or prove the effectiveness of psychotherapy in general by scientific studies. Do you agree that this can be done?

A479: Comparison studies are constantly being done, but the results are usually flawed through neglecting to consider many variables that make such studies unreliable. Although randomization may be utilized in assignments, no two patients are ever alike, even where they suffer from the same syndrome, possess an equivalent severity of symptoms, are of the same approximate age, and come from the same cultural background. No two therapists do the same kind of therapy, even when they have been trained alike, espouse identical theories, and come from a similar cultural background. The gestalt of every patient-therapist relationship is so unique, even within the same theoretical school of practice, that differences usually exceed similarities. On top of these complications is the fact that therapists do react countertransferentially to selected patients, an eventuality that is usually not detectable in a research study. Countertransference will influence the therapeutic process for better or worse.

Applying scientific procedures to validate the effectiveness of psychotherapy is thus fraught with great uncertainty (Wolberg, 1977, pp. 50-67), and most contemporary contributions on this subject are not too reassuring, as Strupp and Hadley (1977) and Parloff (1979) have pointed out. Yet this should not discourage our efforts at refining experimentation in the hopes of eventually rectifying such uncertainty. Single studies need to be replicated and their hypotheses tested by other researchers.

The fact that scientific studies are not yet convincing does not invalidate psychotherapy as a viable approach in emotional problems (Bergin, 1971; Bergin and Lambert, 1978; Gottschalk et al., 1967; Luborsky et al., 1975; Meltzoff and Kornreich, 1970; Parloff, 1979; Parloff et al., 1978; Sloane et al., 1975; Smith et al., 1980; Vorster, 1966). Even the most pessimistic of the foregoing researchers concede that psychotherapy is more effective than no treatment or the administration of a placebo.

Q480: Are there any procedures for the measurement of outcome and can you cite the literature?

A480: General procedures for the measurement of outcome have been detailed by a number of authorities, including Gottman and Markman (1978), and Waskow and Parloff (1975). Of primary concern is identifying the specific variables that are significant to measure and that give us reliable and valid data. Of concern also are the research designs that can best provide answers to our questions about outcome. The instruments that are used for the gauging of outcome must be selected carefully, recognizing that no one instrument is suitable for different patient populations and for varying forms of psychotherapy. Rather, multiple outcome instruments are indicated. Among the measures in use today are: self-reporting which deals with the patient's daily functioning (Cartwright, 1975; Imber, 1975); broad anamnestic material as in the popular Minnesota Multiphasic Personality Interview (Payne and Wiggins, 1972); data from family and friends (Hargreaves et al., 1975; Waskow and Parloff, 1975); a "Community Adjustment Scale" (Ellsworth, 1974); therapist assessment scales (Endicott et al., 1976; Green et al., 1975; Mintz et al., 1979; Newman and Rinkus, 1978); material from community agencies or members (Cummings, 1977; Cummings and Follett, 1968; Halpern and Biner, 1972); and changes in economic and creative output (Riess, 1967; Yates, 1980). Insofar as research designs are concerned, a number of authorities have offered their ideas, for better or worse, including Bandura (1978), Cronbach (1978), Kazdin (1979), Cook and Campbell (1979), Glass et al. (1973), and Luborsky et al. (1975). Difficulties in the testing of outcome are many (Frank, 1979; Wolberg, 1977, pp. 50-67), but this should not deter us from making efforts at refining our designs.

Q481: Are outcome studies comparing patients who have received psychotherapy with those who have received only an initial interview valid? The reason I am asking this is that I read a report recently saying there is no difference in outcome of therapy patients versus no-therapy patients where patients have been randomly assigned to an experimental and control group.

A481: First, the statistics are wrong. Present-day research definitely shows a difference for the better in patients who have received treatment as compared to persons with no treatment (Bergin, 1971; Bergin and Lambert, 1978, Luborsky et al., 1975; Parloff et al., 1978, Parloff, 1979). Second, the "no therapy" group, the members of which had an initial interview, is an invalid concept. An initial interview *is* a form of therapy and patients can benefit significantly from a single contact with a trained professional person. Third, after the initial interview, the patient who is not accepted for therapy does not exist in a vacuum. He will exploit many measures to relieve his symptoms or resolve his problems. These range from tranquilizers to self-help measures to relationships with sundry individuals through whom he may work through some of his difficulties. The idea that he is receiving no therapy then is not true even though the therapy is non-formal. He may experience and report improvement through the measures he exploits. But the *quality* of the improvement has to be examined. Is he gaining relief by withdrawing from potentially traumatic situations? A patient with a travel phobia may feel well so long as he abandons the idea of leaving his home territory. A woman with painful vaginismus may experience peace of mind by deciding that celibacy is the most sensible existence. A man suffering from attacks of anxiety may succeed in repressing his underlying hostility, which diverts into a symptomless but ultimately deadly hypertension. On the other hand, a patient receiving formal psychotherapy may not experience improvement for many reasons—lack of motivation, too great an investment in secondary gains, but most of all treatment by a bad therapist. The balance sheet of results in these two groups of patients may *seem* even, but hidden factors make invalid the assumption that psychotherapy scores no gains over no psychotherapy. Considering all the facts, when we are dealing with an emotional problem there is no substitute for good psychotherapy. (See also Q 487.)

Q482: What are the areas of change to measure in studying outcome and what are common outcome test batteries and how reliable are they?

A482: Therapeutic changes involve many facets of an individual's functioning, not all of which are easily measurable. Among these are symptoms, relationships with people, values, self-esteem, work capacity, self-image, economic status, creativity, etc. No patient progresses equally along all dimensions of possible change. To assess these we would require a variety of instruments. The usual pronouncement of "improvement" or "cure" generally connotes merely a relief of symptoms, and does not indicate what sacrifices are being made to achieve this. For example, a patient with depression initiated by loss of a loved person who served as a maternal object may find his depression "cured" when he finds a new maternal companion. Should he coordinately be in therapy he may falsely ascribe his "cure" to the effect of treatment.

In estimating change we are confronted with the dilemma that the multiple change criteria with which we deal are not standard and that situation-specific behaviors (like efficiency at work) are more easily assessed than personality traits. To bring some order to this muddle attempts have been made to establish a battery of measuring devices. Waskow and Parloff (1975) have recommended as a standard test battery: the Minnesota Multiphasic Personality Inventory (Dahlstrom et al., 1972); the Hopkins Symptom Checklist (Derogatis et al., 1973); the Psychiatric Status Schedule (Spitzer et al., 1967, 1970); Target Complaints (Battle et al., 1966); and a choice of either the Personal Adjustment and Role Skills Scales (Ellsworth, 1975), or the Katz Adjustment Scales (Katz and Lyerly, 1963). The value of these or any other proposed batteries will require more testing.

For the most part outcome assessment will rely on the patient's divulgences, on disclosures of the therapist, as well as on the reports of family and friends, all of which may be highly biased. Nevertheless, we may have no other way of assessing change than through these declarations and through the use of instruments such as the battery of tests cited above by Waskow and Parloff (1975). Lambert (1979) has written an excellent review of measurement batteries, and useful measures have been described by Lorr and McNair, 1965; Malan, 1976;

Meldman et al., 1977; Miles et al., 1951; and Strupp et al., 1969. Insofar as personality tests are concerned, they have not been found too useful (Mischel, 1977).

Q483: Isn't it true that all treatment methods get similar results?

A483: To an extent confusion about the value of different forms of psychotherapy is due to the fact that contingencies responsible for therapeutic improvement are still unclear. Research studies have not been able to shed light on this dilemma. However, they *have* revealed one outstanding finding: Approximately two-thirds of all patients experience improvement irrespective of the kind of psychotherapy employed. The implication of this finding is that psychotherapies differ in their design rather than in their outcome. Psychotherapists, nevertheless, are apt to credit their results not to kindred events common to all psychotherapies, but to casual epiphenomena unique to their own methods of treatment. Accordingly, they have—some with undaunted hubris—made global assumptions about the values of their personal ideologies and techniques.

The thesis that all psychotherapies score similar results is, however, open to a good deal of question. The quality of improvements achieved and permanence of beneficial effects will vary. There is a great deal of difference between an "improved" patient who achieves mere symptom relief and one who in addition to symptom relief is helped to understand and to deal with sources of his symptoms with the object of averting future attacks. These factors are usually not considered in random outcome studies. Nor is, perhaps, the most important variable emphasized, namely the therapist himself—his training, experience, expertise in working with a special technique, and capacity for empathy, sensitivity and perceptivity—ingredients that, in my opinion, are more important than the identifying labels pinned onto treatment interventions. In other words, the value of any psychotherapy is no greater than the competence of the therapist who implements it.

Q484: Is the outcome of reconstructive personality change possible without psychotherapy?

A484: Where anxiety investing such change is not too great, or secondary gains not too rewarding, or basic personality characteristics not too rigid, considerable change is possible through education and constructive life experiences. Sometimes a crisis that superimposes itself and challenges basic security and self-esteem may force the individual to alter his attitudes, philosophies, and patterns of behavior so as to encourage substantial behavioral changes. Where the environment rewards such revisions, the transformation may be permanent. The most difficult areas to influence are personality traits that are ego-syntonic and that satisfy unconscious repudiated needs and conflicts. Here dynamically oriented psychotherapy offers the person the best opportunity for improvement.

Q485: Why do patients from lower socioeconomic levels tend more often to break off therapy than patients from higher socioeconomic levels?

A485: For many reasons. Chief among these is failure in communication, the therapist operating on a different semantic plane than the patient. The therapist must adapt his language to the vernacular of the patient and not expect the reverse. Important also is the fact that the expectations of the patient are unfulfilled. Most patients from lower socioeconomic levels presume that the therapist will function like a physician or dentist. The patient presents his problem and the therapist should then take over and administer the cure. Merely talking about a problem and needing to assume responsibility for working it out does not accord with anticipated hopes. What is usually desired is some material evidence of action or some direct advice. This is why such patients are apt to respond well to demonstrably active measures like hypnosis or biofeedback or medicinal placebos, which may enable them to relate better to the "giving" person in the therapist. The latter's psychotherapeutic maneuvers are then more likely to be accepted.

Another reason is that the therapist is apt to distance himself more from "blue collar" than from "white collar" workers, the values of the latter encouraging greater empathy and better identification. Patients will sense the distancing and defensively withdraw. On their own, patients will also feel the class difference and believe that it is not possible for persons from another background to understand and sympathize with their situation. Eventuating transference resistance may be in terms of stopping treatment. By the same token, we may hypothesize that countertransference is apt to be greater with therapists who come from middle- or uppper-class backgrounds when they come into contact with citizens with "offensive" traits, standards, skin color, race and religion. There is a good deal that the therapist can do toward making the relationship climate more agreeable if he is motivated to take the trouble to do so with patients of a different class.

The common idea that people from lower socioeconomic levels cannot utilize dynamic therapies is not a valid one, as our experience with Medicaid patients at the Postgraduate Center for Mental Health has shown. The crucial variable is the nature of the working relationship. It is the therapist's responsibility to examine his own prejudices and shortcomings that retard his effectiveness with a population that increasingly is demanding and needful of services.

Q486: Is there any scientific evidence that contemporary psychotherapeutic practices are effective?

A486: Whatever value we place on statistics, these bear out the effectiveness of psychotherapy in terms of a 60 to 80 percent improvement rate (Bergin, 1971; Luborsky et al., 1975; Meltzoff and Kornreich, 1970; Sargent et al., 1968).

Q487: How can you consider psychotherapy effective if the same number of neurotic individuals improve without therapy as those who receive it?

A487: There is still a good deal of confusion about the studies that have been published that indicate that two-thirds of all neurotic patients improve whether they receive psychotherapy or no psychotherapy. Eysenck's original studies (1952, 1960b, 1965) which challenge the effectiveness of psychotherapy have been shown to be unreliable (Bergin, 1971). Rachman's (1972) data also have been questioned; his implication that psychotherapy/no psychotherapy outcomes are equivalent is challenged by the studies of Bergin and Suinn (1975), Kellner (1975), and Luborsky et al. (1975). A controlled study by Smith and Glass (1977) covering 25,000 treated and controlled patients indicated that those who received treatment were better off than 75 percent of those who did not.

Many other studies have been published which indicate without question that psychotherapy is superior to no treatment. This does not seem to be an earth-shaking conclusion because if the difference is not significant, one may legitimately wonder if psychotherapy is cost-effective. The answer to this, I believe, lies in the fact that many professionals are doing psychotherapy who have not been adequately trained, or whose personalities block the development of the essential ingredient of all effective psychotherapies, i.e., a good working relationship. An incompetent therapist or one lacking important personality traits will not only fail to help many patients but actually will make them worse. The victims of such therapists would have been better off to rely on the bounties of fate and "spontaneous remission" than on the ministrations of their professional helpers (see Wolberg, 1977, pp. 55-59). The negative results of these ineffective therapists are lumped together with the positive results, making for a percentage far below what would have occurred if only the results of qualified and effective therapists were considered.

In addition, where randomized selection processes are used in a study, there is a tendency to take on all comers. Not all applicants are suitable candidates for psychotherapy. Drug addicts will do much better in a methadone clinic than in a formal psychotherapy set-up. Certain forms of non-professional help other than psychotherapy are better suited for some problems; patients in the control groups are apt to exploit these and to benefit from them more than their privileged competitors assigned to the experimental groups. In spite of all of these negative factors, psychotherapy patients still come out ahead of those who do not receive psychotherapy. The conclusion: Psychotherapy *is* effective. (See also Q481.)

Q488: Can we predict a good outcome in all patients who are highly motivated for therapy?

A488: This depends on the specific goals the patient wishes to achieve. Thus a patient may be motivated for therapy in order to reduce the severity of his symptoms or to eliminate them. However, he may not be motivated to give up patterns of behavior that initiate or sustain his symptoms. We may take as an example a man who suffers from anxiety and depression for which he seeks help. The dynamic core of the problem is the repetitive pursuit of a punitive mother figure who rejects and punishes him. This stirs up great hostility, guilt, fear of abandonment, anxiety, and depression. In therapy he may be brought to an awareness of the operative dynamics and the need to give up a current relationship with a rejecting woman which is responsible for his immediate suffering. He may accept the rationale of a recommended course of action, but his need for a sadomasochistic relationship may be greater than his willingness to give it up, even though he is penalized by symptoms. Were this patient in intensive analysis (assuming he was a suitable candidate for analysis) directed toward creation and working-through of the problem in a transference neurosis, there might be a possibility of cure. But other factors like insufficient ego strength or practical limitations of time and finances may make this form of treatment unfeasible. Here his high motivation to receive therapy to eliminate his symptoms will prove to be of little avail. High motivation is one of the desirable assets in helping a patient resolve the cause of his problems, but resistance may neutralize his incentive to get well.

Q489: Can the efficacy of a therapy be tested by establishing a pre-therapy baseline, starting therapy and continuing until improvement, then stopping treatments to bring a patient back to a baseline? At this point therapy is again started to see whether therapy again achieves improvement.

A489: This is a so-called "return-to-baseline design." It is applicable only in a few therapies like pharmacotherapy and symptom-oriented approaches like biofeedback and some behavior modification methods. In most forms of psychotherapy the initial changes may start a chain reaction that continues after therapy has halted.

Q490: Are there any good studies that have been done on comparing different therapies as to results?

A490: Many publications exist, most of dubious quality. Two good studies can be mentioned: 1) the study by Sloane et al. (1975) at Temple University which compared the outcome of short-term psychoanalytically oriented therapy, behavior therapy, and patients put on a waiting list; and 2) the study by Kernberg et al. (1972) at the Menninger Clinic. The former study suggests that behavior therapy and psychoanalytically oriented therapy, executed by good therapists, yield approximately the same results, i.e., 80 percent global improvement, while 48 percent of the waiting list group improved. Behavior therapy scored somewhat better than the other groups on improvement of general adjustment. In the Kernberg study high ego strength correlated with improvement regardless of the type of therapy done (psychoanalysis, expressive psychotherapy, expressive-supportive psychotherapy, or supportive therapy). The quality of interpersonal relationships was most predictive of results. Patients with high ego strength did best with psychoanalysis; those with ego weakness did best with supportive-expressive therapy; those with severe ego weakness did better with an expressive approach oriented around the present, with focusing on transference and the ordering of their lives outside of therapy.

These studies are both worth reading since they were well designed and executed. Their conclusions, while interesting, are, however, not conclusive, nor as important as the methodologies described that show how clinical material can be adapted to good research studies. They both indicate the bewildering number of variables with which we must deal in doing outcome studies.

Q491: Can any personality test be used to predict outcome?

A491: There is no single personality test or battery of tests, including the Rorschach, TAT and MMPI, that can predict outcome. A few studies have identified some favorable characteristics, but these studies have not been replicated.

Q492: Do patients do better with therapists of the same sex?

A492: Not necessarily. A good therapist can work with both sexes if he or she manages the initial resistances (see Wolberg, 1977, pp. 399; Wolberg, 1980, pp. 36,37).

Q493: Has experience in doing therapy been shown to result in better outcome?

A493: We would like to believe so. Even though studies published are contradictory, my personal opinion is that experience *should* result in better outcome if the therapist learns from his experience and does not persist in repeating mistakes. Other therapist variables may neutralize experience as a positive factor, such as severe personal maladjustment and certain personality qualities like detachment and excessive un-controlled hostility that will interfere with a working relationship. The capacity to develop a good relationship with patients, to empathize with their needs and yet to avoid being drawn into gratifying the patient's neurotic designs is most crucial for success in therapy.

Q494: Can a constructive environment overcome the damage done by an unfortunate, unfulfilling destructive childhood?

A494: Not always. Once patterns have been stabilized in late childhood or early adult life, they sometimes continue irrespective of the environment. Confoundingly, the individual may try to recreate conditions of his childhood, almost as if he is trying to work them out in a different and more favorable setting. In some cases, however, where there is sufficient motivation to change, and a psychological readiness for change, a constructive environment may bring about amazing alterations in the personality structure. This metamorphosis is most expeditiously helped by exposure of the individual to dynamic psychotherapy. (See also Qs 456, 461, and 472.)

Q495: What are the most common reasons for negative effects in psychotherapy?

A495: Reasons are multiple. A therapist who prematurely confronts or interprets on a depth level may frighten a patient away from further treatment and upset and traumatize a patient. Most negative effects are due to improper therapy. *It is better for a patient to have no psychotherapy than to receive treatment from a bad therapist.* A potent common source of negative effects is misinterpretation by the patient of the actions or statements of the therapist. An individual with a devalued self-image is particularly disposed to do this in reinforcing his undermined feeling about himself and interpreting what is said to him in a negative way. Questioning the patient about his ideas and feelings of what is being done for him or said to him and clarifying misconceptions can sometimes help forestall a later bad reaction.

Q496: Can one predict the outcome of psychoanalytically oriented therapy from initial interviews or tests?

A496: Only in a limited way. Luborsky and his associates, in an extensive research study at the University of Pennsylvania on estimating outcome from direct predictions by patient, therapist and clinical observers, as well as from other predictive measures, found that only 5 to 10 percent of the outcome variance was predicted. The most successful predictive measures were patient characteristics such as emotional freedom, initiative, flexibility, optimistic expectations, etc. Therapist measures, pretreatment patient-therapist match measures, and treatment characteristics did not predict significantly. Therapist-selected patients did better than those randomly selected. These poor results do not invalidate the authenticity of some of the variables in psychotherapy that are correlated with effective psychotherapy, which of course can be neutralized by coexisting negative factors. For example, an empathic, trained, experienced therapist with faith in his methods may find himself stymied by a resistive, non-motivated patient who refuses to leave a destructive, irremediable environment. Nor do the results mean that one cannot more reliably predict what will happen after psychotherapy has started and the therapist is able to evaluate the nature of the therapeutic relationship and the responses to his interventions. (See also Q 476.)

Q497: Are there any readings you can recommend that deal with the evaluation of various psychotherapy programs in different settings?

A497: Some good readings I can recommend are those by Attkisson et al., (1978), Cook and Campbell (1979), Liptzin et al. (1977), Parloff et al. (1978a), Riecken and Boruch (1974), Riecken (1977), Schulberg (1976, 1977), Weiss (1972), and Wortman (1975).

XXII. Cost-Effectiveness of Psychotherapy

Concern about finances in community-based programs has focused the searchlight on the cost-effectiveness of psychotherapy. Governmental authorities and insurers are asking for proof regarding the usefulness of the various kinds of psychotherapy. Can we verify the worthwhileness of an expensive project of psychiatric or psychological treatment? The difficulty of supplying scientific evidence of merit is complicated by the fact that, no matter how good a species of psychotherapy may be, it will not prove cost-effective in the hands of a bad therapist. But even if we accept what the most dubious researchers now concede, that psychotherapy is at least minimally effective and better than no treatment or the use of a placebo, most impartial observers would have to consider it a beneficial enterprise. But can we say it is cost-effective and that the benefits justify the expenditure of time, effort, and money? This depends on how we rate the tangible and intangible costs of emotional disturbance and how much monetary value we put on human suffering and the misfortunes psychological illness foists on the community. When we consider the misery wrought by neurotic symptoms—the awesome damage to families, the wrecked marriages, the derailed lives, and the shattered productivity that follow in the wake of a neurosis—and add to these calamities crimes, delinquencies, rapes, arsons, murders, suicides, violence in the streets, and the ravages of alcoholism and drug addiction that are neurotically or psychotically inspired, we may ask: "How costly is it to society *not* to try to prevent these tragedies through some kind of corrective procedure?" Is not even a minimally effective solution better than no solution at all?

Q498: There has recently been a good deal of agitation on the part of insurers and governmental authorities for proof regarding the safety and effectiveness of psychotherapy, with, I suppose, the object of reducing the numbers of procedures that deserve third-party payments. Do you think there is any merit in such a movement?

A498: I believe the motive is an understandable one considering the rising costs of health care. But in my opinion, the direction on which the proposed inquiries are focused is wrong. The various procedures employed today in treating mental and emotional problems, such as dynamically oriented psychotherapy, behavior therapy, family therapy, group therapy, marital therapy, pharmacotherapy and others, are substantially safe and effective *when executed by trained, experienced and skilled professionals.* The best studies in the field have demonstrated the effectiveness of psychotherapy (Smith et al., 1980; Smith and Glass, 1977). What makes a procedure unsafe and ineffective is not the technique itself, but how it is applied. A scalpel in the hands of an unskilled surgeon can be a dangerous and useless instrument. Pardes, Director of the National Institute of Mental Health, has pointed out that the question of solid proof of treatment effectiveness extends across the entire health care field. In a 1978 report from the Congressional Office of Technology Assessment, only 10 to 20 percent of *all* health care technology has been proven effective by formal methods. Many of the commonly employed medical procedures have never been satisfactorily evaluated. Controlled studies in the mental health field definitely show that psychological treatments rate at least no worse than treatments in medicine and surgery.

Q499: Is psychotherapy really cost-effective in your opinion?

A499: There is no question in my mind that good therapy is cost-effective.

Q500: Is psychotherapy cost-effective in the sense that it can reduce medical expenses, for instance, lower the number of visits to physicians or medical clinics paid by the treated patient?

A500: Since physical symptoms caused or aggravated by emotional problems constitute a good bulk of the patients seen by medical practitioners, we would expect that patients receiving psychotherapy would show a reduction in utilization of medical services. This is actually what a number of studies show (Cummings and Follette, 1968; Goldberg et al., 1970; Jameson et al., 1976; Olbrisch, 1977; Pomerleau, 1979).

Q501: Don't such issues as "patient's rights" and "informed consent" interfere with experiments to test the efficacy of psychotherapy?

A501: Obviously, especially where the patient is assigned to a control "no-treatment" group or given a placebo. Ethically, sick patients are entitled to receive therapy and to deny them this to test a procedure involves moral as well as legal issues. One way that has been recommended to circumvent this problem is by "informed consent" procedures apprising the patient of the purposes of the experiment, possible risks, the uses of the data collected, and the fact that the patient can leave the experiment when he wishes to do so. He may also be informed about other therapeutic resources. Will this interfere with the experiment? It may, since suggestion enters into the picture. The patient will know what is demanded of him. The "demand characteristics" of the experiment will undoubtedly influence some of his reactions, the patient responding either in ways to please the researcher (who may have promised him treatment in the future) or reacting oppositionally to frustrate the researcher out of resentment or transference.

Q502: In cost-benefit research do any studies show greater work productivity for patients receiving psychotherapy?

A502: Yes, for example, a study by Riess (1967) done at the Postgraduate Center for Mental Health in New York City shows an increase of 35 percent in income of patients receiving psychotherapy.

Q503: How does community-based treatment compare in cost-benefits and cost-effectiveness with treatment in institutions?

A503: Delivery systems in the community are more cost-beneficial and cost-effective than institutional delivery systems. What is important of course is supervision of the quality of care in day-hospital and other community-based programs. In one study (Cassell et al., 1972), deinstitutionalization with follow-up care, welfare costs, medications, etc., was shown to be about 60 percent less costly than institutional costs, and the outcome was considered more effective. The advantage of community programs has been confirmed by Foreyt et al., 1975, Levenson et al., 1977, Mosher et al., 1975, and others. Again it must be emphasized that dumping patients onto the community without adequate follow-up produces problems for both the patients and the citizens around them. On the other hand, adequate aftercare services are reflected in all-around benefits.

Q504: Why is there resistance among insurers and governmental policymakers toward financing psychotherapy, and can this situation be improved?

A504: Prejudice against psychotherapy is based largely on its indeterminate cost and outcome. There is some question about its true efficacy also as a method, contrasted, for example, with drug therapy. We do not as yet know which therapies do best with which syndromes and with which patients. A psychotherapeutic effort is believed by many to be a "catch as catch can" affair, a therapist utilizing his own standards about how long to keep a patient in treatment and what best to do in a specific situation. Experience with long-term therapy, especially psychoanalysis, has not been reassuring. A patient may be in four or five times a week treatment for five years or longer and the cost can be monumental. Yet, unless the patient has been carefully screened, he may have been completely unsuited for this technique. When we assay the result of this high investment of time, money and effort, we must admit that the cost-effectiveness level here is low. Without knowing that the fault lies in poor selection, people responsible for payments will come to the spurious and global conclusion that psychoanalysis as a method of treatment is fraudulent.

I do believe there are answers. Foremost, some fiscal restraints are essential in financing psychotherapy. This means limiting the number of sessions, except in cases where longer-term therapy is really needed. What would help immeasurably is setting up training standards for professionals who propose to do psychotherapy. Should an individual require help beyond the allotted number of sessions financed by third-party payments, a review committee may have to decide on the feasibility and kind of long-term treatment, with periodic reviews of progress.

XXIII. Prevention

The community mental health movement has been described "as a chaos of good psychiatric intentions rushing off in all directions at once and held together by public funds" (Brodie, 1969). Much of the failure to achieve the original purpose of Congress in creating the community mental health program lay in the fact that providing for the mental health needs of all people was a too ambitious, and perhaps unrealistic, goal that should have awaited a good deal of experiment over many years before it could be even minimally fulfilled.

The development of a broad public health model of prevention has been especially difficult. In addition to fiscal problems, there are relatively few psychiatrists and psychologists who have gone beyond their clinical training to acquire essential skills to work at prevention. But even where the mental health worker has had adequate training, there are regressive forces within the community that will resist change and perhaps attempt to restore the prior pathogenic elements once change is effectuated. Indeed, there are professionals who insist that the present-day community mental health movement is geared predominantly toward social control and toward preserving the political economic system. Charges and countercharges are fired about freely, making for passionate polemics.

Q505: The problem in psychotherapy, as I see it, is that after you have worked out a problem with a patient and he feels better or resolves his difficulty, he usually returns to the same environment that originally produced or encouraged his problem. How can you prepare the patient for what he will be up against so that he will not relapse? This is especially important in patients who have been hospitalized, as well as drug addicts who have struggled to become free of their habit, and alcoholics who have become sober. Are there any articles on this subject?

A505: This is a very important question and one unfortunately that most therapists neglect. Therapy is incomplete unless it deals preventively with the deteriorating effects of the post-therapy period, and particularly the impact of an environment that reinforces sick behavior. As part of the treatment plan we must consider the destructive elements in the patient's living situation, some of which may be alterable. Family therapy and marital therapy are valuable here if the noxious forces reside at home. Counseling and environmental manipulation may also be helpful and the services of a good social worker who knows casework techniques can be invaluable. These adjunctive therapies should be started during the active treatment process with the patient. Sometimes the only way to deal with a bad environment that is irremediable is to help the patient remove himself from it and take up residence in a less emotionally polluted atmosphere. Where the individual cannot escape from a destructive environment and must live in it, some of the techniques of cognitive therapy may be of great help in insulating the person and changing his ideational perspective toward the environment. I would recommend reading the book by Goldfried and Davison (1976) and articles by Coché and Flick (1975), Richards and Perri (1978), Chaney et al. (1978), and Marlatt (1978), the latter two dealing with maintenance strategies in alcoholics that may also be applied to other problem areas.

Q506: Can emotional illness be prevented or at least its incidence lowered through any method?

A506: Prevention of emotional illness rests to a large extent on meeting the developmental needs of each new generation. An understanding of which needs are fundamental and modes of parenting that best insure fulfillment of these needs would seem essential. Unfortunately, the empirical findings issuing from research on development and on child-rearing have not had much effect on current practices. To a large extent we may suspect that contemporary society with its many encumbrances encourages morbidity within the family, the members of which in turn perpetuate social pathology. Family education alone without social change that can reinforce new learnings falls short of our goal. We may beg the question then and ask how social change may best be secured. Is it through political action? Is it through concerted family education, or through other means? Here we find ourselves in the chicken-egg situation. Should our primary focus be on the family or on society?

When we consider family education, the review of well-intended programs in the past does not provide a basis for optimism (Amidon and Brim, 1972; Brim, 1959). Hess (1980), for example, points out that even where parents want to cooperate it is difficult to provide them with information specific for the needs of a particular family "to adapt it to the many varieties of culture and economic conditions, to develop techniques that will give parents insight into the patterns of their family interaction, and to help them alter their patterns over time." He points out the vital barrier that parents "are sometimes the victims of the influences they cannot control."

Insofar as altering society itself so that it can provide an optimum medium of personality growth, there are grave doubts that this can be done in the near future. These negative statements should not deter us from making concerted efforts to promote proper family education and to work for a society geared to helping each individual reach the maximum of his potential. Persistent efforts in this direction may eventually establish foundations for effective preventive programs in the future.

XXIV. Conclusion

There are many questions that plague the student, researcher and clinician regarding the contingencies that influence results in psychotherapy. Answers to these questions are obscured by a complex mosaic of variables, the operative techniques constituting only a small part of the total treatment gestalt. Yet, if our aim is to enhance our results and make treatment more cost-effective, it is vital to understand the multiple factors that enter into the therapeutic process. At the outset it is necessary to recognize that no psychotherapeutic method exists today that is applicable to all patients or germaine to the styles of all therapists. It is presumptuous, to say the least, for any therapist to assume that his special way of doing psychotherapy is consummate and supreme. More and more we are coming to a point where we can recognize similarities between various treatment approaches and where a synthesis of contemporary views is gaining ground.

As disparate as the various approaches to psychotherapy may seem, their impact on the patient is often registered in similar ways. First, they offer a unique kind of interpersonal relationship in which one feels accepted for what one is and where judgments concerning attitudes and behavior do not agree with habitual expectations. Second, there is an explicit and implicit reinforcement of selected responses with the object of overcoming important behavioral deficits and of extinguishing maladaptive habit patterns. Third, there are direct or indirect attempts made at cognitive restructuring, through various instrumentalities, such as 1) persuasive arguments and proffering of philosophical precepts, 2) the exploration of conscious and unconscious conflicts aimed at the inculcation of insight, and 3) the provision of a corrective behavioral and emotional experience within the matrix of the patient-therapist interaction. Irrespective of behavioral parameters that purportedly are selected for inquiry and rectification, the patient will respond to the therapeutic interventions being utilized in accordance with his own needs and readiness for change. For instance, a behavior therapist may confine tactics to a directive remedying of a paralyzing travel phobia. Even though goals may be circumscribed to an elimination of the phobic symptom, the patient may derive added dividends from contact with the humaneness of the therapist through acquisition of more constructive attitudes toward life and more productive relationships with people. A psychoanalyst may work toward the mobilization of transference in the hopes of imparting insight to the patient. But as non-interfering as the analyst may act, idiosyncratic character traits and personal philosophies will filter through to reinforce certain kinds of behavior in the patient.

Moreover, irrespective of the technological sophistication and emotional maturity of the therapist, or noble intentions toward the patient, some patients will respond with devastating negative reactions that will explode therapeutic efforts into thin air. Or they may become enveloped in a morass of more subtle resistances that will retard progress to a snail's pace.

These facts have fathered a common idea among professionals that therapists of different theoretical orientations do essentially the same things. The patient presents his problem; an attempt is made to establish a meaningful relationship; some formulation is presented to the patient as a working hypothesis; and special procedures are implemented to enhance the patient's mastery and eliminate disruptive elements in his adjustment. It is avowed that if one follows certain basic principles of interviewing and relating; if one does not interfere too drastically with the healing agencies that precipitate out spontaneously in any helping situation; if one does not permit personal problems to entangle and complicate the patient's difficulties; and, perhaps most importantly, if one functions with the patient as a constructive and non-punitive authority, the patient will tend to get well, whatever language we use, or concepts we cherish, or explanations we proffer.

We can speak English or French or Spanish or German or Swedish or Swahili; we can employ neurophysiological or interpersonal or social or spiritual models; we can utilize psychoanalytic or existential or behavioral or other concepts—so long as the patient speaks and understands our language, and accepts our explanations, he will move along the bell-shaped curve of improvement. If this be true, then techniques are merely forms of communication secondary to a host of transactional processes that draw from many biological, intrapsychic, and interpersonal vectors.

A reasonable question that may be asked is whether current research can shed some light on how these vectors can be organized and manipulated to make our operations more effective. Specifically, do we have reliable data that will permit us to match patients, therapists and techniques? Offhand we must admit that empirical studies to date have not settled this question. In an extensive review of research on the assessment of psychosocial treatment of mental disorders by an NIMH working group functioning as an advisory committee on mental health to the Institute of Medicine of the National Academy of Sciences, it is concluded that we do not yet have the answers to the basic question of "what kinds of changes are effected by what kinds of techniques applied to what kinds of patients by what kinds of therapists under what kinds of conditions" (Parloff et al., 1978). We have insufficient data to date regarding the relative effectiveness of the different therapeutic modalities as well as the patient-therapist preferences to make a scientific matching feasible. With the possible exception of a few studies in behavior therapy, research has failed to fulfill standards of acceptability. Insofar as psychoanalysis is concerned, "a wide survey of experimentally controlled, comparative outcome studies has failed to reveal a single appropriate study involving classical psychoanalytic treatment." There are many reasons for this, the authors of the report avow, including lack of cooperation of psychoanalysts with independent researchers, the tendency to depend on enigmatic case-study methods, and the fear that the study itself will alter and distort the therapy process. When we consider the choice of the "best" kind of therapy, the report sums up in the following way: "In summary, the data do not show that any of the tested forms of therapy are unconditionally superior to any other form." The report goes on with the statement that the existing single studies have proved inadequate to answer questions that we need to resolve. What is required is a coordinated planning of wide-scale sophisticated research utilizing an agreed upon minimal set of standardized measures for describing and assessing the kinds of problems, the variety of treatment interventions, and the nature and degree of behavior change.

Since help from present-day research is so problematic, we must depend on clinical hunches in sorting out the significance of the many variables in psychotherapy. For convenience we may group these into:

1) patient variables,
2) therapist variables,
3) intercurrent nonspecific variables,
4) social and environmental variables,
5) transferential and countertransferential variables, and
6) resistance variables.

PATIENT VARIABLES

The Syndrome or Symptomatic Complaint

Are there special techniques that coordinate best with selected symptom complexes, methods that are more rewarding with some types of complaints as compared to other types? How really important are techniques in psychotherapy? Can different therapists get the same results by utilizing various kinds of interventions with which they are individually expert?

By and large techniques do operate as a conduit through which a variety of healing and learning processes are liberated. How the techniques are applied, the faith of therapists in their methods, and the confidence of the patient in the procedures being utilized will definitely determine the degree of effectiveness of a special technique. But techniques are nevertheless important in themselves and experience over the years with the work of many therapists strongly indicates that certain methods score better results with special problems than other methods.

Thus symptoms associated with biochemical imbalances, as in *schizophrenia* or *manic-depressive disorders*, may be relieved with proper psychotropic medication, for example, neuroleptics in the case of schizophrenic thinking disorders, antidepressant drugs in depressive states, and lithium for manic excitement and bipolar depressions. While thinking disorders in schizophrenia are helped by neuroleptics, problems in social adjustment are better mediated by behavior therapy, family therapy, and counseling. Indeed, milieu therapy in the form of a therapeutic environment staffed by accepting, supportive persons may often permit an adequate adjustment without the use of drugs. Such a congenial atmosphere must be continued indefinitely, in some cases over a lifelong period. The presence of a hostile or nonaccepting family correlates with an increased rehospitalization rate. Research studies, i.e., controlled outcome studies for individual or group therapy in schizophrenia, provide no strong evidence for or against the value of psychotherapy. Generally with continued aftercare following hospitalization in the form of a behaviorally oriented program and an adequate residential regime (halfway houses, partial hospitals, rehabilitation units and other community support systems), over 90 percent of patients can be discharged in the community with a two-year rehospitalization rate of less than 5 percent (Paul and Lentz, 1977).

Our experience at the Postgraduate Center for Mental Health confirms the value of a rehabilitation program in lowering rehospitalization rates and, in rehospitalized patients, reducing the time of confinement. Behavioral token economies are often valuable in hospitalized patients toward regulating ward behaviors in areas such as self-care, grooming and social adjustment, and to control target behaviors such as job performance. Behavioral extinction procedures have been utilized to manage gross pathological behavior, like violence and destructive tantrums in psychotic autistic children, especially when coupled with differential reinforcement of constructive behavior. Such behavioral gains are consolidated when management techniques are taught to parents or other adults with whom the patient lives. No cure of the basic condition is brought about by these methods, but definite improvement of behavioral repertoires may be achieved.

While drugs influence *depressive symptoms*, they have little effect on patterns of behaving and thinking, which are best mediated through dynamic interpersonal therapy, cognitive therapy, and behavior therapy aimed at reinforcing involvement with pleasant activities and changing target symptoms and behavior toward improvement of interpersonal relations and social functioning. Combined drug and psychosocial therapy is thus best in most depressions. In suicidal depression electroconvulsive therapy has proven to be a life-saving measure.

In *hyperkinetic children* it is generally found that we may be able to reduce the overactivity with psychostimulant medications, like Ritalin and Dexedrine, plus behavioral forms of reinforcement of positive behavior or such mild aversive techniques as removing the child with disturbing behavior to a "time-out" room for a few minutes. To influence neurophysiological dimensions, as reflected in severe *tension states*, simple relaxation procedures like meditation, or relaxing hypnosis, or autogenous training, or emotive release therapy have been instituted.

Certain *psychosomatic conditions*, such as muscle spasms, migraine, hypertension and arrhythmia, may sometimes be helped by biofeedback. Unfortunately, biofeedback has been oversold, its utility being limited to selected patients (Miller, 1978). Behavioral advocates claim that best results with obesity are obtained with measures directed at self and stimulus control. Behavioral operant reinforcement techniques and systematic desensitization are being used in *anorexia nervosa*, although the evidence of their effectiveness is still unclear. *Smoking* control, it is claimed, is best handled by multi-component treatment packages which program a reinforcement of non-smoking behaviors and utilize smoking suppressive tactics (Bernstein and McAlister, 1976). Stimulus satiation, i.e., rapid smoking to satiation, is temporarily effective but the physical side-effects must be considered. Hypnosis is also useful in combination with follow-up behavioral methods. In *enuresis* behavioral approaches (such as a urine alarm bell) are claimed to be superior to dynamic psychotherapy and imipramine.

Sexual disorders (voyeurism, fetishism, sadomasochism, exhibitionism, transvestisim), though difficult to treat, are approached by some therapists with aversive therapy, such as electrical stimulation for transvestism (Marks, 1976) and with certain idiosyncratic methods like having an exhibitionist appear before a female audience to expose himself while talking about his condition, the extraordinary procedure being credited with some success on follow-up (Wickramasekera, 1976). *Sexual dysfunctions* (impotence, frigidity, dyspareunia, vaginismus, anorgasmia, premature ejaculation) do well with various behavior therapies, hypnosis, and dynamic psychotherapy. Of all of these programs, the Masters and Johnson techniques have proven most popular and have in the opinion of some authorities been made more effective when blended with psychodynamic and interpersonal techniques (Sollod and Kaplan, 1976).

Phobias that have their origin in conditioning experiences (i.e., exposure to parental fears, like a mother who is in terror of mice or a father who shies away from heights), or to a catastrophic personal happening (i.e., an accident in an airplane in which a person was traveling, resulting in a fear of flying), or to an anxiety or physiologically distressing experience linking itself to a coincidental stimulus (i.e., nausea or gastric upset occurring at the same time that one is eating a certain food, resulting in a subsequent refusal to eat that food), seem to respond more rapidly to systematic desensitization, flooding or graded exposure to a phobic object than to any other kind of technique. On the other hand, phobias that are the product of deep personality conflicts, the projected symbols of unconscious needs and fears, are in a different class from conditioned phobias and do not respond as well to behavioral methods. In fact, they may stubbornly resist those techniques and are better suited for dynamic approaches. Of all phobias, agoraphobia seems to be the most resistant.

About two-thirds of patients with *anxiety reactions* are helped by both dynamic psychotherapy and behavioral techniques, such as systematic desensitization, progressive relaxation, "participant modeling" (i.e., the therapist modeling how to master anxiety), and temporary drug therapy. Incidentally, behavior therapy is moving toward recognizing the importance of cognitive factors (such as irrational self-statements and false attributes) and the need not only to modify environmental parameters, but also to consider the patient's interpretation of events and thoughts that mold reactions to the environment. In line with this, applications of behavior therapy have expanded toward a wide spectrum of neuroses and personality disorders.

Some *compulsive disorders* come under control with aversive behavioral techniques when they resist every other type of manipulation. Prolonged exposure to thoughts or situations that provoke compulsive rituals combined with blocking of the patient from engaging in such rituals has yielded some successes. In-vivo exposure is superior to exposure to fantasies. We may minimize persuasion as a technique, but it can have a potent effect on some *obsessive states, adjustment reactions*, and related conditions (Truax and Carkhuff, 1967). Stubborn as they are, *personality problems* and most *neurotic disorders* which are bracketed to personality problems are conditions most subject to the utilization of a dynamic orientation which probes for provocative conflicts and defenses. *Relationship difficulties* are particularly suited for group therapy, marital therapy, and, especially where children are involved, family therapy.

Some *addictions* seem to respond best to certain inspirational groups (e.g. drugs with Synanon, alcohol with Alcoholics Anonymous, food gorging with Weight Watchers, gambling with Gamblers Anonymous). These groups are preferably led by a person who has gone through and has conquered a particular addiction and offers himself as a model for identification. Accordingly, where a therapist works with such groups, an ex-addict cotherapist may be a great asset.

Where repressions are extreme, classical psychoanalysis, intense confrontation, hypnoanalysis, narcoanalysis, and encounter groups have been employed in the attempt to blast the way through to the offensive pathogenic areas. Understandably, patients with weak ego structures are not candidates for such active techniques, and therapists implementing these techniques must be stable and experienced. *Psychopathic personalities* subjected to a directive, authoritarian approach with a firm but kindly therapist sometimes manage to restrain their acting-out, but require prolonged supervised overseeing.

Apart from the few selected approaches pointed out above that are preferred methods under certain circumstances, we are led to the conclusion that no one technique is suitable for all problems. Given conditions of adequate patient motivation and proper therapist skills, many different modalities have yielded satisfactory results. It is my feeling, however, that whatever techniques are employed, they must be adapted to the patient's needs and are most advantageously utilized within a dynamic framework. Transference reactions may come through with any of the techniques, even with biofeedback and the physical therapies. The important thing is to watch out for transference and to work with it when it operates as resistance to the working relationship. Unless this is done our best alignment of method and syndrome will prove useless.

The fact that certain techniques have yielded good results with special syndromes and symptoms does not mean they will do so for all therapists or for every patient. Interfering variables, such as will henceforth be described, will uniquely block results or will make the patient susceptible to other less popular methods.

Selective Response of the Patient to the Therapist

At its core the patient's reaction to the therapist often represents how the patient feels about authority in general, such emotions and attitudes being projected onto the therapist even before the patient has had his first sessions. The patient may rehearse in advance what he will say and how he will behave, setting up imaginary situations in the encounter to come. Such a mental set will fashion feelings that can influence the direction of therapy. Thus, if the patient believes that authority is bad or controlling, his oppositional defenses may be apparent during the interview. These global notions about authority and the reactions they sponsor are usually reinforced or neutralized by the response to the therapist as a symbol of an actual person important to the patient in the past. Some characteristic in the therapist may represent a quality in a father or mother or sibling and spark off a reaction akin to that which actually had occurred in past dealings with the person in question. Or the reaction may be counteracted by a defense of gracious compliance or guarded formality.

Where the therapist becomes for the patient an idealized figure, the initial therapeutic impact may be enhanced. Or if the transference is to an irrational authority, resistance is more likely in evidence. The degree of charisma possessed by the therapist also influences the patient's responses. Reputation, clothing, manner and appearance all function to nurture the illusion of miracles to come. Added to these tendencies are habitual personality operations and coping mechanisms which are shaped by drives of detachment, hostility, and dependency. The various patterns that evolve have a powerful and often determining effect on any techniques the therapist may utilize.

Selective Response of the Patient to the Therapist's Techniques

Patients occasionally have preconceptions and prejudices about certain techniques. Hypnosis, for example, may be regarded as a magical device that can dissolve a neurosis. Or it may connote exposing oneself to Svengali-like dangers of control or seduction. Misconceptions about psychoanalysis are rampant in relation to both its powers and its ineffectualities. Frightening may be the idea that out of one's unconscious there will emerge monstrous devils who will take command of one's life—for example, the discovery that one is a potential rapist, pervert or murderer. Should the therapist have an inkling as to what is on the patient's mind, clarification will then be in order. The manner of the therapist's style is also apt to influence reactions of rage at the therapist's passivity, balkiness at what is considered too intense activity, anger at aggressive confrontation. Some patients are frustrated by having to talk about themselves and not being given the answers.

Moreover, responses to different methods will vary. There is a story of a Gideon Bible (which may be apocryphal) that illustrates this. As is known, practically all hotel rooms contain, as part of the general equipment, a Bible placed there by the Gideon Society which in the front pages contains suggested reading for the weary traveler. For instance, if one is in need of salvation, he is referred to John 3:3; or desires peace in the time of anxiety to Psalm 46; or relief in the time of suffering to Psalm 41; or consolation in conditions of loneliness to Psalm 23. In a certain hotel Bible, opposite Psalm 23 there was written in the margin this inscription: "If after reading this Psalm you are still lonesome, upset and feel life is not worthwhile, telephone 824-3921 and ask for Phyllis." This is eclecticism! Sometimes the Bible helps, and sometimes a Phyllis works better. To help in the selection there are minimal techniques an eclectic therapist should know. In my opinion, the following are most useful: dynamically oriented interview procedures, group therapy, marital therapy, family therapy, behavior modification, pharmacotherapy, relaxation methods and hypnosis.

But irrespective of the techniques we select, we must be sure that they accord with the patient's belief systems. A patient who is convinced that spirit infestation is a cause of his illness will do much better with a shaman or witch doctor than with a psychiatrist. His lack of faith in what the psychiatrist does will render worthless the most sophisticated treatment efforts. Knowledge of the cultural concepts that mold a patient's ideas about what emotional suffering is all about may make necessary some preliminary education to prevent embarking on a futile therapeutic journey.

Some attempts have been made to assign patients to certain styles of therapeutic operation according to their unique characterologic patterns (Horowitz, 1977). For example, hysterical personalities are presumed to require a mode of therapist management that differs from that effective in obsessional personalities. This distinction presumes that certain optimal learning patterns correlate with identifiable personality typologies. The relationship between character structure, diagnostic category, and learning abilities, however, never has been fully clarified. Thus, among patients suffering from the same syndrome, let us say obsessive personality, there are great differences in the way they will respond to certain techniques and therapist styles. While some general principles may be applicable to all or most obsessives, the existing differences prevent our using a blanket approach. People possess different modes, even within the same syndrome, of absorbing, processing and responding cognitively, emotionally, and behaviorally to therapeutic interventions.

Since psychotherapy is in a way a form of reeducation, the learning characteristics of a patient should best correspond with the techniques that are to be used. Problem-solving activities are often related to the kind of processes found successful in the past. Some patients learn best by working through a challenge by themselves, depending to a large extent on experiment. Some will solve their dilemmas by reasoning them out through thinking of the best solution in advance. Others learn more easily by following suggestions or incorporating precepts offered by a helpful authority figure. Some are helped best by modeling themselves after an admired person, through identification with that person. Some patients work well with free association, others do not. Some are able to utilize dreams productively, or behavior modification, or sensitivity training, or other methods. It would seem important to make the method fit the patient and not wedge the patient into the method.

The fact that learning patterns are so unique and modes of learning so varied lends justification to an eclectic approach. It would be advantageous, of course, in the initial phases of therapy to find out how a patient might learn best, but no expedient is available today that can give us this information. We usually settle for the fact that when a patient is first seen learning capacities and styles are unknown and the therapist must proceed somewhat blindly. We more or less shoot in the dark in order to coordinate a patient's specific problem and personality with our techniques. We may get some help during interviewing in discovering how the patient has learned best in the past. More pointedly, we get the most reliable data by actually exposing the patient to the interventions we have to offer and observing how he responds to what is being done.

A few other attempts have been made to identify variables that can make the selection of a therapeutic method more feasible. Among these are the patient's response to hypnotic induction (Spiegel and Spiegel, 1978) and the isolation of core conflicts through the making of a developmental diagnosis (Burke et al., 1979). Some interesting speculations may emerge in watching how patients react to the induction of hypnosis, but are these sufficiently reliable to pinpoint either the existing diagnosis or choices in therapeutic method? More experimental substantiation is required.

Some therapists have attempted to utilize the area of developmental arrest as a way of selecting the ideal technique. Where the patient's prime difficulty is centered around resolution of separation-individuation, this is believed best accomplished through a technique such as described by Mann (1973) in which the struggle over short-term termination of treatment threatens the patient's dependency, lights up the separation problem and offers the opportunity to resolve the conflict in a favorable setting. Where the oedipal conflict is primary, the confrontation styles of Sifneos (1972) and Malan (1963, 1976) are believed to be most effective. For problems originating in the latency period that precipitate out in the mid-life transition around issues of productivity and creativity, the "corrective action" approach of Alexander and French (1946) is recommended. However, it is difficult to substantiate these views because of the interference of so many other variables that can vaporize our best choice-of-method intentions.

While empirical studies tell us little about factors that make for a good patient-therapist match, we may speculate that the personalities, values, and physical characteristics of both patient and therapist must be such that severe transference and countertransference problems do not erupt to interfere with the working relationship. A giving, accepting, warm and active but not too interfering or obnoxiously confronting manner in the therapist is most conducive to good results.

Readiness for Change

Another important factor is the individual's readiness for change. This is a vast unexplored subject. A person with a readiness for change will respond to almost any technique and take out of that technique what he is prepared to use. What components enter into a satisfactory readiness for change have not been exactly defined, but they probably include a strong motivation for therapy, an expectation of success, an availability of flexible defenses, a willingness to tolerate a certain amount of anxiety and deprivation, the capacity to yield secondary gains accruing from indulgence of neurotic drives, and the ability either to adapt to or constructively change one's environment.

Patients come to therapy with different degrees of readiness to move ahead. Some have worked out their problems within themselves to the extent that they need only a little clarification to make progress, perhaps only one or two sessions of therapy. Others are scarcely prepared to proceed and they may require many sessions to prepare themselves for some change. We may compare this to climbing a ladder onto a platform. Some people are at the bottom of the ladder and before getting to the top will need to climb many steps. Others will be just one rung from the top, requiring only a little push to send them over to their destination.

In therapy we see people in different stages of readiness for change. And we often at the start are unable to determine exactly how far they have progressed. One may arrive at an understanding of what is behind a patient's problem rapidly. From this we may get an idea that he will get well with little delay. Yet in relation to his readiness for change he may still be at the bottom of the ladder. Others are at a point where almost any technique one happens to be using will score a miracle. We may then overvalue the technique that seems to have worked so well and apply it to many different patients with such conviction that the placebo effect produces results.

We sometimes see patients who have been in therapy for a long time under the guidance of another therapist who on the surface have made no progress at all. Surprisingly, after a few sessions the patient will begin to progress remarkably, creating the impression that the therapist is a genius in being able to do in three sessions what the previous therapist was not able to accomplish in three years. What actually may have happened is that the previous therapeutic effort succeeded in pushing the patient up the ladder to the top rung, requiring only a bit more therapy for him to traverse the last step.

I remember one patient who came to see me who advertised the fact that I had cured her in one session. She had been under the care of physicians for years, suffering from a host of physical complaints, and her last few doctors, who were burdened by her incessant shifting symptoms, had given up on her as an obstinate hypochondriac. No medicines seemed to help and whenever psychiatric referral was mentioned she responded with an angry refusal and a host of new symptoms. Finally, one day she announced in frustration to her doctor that she was ready to see a psychiatrist and the doctor then referred her to me.

At the appointed time a buxom, handsome, middle-aged lady walked into my office and from the moment the door opened started and continued talking without giving me a chance even to introduce myself. My initial interview sheet in hand, I waited for a pause so that I could at least get some statistical data. After what seemed like an interminable span, she stopped for breath and I threw in an introductory: "By the way, how old are you?" Without pause she avoided the question and continued on her odyssey of voyages to doctors' offices around New York. After several futile attempts to interrupt, I gave up, put my sheet down, settled back in my chair and listened, interpolating an occasional "yes" and "hm humm." I broke in at the end of the hour with: "Unfortunately our time is up." "Doctor," she said, "I feel so much better—thank you very much," and she got up and walked out without making another appointment.

I was curious about what had happened, so that a week later, I telephoned her doctor. His startling reply was: "I don't know what you did for her, but it was like a miracle. For the first time since I've known her, she's lost her symptoms and is interested in getting out of the house and doing things. And," he added humorously, "she says you are a brilliant conversationalist." Three months later the doctor called me and confirmed her continued improvement.

I do not know what happened but apparently my respecting her need to talk without interrupting was probably the best approach I could have used. She was under such great tension that had I not permitted her to let off steam verbally I may have succeeded merely in frustrating and antagonizing her. Grilling her with questions might have given me more information, but I am not sure what it would have done for her. She apparently had climbed the readiness ladder by herself up to the top rung and what she needed to push her over the top was to have someone sit back and listen. She undoubtedly wanted to talk freely to somebody who was not a member of her family, who was not going to judge her, who was passively objective, and who was, hopefully, non-judgmental. Whatever qualities she projected onto me, she utilized the relationship in line with her needs.

Obviously, while this passive stance worked well with this woman, it would not have served other patients who might have required more active confrontation over a more protracted period. A person's readiness for change may, more than any other factor, be responsible for how rapidly movement proceeds in psychotherapy.

Degree and Persistence of Childish Distortions

The distorted images that children carry around with them, the ungratified needs, the unwholesome defenses, may persist into adult life and influence the speed, direction, and goals of therapy. These contaminations may obtrude themselves into the therapeutic situation irrespective of what kinds of technique are practiced. Insidiously, they operate as resistance and they can thwart movement toward a mature integration, no matter how persistent and dedicated the therapist may be.

For example, one patient, a successful businessman of 50, came to therapy in a crisis over abandonment by his mistress 25 years his junior who had run off with another man. A deep depression and anxiety were the chief symptoms for which he sought help. He blamed the young lady's defection partly on his inability to compete with his rival and partly on the ubiquitous duplicity of all females. When he described his life, it became apparent that he had from the earliest days of adolescence looked for and pursued a certain physical type: blonde, fair skinned, long-legged, big-bosomed tarts whose teasing sexual provocativeness and irresponsibility added a fillip to his affairs. Invariably he would select young women who were unable to establish a meaningful relationship and who eventually, despite his wealth and generosity, would reject him and finally leave him. This would make the relationship all the more precious in his mind and the rupture of the romance more disastrous.

During therapy he beat at himself, unmercifully proclaiming himself a worthless and destroyed person, a victim of the treachery of womankind. No amount of reassurance, challenge, and interpretation could penetrate his overwhelming despair and antidepressants proved of little benefit. The fact that the great jewel in his life during the heyday of their relationship had led him a merry chase, deceiving and exploiting him mercilessly, made little difference. Her destructive exploits constituted the main content of his discussions with me, but his depreciating her had little effect on his yearning.

After 12 sessions of gripes, the lady returned without warning, complaining that her most recent paramour was unworthy of her, unreliable and, most importantly, penniless. She apologized for having hastily run off after knowing the man only several weeks and she begged the patient to take her back. The effect on the patient was electric. What common sense, medications and psychiatry failed to do she accomplished in one evening. Depression, anxiety, and physical debility vanished. To justify the reunion, the patient offered to bring the lady to me for an interview to prove that she was now reformed.

At the interview there was no question that she had been trading solely on her physical assets, which were indeed ample, but emotionally and intellectually there was much to be desired. In fact, the most generous diagnosis one could bestow on her was that of a borderline case—and this was stretching a point. It was certainly apparent insofar as my patient was concerned that the only motivation he had for therapy was a desire to dull the pain of deprivation, not to inquire into or eliminate its source.

My best efforts to halt the affair were of little avail since the lady could accomplish more with a casual pout than I could with all the armamentaria that Freud, Pavlov and the other great pioneers had to offer. And even though she soon again started her nonsense, he hung on desperately to the relationship at the same time that he bellowed like a wounded buffalo.

In going into the history, the background for his enslavement became apparent. The death of his mother when he was an infant and his placement with a series of relatives who provided him with a succession of nurses had failed to fulfill his need for real mothering. He was told, he said, that he was a colicky baby with respiratory trouble that was diagnosed as asthma. He failed to see any connection between his childhood and what was happening to him in the present. Interpretations of his orally frustrated dreams fell on deaf ears.

One day on inspiration I asked if he had ever seen a picture of his mother. This he denied. However, a later search by a relative through an old album yielded a startling picture that he excitedly handed me—a picture of a blonde beauty who presented an almost exact image of his present girlfriend. It took no great work to convince him that he had practically all his life been searching for a physical duplicate of his mother. This dramatic discovery had not the slightest effect on his futile mission to look for a symbolic breast, because after another abandonment, he started searching for a substitute blonde, long-legged, big-breasted, unreliable paramour, whom unfortunately he found, starting a further round of exploitation, punishment and anxiety.

Where severe traumas and deprivations are sustained in early infancy, especially prior to the acquisition of language, the damage may be so deep that all efforts to acquire that which never developed and to restore what never existed will fail. Transference with the therapist may assume a disturbingly regressive form and, while the genetic discoveries may be dramatic, the patient, despite intellectual understanding, will not integrate his learning and will fail to abandon patterns that end only in disappointment and frustration. Very little can be accomplished under such circumstances in short-term therapy, and even long-term depth therapy may lead to nothing except a transference neurosis that is difficult to manage or resolve. Lest we be too pessimistic about what may be accomplished through psychotherapy, there are some patients who though seriously traumatized may when properly motivated be induced to yield the yearnings of childhood and to control if not reverse the impulses issuing from improper discipline and unsatisfied need gratification. But this desirable achievement will require time, patience and, above all, perseverance.

Aptitude for Dynamically Oriented Psychotherapy

Some of the available research indicates that patients who respond best to psychodynamically oriented therapy need treatment the least. What this would imply is that persons with good ego strength can somehow muddle along without requiring psychotherapy. But, that this is not always so becomes obvious when we examine the quality of adaptation of these near-to-healthy specimens. In view of the shortage of trained manpower we may want to look for characteristics in prospective candidates for therapy that have good prognostic value. As mentioned before, the following positive factors have been emphasized:

1) strong motivation for therapy (actually coming to therapy represents a commitment),

2) existence of some past successes and positive achievements;

3) presence of at least one good relationship in the past;

4) a personality structure that has permitted adequate coping in the past;

5) symptomatic discomfort related more to anxiety and mild depression than to somatic complaints;

6) an ability to feel and express emotion;

7) a capacity for reflection;

8) desire for self-understanding;

9) adequate preparation for therapy prior to referral; and

10) belief systems that accord with the therapist's theories.

The patient's expectations, age and socioeconomic status are not too significant; provided the therapist and patient are able to communicate adequately with each other.

Choice of Goal and Focus

If a patient through therapy expects that he will become a Nobel Prize winner, he will be rudely disappointed and soon lose faith in his therapist. There are certain realistic limits to how much we can accomplish through treatment, the boundaries largely being determined by the patient with whom we have to work and the dedication of the patient to the tasks to which he is assigned. Added to these are the curbs imposed by the many therapist variables soon to be considered. A great deal of tact will be required in dealing with inordinate expectations so as not to further undermine the already existent devalued self-image.

The selection by the patient of the area on which to concentrate during therapy is a legitimate and understandable theater around which initial interventions can be organized. It may not be the most culpable area stirring up trouble for the patient. But to push aside the patient's concerns with a symptom or a disturbing life situation and insist on attacking aspects of his problem the patient does not understand or is not motivated to accept will lead to unnecessary complications and resistances. It is far better to work on zones of the patient's interest at the same time that we make connections for the patient and educate him as to the need to deal with additional dimensions. Thus a man in the manic phase of a bipolar depression may complain of a marital problem and press for its urgent resolution. Should we attempt to bypass his complaint factor and merely press lithium on him, we may be rewarded with an abrupt termination of treatment.

In attempting to choose the most productive arena for intervention we must keep in mind the fact that behavior is a complex integrate of biochemical, neurophysiological, developmental, conditioning, intrapsychic, interpersonal, social and spiritual elements intimately tied together like links in a chain. Problems in one link cybernetically influence other links. In another publication (Wolberg, 1980, p. 136) I have delineated the affiliation between the different links, contingent fields of inquiry, associated therapeutic modalities and related syndromes. Without denigrating the importance of the patient's chosen area of focus, we may most propitiously deal with a link in the behavioral chain that, in our opinion, needs the most urgent attention, that the patient is willing to work on, and that is realistically modifiable with the patient's current or potential resources. Once we strengthen a pathogenic link through therapy, the effects will usually reverberate through the entire behavioral chain.

THERAPIST VARIABLES

Personality Factors

Many years ago when I was Assistant Executive Officer at a large institution devoted to the emergency management of psychiatrically disturbed patients, I had as one of my responsibilities the admission of patients and the making of initial diagnoses. A good number of the admissions were, in addition to acutely mentally sick persons, exacerbations of illness in remitted chronic psychoses. After admission the patients were assigned to the different resident psychiatrists and I was able to follow them along during their stay until either discharge after short-term treatment or transfer to a state mental institution for longer-term care. This was during the era prior to neuroleptic and tranquilizing drugs.

It was interesting to me how some residents consistently were able to help their allocated patients rapidly reach a good level of stability, enabling the patients to leave the hospital after a brief period, while other residents almost consistently failed, their patients then being sent to a mental hospital for further care. One could almost predict the outcome by the personalities of the residents to whom patients were entrusted.

Observations of the determining influence of personality traits in the therapist on outcome have been repeatedly made and reported by Betz (1962), Rogers et al. (1967), Truax and Carkhuff (1967), Truax and Mitchell (1971), and Whitehorn and Betz (1960). One finding is that a relatively untrained person with a concerned manner and empathic personality will get better immediate results, especially with sicker patients, than a highly trained therapist who manifests a "deadpan" detached professional attitude. One should not assume from this that a therapist with a pleasing personality without adequate training will invariably get good results. Some of the available research alerts us to the fact that the level of therapist expectations and the triad of empathy, warmth, and genuineness do not invariably represent the "necessary and sufficient" conditions of effective therapy (Parloff et al., 1978). However, a well-trained therapist who also possesses the proper "therapeutic" personality (see Wolberg, 1977, pp. 55-59, 259) is by far best qualified to do successful therapy.

A good deal of the flesh and blood of what happens in treatment, short-term or long-term, is provided by the relationship the therapist establishes with his patient, the quality of which is largely influenced by the therapist's personality in operation. Personality expressions, good and bad, come through not only in the content of verbal communications but in nonverbal manifestations. The latter are not merely the epiphenomena of interaction but are directly related to the outcome. Nor does the factor of experience always operate to subdue damaging traits. In some cases earnest, dedicated beginners may relate better to patients than do the more experienced, scientifically oriented practitioners. Of course, we may be dealing here with different classes of patients, i.e., patients seeking a warm, giving authority as contrasted to those who want less personal involvement and greater ability to probe for and resolve defenses in quest of more extensive self-understanding.

After many years of training students and observing their work, I would estimate that the most meritorious personality traits sponsoring a good relationship are objectivity, flexibility, empathy, and the absence of serious emotional pathology. Successful therapists possess a bountiful blend of these attributes, unsuccessful therapists a dearth. Where a student therapist in training possesses a healthy combination of such positive personality characteristics, we may anticipate a good career, although this is not guaranteed. Where a candidate is less bountifully blessed, but cherishes rudiments of essential traits, these may be maximized by careful instruction and personal psychotherapy. A few enter training with such rigid defenses that they scarcely budge even after years of intensive analysis.

How to find candidates who personality-wise have a good chance of becoming competent therapists is a challenge confronting all training institutions. In the early days of existence of the Postgraduate Center for Mental Health in New York City, I once asked Paul Hoch, who was then Commissioner of Mental Health of New York State, what he believed the value to be of recommendations for admission to training from a candidate's personal analyst. "From my own experience," replied Hoch waggishly, "when you first start treating or supervising students, your immediate impression is that they are practically psychotic. But shortly thereafter you develop a relationship with them and you believe that they are only neurotic. And a while later you start endorsing them as either completely normal, or even better than normal." Could it be, I inquired, "that therapy changed their personalities for the better?" "More likely," answered Hoch, "as a therapist works with a student, this changes the therapist's judgment for the worse." What he was referring to, of course, was the ubiquitous problem of countertransference which can mask or distort one's appraisal of a partner in a relationship dyad. Other criteria for selection are undoubtedly more reliable than endorsements from one's personal analyst. But the real test of how effective a candidate will be as a therapist is his actual performance with patients with varying syndromes and degrees of pathology, under the surveillance and tutelage of a competent supervisor. Observation of a student's performance behind a one-way mirror and the use of videotape recordings are also of substantial help.

Specifically, especially where the patient requires rapid stabilization, the therapist's manner must convey empathy, confidence, and understanding of the patient's turmoil and what is behind it. The patient, no matter how upset he may seem, will usually discern these qualities in the therapist and react to them. It is important also that therapists be able to control their own difficulties sufficiently so as to avoid the pitfalls of their own countertransferential problems interlocking with the problems of their patients. Particularly important is sensitivity to and the ability to manage irrational projections of patients, hallmarks of transference neuroses.

Considering that desirable character traits, if absent, are difficult to acquire even with personal therapy, it would seem important in the selection of candidates for training that some criteria be available to spot in advance students who possess or will be able to develop appropriate personality characteristics. This is more easily said than done. When we first founded the Postgraduate Center we experimented with many devices, including projective psychological testing and structured and non-structured interviews. We failed to come up with any foolproof selection procedure. This is probably because the role that a candidate plays with an interviewer or psychologist tester is different from that assumed with patients.

My own experience convinces me that two personality qualities are especially undesirable in a therapist doing therapy: First and most insidious is detachment. Where the therapist is detached, he will be unable, within the limited time span of treatment, to relate to his patient or to become involved in the essential transactions of therapeutic process. A detached person finds it difficult to display empathy. To put it simply, one cannot hatch an egg in a refrigerator. A cold emotional relationship will not incubate much change in treatment. The second quality that I believe is inimical to doing good therapy is excessive hostility. Where the therapist is an angry person, he may utilize the patient as a target for his own irritations. The patient has enough trouble with personal hostility and may not be able to handle that of the therapist. A therapist who in his upbringing has been exposed to a restrictive childhood, having been reared by hostile parents, or forbidden to express indignation or rage, is apt to have difficulties when he encounters a patient with problems similar to his own. Thus he may prevent his patient from working through crippling rage by the subtle tactic of changing the subject when the patient talks about feeling angry, or by excessive reassurance, or by an attack on the patient, or by making the patient feel guilty. However, a therapist who is aware of his hostile propensities, who can be objective about these and willing to back down when a patient challenges him, may be able to do fairly good therapy, provided he permits his patient to fight back, and the patient is not too frightened to challenge and stand up to the therapist. But where the therapist refuses to allow the patient to challenge him, and gets upset and vindictive, rejecting or punishing the patient, therapy has a good chance of coming to a halt.

By the same token, a therapist who has serious problems with sexuality may not be able to handle a patient who also has certain sexual impediments. For example, a therapist struggling with a homosexual impulse, of which he is ashamed, may, when a patient with homosexual tendencies brings up the subject, become defensive, overmoralistic, punitive, or so intensely interested in the topic that he will divert the patient from constructively dealing with other important concerns.

All in all, we hope that in doing therapy the therapist will be slightly less neurotic than the patient. The least we may expect is that the therapist will have a reasonable capacity for maintaining objectivity. Some neurosis or character disturbance is probably residual in all of us, but this need not interfere with doing good therapy provided that we have an awareness of our failings and do not permit them to contaminate the therapeutic atmosphere. One of my teachers, an analysand of Freud, once remarked: "If there ever were such a monster as a completely 'normal' human being, he would very soon get psychotic trying to adjust to the rest of us neurotics." "Normal" probably embraces a host of minor neurotic vexations, but where a therapist finds that something within himself *interferes* with his doing good therapy he would do well to get some personal psychotherapy or analysis.

Choice of Techniques

Technical preferences by therapists are territories ruled by personal taste rather than by objective identifiable criteria. As has been previously indicated, it matters little how scientifically based a system of psychotherapy may be or how skillfully it is implemented—if a patient does not accept it, or if it does not deal directly or indirectly with the problems requiring correction, it will fail. Because of the complex nature of human behavior, aspects that are pathologically implicated may require special interventions before any effect is registered. Prescribing a psychotropic drug like lithium for an excited reaction in a psychopathic personality will not have the healing effect that it would have in violent outbursts of a manic-depressive disorder. Unfortunately, some therapists still cling to a monolithic system into which they attempt to wedge all patients, crediting any failure of response to the patient's resistance.

A young analyst, for example, one year after having completed her training in a classical psychoanalytic school, wanted to get some further training in hypnosis. It turned out that her entire patient load was exactly the same one she originally had when she started her personal analysis some years previously. All nine patients were being seen four or five times weekly, associating freely in the couch position, analyzing their dreams, but showing little or no improvement, some even regressing. The therapist, maintaining the traditional passive stance, tried to listen to what they were saying, but found herself getting more and more bored and increasingly discouraged at what was happening. She wanted to learn hypnosis, she said, to be able to get at the early memories of her patients, since few significant infantile revelations had been forthcoming. Her patients simply were not coming to grips with their unconscious. Hopefully, hypnosis might be able to break through their resistance and bring to the surface the noxious memories and conflicts that were responsible for their complaints.

In reviewing her caseload, one could see three obsessive patients—one with a germ phobia who avoided contact with people; the second, a compulsive handwasher who spent most of the day in the bathroom; the third, a salesman with an obsession of death and killing, who, when he came across the number 23, had to engage in elaborate counting and other rituals to neutralize torturesome preoccupations. In all of these cases analysis had succeeded in providing some answers regarding the sources and meaning of these symptoms. The other six patients ranged from severe borderline cases who went over the border periodically, to various species of schizophrenia, with one man, an engineer, actively hallucinating. There was not a single case, in my opinion, that could be considered a suitable candidate for classical psychoanalysis. And yet here was an earnest, dedicated professional digging away at their unconscious in the hopes of uncovering some mnemonic treasures that would ransom them from the prison of their past. My unverbalized hunch was that all hypnosis would do for her stockpile of patients would be to add more fascinating imaginative data to the huge store of information that the therapist had already accumulated, without budging their afflictions one whit.

To expose all of these cases to one technique would be like a surgeon who, because he specializes in appendectomies, removes the appendix in every patient who comes to him with stomachaches, abdominal pains and diarrhea. No one technique can serve to ameliorate all maladies that burden humankind. This is the best argument for a balanced and conservative eclecticism toward which modern psychotherapy has gainfully been moving in the past decades. But there are still a few diehards who, loyal to the traditions of their chosen theoretical school, try to force a circumscribed method on all patients. Such a tactic, following an analogy once proffered by Freud, usually proves no more effective than trying to appease victims of a famine by passing out menus of a French cuisine. For reasons difficult to justify, some earnest students are unable to break away from the strictures of cherished theoretical systems and virtually become trapped along with their patients in its ineffectualities. The only way some can escape from their stagnant caseloads is by moving out of town!

To return to my student, another dilemma confounded her. When she started working with her patients, most of whom were therapeutic failures referred by other therapists only too happy to get them out of their offices, she had, as a beginner, accepted them at a low fee. Considering that they came four and five times weekly, and could scarcely afford paying the accumulated sum each month, the therapist could not, despite the economic havoc inflation imposed on her, bring herself to raise their fees to even the standard minimal level charged by colleagues of her rank. This added to her dilemma and undoubtedly created resentments that promoted depression.

I felt that my first task, prior to teaching her hypnosis, was to teach her how to do psychotherapy with sick patients. We chose as our first prospects the obsessional patient with a germ phobia and a detached borderline case with masochistic fantasies. She was to get them off the couch and allow them to sit up facing her. She was to reduce their sessions to twice weekly and charge them the same fee monthly as before. Most importantly, she was to stop acting like a "phantom therapist" by dropping her anonymity, with little digging and more relating. Because she seemed bewildered at my unorthodoxy, I had to give her the exact words to say to her patients, which were to the effect that a point had been reached where it was no longer necessary to freely associate, where only two sessions weekly were needed, where only reality problems in the here-and-now were to be the focus. She was enjoined to interest herself in what her patients were doing, smiling naturally, interchanging ideas and, if necessary, giving advice and support. Curiously, the student showed no resistance to accepting my advice.

In two weeks a remarkable change developed in both the experimental patients and the therapist. The patients, for the first time, spoke about how much better they felt. And for good reason—they were relating to the therapist as a real person who was interested in them as people rather than as puppets of their unconscious. The therapist found herself liking the patients, and her resentment resolved as the per session fee approximated that of her colleagues. What occurred then was that she got all of her patients off the couch. Sensing that she was losing her confidence in the analytic method, I had to work on her mistaken belief that the techniques I taught her were standard for all patients. While they happened to be suited for the sick caseload she was currently carrying, they might not be right for other cases. Indeed, classical psychoanalysis could be a boon for some patients carefully selected for the procedure. Her supervision with me lasted one year, during which time she acquired new cases, one of which was a patient for classical analysis.

Skill and Experience in the Implementation of Techniques

The history of science is replete with epic struggles between proponents of special conceptual systems. Contemporary psychotherapists are no exception. In a field as elusive as mental health it is little wonder that we encounter a host of therapies, some old, some new, each of which proposes to provide all the answers to the manifold problems plaguing mankind. A scrupulous choice of techniques requires that they be adapted to the needs and learning capacities of patients and be executed with skill and confidence. Understandably, therapists do have predelictions for certain approaches and they do vary in their facility for utilizing them. Faith in and conviction about the value of their methods are vital to the greatest success. Moreover, techniques must be implemented in an atmosphere of objectivity.

To function with greatest effectiveness, the therapist should ideally possess a good distribution of the following:

(a) *Extensive training.* Training, for the most part has become parochial, therapists becoming wedded to special orientations which limit their use of techniques. Accordingly, patients become wedged into restricted interventions and when they do not respond to these the therapeutic stalemate is credited to resistance. Over and over, experience convinces that sophistication in a wide spectrum of techniques can be rewarding, especially if these are executed in a dynamic framework. Whether a personal psychoanalysis is essential or not will depend on what anxieties and personal difficulties the therapist displays in working with patients. The fact that the therapist does not expose himself to the discipline of formal analytic training does not imply that he will do an inferior kind of therapy. Indeed, in some programs, where the analytic design is promoted as the only way of doing therapy, training may be counterproductive. Nevertheless, where a therapist does take advantage of a structured training program, which includes exposure to dynamic thinking and enough personal therapy to work out characterologic handicaps, this will open up rewarding dimensions, if solely to help resolve intrapsychic and interpersonal conflicts that interfere with an effective therapeutic relationship.

Irrespective of training, there is no substitute for management under supervision of the wide variety of problems that potentially present themselves. It is important that the therapist try to recognize his strong and weak points in working with the various syndromes. No matter how well adjusted the therapist may be, there are some critical conditions he may not be able to handle as well as others. The therapist may, when he recognizes which problems give him the greatest difficulties, experiment with ways of buttressing his shortcomings.

(b) *Flexibility in approach.* A lack of personal investment in any one technique is advantageous. This requires an understanding of the values and limitations of various procedures, experience in utilizing a selected technique as a preferred method, and the blending of a variety of approaches for their special combined effect. Application of techniques to the specific needs of patients at certain times, and to particular situations that arise, will require inventiveness and willingness to utilize the important contributions to therapeutic process of the various behavioral sciences, accepting the dictum that no one school has the monopoly on therapeutic wisdom.

INTERCURRENT NONSPECIFIC VARIABLES

There are a number of intercurrent, adventitious variables that operate in all forms of psychotherapy and greatly influence results. Among these are the placebo element, emotional catharsis, the relationship dimension, suggestion, and dyadic group dynamics.

The Placebo Element

At Johns Hopkins Medical School in Baltimore, two psychiatrists, Park and Covi (1965) gave pills containing sugar to 15 patients with a diagnosis of psychoneurosis who suffered principally from anxiety. The patients were told that the pills were innocuous and contained no drug. Thirteen patients reported being helped by the pills, four insisting that the pills were "the most effective ever prescribed for them." A few of the patients even had side effects with this placebo.

Over 60 percent of patients suffering from pain and physical symptoms experience relief when given inert medications, especially if prescribed by a doctor who expresses confidence in their effectiveness. It is common knowledge that physicians who like tranquilizers score much higher successes with them than those who do not. In one study arthritic patients obtained considerable relief through electro-therapeutic machines even when the current was turned off. These effects are products of suggestion inspired by the conviction in the patient that the therapeutic modality will have a certain desired effect. Where the belief is sufficiently strong, a medication, instrument, or psychotherapeutic technique can be enormously helpful or hurtful, depending on the attitude of the patient. The placebo element will, therefore, enhance or negate the modality being employed. Any treatment will work, to some extent at least, if a patient has faith in it. The method may be completely worthless and still the result can be little short of miraculous.

How the placebo exerts its powers is still unknown, but a number of mechanisms are probably operative. First, there is the creation of hope and trust that something helpful will be done and that suffering will be relieved. Such anticipation lessens tension and anxiety. On the physiological level it is possible that the body's regulatory systems are influenced. Recent studies suggest the release of endorphins from the brain and pituitary gland act as an analgesic and could account for the relief of pain, especially in situations of stress, when inert substances, hypnosis, or acupuncture are being administered. Possible also is the placebo regulation of the body's immunologic systems, which may explain the retardation or cure of occasional cases of cancer through relaxing imagery. Second, attention is diverted from one's illness and concerns with suffering and redirected into more constructive channels. Third, there is arousal of comforting feelings of self-worth as a result of a conviction that an authority as vested in the therapist cares and is interested in one's welfare. The accumulated effect is restoration of a sense of mastery.

Avant-garde members of the mental health movement periodically introduce theories and methods, some of which not only violate scientific principles, but also are beyond the reach of common sense. And yet, because of the placebo effect, many patients respond favorably to these aberrant techniques, especially when administered by a charismatic healer. We cannot dismiss the effectiveness of such off-beat methods by derogating them. It is wise to examine why and under what circumstances they work. There may be important lessons we can learn, some truths we may incorporate in our own interventions.

Perhaps the most important caveat is not to minimize the importance of the placebo element in our personal management of patients. Enthusiasm, confidence, and faith in what we are doing can add greatly to the expediency of our efforts. Above all, it is important not to introduce a negative placebo liability by saying to a patient something to the effect that "The last six patients I treated with your condition all committed suicide."

Emotional Catharsis

When a patient comes to see a helping person and spills over with feeling—often exposing things to the therapist that he would not reveal openly to himself—the therapist may have to do little other than listen, with the result that the patient experiences temporary relief. More important than the fact that the patient "spills his guts" or gets things "off his chest" is that he is talking to a symbol of authority. If that authority figure does not respond to the disgorged material in a punitive, deprecatory, or rejecting way, the patient may experience a great deal of benefit, much of which will be lasting, since guilt feelings are assuaged and concepts of authority as neglectful or destructive are somewhat neutralized. The very process of putting evasive feelings into words may clarify underlying distortions. A reevaluation of the wickedness of one's ways and of inherent sinfulness and profligacy may release the patient and enable him to come to grips with painful events that he has tried to banish from his mind. Clarification and interpretation by the therapist help to put the past into proper perspective. Eventually, the patient may develop a different attitude toward his parents, the world and even himself.

These developments bear little relationship to the kind of therapy that is being done, but are intimately dependent on the way the therapist manages the patient's revelations. At first the patient may doubt the validity of the therapist's manner, crediting it to an assumption of a therapeutic role, but by being consistent the therapist may really demonstrate to the patient the genuiness of his attitudes, particularly the absence of arbitrariness and punitiveness. After a while the patient will begin to alter his conceptions of vindictive authority, and this can have a tremendous impact upon other dimensions of his personality.

On the other hand, where the therapist is unable to respond objectively to the patient's verbalizations and provide the patient with different ways of looking at himself and his experiences, this will adversely influence the direction of treatment, negating the impact of the technical maneuvers.

The Relationship Dimension

"Some patients, though conscious that their condition is perilous, recover their health simply through their contentment with the goodness of the physician." These words of the immortal Hippocrates accent the vital importance of the relationship between patient and therapist, which acts as a prime ingredient in the restoration of health and well-being.

Even in non-analytic therapies there is gradually developing a recognition of the vital part played by the therapeutic alliance. For example, Sloane et al. (1977) have shown in a study that patients receiving behavior therapy report benefit from forces similar to those experienced by patients receiving dynamic psychotherapy. Among the ingredients considered by them to be most important in improvement were the personality of the therapist, being helped to recognize the nature of their problems, being encouraged gradually to face their difficulties, and being able to talk to an understanding person. "It would appear that behavior therapy patients put more emphasis on the therapeutic relationship than do their therapists." The latter thus "underutilize a powerful force that is nevertheless operating, unacknowledged, in their treatment." In all forms of therapy one cannot eliminate the impact of the relationship with the therapist.

When a patient comes to therapy he usually has exhausted his own resources for dealing with his problems and a part of him yearns for a dependent alliance with a kind, protective, and intelligent authority who can assuage suffering and provide a new direction in life. He wants somebody to help him, to take care of him, or to function like a guiding, omnipotent, magical, giving authority figure. Even though the projection into the therapeutic relationship of these anachronistic needs augurs of trouble for both the patient and therapist at the beginning of therapy, we may be unable to avoid them. We hope that as his helplessness resolves and he feels stronger, the patient will move the therapist out of this godlike position. The sicker the patient, the more he seeks an idealized authority figure. The initial improvement may be quite dramatic, simply on the basis of the relationship dimension. This can be important in therapy, because the resolution of anxiety and restoration of a sense of mastery may enable the patient to restore habitual defenses and to resume his life in a productive way. In many cases such an accomplishment may be all that the patient desires, and if he avoids stressful predicaments he may manage to get along without further need of help.

In addition to its supportive effect, the relationship may contribute to more substantial changes. A question pondered by researchers deals with what specific aspects of the patient-therapist relationship promote therapeutic learnings. Obviously, during psychotherapy this has something to do with the therapist exerting a corrective influence on the patient. But the process by which a therapist exerts his influence is puzzling, since only some of the operative factors are explicit. One explanation is offered by Strupp (1972), who speculates that what makes a patient susceptible to a therapist's influence is his "basic trust," a residue of his childhood which embodies blind faith in and obedience to a powerful, parental-like authority. The more anxious, helpless and dependent the patient, the more likely will he reach out for the therapist's control. This does not subdue his coordinate need for autonomy and the impulse to retain self-control which will more or less force him to resist and modulate external controls.

What helps to produce change is the patient's realization in depth that the interpersonal strategies (symptoms, defenses, character drives) he has habitually employed to control loved but dangerous authority are self-defeating and unrewarding. Appreciation of the groundlessness of his helplessness and the futility of projecting into adult life distrustful attitudes toward authority that seemed appropriate in childhood, but certainly are not needed now, is what helps make him well. It is essential, then, to restore basic trust in the patient and toward this end the therapist exercises his own interpersonal talents irrespective of the techniques he employs.

Suggestion

Suggestion operates in all therapies, the therapist deliberately or obliquely throwing out ideas and directives that the patient often will pick up and utilize. Sometimes these suggestions are helpful and constructive; at other times less so. The therapist may not be aware that cues are constantly being released to the patient, not only from verbal statements, but also from nonverbal signals like facial expressions of approval or disapproval, hesitancies, silences, the accenting of some of the patient's comments, nodding, shaking the head, grunting, and various physical movements. In this way suggestive elements may come through, even where the therapist believes that he is saying little or nothing.

A simple nod in relation to something the patient has said or done will give the patient the idea that what is being said or done is good and that he should continue in this approved vein. But if the therapist says nothing or shakes his head, this may constitute an aversive suggestion for the patient, and deliberately or unconsciously discourage certain types of activity. The technique of paying no attention to a psychotic person's delusional ramblings or hallucinations, but expressing interest in the patient when acting reality oriented will tend to reinforce constructive activities. All patients pick up from verbal and nonverbal cues of the therapist certain things they should do and believe in. This includes insights the patient gains which often act like a placebo. Even if an insight is wrong, if the person believes in it and imagines that it can help him, he may start feeling better.

Authoritative suggestions are directly proffered in supportive and some forms of ego-building reeducative therapy. The most striking example is suggestive hypnosis for purposes of symptom removal. How effective this can be is illustrated by the case of a child of three who was sent to me because he was virtually starving to death. He refused to eat solid food and gagged when forced to do so. Finally, his diet became completely liquid, which he would often regurgitate, to the distress of his mother. I consented to use hypnosis, and after the consultation, during which I induced a trance, I never saw the patient again. Because I was so deeply involved with other matters at the time, I never followed up the case, assuming that the parents had decided against treatment. Five years later, the pediatrician who had referred the patient telephoned me and said, "Since you did such a wonderful job with that child who gagged, maybe you can help another one of my patients." I vaguely remembered the old referral. Having the name and address of the patient's mother, I wrote to her inquiring about what had happened. Her written reply was accompanied by a photograph of a plump little boy of eight. In the letter she said that when her son came out of my office into the waiting room, he had asked his mother for some cooked potatoes, the first time he had requested such food. And he had been eating very well ever since. "And, doctor," she continued, "you do not know this, but while you were in your office with my son, I walked over to your door and put my ear to it to listen to what was going on. I heard you say, 'You will want to eat. You will have a strong desire to eat because you want to, not because anybody else wants you to.' And, doctor, *I* gained 24 pounds."

The moral of the story is not only that suggestions can be effective even through a closed door, but also that a thorough, deep exploration of inner problems is not always essential for symptom relief. This point of view is not completely accepted in some psychological circles. There are those who still believe in the old idea that all symptoms are like a safety valve for steam. Block the release, and steam will build up and break out in new and perhaps more disabling damage. By and large, the time-honored dictum that symptoms removed by hypnosis must return in the same or substitute form, or that the psychic equilibrium will be upset, precipitating a psychosis, is purely fictional. Relief can be permanent, and advantage may be taken of the symptom-free interlude to encourage a better life adjustment.

In dynamically oriented psychotherapy direct suggestions are kept at a minimum, the patient being encouraged to think through his own solutions. Nevertheless, the factor of prejudicial, inexpedient or unwise suggestions unwittingly being made must always be kept in mind. On the other hand, if the suggestions are productive ones, the patient may benefit from pursuing them. Nor is it essential in therapy always to abstain from direct suggestions or ego-building persuasive formulations. Homework given the patient is an example of the constructive use of suggestion. The therapist will have to gauge the patient's readiness to experiment with any anxiety-provoking action before making a direct or indirect suggestion that the patient undertake it. A premature exposure resulting in failure may merely intensify a phobia.

Dyadic Group Dynamics

An aspect of learning that plays some part in therapy relates to the absorption by the patient of the attitudes and values of the therapist. In long-term therapy this dimension can be prominent, the patient modeling himself after the therapist as he perceives him to be. In short-term therapy interpersonal dynamics involving the therapist must be considered also as a factor in reeducation. Karl Menninger (1952) has emphasized that "The psychiatrist as a person is more important than the psychiatrist as a technician or scientist. What he *is* has more effect upon his patient than anything he *does*. Because of the intimate relationship between patient and psychiatrist, the value systems, standards, interests and ideals of the doctor become important."

A therapist cannot help but communicate his values to his patients. This will occur no matter how passive, non-interfering and nonjudgmental the therapist imagines himself to be. He may try to suppress his verbal valuations, but his nonverbal communications will nevertheless come through. His nods, grunts, frowns, and smiles, immobility, fidgetiness, pauses, choice of topics for questioning, emphasis, repetitions, and interpretations will soon convey to the patient the therapist's world-views and tendencies toward deviance and conformity. Subtle indications such as the kind of waiting room furniture, pictures and magazines, the therapist's hair style and clothing preferences, and the manner in which office routines, billing, and appointments are conducted are as eloquent in revealing standards as any direct verbal avowal of values. It is useless to try to conceal the fact from the patient that the therapist has a definite point of view and possesses certain tastes and prejudices. Indeed, the patient may even divine the therapist's unconscious values and during transference confront him with a bill of particulars, the validity of which may be staggering.

If a therapist's values are apparent to the patient, is it not advisable then to express them verbally as articles of personal conviction, at least those of which the therapist is aware? It is obvious to most therapists who believe this that they must nevertheless not force their values on patients, even when the therapist is convinced of their moral and pragmatic worth. The patient's right to accept or reject the therapist's standards is usually respected. Moreover, the therapist, assuming that he possesses the ability to be objective, may subject his personal value systems to soul searching to discern which of these warp his own maturity.

A frank encounter with oneself, buttressed if necessary by personal therapy, may be boon to both therapist and patient, since many patients will incorporate the therapist's theories and moral precepts more or less uncritically on the basis of a need to please, in order to learn from and amalgamate with the idealized authority figure who is rendering help. This is probably allied to mechanisms that take place in any educational process.

SOCIAL AND ENVIRONMENTAL VARIABLES

Anyone who believes that the innate lenity of man can transcend some of the abuses and indignities that society heaps on him is a victim of Utopian self-deception. Social and environmental variables are probably the most neglected of factors in psychotherapy and among the most important. If in doing therapy we do not consider the environment in which the patient will have to live and function, we will run the risk of annulling therapeutic gains. An environment which does not support and encourage the patient's newly developed patterns or which punishes the patient for his behavior will tend to reverse the gains brought about by the therapeutic process. On the other hand, an environment which rewards for constructive behavior will reinforce therapeutic gains.

Treatment may be considered incomplete if it does not prepare the patient for contingencies he will have to face when treatment is over. Adolescents who belong to gangs, for example, who learn to control delinquent behavior, may find themselves rejected by their peers for abiding by the law. A young adult living at home under the yoke of domineering parents may not be permitted to assume an independent role after the therapeutic resolution of her pathological dependency drive. An alcoholic helped to give up drink may not be able to remain dry so long as he retains his membership in a wine-tasting club.

During therapy a thorough review of what the patient will be up against after termination will be urgently needed. Either the patient will have to modify a destructive environment, if this is possible, or he will have to separate himself from it. Thus the adolescent and the alcoholic will need to find new friends. The young lady will have to get a job and take up residence in a more permissive atmosphere, that is, unless her parents are willing to enter into family therapy and respond sufficiently to permit her to have greater freedom. Too frequently it is assumed that the patient will somehow get along once the treatment sessions have ended. Because the environment will rarely take care of itself, its future impact on the patient must be studied as part of the treatment program.

TRANSFERENTIAL AND COUNTERTRANSFERENTIAL VARIABLES

In therapy the initial positive relationship often serves during the first few sessions to quiet the patient's tensions and to restore a sense of mastery. A good deal of the responsibility for this happening resides in the patient's need for an omnipotent idealized authority, which need is projected onto the therapist. Some therapists advocate ending treatment abruptly when the patient has achieved a windfall of symptom relief, encouraging the patient to resume the customary threads of his life and providing him with some awareness of the circumstances that contributed to his present disorder. Where therapy is terminated after a few sessions the patient may continue to retain the initial image of the therapist as a powerful, benevolent and perhaps magical figure, having utilized this image, however unrealistic it may be, as a vehicle for restoring himself to his customary stability.

Where the therapist is more ambitious, or the patient requires more sessions to get well, around the eighth session a change often occurs in the image of the therapist that can precipitate a crisis in treatment. The patient begins to realize that the therapist is not a god, that he does not have all the answers, that he even possesses feet of clay. This disillusionment may exhibit itself in a forceful return of symptoms, and a crediting to the therapist of ineffectual or evil qualities. They draw their substance from a deep reservoir of fear and hate into which malevolent attitudes toward authority, some dating to childhood, have been stored. This transferential pollution may go on unconsciously and be manifested solely in dreams or acting-out away from the therapeutic situation. The only sign the therapist may detect from the patient's manifest behavior is in the form of resistance to treatment. The patient will complain he is not getting well. He may break appointments or come late for his sessions. He may not pay his bills.

A dynamically oriented therapist searches for transferential signs because he realizes both the potential for helping the patient resolve some of his deepest problems through the insightful understanding of transference, and the destructive effect that unrecognized capricious transference can have on the therapeutic process. A therapist who has no awareness of transference will be truly handicapped in managing patients whose reactions to treatment become paradoxical or inappropriate.

Understandably, the more serious the early problems with authority have been, the more likely will transference become apparent, and the more tumultuous its manifestations.

Where the therapist shares the initial illusions with his patient to the effect that he is a demigod, he will be especially disturbed in being converted into a devil. Such therapists try to avoid trouble by confining themselves to the briefest forms of short-term therapy, terminating all treatments before the sixth session. But sometimes this does not help, especially in vulnerable borderline or schizophrenic patients who develop transference reactions toward the therapist even before seeing the therapist at the initial interview. It is far better that the professional who wishes to do good therapy work through his godlike image, if it is at all resolvable, by himself or in personal therapy. At any rate, a good degree of stability is required on the part of the therapist in order to handle transference reactions when they occur. An unstable therapist finds it difficult, because of countertransference, to control his responses when he is challenged or unfairly accused by a patient in transference. He may impulsively discharge the patient or furiously cow the patient into submission, which will obviously rob the patient of an opportunity to work through problems with authority.

Whether personal psychotherapy is mandatory for all therapists in training as a means of preventing obstructive countertransference is a question about which there is much debate. If one is a good therapist, personal therapy will probably help make one a better therapist. But it will not accomplish miracles. There are certain problems that are so deep that personal therapy may not be able to budge them. For example, intense childish distortions developed in very early infancy may resist correction. The individual may get an awareness of these distortions through personal therapy, yet be unable at times to control their surfacing. Yet, through personal therapy, one may be able to manage one's reactions sufficiently so that they do not interfere too much with one's functioning with patients. Personal psychotherapy will accomplish its mission if it can control the therapist's use of the patient for his own designs and projections. Countertransference is probably present to some extent in all therapists, but this need not necessarily be destructive if the therapist is aware of its presence, recognizes how it is manifesting itself, and takes steps to resolve it.

Countertransference is not always harmful. It may alert the therapist to traits and maneuvers of the patient that arouse important feelings in other people besides himself. The important thing is how the therapist utilizes his countertransference. If he brings out the unconscious needs and conflicts of the patient and describes the effect they can have on himself as well as on others, the patient may learn something important. For example, a great deal of tolerance is required on the part of the therapist in adjusting to the habits of some patients. Most therapists are punctual in appointments (as they should be) even though certain patients are lax in appearing promptly at the scheduled hour. These patients are prone to subject the therapist to a bit of delinquency as a vehicle of testing or defiance. The therapist may particularly be irritated by patients who come to clinics, paying little or nothing yet seeming unappreciative of what is being done for them. There is no reason why the therapist should not focus on the patient's offensive behavior, not as a way of reprimanding the patient, but to clarify the meaning of what is going on. There are certain patients we relish working with and others who are less than a joy to treat. Thus there are therapists who are completely unable to handle adolescents while others do their best work with young people. Schizophrenic, violent, obsessional, paranoidal, psychopathic, hypochondriacal, suicidal, and delinquent patients stimulate aversive response in many therapists. Yet other therapists not only tolerate these syndromes but enjoy handling them.

Countertransferential elements encourage a therapist to project onto the patient aspects of his own inner needs of which the therapist is partly or wholly unaware. One therapist whom I was supervising in a class reported that his patient was getting progressively more depressed. An audio cassette of a session brought out a repetitious theme voiced by the patient that nobody cared for her, nobody paid attention to her, nobody liked her; that she was the neglected child in the family, whose destiny was to spend her life in misery as an isolate. She insisted that she could never command respect or attention from anybody. She went on and on in this depressive vein, and the therapist from his conversation seemed to be responding correctly to what the patient was saying. We decided then that the therapist should interview the patient behind a one-way-mirror with the class observing. The therapist was instructed to set up the furniture similar to the arrangement in his office. When the patient entered the room she seemed fairly animated, but as she talked she appeared to get progressively more and more depressed, the content of her verbalizations centering around feeling rejected by her family, by people, and by the world. What was startling was that the therapist, without realizing it, was actually playing into her theme of rejection. He had placed his chair at an angle so that he did not face her, and while he would from time to time fire an interpretation at her, he was constantly busy writing or looking away toward the opposite corner of the room. Periodically the patient would glance at the therapist, who by all appearances was off in space. One got the impression that she was being treated like a scientific specimen, not like a needful human being. Having been reared by a schizoid mother who in later life was admitted to a mental institution, she interpreted the therapist's manner as rejection.

The interesting thing was that a sophisticated professional in his last year of postgraduate training did not realize that he was providing the patient with a stimulus that activated her habitual rejection theme. On questioning, the therapist admitted that he was losing interest in the patient because she was beating at him constantly with her griping and complaining and getting no better. He was unaware that the placement of his chair was a gesture that signaled his disinterest, nor did he realize that the sessions were as traumatic for the patient as they were for him. He was sufficiently advanced in his training and personal analysis to explore his feelings toward the patient and affiliate them with attitudes toward a hypochondriacal mother who drove his own father to distraction. In this way his countertransference interlocked with the transference projections of the patient.

What the patient was doing with her therapist she did with all people with whom she became intimate. She expected rejection so much that in testing their sincerity she did exactly the things that resulted in her being rejected. People then responded by avoiding her. I suggested that the next time the patient came for a session the interview be conducted face to face. The therapist was to put aside his pad and just talk about the patient's interests and experiences without probing her feelings—in other words to work on building a relationship. In a very short time the whole nature of the therapy sessions changed. The patient became livelier, more interested in what she was doing, and more able to joke and smile. And the therapist developed greater enthusiasm about the patient. Eventually the patient's depression lifted and the patient was able to manage the termination phases of therapy without too great difficulty.

Not all of a therapist's reactions are countertransferential. They may be prompted by deliberate, destructive and outlandish conduct. I recall one patient whose behavior was so provocative as to challenge my capacity for disciplined objectivity. It was all I could do during some sessions when she acted particularly nasty and insulting to stop myself from responding defensively or punitively. The patient was a married woman in her late thirties who came to me not of her own free will but because of the pressures imposed on her by her friends and family, who realized that she was seriously depressed and disturbed. She was the only child of a wealthy couple who adulated, pampered and spoiled her so that she soon ruled the household like a tyrannical princess with an iron fist without the traditional velvet glove. Screaming tantrums forced her parents and private tutors to yield to her slightest whim.

When she grew up she transferred these tactics to people around her, responding to not getting her way with violence, headaches and paranoidal-like projections. Her marriage, she revealed, started off sizzling on a King-sized bed. But soon, after she had succeeded in verbally whip-lashing her husband into partial impotence, the couple retreated into twin beds, and, following the birth of her two children, they sought refuge in separate rooms from which they sauntered out to combat. Added to this the inanities of suburban life were more, she claimed, than human flesh could endure.

Her initial contacts with me were organized around exploratory maneuvers to determine how much she could win me over and manipulate me. Interpretations fell on deaf ears. She was certain that I was siding with the enemy at home who blamed her for the prevailing mess she was in. Hostility was expressed in subtle and not so subtle ways. On one occasion, she asked me to refer her to the *best* dermatologist in town. She appeared at his office with her dog whom she brought into the consulting room. It turned out that she wanted treatment not for herself but for her dog "who deserved the best." The dermatologist, who was a dear friend of mine, winked to his nurse and they proceeded to put the dog on the examining table and to treat him like a regular patient, right to the rendering of a prescription with the dog's name on it. Fortunately, the doctor, a dermatologic authority, had a great sense of humor and he went along with the "gag." On another occasion, being more careful to explore her complaint of backaches, I referred her to an orthopedic surgeon who on walking through the waiting room found her sitting in a chair with her feet on a new expensive coffee table. In not too gentle tones, he commanded her: "Won't you take your feet off my table?" Haughtily she turned on him with "It took me four months to hate Wolberg. You I hate right away."

With this as a background, I want to describe an incident where my loss of objectivity resulted in a significant therapeutic gain. During an interview, as she sat facing me, I confronted her with her responsibility in promoting a quarrel with her best friend. Furiously the patient removed a diamond ring from her finger and fired it at me. As the ring, a huge eight-carat gift from her father, whizzed by my ear, I tried to conceal my surprise and dismay by acting nonchalant and by not commenting on her behavior. I could see that she was nonplussed and irritated by my lack of concern. "Give me back my ring," she commanded imperiously. "*You* threw it," I replied, "*You* find it." After several such exchanges, she stormed over to my chair and began to search for the ring. It was nowhere in sight! "You better find my ring," she shrieked, but she got no response from me. However, after several minutes had passed in futile search, the ring remained undiscovered, and I leisurely proceeded to help her. But the ring was nowhere to be seen. By this time, I too was concerned. Yet a minute search of the room produced nothing. The patient burst into tears and I then tried to reassure her, utilizing the incident to accent my previous interpretations that her loss of temper hurt her more than it did other people.

After the patient left my office ringless, I went over the room minutely and finally I found the ring, which apparently had fallen on the couch and bounced off to the side, becoming wedged in between the mattress and the wooden side. The patient was relieved at my telephone call and thanked me. My victory, however, was short-lived. The next day when the patient came for her ring she burst angrily into my office and slammed the door shut with her foot, registering a dirty footprint on my newly painted door. I could feel my anger bubbling up. "You wash that footprint off that door," I ordered. "Ha, ha, ha," she retorted defiantly, "You make me." Reflexly, I grabbed her by the back of her neck and marched a frightened patient into the bathroom, stuck a wet soapy washcloth in her hand, and firmly marched her back to the door. She obediently washed the door, then quietly sat down; then we had our first constructive talk. She acted contented and even smiled. What the patient seemed to have done was to force me to set limits on her behavior that her father had failed to do. What she wanted and needed was some discipline. The positive effect on our relationship was amazing and we were able to achieve changes in her life that earned for me the gratitude of the patient and her family.

If through the relationship the patient is able to modify the introjected image of authority, the therapeutic process will have scored a great gain. Such modification comes about by a replacement of the patient's imprinted authority figure, which is often harsh or overprotective, or negligent, or distorted, with a new, more rational and constructive figure as vested in the therapist. An opportunity for this may come about through transference on the therapist of feelings or attitudes that relate to the authoritative introject. Manifestations of the transference appear in direct or disguised form, in oppositional resistance to the therapist or to the techniques being employed, in unreasonable demands for favors or affection, in fantasies or dreams, or in acting-out away from treatment with persons other than the therapist. The ability of the therapist to recognize transference when it appears, particularly in its disguised forms, and to deal with it through interpretation and proper management of the relationship will have a determining effect on the direction and results of treatment.

RESISTANCE VARIABLES

Shorr (1972) cited Saul Bellow, who in *Herzog* describes the common resistance to normality so often encountered in therapy: *"To tell the truth, I never had it so good . . . but I lacked the strength of character to bear such joy.* That was hardly a joke. When a man's breast feels like a cage from which all the dark birds have flown—he is free, he is light. And he longs to have his vultures back again. He wants his customary struggles, his nameless empty works, his anger, his afflictions, and his sins." Paradoxically, some people are loath to give up the very chains that bind them to neurotic slavery.

Reluctance to accept normality is merely one of the many resistances that precipitate out in the course of therapy. Some resistances, inspired by lack of motivation and refusal to give up a stereotype of a nonrealistic therapist, occur at the start of therapy. Some, such as transference resistances, convert the therapeutic alliance into a battlefield of archaic projections and interfere with the treatment process itself. Others, like regressive dependency, mobilize anger and grief, and obstruct proper termination of therapy.

Resistances can take many forms, often following defensive maneuvers customary for the individual. Thus the patient may become evasive or forgetful, breaking, cancelling or coming late for appointments, or he may engage in prolonged silences during sessions. He may indulge in superficial, rambling talk. He may try to disarm the therapist with praise, or he may become aggressive, argumentative, and accusatory. Women may become sexually seductive toward their male therapists and men toward their female therapists.

Destructive as they are, certain resistances protect the individual

from catastrophic helplessness and anxiety. They are means of preserving important neurotic coping mechanisms. A phobia, for example,
may disable the individual, but it still has a protective quality. A
hysterical arm paralysis can shield the individual from awareness of
murderous impulses, although he may blandly protest the inconveni-
ence of being unable to utilize his limb. Frigidity may mask overwhelming fear in a woman of assuming a feminine role. In all of these
cases the yielding of important defenses promises exposure to dangers
far greater than the torments the patient already suffers. Moreover,
certain secondary gains of a positive nature may accrue to the indulgence of a neurosis. In industrial accidents the victim who is on disability
payments may in giving up pain and physical illness lose not only his
financial security, but also sympathy, freedom from responsibility, and
the opportunity of occupying center stage with his repetitive tales of
what he has endured at the hands of doctors. Having been referred to
a therapist by an insurance company, which insists on his getting
treatment, or brought in by his family who tire of his complaints, he
is exposed to the threat of health, which is a barren bounty compared
to the advantages of his disability.

Experience with large numbers of patients convinces that three common dynamic problems most often initiate emotional difficulties and
also create resistance to psychotherapy. They are: 1) inadequate separation-individuation; 2) a hypertrophied sadistic conscience; and 3)
devaluated self-esteem. These are never isolated units. Rather, they
coexist and reinforce each other, and they create needs to fasten onto
and to distrust authority, to torment and punish oneself masochisti-
cally, and to wallow in a swamp of hopeless feelings of inferiority and
ineffectuality. They frequently sabotage a therapist's most skilled
treatment interventions, and when they manifest themselves, unless
dealt with deliberately and firmly, the treatment process will bog down
in a stalemate. The most the therapist may be able to do is to point
out evidences of operation of resistance saboteurs, to delineate their
origin in early life experience, to indicate their destructive impact on
the achievement of reasonable adaptive goals, to warn that they may
make a shambles out of the present treatment effort, and to encourage
the patient to recognize his personal responsibility in perpetuating
their machinations. The frightening hold a self-devaluating resistance
can have on a patient is illustrated by the following fragment of an
interview.

The patient, a writer, 42 years of age, who made a skimpy living as
an editor in a publishing house, came to therapy for depression and

for help in working on a novel that had defied completion for years. Anger, guilt, shame, and a host of other emotions bubbled over whenever he compared himself with his more successful colleagues. He was in a customarily frustrated, despondent mood when he complained:

Pt: I just can't get my ass moving on anything. I sit down and my mind goes blank. Staring at a blank piece of paper for hours. I finally give up.

Th: This must be terribly frustrating to you.

Pt: (angrily) Frustrating is a mild word, doctor. I can kill myself for being such a shit.

Th: You really think you are a shit?

Pt: (angrily) Not only do I think I am a shit, I am a shit and nobody can convince me that I'm not.

Th: Frankly, Fred, I'm not even going to try. But you must have had some hope for yourself; otherwise you never would have come here.

Pt: I figured you would get me out of this, but I know it's no use. I've always been a tail ender.

Th: (confronting the patient) You know, I get the impression that you've got an investment in holding on to the impression you are a shit. What do you think you get out of this?

Pt: Nothing, absolutely nothing. Why should I need this?

Th: You tell me. (In his upbringing the patient was exposed to a rejecting father who demanded perfection from his son, who was never satisfied with his even better than average marks at school, who compared him unfavorably with boys in the neighborhood who were prominent in athletics and received commendations for their schoolwork. It seemed to me that the paternal introject was operating in the patient long after he left home, carrying the same belittling activities that had plagued his existence when he was growing up.)

Pt: (pause) There is no reason. (pause)

Th: You know I get the impression that you are doing the same job on yourself now that your father did on you when you were a boy. It's like you've got him in your head. (In the last session the patient had talked about the unreasonableness of his father and his inability to please his father.)

Pt: I am sure I do, but knowing this doesn't help.

Th: Could it be that if you make yourself helpless somebody will come along and help you out: (I was convinced the patient was trying

*to foster a dependent relationship with me, one in which I would
carry him to success that defied his own efforts.)*

Pt: You mean, you?

Th: Isn't that what you said at the beginning, that you came to me to
get you out of this thing? You see, if I let you get dependent on
me it wouldn't really solve your problem. What I want to do is
help you help yourself. This will strengthen you.

Pt: But if I can't help myself, what then?

Th: From what I see there isn't any reason why you can't get out of
this thing—this self-sabotage. *(The patient responds with a dubious expression on his face and then quickly tries to change the
subject.)*

In the conduct of treatment one may not have to deal with conflicts
such as those above *so long as the patient is moving along and making
progress. It is only when therapy is in a stalemate that sources of resistance must be uncovered.* These, as has been indicated, are usually
rooted in the immature needs and defenses of dependent, masochistic,
self-devaluating promptings. At some point an explanation of where
such promptings originated and how they are now operating will have
to be given the patient. This explanation may at first fall on deaf ears,
but, as the therapist consistently demonstrates their existence from
the patient's reactions and patterns, the patient may eventually grasp
their significance. The impulse to make oneself dependent and the
destructiveness of this impulse, the connection of suffering and symptoms with a pervasive need for punishment, the masochistic desire to
appease a sadistic conscience that derives from a bad parental introject,
the operation of a devalued self-image, with the subversive gains that
accrue from victimizing oneself, must be repeated at every opportunity,
confronting the patient with questions as to why he continues to sponsor such activities.

When we consider the many patient, therapist, intercurrent, environmental, transference and resistance variables that have been described above, and that are parcels of all therapies, irrespective of type,
it becomes apparent that empirical research into their effects may do
a great deal in promoting more effective practice and in advancing
psychotherapy to its rightful place in the family of scientific methodologies.

References

Ables, B.S., & Brandsma, J.M.: *Therapy for Couples: A Clinician's Guide for Effective Treatment.* San Francisco: Jossey-Bass, 1977.

Abroms, G.M.: The new eclecticism. *Arch. Gen. Psychiat.,* 20:514-523, 1969.

Abroms, G.M.: Who prescribes drugs? (cassette recording). Paper presented at the May 1972 meeting of the American Psychiatric Assn. Glendale, CA: Audio-digest Foundation, Vol. 1 No. 1, 1972.

Agras, W.S., Taylor, C.B., Kralnie, H.C., Allen, A., et al.: Twenty-four hour blood pressure reductions. *Arch. Gen. Psychiat.,* 37:859-863, 1980.

Alberti, R.E., & Emmons, M.L.: *Your Perfect Right: A Guide to Assertive Behavior,* 2nd ed. San Luis Obispo, CA: Import Press, 1974.

Alexander, F.: The psychology of dreaming. In Herma, H. & Kurth, G.M. (Eds.). *Elements of Psychoanalysis.* New York: World Publishing Company, 1950, pp. 58-75.

Alexander, F., French, T.M., et al.: *Psychoanalytic Therapy.* New York: Ronald, 1946.

Amidon, A. & Brim, O.G.: What do children have to gain from parent education? Prepared for the Advisory Committee in Child Development, National Academy of Sciences, 1972.

Anderson, A.: Anorexia Nervosa. *Weekly Psychiatry Update Series,* Vol. 3, Lesson 1. Princeton, NJ: Biomedia, Inc., 1979.

Applebaum, A.: Transactions of the Topeka Psychoanalytic Society. *Bull. Menninger Clinic,* 39:384-390, 1975.

Aronson, M.L.: Resistance in individual and group psychotherapy, *Am. J. Psychother.,* 21:95-96, 1967.

Aronson, M.L.: Group process: Techniques to raise intensity. *Psychiatric Annals,* 2:39-51, 1972.

Attkisson, C.C., Hargreaves, W., Horowitz, M.J., & Sorensen, J.E.: Evaluation: Current strengths and future directions. In Attkisson, C.C., Hargreaves, W.A., Horowitz, M.J., & Sorenson, J.E. (Eds.). *Evaluation of Human Service Programs.* New York: Academic Press, 1978.

379

Bachrach, H.M., & Leaff, L.A.: Analyzability: A systematic review of the clinical and quantitative literature. *J. Am. Psychoanal. Assn.*, 26:881-920, 1978.

Bachrach, L.L.: Overview: Model programs for chronic mental patients. *Am. J. Psychiatry*, 137:1023-1031, 1980.

Baldwin, B.: Formal training in crisis intervention. Presented to the Southeastern Psychological Association, New Orleans, LA, 1979.

Bandura, A.: *Principles of Behavior Modification.* New York: Holt, Rinehart & Winston, 1969.

Bandura, A.: *Social Learning Theory.* Englewood Cliffs, N.J.: Prentice-Hall, 1977.

Bandura, A.: On paradigms and recycled ideologies. *Cognitive Theory Res.*, 2:79, 1978.

Bandura, A., Blanchard, E.E., & Ritter, B.: Relative efficacy of desensitization and modeling approaches for inducing behavioral affective and attitudinal changes. *J. Personality Social Psychol.*, 13:172-199, 1969.

Battle, C.C., Imber, S.D., Hoehn-Saric, R., Stone, A.R., Nash, C., & Frank, J.D.: Target complaints as criteria of improvements. *Am. J. Psychother.*, 20:184-92, 1966.

Beck, A.T.: *Cognitive Theory and Emotional Disorders.* New York: International Universities Press, 1976.

Beck, A.T., & Rush, A.J.: Cognitive approaches to depression and suicide. In Serban, G. (Ed.). *Cognitive Defects in the Development of Mental Illness.* New York: Brunner/Mazel, 1978.

Bemis, K.M.H.: Current approaches to the etiology and treatment of anorexia nervosa. *Psychol. Bull.*, 85:593-617, 1978.

Bergin, A.E.: The evaluation of therapeutic outcome. In Bergin, A.E., & Garfield, S.L. (Eds.). *Handbook of Psychotherapy and Behavior Change: An Empirical Analysis.* New York: John Wiley & Sons, 1971.

Bergin, A.E., & Lambert, M.J.: The evaluation of therapeutic outcomes. In Bergin, A.E., & Garfield, S.L. (Eds.). *Handbook of Psychotherapy and Behavior Change: An Empirical Analysis.* New York: John Wiley & Sons, 1971.

Bergin, A.E., & Lambert, M.J.: The evaluation of therapeutic outcomes. In Garfield, S.L., & Bergin, A.E. (Eds.). *Handbook of Psychotherapy and Behavior Change: An Empirical Analysis.* 2nd ed. New York: John Wiley & Sons, 1978.

Bergin, H.E., & Suinn, R.M.: Individual psychotherapy and behavior therapy. *Annual Rev. Psychol.*, 26:509-56, 1975.

Bergin, I.I.: Therapist patient matching. In Gurman, A.S., & Razin, A.M. (Eds.). *Effective Psychotherapy: A Handbook of Research.* New York: Pergamon, 1977.

Bernstein, D.: Modification of smoking behavior: An evaluation review. *Psychol. Bull.*, 71:418-40, 1969.

Bernstein, D.A., & McAlister, A.: The modification of smoking behavior: Progress and problems. *Addictive Behaviors*, 1:89-102, 1976.

Betz, B.J.: Experiences in psychotherapy with schizophrenic patients. In Strupp, H.H., & Luborsky, L. (Eds.). *Research in Psychotherapy*, Vol. 2. Washington DC: American Psychological Association, 1962.

Bierman, R.: Dimensions for interpersonal facilitation in psychotherapy and child development. *Psychol. Bull.*, 72:338-352, 1969.

Bion, W.R.: *Attention and Interpretation.* London: Tavistock, 1970.

Bleuler, M.: *Roche Report*, Nov. 1, 1976, p. 6.

Booraem, C.D., & Flowers, J.V.: A procedural model for the training of assertive behavior. In Whiteley, J.M., & Flowers, J.V. (Eds.). *Approaches to Assertive Training.* Monterey, CA: Brooks/Cole, 1977.

Bower, T.G.R.: *A Primer of Infant Development.* San Francisco: W. H. Freeman, 1977.

Brenman, M., & Gill, M.M.: Hypnotherapy: A survey of the literature. *The Menninger Foundation Monograph Series.* No. 5. New York: Wiley, 1964.

Brenner, C.: Some comments on technical precepts in psychoanalysis. *J. Am. Psychoanal. Assn.*, 17:333-352, 1969.

References 381

Breuer, J., & Freud, S.: *Studies in Hysteria*. Washington, DC: Nervous and Mental Disease Publishing Co., 1936.

Brim, O.G.: *Education for Child Rearing*. New York: Russell Sage Foundation, 1959.

Brody, B.: Community mental health. The perspective from the viewpoint of psychotherapy. *Int. J. Psychiatry*, 7:323, 1969.

Bruch, H.: *Eating Disorders: Obesity, Anorexia Nervosa and the Person Within*. New York: Basic Books, 1973.

Bruch, H.: How to treat anorexia nervosa. *Roche Report*, 5(8), 1975.

Budman, S.H. (Ed.): *Forms of Brief Therapy*. New York: Guilford, 1981.

Burke, J.D., White, A.H., & Havens, L.L.: Matching patient and method. *Arch. Gen. Psychiat.*, 35:177-186, 1979.

Butcher, J., & Maudal, G.: Crisis intervention. In Weiner, I (Ed.). *Clinical Methods in Psychology*. New York: John Wiley & Sons, 1976.

Cadoret, R.J., Cain, C.H., & Grove W.: Development of alcoholism in adoptees raised apart from alcoholic biological relative. *Arch. Gen. Psychiatry*, 37:561-563, 1980.

Calef, V., & Weinshel, E.M.: The new psychoanalysis and psychoanalytic revisionism. *Psychoanal. Quart.*, 48:470-491, 1979.

Cartwright, D.S.: Patient self-report measures. In Waskow, I.E., & Parloff, M.B. (Eds.). *Psychotherapy Change Measures*. Washington, DC: DHEW Publication No. (ADM) 74-120, 1975.

Cassell, W.A., Smith, C.M. Grunberg, F., et al.: Comparing costs of hospital and community care. *Hosp. Community Psychiatry*, 23:197, 1972.

Cautela, J.R., & Kastenbaum, R.A.: A reinforcement survey schedule for use in therapy, training and research. *Psychological Reports*, 20:1115-1130, 1967.

Cautela, J.R., & Upper, D.: The process of individual behavior therapy. In Hersen, R.M., Eisler, R.M., & Miller, P.M. (Eds.). *Progress in Behavior Modification*, Vol 1. New York: Academic Press, 1975.

Chaney, E.F., O'Leary, M.R., & Marlatt, G.A.: Skill training with alcoholics, *J. Consult. Clin. Psychol.*, 46:1092-1104, 1978.

Chertok, L.: *Hypnosis*. Elmsford, N.Y.: Pergamon Press, 1966.

Clarke, A.M., & Clarke, A.D.B.: *Early Experience: Myth and Evidence*. London: Open Books, 1976.

Coché, E., & Flick, A.: Problem solving training groups for hospitalized psychiatric patients. *J. Psychol.*, 91:19-29, 1975.

Cohen, M., & Ewalt, P.L.: An intensive program for severely retarded children. *Soc. Casework*, 56:337, 1975.

Condon, W.S., & Sander, L.W.: Neonate movement is synchronized with adult speech: Interventional participation and language requisition. *Science*, 183:99-101, 1974.

Cook, T.D., & Campbell, D.T.: *Quasi-experimentation: Design Analysis Issues for Field Settings*. Chicago: Rand McNally, 1979.

Cronbach, L.J.: *Designing Evaluations*. Stanford, CA: Stanford Evaluation Consortium, 1978.

Csapo, M.: Peer models reverse the "one bad apple spoils the barrel" theory. *Teaching Exceptional Children*, 4:20-24, 1972.

Cummings, N.A.: Prolonged (Ideal) versus short-term (Realistic) psychotherapy. *Professional Psychology*, 8:491, 1977.

Cummings, N.A., Follett, W.T.: Psychiatric services and medical utilization in a prepaid health plan setting (Pt. 2). *Medical Care*, 5:31, 1968.

Dahlstrom, W.G., Walsh, G.A., & Dahlstrom, L.E.: *MMPI Handbook: Vol. I, Clinical Applications* (rev. ed.). Minneapolis: University of Minnesota Press, 1972.

Darbonne, A.R.: Crisis: A review of theory, practice and research. *Psychoth. Res. Prac.*, 4:49-56, 1967.

Delaney, J.A., et al.: Crisis intervention and the prevention of institutionalization: An interrupted time series analysis. *Am. J. Community Psychol.*, 6:33, 1978.

De La Torre, J.: The therapist tells a story: A technique in brief psychotherapy. *Bull. Menninger Clin.*, 36:609-616, 1972.

Derogatis, L.R., Lipman, R.S., & Covi, L.: SCL-90: An outpatient psychiatric rating scale. *Psychopharmacol. Bull.*, 9:13-27, 1973.

Dince, P.R.: *Psychotherapy for the Difficult-to-Engage Adolescent.* (Casette Recording) Glendale, CA: Audio-digest Foundation, Vol. 10, No. 5, March 9, 1981.

Dolliver, R.H.: Personal sources for theories of psychotherapy. *J. Con. Psychol.*, 12:53-59, 1981.

Dunn, J.: *Distress and Comfort.* Cambridge, MA: Harvard University Press, 1977.

Dykes, H.M.: Evaluation of three anorexiants. *J.A.M.A.*, 230:270-272, 1974.

Edelstien, M.G.: *Trauma, Trance, and Transformation: A Clinical Guide to Hypnotherapy.* New York: Brunner/Mazel, 1981.

Eisenberg, L.: Development as a unifying concept in psychiatry. *Br. J. Psychiatry*, 131:225-237, 1977.

Ellis, A.: *Reason and Emotion in Psychotherapy.* New York: Lyle Stuart, 1962.

Ellsworth, R.B.: *PARS V Community Adjustment Scale.* Roanoke, VA: Institute for Program Evaluation, 1974.

Ellsworth, R.B.: Consumer feedback in measuring the effectiveness of mental health programs. In Struening, E.L., & Guttentag, M. (Eds.). *Handbook of Evaluation Research.* Vol. 2. Beverly Hills, CA: Sage Publications, 1975.

Endicott, J., Spitzer, R.L., Fleiss, R.L., & Cohen, J.: The global assessment scale. *Arch. Gen. Psychiatry*, 33:766, 1976.

Erickson, M.H., & Rossi, E. (Eds.): *Innovative Hypnotherapy. Collected papers of Milton H. Erickson on Hypnosis,* Vol. 4. New York: Halsted Press, 1980.

Erikson, E.H.: *Childhood and Society.* New York: Norton, 1950, 2nd ed., 1963.

Eysenck, H.J.: The effects of psychotherapy: An evaluation. *J. Consult. Psychol.*, 16:319-24, 1952.

Eysenck, H.J.: *Behavior Therapy and the Neuroses.* New York: Pergamon Press, 1960(a).

Eysenck, H.J.: *Handbook of Abnormal Psychology.* London: Pitman, 1960(b).

Eysenck, H.J.: The effects of psychotherapy. *Int. J. Psychiat.*, 1:97-143, 1965.

Fensterheim, H., & Baer, J.: *Don't Say Yes When You Want to Say No.* New York: David McKay, 1975.

Ferenczi, S.: Kontraindikationen der aktiven psychoanalytischen Technik. *Int. Zeitschrift Psychoanalyse*, 12:3-14, 1926.

Flavell, J.H.: An analysis of cognitive developmental sequences. *Genetic Psychol. Monog.*, 86:279-350, 1972.

Flowers, J.V., & Booraem, C.D.: Simulation and role playing methods. In Kanfer, F.H., & Goldstein, A.P. (Eds.). *Helping People Change,* 2nd ed. New York: Pergamon, 1980.

Foreyt, J.P., Rockwood, C.E., Davis, J.C., et al.: Benefit-cost analysis of a token economy. *Professional Psychology*, 6:26, 1975.

Frank, J.D.: The present status of outcome studies. *J. Consult. Clin. Psychol.*, 47:310, 1979.

Frankel, F.H., & Zamansky, E. (Eds.): *Hypnosis At Its Bicentennial: Selected Papers.* New York: Plenum, 1978.

Frankl, V.E.: Paradoxical intentions: A logotherapeutic technique. *Am. J. Psychother.*, 14:520-535, 1960.

Frankl, V.E.: Paradoxical intention and dereflection. *Psychother. Theory Res. Prac.*, 12:226-237, 1975.

Frantz, R.L., & Nevis, S.: Pattern preferences and perceptual cognitive development in early infancy. *Merrill-Palmer Quarterly*, 13:77-108, 1967.

Freud, S.: *Standard Edition of the Complete Psychological Works of Sigmund Freud,* (Strachey, J., Ed.). London: Hogarth Press, 1953-1974, 24 vols.

Focus: How to make psychiatric services more effective and efficient. Part 1: Dr. Jack F. Wilder takes the group on a trip to a troubled clinic. *Frontiers of Psychiatry*, 9(1):1-2, 10, 1979.

References

Gaarder, K.R., & Montgomery, P.S.: *Clinical Biofeedback: A Procedural Manual*. Baltimore: Williams & Wilkins, 1977.

Gambrill, E.D., & Richey, C.A.: An assertive inventory for use in assessment and research. *Behav. Ther.*, 6:547-549, 1975.

Gedo, J.E.: A psychoanalyst reports at mid-career. *Am. J. Psychiatry*, 136:646-649, 1979.

Gill, M.M.: Metapsychology is not psychology. In Gill, M.M., & Holzman, P., (Eds.). *Psychology vs. Metapsychology: Psychoanalytic Essays in Memory of George S. Klein*. Psychological Issues, Monograph No. 36. New York: International Universities Press, 1976.

Gill, M.M., & Muslin, M.L.: Early interpretation of transference. *J. Am. Psychoanal. Assn.*, 24:788, 1976.

Glass, G.V., Wilson, V.L. & Gottman, J.M.: *Design and Analysis of Time-Series Experiments*. Boulder, CO: Laboratory of Educational Research, 1973.

Glick, R.A., Meyerson, A.T., Robbins, E., & Talbott, J.A. (Eds.): *Psychiatric Emergencies*. New York: Grune & Stratton, 1976.

Goldberg, I., Krants, G., & Locke, B.: Effect of a short-term outpatient psychiatric therapy benefit on the utilization of medical services in a prepaid practice medical program. *Medical Care*, 8:423, 1970.

Goldensohn, S.S.: Psychotherapy for the economically disadvantaged: Contributions from the social sciences. *J. Am. Academy Psychoanal.*, 9:291-302, 1981.

Goldensohn, S.S., & Haar, E.: Transference and countertransference in a third party payment system (HMO). *Am. J. Psychiatry*, 131:256-260, 1974.

Goldfried, M.R., & Davison, G.C.: *Clinical Behavior Therapy*. New York: Holt, Rinehart & Winston, 1976.

Goldstein, A.P: Relationships-enhancement methods. In Kanfer, F.G., & Goldstein, A.P. (Eds.). *Helping People Change*, 2nd ed. New York: Pergamon, 1980.

Goldstein, A.P., Sprafkin, R.P., & Gershaw, J.: *Skill Training for Community Living: Applying Structured Learning Therapy*. New York: Pergamon Press, Structured Learning Associates, 1976.

Goldstein, A., & Wolpe, J.: Behavior therapy in groups. In Kaplan, H.I., & Sadock, B.J., (Eds.). *Comprehensive Group Psychotherapy*. Baltimore: Williams & Wilkins, 1971, pp. 292-327.

Goodwin, D.W.: Alcoholism and heredity: A review and hypothesis. *Arch. Gen. Psychiatry*, 36:57-61, 1979.

Gottman, J.M., & Markman, H.J.: Experimental designs in psychotherapy research. In Garfield, S.L., & Bergin, A.E. (Eds.). *Handbook of Psychotherapy and Behavior Change: An Empirical Analysis*. New York: John Wiley & Sons, 1978.

Gottesman, I.I.: Schizophrenia and genetics: Toward understanding uncertainty. *Psychiatric Annals*, 9(1):54, 1979.

Gottschalk, L.A., Mayerson, P., & Gottlieb, A.A.: Prediction and evaluation of outcome in an emergency brief psychotherapy clinic. *J. Nerv. Ment. Dis.*, 144:77, 1967.

Green, B.L., Gleser, G.C., Stone, W.N., et al.: Relationships among diverse relationships of psychotherapy outcome. *J. Consult. Clin. Psychol.*, 43:689, 1975

Greenson, R.R.: Empathy and its vicissitudes. *Int. J. Psycho. Anal.*, 41:418-424, 1960.

Grinspoon, L., Ewalt, J., & Shader, R.: *Schizophrenia: Pharmacotherapy and Psychotherapy*. Baltimore: Williams & Wilkins, 1972.

Grotjahn, M.: The best and the worst in analytic group therapy: Clinical observations about suitability. In Wolberg, L.R., & Aronson, M.L. (Eds.). *Group and Family Therapy 1980*. New York: Brunner/Mazel, 1980.

Guerney, B.G.: *Relationship Enhancement: Skill Training Programs for Therapy, Problem Prevention and Enrichment*. San Francisco: Jossey-Bass, 1977.

Gutride, M.E., Goldstein, A.P., & Hunter, G.F.: The use of structured learning theory and transfer training in the treatment of chronic psychiatric inpatients. *J. Clin. Psychol.*, 30:277-279, 1974.

Haggstrom, W.C.: The power of the poor. In Riessman, F., Cohen, J., & Pearl, A. (Eds.).

Mental Health of the Poor. New York: Free Press, 1964, pp. 225-223.

Haley, J.: Marriage therapy. *Arch. Gen. Psychiatry.,* 8:213-234, 1963.

Haley, J.: *Uncommon Therapy: The Psychiatric Techniques of Milton H. Erickson, M.D.* New York: Norton, 1973.

Haley, J.: *Problem-solving Therapy: New Strategies for Effective Family Therapy.* San Francisco: Jossey-Bass, 1976.

Halleck, S.L.: Future trends in the mental health profession. *Psychiatric Opinion,* 11:5-11, 1974.

Halpern, J., & Biner, J.R.: A model for an output value analysis of mental health programs. *Administration in Mental Health.* DHEW Pub. No. (HSM 73-9050), Winter, pp. 40-51, 1972.

Hargreaves, W., Attkisson, C.C., Siegel, L.M., et al.: *Resource Materials for Community Mental Health Program Evaluation: Part 3—Evaluation Effectiveness of Services.* Rockville, MD: National Institute of Mental Health, DHEW Publications No. (ADM) 75-222, 1975.

Heimann, P.: On countertransference. *Int. J. Psycho. Anal.,* 31:81-84, 1950.

Heimann, P.: Discussion of O. Kernberg's paper: Instincts, Affects, and Object Relations at the meeting of the New York Psychoanalytic Society, October 15, 1966.

Hess, R.D.: Experts and amateurs: Some unintended consequences of parent education. In: Fantini, M.D., & Cardenas, R. (Eds.). *Parenting in a Multicultural Society.* New York: Longman, 1980, p. 151.

Hingtgen, J.N., Coulter, S.K., & Churchill, D.W.: Intensive reinforcement of imitative behavior in mute autistic children. *Arch. Gen. Psychiat.,* 17:36-43, 1967.

Holt, R.R.: Drive or wish. A reconsideration of the psychoanalytic theory. In Gill, M.M., & Holzman, P.S. (Eds.). *Psychology vs. Metapsychology: Psychoanalytic Essays in Memory of George S. Klein.* Psychological Issues, Monograph No. 36. New York: International Universities Press, 1976, pp. 158-197.

Homme, L.E.: Control of covenants, the operants of the mind. *Psychological Record,* 15:501-511, 1965.

Horowitz, M.J.: *Stress Response Syndrome,* New York: Aronson, 1976.

Horowitz, M.J.: *Stress Response Syndromes and Brief Psychotherapy.* Strecher Monograph Series No. 14. Philadelphia: Institute of the Pennsylvania Hospital, 1977.

Imber, S.D.: Patient direct self-report techniques. In Waskow, I.E., & Parloff, M.S. (Eds.). *Psychotherapy Change Measures.* Washington, DC: DHEW Publ. No. (ADM) 74-120, 1975.

Jacobson, N.S., & Margolin, G.: *Marital Therapy: Strategies Based on Social Learning and Behavior Exchange Principles.* New York: Brunner/Mazel, 1979.

Jameson, J., Shuman, L.J., & Young, W.W.: The effects of outpatient psychiatric utilization on the costs of providing third-party coverage. *Research Series* 18. Blue Cross of Weston, Pa., 1976.

Janda, C.H., & Rimm, D.C.: Covert sensitization in the treatment of obesity. *J. Abnor. Soc. Psychol.,* 80:37-42, 1972.

Johnson, D.W.: Attitude modification methods. In Kanfer, F.H., & Goldstein, A.P. (Eds.). *Helping People Change,* 2nd ed. New York: Pergamon, 1980.

Jones, K., Sidebotham, R, Wadsworth, W.V., et al.: Cost and efficiency in mental hospitals. *The Hospital,* 57:23, 1961.

Kagan, J.: *Change and Continuity in Infancy.* New York: John Wiley & Sons, 1971.

Kagan, J., Kearsley, R.B., & Zelazo, P.R.: *Infancy, Its Place in Human Development.* Cambridge: Harvard University Press, 1978.

Kanfer, F.H.: Self management methods. In Kanfer, F.H., & Goldstein, A.P.: *Helping People Change,* 2nd ed. New York: Pergamon, 1980, pp. 334-389.

Kapp, R., & Weiss, S.: An interdisciplinary, crisis-oriented graduate training program with a student health service mental health clinic. *J. Amer. College Health Assoc.,* 3(5):340-344, 1975.

Karoly, P.: Operant methods. In Kanfer, F.H., & Goldstein, A.P. (Eds.). *Helping People Change*, 2nd ed. New York: Pergamon, 1980, pp. 210-247.

Karon, B.P., & Vanden Bos, G.R.: The consequence of psychotherapy for schizophrenic patients. *Psychother. Theory Res. Prac.*, 9:111-119, 1972.

Katz, M.M., & Lyerly, S.B.: Methods for measuring adjustment and social behavior in the community: Rationale description, discriminative validity and scale development. *Psychol. Res.*, 13:1503-55, 1963.

Katz, R.L.: *Empathy—Its Nature and Uses*. New York: Free Press, 1963.

Kayton, L.: Clinical features of improved schizophrenics. In Gunderson, J.G., & Mosher, L.R. (Eds.). *Psychotherapy of Schizophrenia*. New York: Aronson, 1975, pp. 361-395.

Kazdin, A.E.: Therapy outcome questions requiring control of credibility and treatment-generated expectancies. *Behav. Ther.*, 10:81, 1979.

Kellner, R.: Psychotherapy in psychosomatic disorders: A survey of controlled studies. *Arch. Gen. Psychiatry*, 32:1021-28, 1975.

Kernberg, O.: *Borderline Conditions and Pathological Narcissism*. New York: Jason Aronson, 1975.

Kernberg, O.: Technical considerations in the treatment of borderline personality organization. *J. Am. Psychoanal. Assoc.*, 24:795-828, 1976.

Kernberg, O.: Character structure and analyzability. *Bull. Assoc. Psychoanal. Medicine*, 19(3):117, 1980(a).

Kernberg, O.: Psychotherapy with borderline patients. In Karasu, T.B. & Bellak, L. (Eds.). *Specialized Techniques in Individual Psychotherapy*. New York: Brunner/Mazel, 1980(b), pp. 85-117.

Kernberg, O., Burstein, E.D., Applebaum, A., Horwitz, L., & Voth, H.: Psychotherapy and psychoanalysis: Final report of the Menninger Foundation's Psychotherapy Research Project. *Bull. Menninger Clinic*, 36:1-276, 1972.

Kimmel, D., van der Veen, F.: Factors of marital adjustment in Locke's marital adjustment test. *J. Marriage Fam.*, 36:57-63, 1974.

Klein, G.S.: *Psychoanalytic Theory: An Exploration of Essentials*. New York: International Universities Press, 1976

Kniskern, D.P., & Gurman, A.S.: Clinical implications of recent research in family therapy. In Wolberg, L.R., & Aronson, M.L., (Eds.). *Group and Family Therapy 1980*. New York: Brunner/Mazel, 1980.

Kohut, H.: *The Analysis of the Self. A Systematic Approach to the Psychoanalytic Treatment of Narcissistic Personality Disorders*. New York: International Universities Press, 1971.

Kriegsfeld, M.: How now: A Gestalt approach. In Grayson, H. (Ed.). *Short-term Approaches to Psychotherapy*. New York: Human Sciences Press, 1979.

Kubie, L.: The language tools of psychoanalysis: A search for better tools drawn from better models. *Int. Rev. Psa.*, 2:11-24, 1975.

Laing, R.D.: *The Divided Self*. London: Tavistock, 1960.

Laing, R.D.: *The Politics of Experience*. New York: Pantheon, 1967.

Lambert, M.J.: *The Effects of Psychotherapy*. Montreal: Eden Press, 1979, pp. 109-122.

Langs, R.: *The Therapeutic Interaction*. New York: Basic Books, 1972.

Levene, H., Breger, L., & Patterson, V.: A training and research program in brief psychotherapy. *Am. J. Psychother.*, 26:90, 1972.

Levenson, A.J., Lord, C.J., Sermas, C.E., et al.: Acute schizophrenia: An efficacious outpatient treatment approach as an alternative to full-time hospitalization. *Diseases of the Nervous System*, 38:242, 1977.

Lewin, R. (Ed.): *Child Alive: New Insights Into the Development of Young Children*. London: Temple Smith, 1975.

Lichtenstein, E., & Keutzer, C.: Modification of smoking behavior: A later look. In Ruben, R., Fensterheim, H., Lazarus, H.A., & Franks, C., (Eds.): *Advances in Behavior Therapy*. New York: Academic Press, 1971.

Liebman, R., Minuchin, S., & Baker, L.: An integrated program for anorexia nervosa. *Am. J. Psychiatry*, 131:432-436, 1974.

Liptzin, B., Stockedill, J.W., & Brown, B.S.: A federal view of mental health program evaluation. *Professional Psychology*, 8:543, 1977.

Little, M.: Countertransference and the patient's response to it. *Int. J. Psycho. Anal.*, 32:32-40, 1951.

Locke, H.J., & Wallace, K.M.: Short marital adjustment and prediction: Their reliability and validity. *Marriage Family Living*, 21:251-255, 1959.

Lorr, M., & McNair, D.M.: Expansion of the interpersonal behavioral circle. *J Personality Soc. Psychol.*, 2:823-30, 1965.

Luborsky, L., Singer, B., & Luborsky, L.: Comparative studies of psychotherapies. *Arch. Gen. Psychiatry*, 32:995-1008, 1975.

Luborsky, L., Mintz, J., Auerbach, A., et al.: Predicting the outcome of psychotherapy: Findings of the Penn Psychotherapy Project. *Arch. Gen. Psychiatry.*, 37(4):471-481, 1980.

Ludwig, A.M.: Altered states of consciousness. *Arch. Gen. Psychiatry*, 15:225-234, 1966.

Mahler, M.S.: On two crucial phases of integration of the sense of identity: Separation-individuation and bisexual identity. Abstracted in: Panel on Problems of Identity, Rubinfine, D.I. (Ed.). *J. Am. Psychoanal. Assoc.*, 6:136-139, 1958.

Mahler, M.S., & Furer, M.: *On Human Symbiosis and the Vicissitudes of Individuation.* New York: International Universities Press, 1968.

Malan, D.H.: *A Study of Brief Psychotherapy.* Springfield, IL: Thomas, 1963.

Malan, D.H.: *Toward the Validation of Dynamic Psychotherapy: A Replication.* New York: Plenum Press, 1976.

Malan, D.H.: *The Frontier of Brief Psychotherapy.* New York: Plenum, 1976.

Malcolm, R., Riddle, E., Currey, H.S., & Sexauer, J.D.: Behavior modification in the management of obesity. *J.S.C. Med. Assoc.*, 73:197-199, 1977.

Mann, J.: *Time-limited Psychotherapy.* Cambridge: Harvard University Press, 1973.

Mann, J.: *A Casebook of Time-limited Psychotherapy.* New York: McGraw-Hill 1981.

Mann, R.A.: The behavior-therapeutic use of contingency contracting to control an adult behavior problem: Weight control. *J. Appl. Behav. Anal.*, 5:99-109, 1972.

Marder, S.R., van Kammen, D.P., Docherty, J.P., Ragner, J., Bunney, W.E., Jr.: Predicting drug-free improvement in schizophrenia psychosis. *Arch. Gen. Psychiatry*, 36:1080-1085, 1979.

Marks, I.M.: Management of sexual disorders. In Leitenberg, H. (Ed.) *Handbook of Behavior Modification and Behavior Therapy.* Englewood Cliffs, NJ: Prentice-Hall, 1976.

Marlatt, G.A.: Craving for alcohol, loss of control and relapse: A cognitive behavioral analysis. In Nathan, P.E., Marlatt, G.A., & Lobert, T. (Eds.). *Alcoholism: New Directions in Behavioral Research and Treatment.* New York: Plenum, 1978.

Marmor, J.: *Psychiatry in Transition: Selected Papers.* New York: Brunner/Mazel, 1974.

Marmor, J.: Recent trends in psychotherapy. *Am. J. Psychiat.*, 137:409-416, 1980.

Marohn, R.C.: *The Delinquent Adolescent* (Cassette recording). Glendale, CA: Audio-digest Foundation, Vol. 6, No. 23, Dec. 5, 1977.

May, P.R.A.: *Treatment of Schizophrenia: A Comparative Study of Five Treatment Methods.* New York: Science House, 1968.

May, P.R.A., & Goldberg, S.C.: Prediction of schizophrenic patient's response to pharmacotherapy. In Lipton, M.A., DiMascio, A., & Killam, K.F. (Eds.). *Psychopharmacology: A Generation of Progress.* New York: Raven Press, 1978, pp. 1139-1153.

Meichenbaum, D.H.: Examination of model characteristics in reducing avoidance behavior. *J. Personality Social Psychol.*, 17-298-307, 1971.

Meichenbaum, D.H.: *Cognitive Behavior Modification.* New York: Plenum, 1977.

Meichenbaum, D.H., & Cameron, R.: The clinical potential of modifying what clients pay to themselves. *Psychother. Theory Res. Prac.*, 11:103-117, 1974.

Melamed, B.G., & Siegel, L.J.: Reduction of anxiety in children facing hospitalization and surgery by use of filmed modeling. *J. Consult. Psychol.,* 43:511-521, 1975.

Meldman, M.H., Harris, D., Pellicore, R.J., & Johnson, E.L.: A computer assisted, goal oriented psychiatric progress note system. *Am. J. Psychiatry,* 134:38-41, 1977.

Meltzoff, J., & Kornreich, M.: *Research in Psychotherapy.* New York: Atherton Press, 1970.

Mendel, W., Houle, J., & Osman, S.: Mainstreaming: An approach to the treatment of chronically and severely mentally ill patients in the community. *Hillside Journal of Clinical Psychiatry,* 2:95-128, 1980.

Menninger, K.A.: What are the goals of psychiatric education? *Bull. Menninger Clinic,* 16:153-158, 1952.

Michels, R.: Character structure and analyzability. *Bull. Assoc. Psychoanal. Medicine,* 19:81-86, 1980.

Miles, H., Barrabee, E.L., & Finesinger, J.E.: Evaluation of psychotherapy. *Psychosom. Med.,* 13:83-105, 1951.

Miller, D.H.: Parameters of therapy in seriously disturbed adolescents. (Cassette recording) Glendale, CA: Audio-digest Foundation, Vol. 9, No. 13, July 14, 1980.

Miller, N.E.: Biofeedback and visceral learning. *Annual Review Psychology,* 29:373-404, 1978.

Millman, R.B.: An editorial reply. *The Bulletin,* 21(4):1, 1979.

Mintz, J., Luborsky, L., & Christoph, P.: Measuring the outcome of psychotherapy: Findings of the Penn Psychotherapy Project. *J. Consult. Clin. Psychol.,* 47:319, 1979.

Minuchin, S.: Psychoanalytic therapies and the lower socio-economic population. In Marmor, J. (Ed.). *Modern Psychoanalysis.* New York: Basic Books, 1968, pp. 532-550.

Minuchin, S.: *Families and Family Therapy.* Cambridge: Harvard University Press, 1974.

Minuchin, S., & Fishman, H.C.: *Family Therapy Techniques.* Cambridge: Harvard University Press, 1981.

Mischel, W.: On the future of personality research. *Am. Psychol.,* 32:246-54, 1977.

Modell, A.A.: Character structure and analyzability. *Bull. Assoc. Psychoanal. Med.,* 19(3):97-103, 1980.

Morris, K.T., & Cinnamon, K.M.: *A Handbook of Verbal Group Exercises.* Springfield, IL: Thomas, 1974.

Mosher, L.R., Menn, A., & Matthews, S.M.: Soteria: Evaluation of a home-based treatment for schizophrenia. *Am. J. Orthopsychiatry,* 45:455, 1975.

Muench, G.A., & Schumacher, R.: A clinical expedient with rotational time-limited psychotherapy. *Psychother. Theory Res. Prac.,* 5, 81-84, 1968.

Newman, F.L., & Rinkus, A.J.: Level of functioning, clinical judgment and mental health services. *Evaluation and the Health Professions,* 1:175, 1978.

Olbrisch, M.E.: Psychotherapeutic interventions in physical health: Effectiveness and economic efficiency. *Amer. Psychologist,* 32:761, 1977.

Ormont, L.: Group resistance and the therapeutic contract. *Int. J. Group Psychother.,* 19:420-432, 1968.

Orne, M.T., & Wender, P.H.: Anticipating socialization for psychotherapy. *Am. J. Psychiatry,* 124:1202-1212, 1968.

Paolino, T.J., & McCrady, B.C. (Eds.): *Marriage and Marital Therapy: Psychoanalytic, Behavioral, and Systems Theory Perspectives.* New York: Brunner/Mazel, 1978.

Park, L.C., & Covi, L.: Nonblind placebo trial. *Arch. Gen. Psychiatry,* 12:336-345, 1965.

Parloff, M.B.: Can psychotherapy research guide the policymaker? A little knowledge may be a dangerous thing. *Amer. Psychologist,* 34:296, 1979.

Parloff, M.B., Wolfe, B., Haldey, S., & Waskow, I.E.: *Assessment of Psychosocial Treatment of Mental Disorders: Current Status and Prospects.* Report by NIMH Working Group, Advisory Committee on Mental Health, Institute of Medicine, National Academy of Sciences, 1978(a).

Parloff, M.B., Waskow, I.E., & Wolfe, B.E.: Research on therapist variables in relation to process and outcome. In Garfield, S.L., & Bergin, A.E. (Eds.). *Handbook of Psychotherapy and Behavior Change: An Empirical Analysis*, 2nd ed., New York: John Wiley & Sons, 1978(b).

Patterson, G.R.: Some procedures for assessing changes in mental interaction patterns. *Oregon Research Institute Research Bulletin*, 16, 7, 1976.

Patterson, G.R., Hops, H., & Coercin, H.: A game for two: Intervention techniques for marital conflicts. In Ulrich, R.E., & Mountjoy, P. (Eds.): *The Experimental Analysis of Social Behavior.* New York: Appleton-Century-Crofts, 1972.

Paul, G.L., & Lentz, R.J.: *Psychosocial Treatment of Chronic Mental Patients: Milieu vs. Social-Learning Programs.* Cambridge, MA: Harvard University Press, 1977.

Payne, F.D., & Wiggins, J.S.: MMPI profile types and the self-report of psychiatric patients. *J. Abnormal. Psychology*, 79:1, 1972.

Perls, F.: *Gestalt Therapy Verbatim.* Lafayette, CA: Real People Press, 1969.

Perry, M.A.: Modeling and instructions in training for counselor empathy. *J. Counseling Psychology*, 22:173-179, 1975.

Perry, M.A., & Cerreto, M.C.: Structured learning training of social skills for the retarded. *Mental Retardation*, 15:31-34, 1977.

Perry, M.A., & Furukawa, M.J.: Modeling methods. In Kanfer, F.H., & Goldstein, A.P. (Eds.). *Helping People Change*, 2nd ed. New York: Pergamon, 1980, pp. 131-171.

Peterfreund, E.: The need for a new general theoretical frame of reference for psychoanalysis. *Psa. Quart.*, 44:544-549, 1975.

Pfeiffer, J.W., & Jones, J.E.: *A Handbook of Structured Experiences for Human Relations Training.* Iowa City: University Associates Press, 1970.

Philips, J.S., & Kanfer, F.H.: The viability and vicissitudes of behavior therapy. In Frederick, C.J. (Ed.): *The Future of Psychotherapy.* Boston: Little, Brown, 1969, pp. 75-131.

Piaget, J., & Inhelder, B.: *The Growth of Logical Thinking from Childhood to Adolescence.* New York: Basic Books, 1958.

Pomerleau, O.F.: Behavioral medicine: The contributions of the experimental analysis of behavior to medical care. *Amer. Psychologist*, 34:654, 1979.

Rachman, S.: *The Effects of Psychotherapy.* International Series of Monographs in Experimental Psychology, Vol. 15, New York: Pergamon, 1972.

Racker, H.: The meanings and uses of countertransference. *Psychoanal. Quart.*, 26:303-357, 1957.

Raskin, D.E.: Losing a symptom through keeping it. *Arch. Gen. Psychiatry*, 33:548-555, 1976.

Redl, F.: Resistance in therapy groups. *Human Rel.*, 1:307-320, 1948.

Reeder, C.W., & Kunce, J.T.: Modeling techniques, drug abstinence behavior, and heroin addicts: A pilot study. *J. Counseling Psychology*, 23:560-562, 1976.

Resnik, H.L.P., & Ruben, H.L. (Eds.): *Emergency Psychiatric Care: The Management of Mental Health Crises.* Bowie, MD: Charles, 1975.

Richards, C.S., & Perri, M.G.: Do self-control treatments last? An evaluation of behavioral problem solving and faded counselor contact as treatment maintenance strategies. *J. Counseling Psychol.* 25:376-383, 1978.

Riecken, H.W.: Principal components of the evaluation process. *Professional Psychology*, 8:392, 1977.

Riecken, H.W., & Boruch, R.F. (Eds.): *Social Experimentation: A Method for Planning and Evaluating Social Intervention.* New York: Academic Press, 1974.

Riess, B.F.: Changes in patient income concomitant with psychotherapy. *J. Consulting Psychology*, 31:130, 1967.

Robins, L.N.: *Deviant Children Grown Up.* Baltimore: Williams & Wilkins, 1966.

Rogers, C.R., Gendlin, E.G., Kiesler, D.J., et al.: *The Therapeutic Relationship and Its Impact: A Study of Psychotherapy with Schizophrenics.* Madison, WI: University of Wisconsin Press, 1967.

Rogers, C.R., & Truax, C.B.: The therapeutic conditions antecedent to change: A theoretical view. In Rogers, C.R. (Ed.) *The Therapeutic Relationship and Its Impact: A Study of Psychotherapy with Schizophrenics.* Madison, WI: University of Wisconsin Press, 1967.

Rosman, B., Minuchin, S., & Liebman, R: Family lunch session: An introduction to family therapy in anorexia nervosa. *Am. J. Orthopsychiatry,* 45:846-853, 1975.

Rosenthal, L.: The resolution of group-destructive resistance in modern group analysis. *Modern Psychoanal.,* 1:243-256, 1976.

Rosenthal, L.: Resistance in group psychotherapy: The inter-relationship of individual and group resistance. In Wolberg, L.R., & Aronson, M.L. (Eds.). *Group and Family Therapy, 1980.* New York: Brunner/Mazel, 1980.

Ross, D.W.: How to get a neurotic worker back on the job successfully. *Occupational Health and Safety,* 46:20-23, 1977.

Rubins, J.L.: Five year results of psychoanalytic therapy and day care for acute schizophrenic patients. *Am. J. Psychoanal.,* 36:3-26, 1976.

Rubinstein, B.: Explanation and mere description: A metascientific examination of certain aspects of the psychoanalytic theory of motivation. In Holt, R.R. (Ed.). *Motives and Thought: Psychoanalytic Essays in Honor of David Rapaport.* Psychological Issues Monograph No. 18/19. New York: International Universities Press, 1967, pp. 20-77.

Rush, A.J.: Cognitive therapy. *Weekly Psychiatry Update Series,* Lesson 52. Princeton, NJ: Biomedia, Inc., 1978.

Rush, A.J., Beck, A.T., Kovacs, M., & Hollon, S.: Comparative efficacy of cognitive therapy and pharmocotherapy in the treatment of depressed outpatients. *Cog. Ther. Res.,* 1:17-37, 1977.

Rusk, T.: Opportunity and technique in crisis psychiatry. *Comprehensive Psychiatry,* 12:249-263, 1971.

Rutter, M.: *Maternal Deprivation Reassessed.* Middlesex, England: Penguin Books, 1972.

Sager, C.: *Marriage Contracts and Couple Therapy.* New York: Brunner/Mazel, 1976.

Sarason, I.G., & Ganzer, V.J.: Modeling and group discussion in the rehabilitation of juvenile delinquents. *J. Counseling Psychol.,* 20:422-429, 1973.

Sargent, H., Horwitz, L., Wallerstein, R., et al.: Prediction in psychotherapy research: A method of transferring clinical judgments into testable hypothesis. *Psychol. Issues,* 6:1-146, 1968.

Schafer, R.: Generative empathy in the treatment situation. *Psychoanal. Quart.,* 28:342-373, 1959.

Scheidlinger, S.: The concept of empathy in group psychotherapy. *Int. J. Group Psychother.,* 16:413-424, 1966.

Schreiber, K.A.: Does training prepare for practice; a case in point. *The Bulletin,* 21(4): 1, 1979.

Schulberg, H.C.: Quality-of-care standards and professional norms. *Am. J. Psychiatry,* 133:1047, 1976.

Schulberg, H.C.: Issues in the evaluation of community mental health programs. *Professional Psychology,* 8:560, 1977.

Searles, H.F.: *Collected Papers on Schizophrenia and Related Subjects.* New York: International Universities Press, 1966.

Seligman, E.: Behavior therapy. In Grayson, H. (Ed.). *Short-term Approaches to Psychotherapy.* New York: Human Sciences Press, 1979, pp. 11-55.

Seligman, E.: Assertive training. In Grayson, H. (Ed.). *Short-term Approaches to Psychotherapy.* New York: Human Sciences Press, 1979, pp. 167-175.

Sermat, V., & Smyth, M.: Content analysis of verbal communication in the development of a relationship: Conditions influencing self-disclosure. *J. Personality and Social Psychol.* 26:332-346, 1973.

Shapiro, T.: The development and distortions of empathy. *Psychoanal. Quart.,* 43:4-25, 1974.

Shorr, J.E.: *Psycho-imagination Therapy.* New York: Intercontinental Medical Book

Corporation, 1972.

Sifneos, P.E.: *Short-term Psychotherapy and Emotional Crisis.* Cambridge: Harvard University Press, 1972.

Simpson, D.D., & Savage, L.J.: Drug abuse treatment readmissions and outcomes. *Arch. Gen. Psychiatry,* 37:896-901, 1980.

Slater, E., & Cowie, V.: *The Genetics of Mental Disorders.* London: Oxford University Press, 1971.

Sloane, R.B., Staples, F.R., Cristol, A.N., Yorkston, N.J., & Whipple, K: *Psychotherapy Versus Behavior Therapy.* Cambridge: Harvard University Press, 1975.

Sloane, R.B., Staples, F.R., Whipple, K., et al.: Patients' attitudes toward behavior therapy and psychotherapy. *Am. J. Psychiatry,* 134(2):134-137, 1977.

Smith, E.W.L. (Ed.): *The Growing Edge of Gestalt Therapy.* New York: Brunner/Mazel, 1976.

Smith, M.J.: *When I Say No, I Feel Guilty.* New York: Dial Press, 1975.

Smith, M.L., & Glass, G.V.: Meta-analysis of psychotherapy outcome studies. *Am. Psychol.,* 32:752-60, 1977.

Smith, M.L., Glass, G.V., & Miller, T.I.: *The Benefits of Psychotherapy.* Baltimore: Johns Hopkins University Press, 1980.

Sollod, R.N., & Kaplan, H.S.: The new sex therapy: An integration of behavioral, psychodynamic, and interpersonal approaches. In Claghorn, J.L. (Ed.) *Successful Psychotherapy.* New York: Brunner/Mazel, 1976.

Solow, C., Silverfarb, P.M., & Swift, K.: Psychosocial effects of intestinal bypass surgery for severe obesity. *New Eng J. Med.,* 290:300-304, 1974.

Spangaard, J.: The manifest dream content and its significance for the interpretation of dreaming. *Int. J. Psycho-Analysis,* 50:221-235, 1969.

Spanier, G.B.: Measuring dyadic adjustment: New scales for assessing the quality of marriage and similar dyads. *J. Marr. Fam.,* 38:15-28, 1976.

Spiegel, H., & Spiegel, D.: *Trance and Treatment: Clinical Uses of Hypnosis.* New York: Basic Books, 1978.

Spiegel, J.P.: Cultural aspects of transference and countertransference revisited. *J. Am. Acad. Psychoanal.,* 4:447-467, 1976.

Spitzer, R.L., Endicott, J., & Cohen, J.: *The Psychiatric Status Schedule: Technique for Evaluating Social and Role Functioning and Mental Status.* New York: N.Y. State Psychiatric Institute and Biometrics Research, 1967.

Spitzer, R.L., Endicott, J., Fleiss, R.L., & Cohen, J.: The psychiatric status schedule: A technique for evaluating psychopathology and impairment in role functioning. *Arch. Gen., Psychiatry,* 23:41-55, 1970.

Spivack, G., Platt, J.J., & Shure, M.B.: *The Problem-Solving Approach to Adjustment.* San Francisco: Jossey-Bass, 1976.

Spotnitz, H.: Resistance phenomena in group psychotherapy. In Ruitenbeek, H.M. (Ed.) *Group Therapy Today: Styles, Methods and Techniques.* New York: Atherton Press, 1969.

Stanton, H.E.: Weight loss through hypnosis. *Am. J. Clin. Hypnosis,* 18:94-97, 1975.

Stein, L.I., & Test, M.A. (Eds.): *Alternatives to Mental Hospital Treatment.* New York: Plenum, 1978.

Stern, B.E., & Stern, E.S.: Efficiency of mental hospitals. *Br. J. Preventive Social Med.,* 17:111, 1963.

Stolorow, R.D., & Atwood, G.E.: *Faces in a Cloud.* New York: Jason Aronson, 1979.

Stone, L.: Discussion-character structure and analyzability. *Bull. Assoc. Psychoanal. Med.,* 19(3):104-115, 1980.

Strachey, J.: The nature of the therapeutic action of psychoanalysis. *Int. J. Psycho-Anal.* 50:275-292, 1969.

Strupp, H.H.: Needed: A reformulation of the psychotherapeutic influence. *Int. J. Psychiatry,* 10:119, 1972.

Strupp, H.H.: Some critical comments on the future of psychoanalytic therapy. *Bull.*

Menninger Clinic, 40:242, 1976.

Strupp, H.H., Fox, R.E., & Lessor, K.: *Patients View Their Psychotherapy.* Baltimore: Johns Hopkins University Press, 1969.

Strupp, H.H., & Hadley, S.W.: A tripartite model of mental health and therapeutic outcomes. *Am. Psychologist,* 32:187, 1977.

Stuart, R.B., & Davis, B.: *Slim Chance in a Fat World: Behavioral Control of Obesity.* Champaign, IL: Research Press, 1972.

Szalita, A.B.: Some thoughts on empathy. *Psychiatry,* 39:142-152, 1976.

Tabachnick, N.: Research Committee Report on Psychoanalytic Practice. *The Academy,* 17:9-12, 1973.

Talbott, J.A. (Ed.): *The Chronic Mentally Ill: Treatment, Programs, Systems.* New York: Human Sciences Press, 1981.

Thomas, A., & Chess, S.: *The Dynamics of Psychological Development.* New York: Brunner/Mazel, 1980.

Truax, C.B., & Carkhuff, R.R.: *Toward Effective Counseling and Psychotherapy: Training and Practice.* Chicago: Aldine, 1967.

Truax, C.B., & Mitchell, K.M.: Research on certain therapist interpersonal skills in relation to process and outcome. In Bergin, A.E., & Garfield, S.L. (Eds.). *Handbook of Psychotherapy and Behavior Change: An Empirical Analysis.* New York: Wiley, 1971.

Tullis, F.: Rational diet construction for mild and grand obesity. *J.A.M.A.,* 226:70-71, 1973.

Vaillant, G.E.: *Adaptation to Life.* Boston: Little, Brown, 1977.

Vaillant, G.E., Semrad, E.V., & Ewalt, J.R.: Current therapeutic results in schizophrenia. *New Eng. J. Med.,* 271: 280-283, 1964.

Vorster, D.: Psychotherapy and the results of psychotherapy. *South African Med. J.,* 40:934, 1966.

Wadsworth, W.V., et al.: Cost of treatment of affective disorders: A comparison of three hospitals. *Lancet,* 273:533, 1957.

Wallace, M., & Morley, W.: Teaching crisis intervention. *Am. J. Nursing,* 70:1484-1487, 1970.

Walsh, W.B.: Validity of self-report. *J. Counseling Psychol.,* 14:18-23, 1967.

Walsh, W.B.: Validity of self-report: Another look. *J. Counseling Psychol.* 15:180-186, 1968.

Waskow, I.E., Parloff, M.B. (Eds.): *Psychotherapy Change Measures.* Washington, DC: DHEW Pub. No. (ADM) 74-120, 1975.

Watzlawick, P., Beavin, J., & Jackson, D.: *Pragmatics of Human Communication.* New York: Norton, 1967.

Watzlawick, P., Weakland, J.H., & Fisch, R.: *Change: Principles of Problem Formation and Problem Resolution.* New York: Norton, 1974.

Weise, C.C., Stein, M.K., Pereira-Ogan, J., Csanalosi, I., & Rickels, K.: Amitryptiline once daily vs. three times daily in depressed outpatients. *Arch. Gen. Psychiatry,* 37:555-560, 1980.

Weiss, C.H.: *Evaluation Research: Methods of Assessing Program Effectiveness.* Englewood Cliffs, NJ: Prentice-Hall, 1972.

Weiss, R.L.: The conceptualization of marriage from a behavioral perspective. In Paolino, T.J., Jr., & McCrady, B.S. (Eds.): *Marriage and Marital Therapy: Psychoanalytic, Behavioral and Systems Theory Perspectives.* New York: Brunner/Mazel, 1978.

Weiss, R.L., Hops, H., & Patterson, G.R.: A framework for conceptualizing marital conflict, a technology for altering it, some data for evaluating it. In Hamerlynck, L.A., Handy, L.C., & Mash, E.J. (Eds.). *Behavior Change: Methodology, Concepts and Practice.* Champaign, IL: Research Press, 1973.

Weitzenhoffer, A.M.: *General Techniques of Hypnotism.* New York: Grune & Stratton, 1957.

Whitehorn, J.C., & Betz, B.J.: Further studies of the doctor as a crucial variable in the outcome treatment with schizophrenic patients. *Am. J. Psychiatry,* 117:215, 1960.

Whiteley, J.M., & Flowers, J.V.: *Approaches to Assertion Training.* Monterey, CA: Brooks-Cole, 1977.

Wickramasekera, I.: Aversive behavior rehearsal for sexual exhibitionism. *Behavior Therapy,* 7:167-176, 1976.

Wilder, F.: Roche Report: Frontiers of Psychiatry, 9(1):1, 1979.

Will, O.A.: Schizophrenia: The problem of origins. In Romano, J. (Ed.). *The Origins of Schizophrenia.* Amsterdam: Excerpta Medica Foundation, 1967, pp. 214-227.

Wolberg, A.: *The Borderline Patient.* New York: Intercontinental Medical Book Corp., 1973, pp. 185-234.

Wolberg, A.: *The Psychoanalytic Psychotherapy of the Borderline Patient.* New York: Thieme-Stratton, 1982.

Wolberg, L.R.: *Medical Hypnosis.* New York: Grune & Stratton, 1948.

Wolberg, L.R.: *Hypnoanalysis.* New York: Grune & Stratton, 2nd ed., 1964.

Wolberg, L.R.: *The Technique of Psychotherapy,* 3rd ed. New York: Grune & Stratton, 1977.

Wolberg, L.R.: Editorial—DSM-III and the Taxonomic Stew. *J. Am. Acad. Psychoanal.,* 7:139-141, 1979.

Wolberg, L.R.: *The Handbook of Short-term Psychotherapy.* New York: Thieme-Stratton, 1980.

Wolberg, L.R., & Kildahl, J.: *The Dynamics of Personality.* New York: Grune & Stratton, 1970.

Wolf, A., & Schwartz, E.K.: *Psychoanalysis in Groups.* New York: Grune & Stratton, 1962.

Wolpe, J.: *Psychotherapy by Reciprocal Inhibition.* Stanford CA: Stanford University Press, 1958.

Wolpe, J., & Lang, P.J.: A fear survey schedule for use in behavior therapy. *Behav. Res. Therapy,* 2:27-30, 1964.

Wolpe, J., & Lazarus, A.A.: *Behavior Therapy Techniques.* New York: Pergamon, 1966.

Wortman, P.M.: Evaluation research: A psychological perspective. *Amer. Psychologist,* 30:562, 1975.

Yates, B.T.: *Improving Effectiveness and Reducing Costs in Mental Health.* Springfield, IL: Thomas, 1980.

Zimberg, S., Wallace, J., & Blume, S.B. (Eds.): *Practical Approaches to Alcoholism Psychotherapy.* New York: Plenum, 1978.

Name Index

Subject Index

Italic numbers indicate major discussion of the entry.